Smart Business Networks

Peter Vervest · Eric van Heck
Kenneth Preiss · Louis-François Pau
(Editors)

Smart Business Networks

With 90 Figures

Springer

Professor Peter Vervest
Professor Eric van Heck
Professor Louis-François Pau

Erasmus University Rotterdam
P.O. Box 1738
3000 DR Rotterdam
The Netherlands

pvervest@fbk.eur.nl
eheck@fbk.eur.nl
lpau@fbk.eur.nl

Professor Kenneth Preiss
Ben Gurion University
P.O. Box 653
Beer Sheva 84105
Israel

preiss@bgumail.bgu.ac.il

Cataloging-in-Publication Data
Library of Congress Control Number: 2004110716

ISBN 3-540-22840-3 Springer Berlin Heidelberg New York

Springer is a part of Springer Science+Business Media

springeronline.com

Printed in Germany

Hardcover-Design: Design & Production GmbH, Heidelberg

SPIN 11312260   42/3130-5 4 3 2 1 0 – Printed on acid-free paper

Preface

Jan Baan

Based on my experiences in the world of Enterprise Resource Planning (ERP) a question has been on my mind for a number of years: "Why is that software so often hinders collaboration between people, systems and organisations? What makes it so complicated and what can be done to resolve this?"

As modern communication, such as the Internet, enables many more distributed ways for cooperating, organisations need fast and reliable ways to connect - and disconnect - their processes. ERP cannot do this. We need a more advanced technology. Not one that "hard codes' organisational processes leaving little or no opportunity to change them, rather one that allows organisations to capitalise on new business opportunities by respecting former IT investments, leveraging their existing systems and developing new business process driven functionalities. At Cordys we believe that we have developed a compelling solution to these challenges. We speak of lightweight, composite application frameworks: a thin layer of software using existing organisational systems and managing them in an intelligent way.

I am attracted by the term "business operating system". In the 1980s computer operating systems were invented to allow application software to be run on different hardware platforms. Today we require equivalent "business operating systems" to run business processes on different organisational platforms. Each process starts a complicated path of activities picked from the members of its business network. We posed the question: what should be done to make the outcomes of this network "smart", that is, just a little better than that of your competitor? More agile and self-learning, giving more return to all the members of the network, now and over time?

The near future will be about event-driven smart business networks bringing together the qualities of independent professionals and smart companies doing everything they possibly can to serve their demanding clients in the best possible way. Potentially, smart business networks can contribute greatly to the well being of people and to business success. And, if the concept is worked out thoroughly and sensibly, we can enter a new age of global collaboration that will benefit all participants.

This book is the result of research carried out on the question *"how do you make business networks smart"* and the resulting discussions at our castle, "The Vanenburg", in Putten. From 26-28 May 2004, scientists and business people worked together to exchange their experiences and research, to make predictions on the future of smart business networks. The meeting was inspiring. Let this book inspire you!

We are talking about new possibilities for the worldwide collaboration of people, systems and organisations for their joint benefit. Since we are now on the verge of a new era, I encourage scientists as well as business researchers to join hands and explore the new opportunities that this technology presents. Just collaborate.

Jan Baan
Founder and
Chief Executive Officer
Cordys

Han van Dissel

Innovation is at the heart of business success. The Internet and mobile and wireless communication technologies are critical enablers of todays business innovation. As we gain deeper understanding of the technological possibilities, it is becoming clear that their successful application requires more than simply exploring and exploiting new products or services. What decides real success is the ability to organise, to build and to sustain a value network of different business organisations. This book addresses this "organising capability" as it speaks of "smart business networks". I believe the concept of a *smart* business network will create many progressive and far-reaching changes: smart organisational networks will have a lasting impact on our ability to generate wealth in an increasingly global business world.

The first wave of Internet-enabled business innovation concentrated on new ways of interacting with the customer, on the "web-storefront", online information provisioning and order taking. But great web sites do not necessarily result in great profits. Without the ability to act effectively on what the customer wants and expects, many of such websites have failed to deliver compelling business results. A new way is required to organise and manage the many parties involved in the creation, and fulfilment, of a customer order. This is what we call the "business network". It becomes smart if the network allows customisation, personalisation, and relationship building; if it enables cross-boundary logistics and the strengthening of brand identity. Logistics should play a dominant role in the enablement of smart business networks - the more so as the Internet and mobile communications change the market to a web of interlinked supply chains.

In my view a smart business network is critically dependent on the excellence of the business process management of the cooperating firms. As each firm will have access to the same technology, its own competitive edge will depend on its unique ability to fuse people, business processes and technology. The decisive factor may well be a firm's competence to "out-source" business processes and to "out-task" functions to best-practice, online players, while at the same time building, enhancing and sustaining relationships.

Process excellence in smart business networks creates many challenges for the firm as well as for academia. Let me propose some themes:

1. Most organisations divide logistics over many functions. Implementing smart business networks will require a much more holistic view on logistics in order to make business processes more modular and dynamic

and to gain sourcing flexibility and asset efficiency. We know little about how to transform existing organisations into smart business networks, how these networks should be governed, and how to leverage their value potential for an individual firm participating in the network.

2. New technological solutions tend to bring new functionalities without immediate attention to their integration with legacy systems. The inability to integrate legacy systems into smart business networks may be a barrier to their success.
3. The sourcing of business processes to best practice providers may, in the short term, bring a favourable change to a firm's capital structure but increases the dependency on the process provider. The provider may be the one who harvests the profits of moving to the next practices. The longer term implications of business process outsourcing in smart business networks are largely unknown.
4. Embedding business rules in the software of the business network enables customer self-service but, at the same time, a firm runs the risk of removing the distinctive, humanised content from its offerings. At the end of the day, the social capital within and surrounding the business networks may be a very important factor in determining a firm's competitive position.

The concept of smart business networks provides a strong, new direction for business research. We, at RSM, are keen to take a lead. As a research-driven school we must continually investigate new areas in order to provide the business community with guidance and world-class education for business excellence. Smart business networks must begin with smart, educated people. This book brings together experience, research, and predictions on smart businesses. Its creation is a result of the work and enthusiasm of the many contributors and, in particular the interest and continuing support of Mr. Jan Baan, Founder and Chief Executive Officer of Cordys. This book offers a venue for everybody interested in exploring and participating this new competitive frontier. I trust you will enjoy reading it.

Han van Dissel
Dean RSM
Erasmus University Rotterdam

Table of Contents

Section 2: Execution of Smart Business Networks

Section 3: Governance of Smart Business Networks

Section 4: Design of Smart Business Networks

Introduction

1 Welcome to Smart Business Networks

Introduction

Rotterdam School of Management is less than a mile away from the biggest cargo port in the world. During 2003 this Port of Rotterdam handled 327 million metric tons of cargo. Over 29,000 sea-going vessels docked at the port. Over 7 million containers ("TEU's" i.e. 20 foot equivalent units) were carried through an area less than the size of the center of New York: 20,000 containers each day! (Port Authority of Rotterdam, 2004).

In August 2003 a group of the School's researchers[1] put the following question: imagine that, all over the port of Rotterdam, one could have instant wireless access to the state of all ships, trucks, containers and cargo, and anyone and anything related to this. If so, could one manage the processes better, faster, more effectively, and more efficiently? What could one do that was not possible before? What would be required to do so?

This book is a first result of exploring these questions. Perhaps not surprisingly, our research took us far from transport and logistics into very different areas. Managing the movement of physical objects, or managing digital goods or services, all seem to have the following in common: it involves many different parties, linked together in a web of activities, using different processes with no single organisation in full control over the others. What makes this cooperation "smart"? Is the physical logistics smartness the consequence of information smartness?

Embedded Smartness

For many years the Rotterdam School of Management has studied integrated transport logistics, from diverse viewpoints such as operations research, information management, and networking, or telecommunications. Over the years, the port changed from a pure transportation hub to a "value-adding hub". Concepts such as "integral value chain management" were coined to describe the management of value-adding processes that are disjoint but need to be "linked": our view was that processes such as sale and purchase, transport, and payment can be integrated and "man-

[1] The group of scientists included professor Peter Vervest, professor Eric van Heck, professor Louis Pau, Lorike Hagdorn, Martijn Hoogeweegen, Otto Koppius, Diederik van Liere, Jeffrey Teich, Jimmy Tseng, as members of the Department Information and Decision Sciences, Erasmus University's Rotterdam School of Management and specialising in the telecommunications of business.

aged" across different parties over time. It is said that handling cargo is difficult because it is not self-correcting. Cargo people refer to passage as "self-stowing cargo". Passengers themselves correct the transport processes if something goes wrong ("they complain"). Not so with cargo! However, this can change. With much more sophisticated telecommunications with simple and affordable identifiers everything could "communicate"; processes would be self-organising, a system could be "intelligent".

This is not an idea restricted to the transport business. It can be a general concept. Consider insurance. Cars and bicycles are already being equipped with identifier-chips. Theoretically, an insurance company is now able to continually manage its exposure to car and bicycle risks and everything that goes with it; from selling insurance products and administering risks, to handling claims.

With new communication technology comes new competitive capabilities. We are advancing from the ability to move information quickly in a given supply chain as mentioned above, to the ability to take advantage of being part of a technological network to rapidly connect to and disconnect from different chains. This requires a different level of smartness and is a central theme of this book – but more of this in later chapters.

Networks - Not Chains

A transport process is an interesting phenomenon since it typically involves many different parties that must work together (or cooperate) to realise the actual movement of physical goods in the right direction. The concept of Porter's value chain (1985) can easily be recognised: a chain of actors (or organisations) each carrying responsibility for a certain part of the chain of activities. Cooperation techniques initially focused on the relaying of the chain, i.e. ensuring that the handover from one party to the other goes well. Once many parties become involved, some with overlapping or competing, capabilities, a selection, or choice needs to be made. The chain becomes a "network" of cooperating or competing parties. These parties are the "nodes" or "actors" while the routes are the "links" or "paths". We speak of "networks" in the classical sense, see Jay and Goetz (1984), as a series of points interconnected by communication channels. Business networks are defined as networks with the "nodes" being business entities or "actors" interconnected by "links", see Miles and Snow (1992) and Kambil and Short (1994). Much work has gone into analysing the information flows in organisational communications (Monge and Contractor, 2003) and the governance of cooperation (Thompson, 2003). But what makes a business network "smart"? What makes a business network generate more sustainable and profitable outcomes than other forms of competitive, or cooperative, strategy?

Smart - or Stupid - Business Networks

It may not be easy to "see" smart business networks. Smartness may be the result of actions and not always foreseen by the individual actors. Could it be that even stupid actors could create a smart network together? Could a stupid network be the result of smart actors? What defines stupidity? In our discussions we agreed that we did not know! We also postulated that one, critical component would be the following: a smart business network segregates the business logic from the executional processes and activities; i.e. the actors of a smart business network create a *business operating system*. This business operating system coordinates the processes among the networked businesses and its logic is embedded in the systems used by these businesses. In practice we see the first glimpses of smart business networking appearing. For example, Wal-Mart (among many others) is using radio frequency identification (RFID) technology for smarter product tracking and tracing. Dell's modular products and IT infrastructure allow it to configure its supply chain "on the fly" based on the specific customer order. Philips is developing ambient intelligence applications for the next decade consumer homes.

The Research Themes

We set out to explore the scientific and practical implications of the design and management of, what we called, *Smart Business Networks*. We identified the following components:

- Outcome of smart business networks. How do smart business networks outperform traditional networked businesses?
- Execution of smart business networks. How are smart business networks designing and implementing their critical execution processes?
- Governance of smart business networks. How are smart networks coordinated and by what or whom?
- Design of smart business networks. What are the rules embedded in the business operating system and how are they embedded? What can be standardised and how?

We have not attempted to deal with the underlying technologies of smart business networks, but rather with how to design and manage smart networks and to realise business goals using them.

A Different Approach

The Journal of Information Technology[2] invited us to create a special issue on Smart Business Networks. Cordys Company kindly offered its support in developing the contents. We sent out a call for papers via the Association for Information Systems[3] and other forums. Reactions came from many different fields; from technology fields such as webservices, workflow, business process management, and (mobile) telecommunications, as well as management fields such as information systems research, innovation management, and general management strategies. Some offered very new approaches such as studying interaction patterns as a result of network topology based on the work of Buchanan (2002) and Barabási (2003).

We decided to invite a selection of researchers to combine and consolidate key knowledge and insights in this relatively new field of research. We preferred that the participants should not have been previously acquainted, and that they should have a "low" professional degree of removal to each other, analogous to the well-known concept of the Erdòs number. This worked. We did not predetermine the contents. The contributions could be based on a variety of research methods and include both scientific oriented and practice based research. It had been specifically intended to combine theoretical approaches with in-depth case studies, empirical validations or demonstrations. Such cases could come from a variety of organisations and industries, for example:

- Manufacturing industries capturing business process logic in company-wide repositories that are shared via their intranets and extranets,
- Industries with high modularity of product portfolios that allows them to manage high product variety at manageable cost,
- Government institutes using smart business network principles to interact with business and citizens in a more customer-centric way,
- Transport and logistics companies providing the latest tracking and tracing solutions that can enable high flexibility of supply chains and networks.

---

2 Journal of Information Technology, edited by Leslie Willcocks, from Warwick Business School, and Chris Sauer, from Oxford University, UK. See www.palgrave-journals.com/jit. The Special Issue on Smart Business Networks appears in their December 2004 publication.

3 See the Association for Information Systems at www.isworld.org

The Vanenburg Science Seminar

From 26 to 28 May 2004 approximately 30 selected scientists gathered at Vanenburg castle in The Netherlands on invitation of Mr. Jan Baan, Founder and Chief Executive Officer of Cordys Group, to present and discuss a selection of the papers which the participants prepared and shared in advance. A strict format was applied. On arrival we gathered in table groups each selecting a theme and developing this into a number of "propositions". Selected papers were discussed with a rigid process of short presentations by the author and a pointed assessment by a reviewer. Every session ended with questions-and-answers with the participants. A rapporteur summarised the session. At the close the table groups reported on their themes. This formed the basis of a vivid interaction with Cordys senior management during the "Cordys Panel" discussion.

The outcomes of these highly interactive, and at times intense discussions are recorded in the *Introduction* of this book. The four constituent components of smart business networks, as given above, are the *Sections* of the book. The papers by participants are the *Chapters* and have been grouped according to the Sections - but we must ask you not to regard this grouping too strictly! We believe the result is interesting and highly commendable reading, providing critical insights for management practice and theory, today and in the near future.

Readers Guide

The book aims to bring a novel approach to digital business and value chain management for:

- Executives, high-level organisational managers, strategists and senior marketers,
- Information managers and IT specialists in large companies and government,
- Industry specialists and consultants in business process management, logistics, webservices, and software,
- Business scientists and researchers involved in the fields of management of Information and Communication Technology (ICT), innovation management, social networking and global value-chain management.

Table 1.1 is intended to guide readers to those sections that should be of most interest to them according to their professional interests.

Table 1.1 Reader's guide

Target readers / Section	Executives, managers, strategists, marketeers	Information managers and IT specialists	Industry specialists and consultants	Business scientists and researchers
Introduction	●●●●	●●●●	●●●●	●●●●
Section 1. Outcomes	●●●	●●	●●●	●●●●
Section 2. Execution	●	●●●	●	●
Section 3. Governance	●●	●●	●●●	●●●●
Section 4. Design	●	●●●●	●●	●●●●

● .... the number of dots indicates the relative importance for the reader group

Introduction

The Introduction is general in nature and should appeal to business persons as well as to researchers. Chapter 2 lists the participants and contributors, the "actors" to this production. The Program Committee presents its perspective on the importance of smart business networks for today's business in Chapter 3. The result of the five "table discussions" during the seminar is given in Chapter 4. This is a thought-provoking set of concepts derived from the real-time interaction of all participants. The final chapter in the Introduction brings you the results of the panel discussion of business and science, and emphasises the creation of "light" cooperation technologies and the development of a pervasive business operating system. This chapter also contains two papers by Cordys Group on the market requirements and enabling technologies.

Section One: Outcomes

Section One concentrates on the outcome of smart business networks: Why would such smart networks perform "better" than traditional business networks? What is "better"? *Benn Konsynski* and *Amrit Tiwana* present the spontaneous character and unique pattern of practice that is served by collaborative networks. *Kenneth Preiss* discusses where "smartness" would be located in a smart business network: in the actors, in the links, in the network, or elsewhere? A novel approach has been shown by *Dan Braha* and *Yaneer Bar-Yam* who derive new rules for designing cooperation based on recent developments in network topology theories. Their application to complicated product development processes in the car industry is very important and challenging. *Roger Nagel, Jason Walters, Greg Gurevich,* and *Patrick Schmid* define where and how smart business networks enable strategic opportunities not found in traditional business networking. Their framework could indicate a way to see "smartness" related to the degree of information integration between the actors in the network. *Al Dunn* presents a pragmatic framework for effective change in the behaviour of the participating actors of a smart business network. *Jo van Nunen, Rob Zuidwijk,* and *Hans Moonen* discuss sustainable smart supply chains and provide examples of research projects and results.

Section Two: Execution

Section Two on the execution of smart business networks presents a number of cases on the design and implementation of critical execution processes. Since these cases are real-life situations it is not surprising that they usually make use of functionality in static supply chains: the cases are mostly not an example of agile connecting and disconnecting to different chains in a dynamically changing network. They describe, after all, successful current businesses. *Christopher Holland, Duncan Shaw,* and *Westwood* take the refreshing example of a company turning its value chain into a smart business network for international translation services. *Martin Hughes, William Golden,* and *Helen Burke* look at the second-hand book trade with a novel way to transform a traditional business into a smart network. *Katarina Pramatari, Georgios Doukadis,* and *Panos Kouronthansassis* assess the changes in the retail industry as a result of smarter networking enabled by RFID technology. *Matthijs Wolters, Peter Vervest,* and *Eric van Heck* adopt a similar approach for the Dutch home construction industry, applying the concepts of modularity to user-driven housing. *Peter Muller* and *Gerrit Schipper* analyse a case in the insurance industry, taking a systems view on controlling and building "off the shelf" business networks. *Arun Rai, Jonathan Wareham,* and *V. Sambamurthy* analyse supply networks for in-flight services and claim that four digital capabilities are key enablers of the design of control systems and learning in intelligent supply network behaviour: visibility, process integration, granular measurement, and knowledge discovery.

Section Three: Governance

Section Three looks at the complicated issues of the governance, or control, of smart business networks: how smart business networks are coordinated, by whom, or perhaps, by what. *Diederik van Liere, Lorike Hagdorn, Martijn Hoogeweegen* and *Peter Vervest* present a way of embedding coordination in a business network by seeing actor organisations as "activity component networks" enabled by resources and capability networks. This approach is applied to the insurance industry. *Otto Koppius* and *Eric van Heck* describe the function of electronic markets as network orchestrators in two cases. They propose that a smart business network will ensure adaptation and adaptability by employing both supply-driven as well as demand-driven coordination mechanisms. *Duncan Shaw, Bob Snowdon, Christopher Holland, Peter Kawalek,* and *Brian Warboys* apply the Viable Systems Model of Stafford Beer to the deregulation of the UK electricity market. They have tried to understand how unforecastable, unplanned for and potentially devastating exogenous shocks to business can be mitigated by being part of a smart business network. *Jens Eschenbacher, Falk Graser,* and *Axel Hahn* analyse how business networks such as the aeronautical industry, handle innovation across the full spectrum of the network. They claim that Distributed Innovation Management is critical to successful governance of a smart business network.

Section Four: Design

Section Four discusses the design of smart business networks. *Amit Basu* introduces the theory and application of meta-graph representation of business processes: this formal description of processes is a prerequisite to share process knowledge within and across organisational boundaries. *Martijn Hoogeweegen* and *Peter Vervest* put the question "how much business modularity?". Coordination of complicated business processes is often achieved by way of componentisation or modularisation of the products and processes but how far should one go? This argument takes us to webservices-advocates *Jos van Hillegersberg, Ruud Boeke,* and *Willem-Jan van den Heuvel.* The authors develop their own "scenario" to test whether the technology supporting webservices will indeed enable more dynamic business arrangements. Their answer is a positive yes but they make an important qualification: as business networks often lack a formal "chain director", intelligence should be added to support "automated" collaboration. *Louis Pau* and *Peter Vervest* discuss the embedding of business logic in the lower stacks of communications networks providing examples and arguments for mobile communications networks. *Jimmy Tseng* gives a view on what is smart about credit card payments. *Jukka Heikkilä, Marikka Heikkilä, Jari Lehmonen,* and *Samuli Pekkola* describe how three different focal companies are networking their ICT infrastructure to enable international expansion - and why this fails. *Hannes Werthner, Oliver Fodor,* and *Marcus Herzog* describe an ontology-based mediation platform enabling information exchange between participants and thus forming the "semantic" basis for business networking. This is applied to the tourism industry. *Rob Peters* and *Marijn Janssen* present a case of the design of smarter cooperation structures in the public domain. They develop a conceptual framework of interoperable and retrievable law, applied to a number of cases.

The reviewers' summaries of those papers that were reviewed during the seminar are included with the relevant papers.

Acknowledgements

A year ago we began an uncharted journey. The phrase *Smart Business Networks* did not then exist. Today it does. We met many people on that journey who shared our interest, to become believers and advocates of these new ideas. Or, for some, not yet! It has been important to recognise that there was much that we did not know and that we should be ready to discover the right questions. This is exposed in this book. There are still many issues, many themes and many more formal theories to be developed. The smartness of the business networks may not be in the nodes (the actor organisations) nor in the ways in which these nodes are linked together. Smartness may be in the overall behaviour of the combination of the nodes and the links, making it difficult to identify where the "real" smartness resides.

We wish to thank the many people that have assisted us in this journey. From the Cordys Group, Jan Baan, Diberna Ligtenberg, Henk Ten Voorde and many others have helped us to achieve this. Thank you for your support! We wish you every success with your Cordys approach. We know "Cordys Cordial" - your launch event where this book will be presented to the world - will be truly cordial! We have experienced this cordiality and the high quality of service professionalism from Jan-Willem Baan, the manager of the Vanenburg castle, whose choice - and timing - of food and drinks can arouse even the most sceptical minds of science!

We would like to thank all the participants of the Science Seminar at "The Vanenburg". They are "actors" in a play that has not yet been written but their names, histories and beliefs are in this book. Thank you for living up to near impossible deadlines. We would like to thank Chantal Schoof and Naima Zerhane, our office assistants at the Rotterdam School of Management and Jeroen Tiekstra, the student assistant. We also thank Al Dunn for checking so many variants of the English language; Dr. Alfred Müller, the Editor in charge for Springer Verlag for his support in publishing and promoting this book; and Leslie Willcocks and Chris Sauer, Editors-in-

Chief of the Journal of Information Technology for giving us a platform to expose our ideas.

As the Program Committee this has been the first time we have worked together in this setting, with this objective and with these unrealistic time schedules and objectives. Using email and late-night telephone calls from all over the world we worked well, hopefully smartly together. So far we made our targets. Let this be a beginning!

Rotterdam, August 2004

Peter Vervest
Eric van Heck
Kenneth Preiss
Louis Pau

References

Barabási, A-L. (2003). *Linked - How Everything Is Connected to Everything Else and What it Means for Business, Science, and Everyday Life*, Penguin Group, New York, 2003.

Buchanan, M. (2002). *Nexus: Small Worlds and the Groundbreaking Science of Networks*, Norton & Company, New York, 2002

Jay, F., J.A. Goetz, (1984). *IEEE Standard Dictionary of Electrical and Electronics Terms*, The Institute of Electrical and Electronics Engineers, Inc., Wiley & Sons, New York.

Kambil, A., J.E. Short, (1994). "Electronic Integration and Business Network Redesign: A Roles - Linkages Perspective", *Journal of Management Information Systems*, 10, 4, pp. 59-83.

Miles, R.E., C.C. Snow, (1992). "Causes of Failure in Network Organizations", *California Management Review*, (Summer), pp. 53-72.

Monge, P.R., N.S. Contractor, (2003). *Theories of Communication Networks*, Oxford University Press, New York.

Thompson, G.F. (2003). *Between Hierarchies and Markets - The Logic and Limits of Network Forms of Organization*, Oxford University Press, New York.

Port Authority Of Rotterdam (2004). *Port Statistics 2003*, Rotterdam, www. PortofRotterdam.com.

Porter, Michael E.(1985). *Competitive Advantage - Creating and Sustaining Superior Performance*, The Free Press, New York.

2 The Actors

Participants of the Vanenburg Science Seminar 26 - 28 May 2004

Jan Baan
Founder and Chief Executive Officer
Cordys (NL)

Amit Basu
Charles Wyly Professor of Information Systems
SMU Cox School of Business (TX, USA)

Dan Braha
Professor of Industrial Engineering
Ben Gurion University (Israel)

Hong Chen
PhD student
RSM – Erasmus University Rotterdam (NL)

Al Dunn
Partner
D-Age Management (United Kingdom)

Willie Golden
Research Director
Centre for Innovation and Structural Change, NUI Galway (Ireland)

Falk Graser
Researcher
Bremen Institute of Industrial Engineering and Applied Work Sciences (BIBA) (Germany)

Lorike Hagdorn
Associate Professor
RSM – Erasmus University Rotter-dam (NL)
Partner, Boer & Croon (NL)

Juppa Heikkilä
Professor of Electronic Commerce
University of Jyväskylä (Finland)

Winfried van Holland
Manager Product Marketing
Cordys (NL)

Marcus Herzog
Associate Professor
Information Systems Institute
Vienna University of Technology (Austria)

Martijn Hoogeweegen
Assistant Professor
RSM – Erasmus University Rotterdam (NL)
Manager, AT Kearney (NL)

Jos van Hillegersberg
Associate Professor
RSM – Erasmus University Rotterdam (NL)

Eric van Heck
Professor of Electronic Markets
RSM – Erasmus University Rotterdam (NL)

Christopher Holland
Professor of Information Systems
Manchester Business School (United Kingdom)

Euwe Kamsteeg
Product Marketing Manager
Cordys (NL)

Deepak Kini
Vice President
Presales Europe
Cordys (NL)

Diberna Ligtenberg
Marketing Executive
Cordys (NL)

Benn Konsynski
George S. Craft Professor of Business Administration for Decision and Information Analysis
Emory University (GA,USA)

Lucas Michels
Vice President
Marketing & Communication
Cordys (NL)

Otto Koppius
Assistant Professor
RSM – Erasmus University Rotterdam (NL)

Peter Muller
Director of Business Architecture
ABZ – an ADP company (NL, USA).

Diederik van Liere
PhD student
RSM – Erasmus University Rotterdam (NL)

Roger Nagel
Senior Fellow and Wagner Professor
Lehigh University (CA, USA)

Jo van Nunen
Professor of Logistics and Decision Sciences
RSM – Erasmus University Rotterdam (NL)

Marcel van Oosterhout
Research manager
RSM – Erasmus University Rotterdam (NL)

Louis-François Pau
Professor of Mobile Business
RSM – Erasmus University Rotterdam (NL)

Rob Peeters
Researcher
Leibniz Center for Law
University of Amsterdam (NL)

Katerina Pramatari
Researcher
Athens University of Economics and Business (Greece)

Kenneth Preiss
The Sir Leon Bagrit Professor: Technology and Global Competitiveness
Ben Gurion University (Israel)

Ulad Radkevitch
PhD student
RSM – Erasmus University Rotterdam (NL)

Arun Rai
The Harkins Chair Professor
J.Mack Robinson College of Business
Georgia State University (GA,USA)

Henk de Ruiter
Executive Vice President Sales and Marketing
Cordys (NL)

Hans de Visser
Manager Research & Development
Cordys (NL)

Duncan Shaw
Research fellow
Manchester Business School (United Kingdom)

Henk ten Voorde
Program Manager
Cordys (NL)

Jimmy Tseng
Assistant Professor
RSM – Erasmus University Rotterdam (NL)

Matthijs Wolters
Assistant Professor
Free University Amsterdam (NL)

Peter Vervest
Professor of Business Telecommunications
RSM Erasmus University Rotterdam (NL)

3 The Emergence of Smart Business Networks

Peter Vervest[1], Kenneth Preiss[2], Eric van Heck[1], Louis Pau[1]

A Joint Vision

Sawhney and Parikh (2001) call network intelligence the Rosetta Stone that can enable executives and entrepreneurs to decipher many of the phenomena shaping the future of business. They define the network as a "conduit of information". The intelligence of the network is its functionality - its ability to distribute, store, assemble, or modify information. "Dumb" networks are simple pipes that transport information without enhancing it. A complex digital network, like the Internet, is "smart"; it can improve the utility of information in multiple ways. That, according to Sawhney and Parikh, is synonymous with creating economic value.

The pivotal question of this book concerns this relationship between the intelligence of networks and the smartness of the businesses that use these networks. We aim to connect a long term vision of smart business networks with short term implementation issues. Defining the long term without short term details would not give practical results since the implementation path would be unknown. On the other hand, defining implementation details without a long term view would yield an undefined, and uncertain direction that business executives may not wish to follow. Hence the correct approach is to deal simultaneously with both short term implementation issues and long term vision.

We should note that practice precedes theory in the development of most technologies. For example, many iron bridges were built during the eighteenth and nineteenth centuries without using theory and before the method of engineering statics and equilibrium was known. Even after todays method of static force polygons had been invented, bridge designers did not use it. Eventually the theory of static forces was used, an important step that allowed bridge designers to extrapolate to much larger spans and enabled the optimisation of the use of materials. A similar process happens in the case of smart business networks: These networks are being con-

---

1 Erasmus University's Rotterdam School of Management, PO Box 1738, 3000 DR Rotterdam, The Netherlands: vervest@d-age.com, e.heck@fbk.eur.nl, l.pau@fbk.eur.nl

2 Ben Gurion University of the Negev, School of Management and Faculty of Engineering, Beer Sheva, Israel, preiss@bgu.ac.il

structed, and the practical construction is followed by the development of suitable theories. Eventually the theory should promote improved business efficiency of such networks and should enable the expansion of business networks to much larger sizes. This paper aims to contribute to the theory of smart business networks.

What Are Smart Business Networks?

We apply the word "smart" to an action that is novel and different, hence thought of as innovative. Smart actions create remarkable, "better than usual" results. Smart has a connotation with fashionable and distinguished, but also with short-lived. What is smart today will be considered common tomorrow. The word "smart" in smart business networks is therefore not an absolute but a relative term. Smartness is a property whereby the network can create "better" results than other, less smart business networks, or other forms of business arrangements. While intelligence in the communications systems and networks may have a more absolute meaning, smartness of business networks is relative, time-bound and situation-bound. To be smart in business is to be smarter than the competitors, just as an athlete considered fast means (s)he is faster than the others.

All three words in the title "smart business networks" are necessary. The pair of words "smart business" can apply to any business without a network. A "smart network" can apply to a network that is not used for business or organisation. A "business network" is generic and includes both smart and not-so-smart business networks. We define a smart business network as:

- A group of participating businesses - organisational entities or "actors" - that form the nodes,
- Linked together via one or more communication networks forming the links, or lines, between the nodes,
- With compatible goals,
- Interacting in novel ways,
- Perceived by each participant as increasing its own value,
- Sustainable over time as a network.

Smart Networks, Supply Trees, and Supply Chains

A network is a generalised graph consisting of nodes connected by links. A fully connected network is a graph where each node is connected to all the others. According to social network analysis the nodal degree would be g-1 for each node (g being the total number of nodes) and the network density would be 1 (Iacobucci, 1999). A business network is unlikely to be fully connected but will be partially connected. A tree is a hierarchical graph. It has no cycles and each node has only one parent. A chain is a subgraph of a tree where each link connects exactly to one other link. These constructs of "supply network", "supply tree" or "supply chain" are often confused. Let us try to explain. Imagine that we draw a graph of three nodes, A, B and C, where each node represents a company, and we draw a link between two nodes if one company (A) is a qualified supplier or a qualified customer of the other company (B). This graph will almost always be a network, see Figure 3.1.

For example, there would be links between nodes A and B, B and C, and A and C. Note that the qualification of a customer or supplier is a process that requires time and money; it is far from an instantaneous process. When a customer chooses specific suppliers from the list of qualified suppliers in order to assemble a good or service, the graph as seen from the customer's view will often (but not always) be a tree. For example the Eaton Corporation supplies automotive subassemblies to GM, and Dana Corporation supplies subassemblies both to GM and to Eaton, making the relevant graph a network and not a tree. If the supplier looks upward into the graph for a particular product, he will only see his own customer, that customer's customer, and so on. This structure is a chain. Hence we see that the term "supply chain" refers to the supplier's view of where his product or service is taken into the end customer. This term is however often used when the customer's view is intended, where the correct term is "supply tree" or "supply network".

The pre-network economy changed slowly. Product shelf life or turnover was slow. Once suppliers were chosen for a product, that structure remained in place for a long time. The customer's attention focused on the supply tree, and the supplier's attention focused on the supply chain, since those were the long-lasting entities in the business structure that required management attention. The business network of qualified customers and suppliers existed, but required little management attention. However, the networked business environment is fast and agile. Supply trees are selected from the network frequently and rapidly, and they usually have short lifetimes because the fleeting commercial opportunities have short lifetimes.

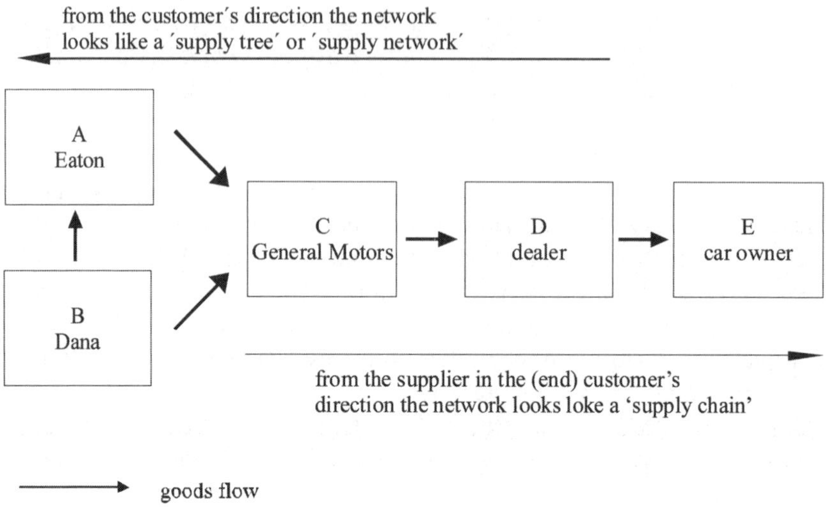

Fig 3.1 Seeing directional graph networks up or down the business network

Management attention then focuses on managing the network, on the processes for joining or leaving a network, and on processes by which to select supplier trees from the network. Business networks and supply trees and chains existed before and exist now; it is the center of gravity of the structures and hence the focus of management attention that has changed. Fine (1998), based on research into several industry sectors including automotive and electronics, wrote that the fundamental competitive capability was not product or process, but the ability to construct and manage a supply chain. We can now go one stage further and say that the fundamental competitive capability is to construct and manage a smart business network.

Note that many of the papers in this book that mention supply chains, should have used the term supply trees. Such supply trees or chains are particular instantiations from smart business networks. Business networks that are smart, however, display quick connect and quick disconnect capabilities; they can pick the best capabilities from many network actors, plug these capabilities together, and make these play in unison; they also control, or own, the business logic for cross-actor execution of business processes.

What Smart Business Networks Should Be Able to Do:

The following capabilities are seen in smart business networks:

- Establishment of common understandings: of meanings, words, of ethics and informal commitments, and of the principles followed in contractual obligations,
- Membership selection: the capabilities to decide which business entities can act as nodes of the network,
- Linking: the positioning and connecting of nodes to the other parts of the network. The linking processes can include the directories (search and select) and routing (path finding) through the network as well as typical communications tasks such as handshake, authentication, and trust establishment,
- Goal setting: the coordination mechanisms that determine the goals of the business network and the tasks and responsibilities assigned to each member node,
- Interaction: the interactive, learning, and self-organising capabilities that make the network generate novel results, preferably those that no single member could achieve on its own,
- Risk and reward management: the division of material results (profit and loss in a monetary but also in a fairly loose and generic sense) and the perceived value by each of the participating business entities of its share,
- Continual improvement: the capabilities and processes of joining and leaving the network over time, of network renewal and sustainability.

Quick Connect, and Disconnect

It is particularly important that actors of a smart business network can "connect" to other actors in the network. Goldman, Nagel and Preiss (1995) described this useful concept in 1995. Sanchez (1995) defines it as "quick-connect electronic interfaces to coordinate product creation resource chains... to a network of product creation resources". This capability of quickly-connected plug-compatibility enables superior response speed and greater component variety when presented with new product opportunities.

The concept of "quick connect" is useful to smart business networks: It includes a search-and-select behaviour by the actors. Once the appropriate actor, or node, is found, and the connection has been established, the process of performing a business transaction can begin. Venkatraman (1994) defines the scope for business network redesign as transaction processing and inventory management, followed by process linkage (interdependent process linkages for unstructured tasks, for example, design and manufacturing) and knowledge leverage (the creation of a network for leveraging skills and expertise). Clearly such connections are much more complicated to achieve and require higher levels of mutual trust.

What requires more attention is the capability to *quickly disconnect*, a process greatly influenced by risk and reward division (Goldman, Nagel and Preiss, 1995). This will be a vital element of a smart business network. Unnecessarily open connections can create unwanted information flows that make a network act "dumb". We need to understand the topology of business networks to fully realise the importance of this. Braha and Bar-Yam (2004) have done so. They examined the statistical properties of networks of people engaged in distributed product development. The patterns of information flows in such networks, say Braha and Bar-Yam, display similar statistical patterns as in other real-world networks of different origins such as information, biological, and technological networks. Interestingly the distribution of incoming communication links always has a cut-off, while the distribution of outgoing communication links is scale-free (Barabási, 2003). This could be consistent with Herbert Simon's bounded rationality-argument (Simon, 1969). It seems easier to transmit information (related to a network's out-degree) than to process information (related to a network's in-degree). Smartness would therefore be related to the organising capability of the information flows within the business network as well as to the topological structure of the network.

Pick, Plug, and Play

Establishing the - temporary - connection is not to say that the network actors, or nodes, will interoperate. Interoperability can be facilitated by modularity. Garud et al. (2003) define modularity as decomposability of a system by grouping elements into a smaller number of subsystems. Schilling (2000) defines modularity as a continuous variable of a system to separate and recombine its components as well as the rules governing the architecture for mixing and matching of these components. Products would be the result of modular, Lego-like blocks combined in a specific way (Baldwin and Clark, 2000). According to Hoogeweegen (1997) this would give the benefits of versatility (the diverse set of products that an organisation can produce) and agility (the ability to respond quickly to fulfil an unpredictable customer order) while at the same time, delivering within the boundaries of value chain total costs and total leadtimes. Hoogeweegen et al. (1999) develop a method to design modular business networks and to optimise the allocation of tasks in the network. Wolters (2002) discerns three dimensions of modularity: product modularity, process modularity, and value chain (business network) modularity. Successful modular design, according to Wolters, should not be restricted to products but must be concurrent in all three dimensions. It requires definition of the function of each module and of the communication protocol between modules. It sees each module as a "black box" that will provide the functionality as required by the modular design.

However, modular designs require much more coordination than non-modular designs. What is an optimal degree of modularity (see Hoogeweegen and Vervest, 2004), or granularity of a system, or business network? Simon (1962) gives an important clue: formal process descriptions make us understand the relatively simple, dynamic laws that can change states found in systems. Managing high degrees of modularity requires much more understanding of the processes that govern the plug compatibility of modular network components.

Once a business network has been able to pick and plug the appropriate product and process modules together, it needs to be able to run, or "play" these modules in the operational environments of the network actors. This is what Webservices aim to achieve, apparently with some considerable success, see Van Hillegersberg, et al. (2004).

Own Business Logic

While workflows define how a process should run, the business logic enacts, monitors and controls the process flow in the technical environments of each of the business network actors; where necessary it passes control over to external systems through agents or adapters to perform a task. This logic is controlled by business rules that take decisions on events depending on the state of the various machines and processes linked to it. There are two critical components to this: the monitoring of all resources in the business network, and management through rule-based event-correlation, see Figure 3.2. It checks the events it receives against the current rules and "fires" the rules when their conditions are met (Smith and Fingar, 2004).

The creation of logic by individual actors in the business networks takes a new meaning once this is linked together and managed through automata, independent of the originating actor(s). Such a business network operates a "business operating system" to run business processes on different organisational platforms. Think of computer operating systems developed in the late 1970s to be able to run application software on different hardware platforms. A business network operating system brings the advantages of making business processes portable and facilitates the end-to-end management of processes running across many different organisations in many different forms. It coordinates the processes among the networked businesses and its logic is embedded in the systems used by these businesses.

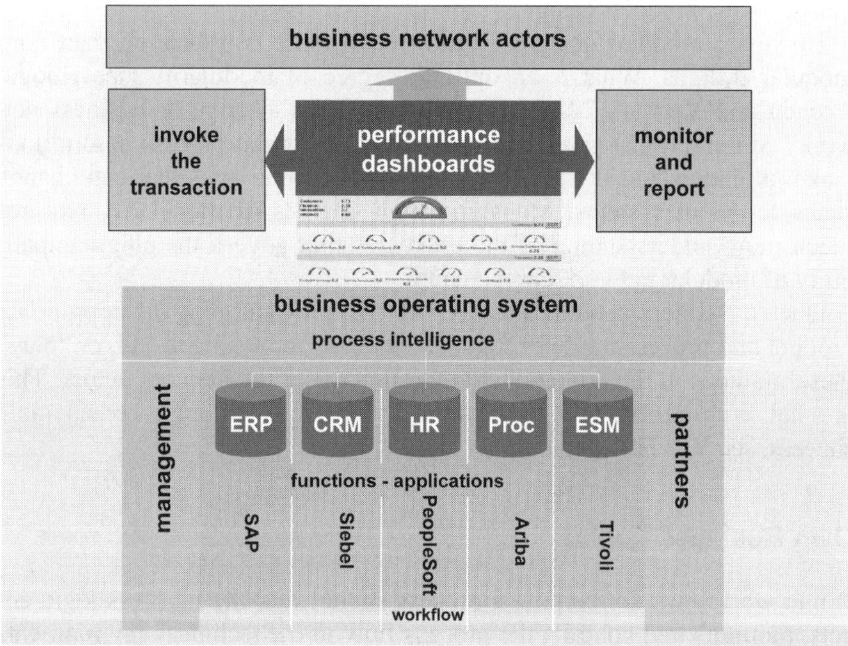

Fig 3.2 The network business operating system contains the overall business logic

Emerging Structures of Smart Business Networks

The levels at which one can analyse and understand the structure of business networks, are, from lower to top level:

1. The hardware and systems software infrastructure(s),
2. The application software,
3. Management of an individual business - described in a networked systems concept as asset and event management,
4. The dynamic control and governance of the business network.

Studies such as Braha and Bar-Yam (2004) and Barabási (2003) suggest that the structure of a smart business network emerges not only from the realities of the business commerce which it enables, or the technology being used, but also from the properties of the network considered as a whole. A number of new determinants for business network structure are proposed in:

- Bounded group rationality that limits the actors' group mind share in a same way as for individuals (Simon, 1969). Measurements suggest that not only individual human beings are limited by an inability to digest intense input of data: A group of people, or a network of nodes, shows comparable limitations,
- Dynamic emergence and decay of key information brokers, information creators, and information users. Measurement on networks shows that most nodes can be categorised as one of these three types,
- Resilience to the effects of both random and malicious malfunction including business malfunctionings, e.g. bankruptcy and contractual breaches.

Each node in a business network has a minimum set of attributes that define the node and link functions. A minimal set of node functions includes capabilities for information generation, information use, and information brokerage, the computational capabilities for each of these, and the allocation of attributes to each of these (such as permissions and rights to the capabilities, the right to create and delete nodes and links, and filtering parameters). Link attributes include weights and amplification factors.

What Smart Business Networks Can Do That No Other Organisational Form Can Do

We require a characterisation of smart business networks based on empirical observations. Examples from the past give some clue. Li&Fung is Hong Kong's largest export trader and innovator in the development of global supply chain management (Magretta, 1998). It manages an expanding network of currently approximately 7,500 suppliers around the world. "What we do is close to creating a customised value chain for every customer order" says Victor Fung. The Li&Fung operation captures the customer critical front end (design, engineering, production planning) and back end (quality control, testing, logistics) tasks. "We are smart about dissecting the value chain". However, smart business networks create a new competitive game. The agile ability to quickly connect and disconnect with a specific tree or chain in a network, and the fact that a given entity (company or profit center) may belong to different business networks for different strategic goals, leads to three simultaneous levels of competition. A smart business network may compete with another smart business network; a smart business network may compete with other strategies of one of its members, and the members of a smart business network may compete in other strategies while cooperating within the smart business network.

There are more examples of smart business networking. Often, such examples are from using intelligent technologies, identifiers, or "conscious" machines. The interest of business is rapidly growing. Bonabeau and Meyer (2001) present studies of "social insects" by companies such as Unilever, Southwest Airlines, Capital One, because social insects work without supervision, are self-organising, and can generate efficient solutions to difficult problems, although the interactions themselves might be simple. Complex collective behaviour can emerge from individual network actors following simple rules (Brooks 2002)! That is a powerful notion.

The Research Challenges Ahead

Smartness does not happen by itself, but it may also emerge spontaneously and not be intentionally designed. Today's pervasive communications technologies will have a much more profound impact on how businesses cooperate and compete than we may be aware of today. We propose that smart business networks should be a recognised direction for management and technology research. As a matter of priority the following research questions are offered to advance the art of smart business networking:

- It is common practice to characterise a single company, usually by defining its product or service sector, possibly with other characteristics. We need a systematic way to characterise smart business networks. Currently we do not yet have the suitable concepts and language to do so,
- Does a requirement develop to embed higher-level functionality into lower levels? If so, should this be done by including the functionality monolithically within the lower level, or should this be done while preserving modularity? The former enhances static efficiency while the latter enhances dynamic adaptability,
- How to design modularity? What spectrum of granularities applies, what modules, architecture, and interface specifications?

- Is today's limitation on the functionality of smart business networks the technical problem of managing complexity, or is it some other question, possibly in the field of social psychology?
- There will come a day when smart business networks are pervasively available and used. By then, complexity management will have a practical solution. What then will govern the design and operation of the smart business network? In other words, today's complexity management appears to constrain the expansion and management of a smart business network, but what will be the limitation then? Research could already focus on this next bottleneck to progress. Will complexity grow without limit, or will trust and human relationships limit the design and operation of a smart business network?

References

Baldwin, C.Y., K.B. Clark, (2000). *Design Rules: The Power of Modularity*, The MIT Press, Cambridge, Mass.

Barabási, A-L, (2003). *Linked - How Everything Is Connected to Everything Else and What is Means for Business, Science, and Everyday Life*, Penguin Group, New York.

Bonabeau, E., Chr. Meyer, (2001). "Swarm Intelligence: A Whole New Way to Think About Business", *Harvard Business Review*, (May), pp.106-114.

Braha, D., Y. Bar-Yam, (2004). "Information Flow Structure in Large-Scale Product Development Organizational Networks", paper presented at the *Smart Business Networks* Science Seminar, The Vanenburg, The Netherlands, 26-28 May 2004. See this book.

Brooks, R.A.,(2002). *Flesh and Machines,* Pantheon Books, New York, NY.

Fine, C.H. (1998). *Clock Speed: Winning Industry Control in the Age of Temporary Advantage*, Perseus Books, Massachusetts - New York.

Garud, R., A. Kumaraswamy, and R.N. Langlois, (2003). *Managing in the Age of Modularity: Architectures, Networks, and Organizations*, Blackwell Publishers, Malden, USA..

Goldman, S.L., R.N. Nagel, and K. Preiss, (1995). *Agile Competitors and Virtual Organizations: Strategies for Enriching the Customer*, Van Nostrand Reinhold, New York.

Van Hillegersberg, J., R. Boeke, and W-J. Van Den Heuvel, (2004). "The Potential of Webservices to Enable Smart Business Networks", paper presented at the *Smart Business Networks* Science Seminar, The Vanenburg, The Netherlands, 26-28 May 2004. See this book.

Hoogeweegen, M., (1997). *Modular Network Design - Assessing the Impact of EDI*, Ph.D. Series in General Management 26, Rotterdam School of Management, TRAIL Research School, Rotterdam.

Hoogeweegen, M., W.J. Teunissen, P.H.M. Vervest, and R. Wagenaar, (1999). "Modular Network Design: Using Information and Communications Technology to Allocate Production Tasks in a Virtual Organization", *Decision Sciences*, Vol. 30, No. 4, Fall 1999, pp. 1073-1103.

Hoogeweegen, M., P.H.M. Vervest, (2004). "How Much Modularity?", paper presented at the *Smart Business Networks* Science Seminar, The Vanenburg, The Netherlands, 26-28 May 2004. See this book.

Iacobucci, D., (1999). "Graphs and Matrices", in: Wasserman, S., K. Faust, *Social Network Analysis: Methods and Applications*, Cambridge University Press, Cambridge.

Magretta, J., (1998). "Fast, Global, and Entrepreneurial: Supply Chain Management Hong Kong Style", *Harvard Business Review*, (September-October), pp.103-114.

Sanchez, R., (1995). "Strategic Flexibility in Product Competition", *Strategic Management Journal*, Vol. 16, pp. 135-159.

Sawhney, M., D. Parikh, (2001). "Where Value Lives in a Networked World", *Harvard Business Review*, (January), pp.79-86.

Schilling, M.A., (2000). "Toward a General Modular Systems Theory and Its Applications to Interfirm Product Modularity", *Academy of Management Review*, Vol. 35, No.2, pp. 312-334.

Simon, H.A., (1969). *The Sciences of the Artificial*, The MIT Press, Cambridge, Mass.

Simon, H., (1962). "The Architecture of Complexity", *Proceedings of the American Philosophical Society*, No. 106, pp. 467-482.

Smith, H., P. Fingar, (2004). "BPM is Not About People, Culture and Change - It is About Technology", Working Paper for the BPMi, (January), See also the *Business Process Management Initiative* www.BPMi.org.

Venkatraman, N., (1994). "IT-enabled Business Transformation: From Automation to Business Scope Redefinition", *MIT Sloan Management Review*, 35, 2, (Winter), pp. 73-87.

Wolters, M.J., (2002). *The Business of Modularity and the Modularity of Business*, ERIM Ph.D. Series in Management, Nr. 11, Trail Thesis Series T2002/1, The Netherlands, TRAIL Research School.

4 Challenges of Smart Business Networks – Five Perspectives

Introduction

At the start of the Vanenburg Science Seminar, during dinner on the first evening, participants were seated at five tables. Each table group was asked to define the phrase *Smart Business Network* (SBN); to choose one aspect of the design, implementation or use of a SBN; to predict what would be the status of that aspect in years 2010 and 2015; and to list the few most significant barriers to achieving the predicted status. Each group continued to work on its document during the days of the conference, then finalised it in the days that followed. The year 2015 is only ten years hence - a distance that is within grasp, and is not too far at all. Two groups chose to deal with the design of a smart business network, two chose to deal with the governance, and one group chose to deal with the business opportunities enabled by a SBN. The groups spontaneously chose subjects that cover the spectrum of important issues that lie ahead, and their reports show different perspectives on similar issues.

The format and the style of each group's document are different - there is indeed no necessity that they be similar. The five documents that follow give much food for thought for both practitioners and researchers interested in bringing smart business networks to reality. Each group document below lists the names of the members of the group. A reader wishing to discuss an issue with any of the seminar participants is referred to the List of Participants and Authors in this book.

Group 1 - Smart Business Networks: Definition and Changes

Willie Golden, Lorike Hagdorn, Rob Peters, Ulad Radkevitch, Arun Rai, and Jimmy Tseng,

Definition of a Smart Business Network

A Smart Business Network (SBN) is a network of organisations coordinating their business processes in a manner that exhibits adaptive, agile and robust behaviour that is generated or reproduced when a robust and necessary set of networked structures and networking processes are established. This definition recognises that smart behaviour of a business network is shaped by its structure, process and technology.

Smart Business Networks are able to generate a continuous stream of innovations and implement mechanisms to generate economic rents by exploiting these innovations in the market. Typically SBNs exhibit a high degree of organic structure and process at inception and evolve and institutionalise formalised structures and processes over time. The Open Source movement has exhibited such a shift from organic structure at inception to a gradual implementation of formalised structures and processes. Through such shifts, SBNs exhibit necessary structural ambidexterity of (a) organic structures and processes necessary for value creation through innovation and (b) formalised structures and processes for value appropriation.

Challenges for Smart Business Networks by 2010

Key challenges identified are grouped into: network structure; coordination process; monitoring and negotiation process; and information technology-enabled integration. Each of these challenges is elaborated below. Network structure challenges identified include:

- Identification of decision criteria to define strong ties and weak ties with partners for core business processes of design, sourcing, logistics, distribution, and after-sales service,
- The mechanisms underlying formation of strong and weak ties include ability of SBN actors to interact in plug-and-play mode when commodity business processes are concerned and to exhibit dynamic negotiation capabilities to tackle sophisticated processes and one off demands,
- Managing agency conflicts associated with the creation and use of intellectual property,
- Contractual structures for the appropriation of economic rents generated because of network effects,
- Power and resources to enforce decisions made collectively, or through arbitration,
- The formation of sustainable alliances given the differences in strategic intent between the various parties, and given changing circumstances.

Coordination process challenges identified include:

- Information sharing processes between SBN partners for coordination of their distributed and interdependent activities,
- Information processing capabilities of a SBN encompasses two major components: 1) translating customer requirements into product or ser-

vice specification and 2) translating specification into production tasks/components,
- Allocation of decision rights for coordination of their distributed and interdependent activities so that expertise and decision rights are co-located,
- Shared cognition to establish and evolve shared expectations about roles, assumptions, and norms of practice. Over time these could become encapsulated as business rules,
- Capability to translate informal coordination mechanisms into institutionalised structural mechanisms that avoid unnecessary transaction costs while not hampering innovative activity.

Monitoring and negotiation process challenges identified include:

- Information sharing between organisations for enhanced transparency of business processes,
- Generation of rich visibility required to monitor activities and flows and stocks of resources across business networks,
- Negotiation of decision rights and contractual conditions for the performance of activities,
- Agreement and standardisation of a language of commitments so that contractual obligations and liability can be expressed in a concise manner (e.g., service level agreements) and disputes resolved in a cost-effective manner.

Information technology-enabled integration challenges identified include:

- Integration of data and information to generate visibility of execution and planning across disparate, but complementary, functional, organisational, and geographic boundaries,
- Integration of knowledge resources across disparate functional, organisational, and geographic boundaries,
- Systems for monitoring performance and generating alerts for manual intervention when automated business processes fail,
- Integration scalability so that solutions and costs required for data, information, and knowledge integration are not one-off investments,
- Business investment logic around process integration protocols, application integration protocols, and other integration technologies.

Challenges for Smart Business Networks by 2015

Key identified challenges focus on the business operating system required to dynamically regulate, organise, and evolve smart business networks. Such a business operating system requires that the following complementary capabilities are established:

- *Dynamic self-regulating behaviour* requires the design of predictive and reactive control systems that effectively uses predictive and reactive control. The business logic will calibrate the cycle times for feedback and feed-forward signals to align with the environmental and network uncertainty that characterise the business network,
- *Dynamic self-organising behaviour* requires the use of federated control structures that exploits centralised control and decentralised control structures to generate adaptive behaviour. The centralised control establishes the architectural rules of the network and decentralised control for the exploitation of each participant's expertise,
- *Dynamic self-renewal behaviour* requires selection processes that identify new network entrants and retire old entrants, by continually assessing compatibility and complementarities of partners. This requires definition of fitness functions for the network and its participants, monitoring mechanisms to assess contributions of partners, and scanning mechanisms to prospecting of new partners.

Group 2 - Design of Smart Business Networks: Smartness Is a Means to an End (and Some Luck Will Help)

Dan Braha, Hong Chen, Benn Konsynski, Katerina Pramatari, Eric van Heck, and Matthijs Wolters

Topic

The central discussion topic of this group was the design and structure of smart business networks. The discussion focused on three issues. Firstly, the discussion was triggered by the paper by Dan Braha and Yaneer Bar-Yam. Secondly, the predicted states of smart business networks in 2015 have been sketched, and thirdly, the barriers lying ahead are analysed.

Trigger

The discussion was triggered by one of the figures in Dan Braha and Yaneer Bar-Yam's paper (see Figure 4.1). The cutoff of in-degree of a node in the product development (PD) network may reflect Herbert Simon's notion of bounded rationality, where complex PD task networks are dominated by a few highly central tasks.

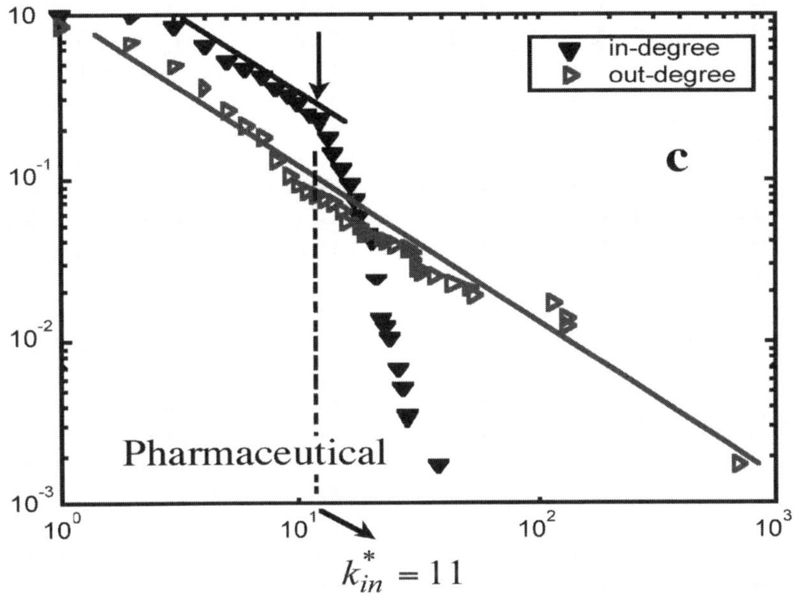

Fig 4.1 Degree distributions for a Pharmaceutical facility development problem solving network with 582 tasks and 4132 arcs

While information keep increasing exponentially, human ability to process it remain basically unchanged, so the design goals of a SBN are:

- Move the cutoff to the right with less highly centralised tasks in the network,
- Achieve optimisation of decision-making based on the design of the structure of the SBN,
- Minimise the process time for information exchange,
- Maximise the capability of information processing.

Key Features in 2015

The key features of the SBN in 2015 are:

- Ubiquitous. One of the enabling technologies of tomorrow's SBN will be ubiquitous computing. With ubiquitous computing, information will be provided any-time any-where. Demands can be captured precisely. (for example, using RFID) and supplies can also be transparent to other nodes in the network,
- More information in the network. The development of technologies will bring down the cost of information generating, transmitting and sharing. But at the same time, more information means more noise in the network,
- Information filtering. Only information that is needed are acquired and processed by the nodes in the SBN, which is only a small portion of the whole amount. The rest of the information will be achieved for later usage or just dumped,
- Membership. A SBN requires memberships. There will not be free riders. The members within a SBN are under continuous assessment; they are competing to cooperate in a closed SBN,
- Plug and Play networks. Each new member to a SBN can join the network without much effort done to his network infrastructure. The interfaces of the nodes of the networks are standardised,
- Network as an asset. In stead of human or physical assets companies value the partnership in smart business networks,
- Fluid networks. The topology of the network can change dynamically. Different nodes in the network will be working together on an ad-hoc task. The contractual relationship between two nodes in a network maybe based on days or weeks, instead of months, neither of years.

Barriers

The barriers lying ahead are:

- IT will increase volume, velocity, veracity and volatility of information. But how to increase the value? How to design information filters that can precisely capture the information needed for ad-hoc demands and at the same time ignore the useless information?
- IT will impact transaction costs and therefore will make shifts in network relationships. What are critical boundaries of transaction costs? What are essential costs and benefits for firms in the network? What will be the impact on different firms in the network?

- How to allocate the decision rights and processes amongst the different nodes within a Smart Business Network? Does a topology exist that will optimise the decision-making process? Will the topology change according to the size of the SBN? What is the suitable size of a SBN?
- Human brainpower and information processing capacity limits. How to adopt ourselves to a fast changing world? When technology has advanced beyond the capability of human being, how can one cope with the reality?
- Legal rules. The laws in different countries are different. This may put restrictions on the nodes and prohibit the formation of a SBN.

The essential building blocks of the Smart Business Network are “plug and play” network components and SBN templates. The latter will serve as the blueprint to configure and build SBNs.

Group 3: On Smart Business Networks and Their Governance

Al Dunn, Jukka Heikkila, Marcus Herzog, and Louis Pau

The group did not reach a consensus on any scenario for smart business networks in 2015. While it is possible to determine the attributes of a business network that might contain or exhibit “smartness” there was a strong view that there will be a diversity of business network adoptions some of which may be described as “smart”. The adoption of such business network models will depend on the conditions in different industry sectors. There is no one 2015. There will be much diversity with different and conflicting models. At this stage the group believes that it is dangerous to over-generalise.

Smart business networks are enabled when organisations combine to amplify their cooperative abilities to deliver a specific value to a specific customer. Therefore to determine the characteristics of the SBN one must address:

- *Amplification*: what is the form and metric of this amplification – is it internal performance or exhibited in its output. It is clear that any amplification is enabled by Information and Communication Technology (ICT),
- *Combining cooperative abilities*: this requires coordination of the events and therefore the participants in the network. ICT enables the ability to coordinate effectively. The form of this coordination will determine the smart business network model,

- *Deliver value to a specific customer*: the "customer" is the consumer of the output of the smart business network according to agreed conditions. This can be the personal consumer (retail), a specific business (wholesale) or may be "internal" (i.e. product development). The delivery of value demands a shared goal that is dispersed and acted upon by the participants in the smart business network according to agreed performance conditions. This places the emphasis on the governance model.

The key characteristic of a smart business network is that it must establish collaboration between its participants to ensure that the agreed deliverable (the external goal) to the "customer" is met according to the individual goals of the participants in the network. In particular, the embedding of business processes into and between organisations, i.e. embedding the business logic into the infrastructure they control, will give an edge to those who take the technology initiatives.

The coordination of smart business networks will not be based on cooperation; rather it will be based on finding an agreed equilibrium in the conflicting goals of the individual participants according to the network goal. This joint goal, usually tactical and short term, must be transparently communicated to all participants. Coordination must resolve these conflicting goals to maintain the joint and individual benefits to each of the participants.

This balancing of the individual goals must be based on ensuring individual confidence and trust and the organisational and contractual arrangements. This means that, whenever an individual participant's short-term goals are not in line with the long-term network goal, it must be compensated with the individual participant's commitment to the network. This will demand increased coordination.

It is noted that this emphasises the static part of the business network (which can be the chosen subset of a dynamic network). While there is an orientation on market-based exchange mechanisms older and less flexible industries will tend to retain their current business network behaviours.

This will reinforce pervasive "smart" stable networks that, by not exhibiting the characteristics of smart business networks, will provide only added costs and a range of disadvantages. They are collusive oligopolies and, as a result, lock-in mechanisms. As a result dominant players in specific industries will favour them.

Smart business networks – i.e. ICT-facilitated (global) network models – are feasible. However there are many barriers including the determining of the economic value of such networks; the implementation of smart

business network models; violations of participant value; and matching to the culture of customers and network partners.
The requirements to design and act "smartly" – ensure situational awareness are to be prepared for (unexpected) changes; to be sensitive to customer desires and to the joint and individual business codes of conduct; as well as to be cost efficient.

Effective governance expands the scope of the organisation with respect to economics, culture, society and technology. Governance of smart business networks requires the coordination by the parties using a generic meta-framework for learning adaptive information handling; for creating and maintaining trust on the domains; for establishing situational awareness; and for feedback, aiming at coordination and controlled, dynamic equilibrium.

Important boundary conditions are the capabilities and means of the parties to carry out dynamic adaptation; to communicate of self-interested goals, roles and responsibilities in a transparent manner; and entry and exit rules.

Towards 2015

From a smart business network viewpoint, 2015 will be characterised by:

- Ubiquitous/pervasive digital business and digital consumer technologies (visible, invisible),
- Intense and ubiquitous communication (connectionless and wireless),
- Capabilities for access (communication and informational links with customer), linking (consolidating and predicting based on customer activity data to trigger appropriate linkages in the business network), location (geographic and activity identification),
- Smart business networks will link to the customer experience – i.e. become a (invisible/transparent) component of the customer lifeline. As a result the smart business networks must predict and act on customer events (trigger points which create requirements) rather than reacting to customer wants or needs. The demand chain becomes the customer event resolution chain.

This places the following requirements on the 2015 SBN:

- Predictive awareness: capturing and acting on customer behaviour to extrapolate rapidly according to predictive "rules" to determine the experience trigger points (heuristic amplification),

- Flexible conformance: the triggering of the appropriate dynamic business network according to embedded governance (the rules of the game: matching, timeliness, costing, regulatory, behavioural) enacted through shared and enacted individual and joint smart business network rules (smart processes in business operating systems),
- New pricing and payment models – close to real time authentication and payment ("payment operating systems", new pricing networks, and infrastructure-embedded value transfers),
- Ability to absorb and enact regulation (local and international) to ensure conformance.

The group concludes that, with the present understanding of the attributes of the smart business network, it is too early to foresee their structure and organics in, say, 2015. There is much to question and understand. It is argue that the "governance" of such business networks lies beyond the governance models of today and must include new structures for the understanding of value distribution in such networks with a concomitant understanding of the factors that contribute to the increased economic value of such cooperations. The distribution of this value will contribute to determining the equilibrium and resolution of internal network conflicts.

Today's "smart" stable networks are the pre-requisite for tomorrow's smart business networks. In particular they will evolve as organisations seek to realise "internal" smart business networks that will reach out and implement their smartness with immediate business network partners.

Group 4 - The Governance of Smart Business Networks in 2015

Amit Basu, Otto Koppius, Peter Muller, Duncan Shaw, Jos van Hillegersberg, and Peter Vervest

At the heart of the concept of smart business networks is the notion that the simple dyadic supply chain is an inadequate representation of both current business practices as well as projected trends for the future of business. Organisations are embedded in networks of relations with their stakeholders and these stakeholders in turn have relations among each other, resulting in networks that can both enable and constrain the focal organisation. Again it is emphasised that the topology of each network is much more complex than a mere collection of dyadic ties, which results in more interactions and also more complex interactions between network members. As the complexity of interaction in a network increases (and there is no reason to assume that it will not increase further), a crucial issue of a smart business network becomes its governance, i.e. how is action coordination within the network? It is contended that most of what one considers to be "smart" in smart business networks is at its core an issue of smart coordination mechanisms in a network. So, what would an ideal coordination mechanism in a smart business network in the future of 2015 look like? Coordination in a future smart business network, at the minimum, needs to exhibit the following characteristics: awareness, adaptiveness and learning capabilities.

At the heart of coordination is the notion of *awareness*, both of network states and network processes. Without awareness, there is no information about the end-goal of the coordination process (the desired state of the network), what the starting point for coordination is (the current state of the network) and how to get to the end-goal from the starting point (the network processes that are available for taking action). Awareness in networks in 2015 will be partly reactive, but will ideally be proactive as well. Reactive awareness is a necessary condition to respond to changes in the network itself and in the network's environment, but it is proactive awareness that truly makes a network smart. Proactive awareness implies the active monitoring of network states and processes instead of waiting for an external change to impact the network. In other words, it builds anticipation into the network. However, the more complex the network, the more phenomena will have an emergent (as opposed to deterministically predictable) quality to them, making adequate forecasting and anticipation much more difficult but at the same of much greater value.

The necessary technologies for awareness such as RFID are already available at commercially viable costs, so technology will not be a barrier. The real barrier to achieve network awareness is the willingness of organisations in the network to share information. As the information architecture of the network can become more transparent towards 2015 by means of technology, more organisations in the network will be concerned with how the increased availability of potentially sensitive information could be used to their disadvantage. This will require increasingly powerful incentives and revenue-sharing mechanisms to induce organisations to share the information necessary for optimal network awareness. This incentive alignment problem has been a central issue since the beginning of organisation theory and it is therefore unlikely to suddenly be solved by 2015, unless a change in the mindset of organisations can be achieved.

The second essential feature of a smart business network in 2015 will be its adaptiveness. Once a network has awareness of its states and processes, it can react to external changes. The capabilities to react, i.e. the actions a network can take to coordinate the actions of its members towards the new desired end-state, characterise the network's adaptiveness. The smarter the business network, the more coordination mechanisms are available and the more information processing capacity each coordination mechanism has. However, this is only part of adaptiveness. At least as important is the availability of knowledge within the network and the capacity to act upon the knowledge of the best coordination mechanism for each situation. This issue becomes particularly salient when new actors enter the network and/or existing actors leave the network and the network has to be reconfigured. It is highly unlikely that there will be a uniform one-best-way of network coordination. Sometimes centralised coordination is more appropriate, sometimes decentralised coordination. Sometimes market-based coordination is more appropriate, sometimes long-term relations need to be in place. To produce such knowledge, a theory of inter-organisational coordination is needed. Although theory in this area has advanced significantly in the last decade, it is still focused mostly on the dyadic level. The theory of coordination mechanisms in a network setting is still in its infancy, and although progress is certainly expected in the next ten years, it is likely that there will still be large gaps in our knowledge and hence many coordination misfits in smart business networks will still be present in 2015.

The third and perhaps most essential feature of a smart business network in 2015 will be its learning capabilities. This is rooted in the proactive awareness mentioned earlier: a truly smart business network will be aware of upcoming external changes before they actually happen. This second order learning allows the network to anticipate those changes by innovating before being forced to innovate (reactive, first-order learning), i.e. building new capabilities in organisations in the network and coordinating network actions in a just-in-time fashion. This implies not only that organisations in the network need to learn continuously from the feedback they receive on their decisions, but also that these feedback processes occur at the network level, as the network processes themselves need to be self-referencing and self-correcting in 2015. While this second order learning capability of the network is what truly makes it smart, this is also where the most significant barriers exist. Part of these barriers are technological as standards in this area are likely to proliferate over the next decade, making it difficult to judge which standard(s) is/are more appropriate, so 2015 will see a multitude of technological approaches to this issue. Part of these barriers, and possibly the more difficult ones to surmount, are social. Traditional learning processes in social networks require significant effort from human actors, are poorly structured, and have unpredictable outcomes and benefits. Thus, underinvestment in the future becomes a likely possibility. Embedding self-referencing and self-correcting procedures in technology (based on network awareness) may decrease the human effort required, but at the expense of loss of control. If technologies become more autonomous, the consequences will be less predictable (especially given the complexity of a network setting) and there is a risk that the network will spin "out of control". Even though such events could be considered "normal accidents", a consequence may be that organisations will be reluctant to cede part of their autonomy to technological systems. So perhaps the boldest aspect of smart business networks, what truly makes them smart, is also what will be the biggest barrier to achieving that goal in 2015.

Group 5 - Projecting Networking Business into the Future "Scenarios for 2010 and 2015"

Falk Graser, Martijn Hoogeweegen, Roger N. Nagel, Kenneth Preiss, and Diederik van Liere

Introduction

In the last few years, increasingly turbulent market behaviour, reducing technological innovation-cycle times, and diminishing trans-national trade barriers forced enterprises to give up the traditional intra-enterprise production paradigm and to challenge their processes with the "make-or-buy" question. This was the onset of massive outsourcing of inefficient business processes and the beginning of networked production. Even since then, many things have changed in business: first enterprise networks proved to be static with hierarchically structured hub-and-spoke collaborations. With ongoing acceleration in market dynamics, networks must become more flexible to be able to quickly respond to these dynamics. Projecting recent trends into the future reveals a massive lack of applicable management concepts, technologies, and even mutually accepted visions on what these networks must look like to prosper in tomorrow's competition. Nevertheless, one thing is certain: enterprise networks must become more innovative, anticipative and agile. The group sees these properties as "smart", hence the business networks showing these properties are called "Smart Business Networks" (SBN). In order to approach the circumstances that will shape these SBNs the ongoing and foreseeable future shifts in collaborative production paradigms are described, followed by an exposition of driving forces pushing forward the shift from traditional, static, and "dumb" Supply Chains to leading-edge Smart Business Networks. Next the vision for networked production in 2010 and 2015 is presented as well as obstacles to be overcome for smoothing the path from now to then. Finally, an approach chosen by the European Integrated Research Projects ECOLEAD to address the transition of enterprise networks is given.

Changing the Paradigm – General Observations

Inter-network Competition

Generally, future developments in enterprise networking will be determined by an increasing degree of collaboration. Thus, the meaning of networks in production will become even stronger than today, while the prominence of the individual enterprise will diminish. It can be assumed that only those enterprises that are able to integrate their business processes quickly within an inter-enterprise cooperation will face tomorrow's competition successfully.

This implies that tomorrow's competition will not be based on attributes of product-based competition, as it was before networks emerged, nor will it be process-based competition as it is in the age of static supply chains. In the next years networks themselves will become competitors, hence tomorrow's competition becomes inter-network competition.

Decreasing Significance of Difference Between Networks and Nodes

In the traditional concept of the static Supply-Chain distinction between the network and its nodes was simple: networks consisted of nodes, representing enterprises or teams, and links, representing informational, logistical, or financial flows between the nodes. With an increasing degree of collaboration, that distinction will become more difficult: not only single enterprises will act as suppliers in networks (as is now current) but also networks that need to be integrated and harmonised with the super ordinate network. Hence, "networks of networks" will arise; examples for this kind of collaboration are as yet few (e.g. large aircraft manufacturers, like Airbus and Boeing) but this model can be expected to become significant over time.

Driving Forces

Obviously, changes in the environment of production systems (e.g. market demands, technological innovation) impose pressure on enterprises and enterprise networks. Pressures will lead to a new paradigm in collaborative production that is characterised by a more intelligent, smarter way of collaboration. Figure 4.2 summarized the driving forces pushing collaborative production into its next generation.

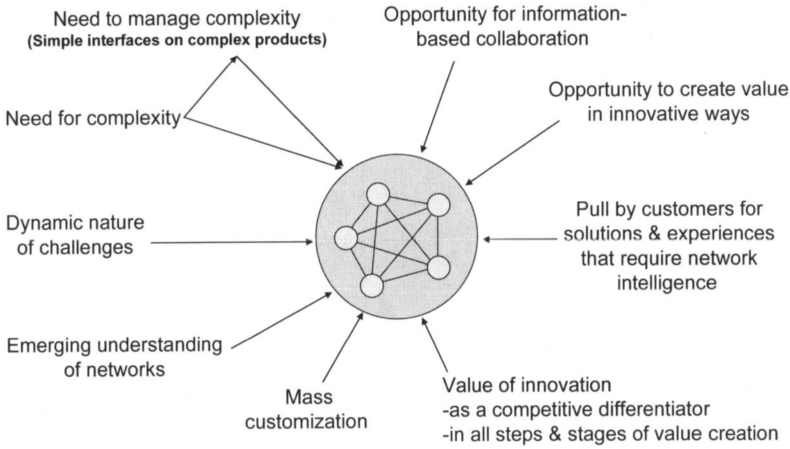

Fig 4.2 Driving forces for shifts in networked production

Smart Business Networks: Visions for 2010 and 2015

Enterprise networks of the future will have to become smarter to withstand upcoming competitive challenges. Thus, Smart Business Networks which will be important in 2010, will by 2015 be more anticipative in recognising market turbulences before they actually occur, more agile towards changes in their environment, and more strongly supported by a variety of intelligent, web-based infrastructures and tools. Some characteristics of collaboration in 2010 and 2015 are outlined in Figure 4.3.

The most important key enabler for entering the next generation of collaborative enterprising is the efficient utilisation of knowledge resources. This applies for the collaboration process itself, and, subsequently, for the output of the collaborative production process. Thus, in the next years, knowledge intensive parts of collaboration may be outsourced to specific SBN providers. Later on, creating a network itself will become a product offered by highly specialised companies. In 2015 networks will innovate and interact with each other through fully virtual markets. Implementation of the mobile ubiquitous computing vision will facilitate and ensure the path to this new way of collaborative business.

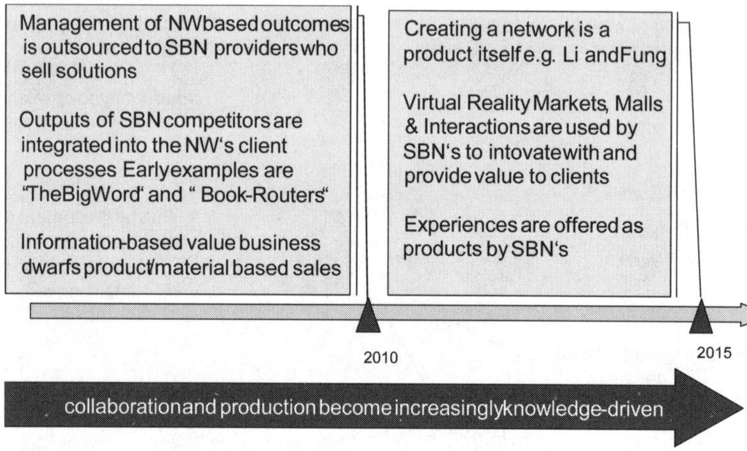

Fig 4.3 Characteristics of collaboration in 2010 and 2015

Smoothing the Path: Obstacles and Solutions

Implementing the visions on networked production in 2010 and 2015 is threatened by a variety of obstacles resulting from organisational, technological and conceptual developments that must successfully be implemented before the visions can come true. Figure 4.4 summarises these potential obstacles. Some obstacles will be explained in more detail below.

Successfully implementing both visions depends strongly upon an agreed understanding of the shape of Smart Business Networks: the concept itself and its necessity need to be understood (2010), perhaps more critical is the need for business leaders to form and articulate in an actionable way the right visions of the evolutionary stages of these kinds of networks in 2015. Both stages must be supported by credible business models. To implement trans-national collaboration international regulations need to be harmonised to overcome existing gaps (2010); further stages (2015) may encounter fears that some of the multi-national networks may become more powerful than national governments. As any reorganisation, transition towards Smart Business Networking in 2010 and 2015 is endangered by organisational inertia and risk-averseness.

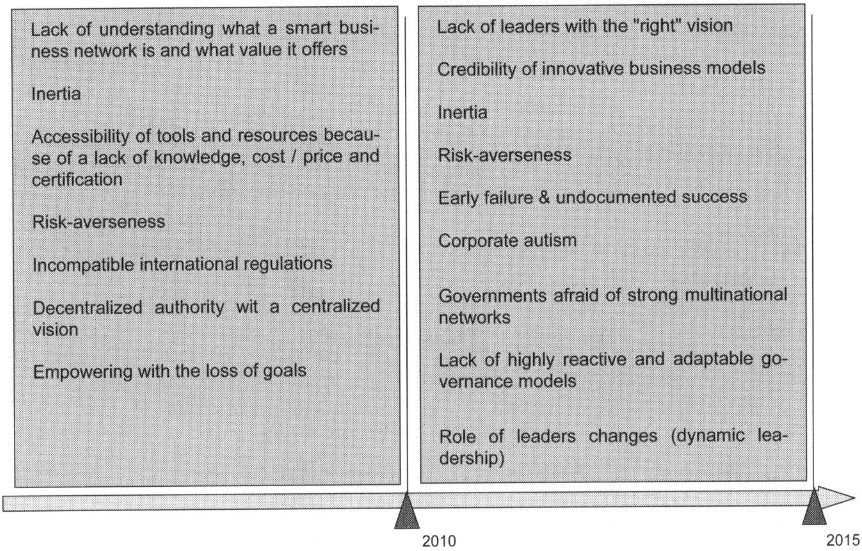

Fig 4.4 Obstacles to Implementation of Visions for 2010 and 2015

Emerging approaches: The ECOLEAD Vision

In April 2004 a major European research initiative on the future of enterprise networks was started. This initiative, named ECOLEAD (European Collaborative Networked Organizations Leadership Initiative) is funded as an Integrated Project within the 6th Framework Program of the European Commission. ECOLEAD developed a roadmap that defines the research gaps between the state-of-the-art and the anticipated state within the next years. This path, from now to then, is highlighted in Figure 4.5.

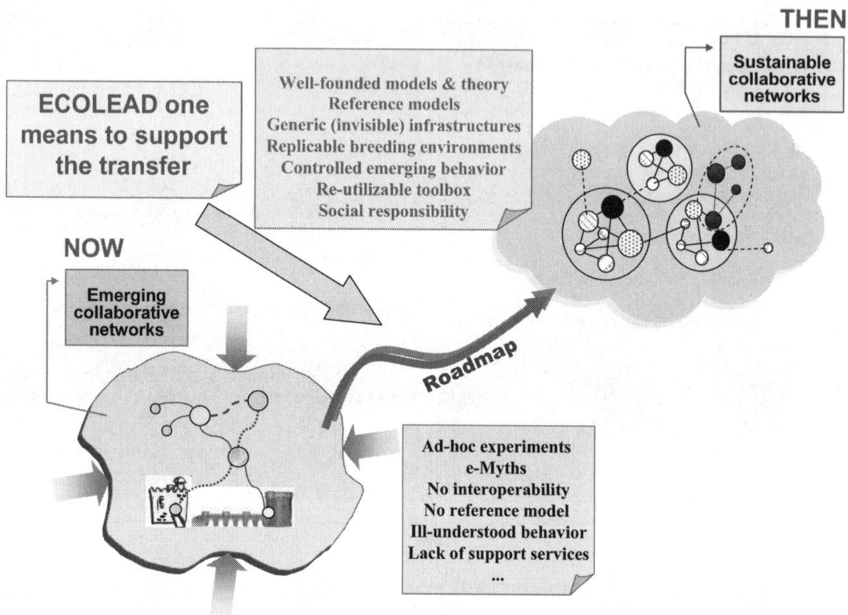

Fig 4.5 The ECOLEAD Roadmap: Requirements to Sustainable collaborative networks (Camarinha-Matos, 2003)

5 The Cordys Panel – Science Meets Business

Introduction

At the end of the Vanenburg Science Seminar the participants presented their themes for discussion (see Chapter 4 for a detail description of the various inputs from the groups). Representatives from Cordys responded and presented their own views on market requirements and the enabling technologies. Their presentations - amplified in the two papers below - formed the basis of an intense discussion between the audience and a panel from Cordys and scientists, moderated by professor Kenneth Preiss. This chapter contains the papers which Cordys presented and the outcomes of the discussion.

5.1 Surf's Up: Are You Ready for the Next Big Technology Wave?

Winfried van Holland[1], Eeuwe Kamsteeg[1] and Vivekanand Sangle[1]

Abstract

Enterprises are struggling with their existing environment to capitalize on new opportunities coming along. For these new opportunities they need to combine existing and new functionality. Composite Applications provide the solution and need specific technology to become extremely beneficial. A Service Oriented Architecture in combination with web-services and an Enterprise Service Bus is needed for that. Existing and new functionality needs to be combined in a process-centric way to create a fast and flexible enterprise. This is needed within your enterprise, and is a must in a Smart Business Network where you need seamless collaboration between people, systems and organizations. Cordys provides this functionality all build on top of the same technology.

[1] Product Marketing, Cordys R&D, Putten, The Netherlands, Hyderabad, India, WvHolland@cordys.com, EKamsteeg@cordys.com, VSangle@cordys.com, phone: +31 341 37555

Another Technology Wave?

We all learned it the hard way. We've all gone through several periods of disillusionment with respect to technology waves. The waves of "standard" packaged applications and the Internet, especially, failed to bring the expected ROI.

On the one hand, enterprises learned that a wave on its own won't provide the answers if you don't focus on the business benefits. On the other hand, they learned to be pretty sceptical about anyone who claims to be delivering the next solution surfing on a new technology wave, especially if it's a software-related wave.

Enterprises have matured now with respect to IT; they are capable of calculating both costs and benefits in order to come to a valid business decision to start new, continue or stop existing projects. Technology waves in general tend to be a synonym for rebuilding the functionality with new technology, i.e., throwing away most of the investments made in the past. That rebuild-and-throw-away part, especially, will make it extremely hard for future technology projects.

In the ever changing world of today, enterprises need to change both their own business and the way in which they cooperate with others. Because of mergers and acquisitions, enterprises are forced to bundle systems with different histories together. In larger enterprises, these merger challenges are even visible on intra-enterprise scale; and as evidenced by the upcoming demands from Smart Business Networks, where different enterprises enhance there cooperation by opening up their internal systems and provide proper information throughout the whole value chain, they are certainly there on an inter-enterprise scale. The question is: how to compose these pre-existing packaged applications and combine them with new functionality. Gartner (amongst others, Pezzini 2003, Schulte 2003) already identified this problem a long time ago and came up with the solution, among others, of a Composite Application.

Providing integration in the back-end systems alone will not suffice. People working with composite applications don't want to be bothered with the fact that they are actually working with various underlying systems. They're asking for one virtual desktop, where the composite application presents itself in one common look and feels like one quick-and-easy user interface. Current enterprises require a seamless collaboration between people, systems and organizations. The collaboration between people needs special attention because enterprises need to deal with informal relations and non-structured information. Within and, especially in the context of a Smart Business Network, outside the boundaries of the enterprise, the collaboration between people must support virtual working groups, quick-and-easy expert locators, discussion boards with peers, and workflow systems that alert peers and co-workers to new processes that need to be executed.

A truly flexible enterprise is capable of changing its internal procedures very quickly. This must be accomplished by stepping away from traditional application development and embracing process-centric application development. A strong prerequisite for the needed flexibility in process-centric development is that the people who understand the business are capable of carrying out the necessary changes. Traditionally, the world is separated into the world of Business Analysts, with an understanding of the business, and the world of IT specialists with an understanding of the supporting software systems and the expertise needed to reorganize them according to new demands from the Business Analyst. They both live in their own worlds, with their own language and their own systems. Flexible enterprises need to have process-centric applications where the Business Analysts are really in the driving seat with respect to changing the systems.

Many enterprises are waiting for the wave that will fulfil their demands for seamless collaboration between people, systems and organizations. That wave will, by respecting existing systems, smartly combine existing and new technologies, together with a flexible process-centric environment that is adaptable to the constant flow of business changes, and all of this at acceptable cost and at their own pace.

If you're ready, you can now benefit from this next technology wave by placing Cordys in your enterprise.

Composite Applications: Smartly Combining New and Existing Systems

As described above, enterprises are not eager for a new big-bang solution in which their existing systems must be rebuilt and thrown away. This creates a strong demand for reusing existing investments, or in other words, to extend their lifecycle. At the time when these investments were made, the systems were not designed or built to cooperate in an environment with other systems. Nowadays, we need to access these pre-existing systems as if they were providing services. The outside world is accessing them as if they were a stand-alone service provider and expects a result in an understandable format. Most of the time, these systems were not even aware that one could access them as a service, and thus without the tightly linked user interface.

The moment that enterprises can open up their pre-existing systems as services and provide them with standard interoperability, they will really become able to reuse their current investments. This creates a need for a Service Oriented Architecture (amongst others, Abrams 2004, Bloomberg 2004), capable of linking different services.

The standardization with web-services and their availability via the Internet makes web-services valid candidates to service enable pre-existing systems. Composite Applications (McCoy and Natis 2003) uses services from different pre-existing systems, which were not initially created for that purpose, and smartly combines them to provide new functions. The composite is delivered to the end-user as if it were created as one application. It is provided in the user's virtual desktop with a single look and feel, combining the strengths and features of the individual services in the right way.

A Service Oriented Architecture requires other capabilities in the area of transactions, security and scalability than the ones currently available in the safe environments of the individual packaged applications. The moment the architecture is able to take care of transactions outside the packaged applications, provide the right level of security given the chosen transportation layer, and provide the power to scale up in response to increasing demand, we will be dealing with an enterprise-class service oriented architecture. Such an enterprise-class environment must operate in a really decentralized manner in which the responsibilities are distributed and no one place can become the single point of failure in the architecture. Such an enterprise-class environment can be established by an Enterprise Service Bus (Schulte 2003) into which all the available services can be plugged, instead of creating one Application Server as a huge spider in the web.

In most cases, it will not be enough to combine existing functions into a new composite application. Most of the time, enterprises will need to combine the existing functions with new functions. These new functions will immediately be created in a service-oriented approach. It will be highly beneficial if the new functions can be created in the same environment used to create the existing ones, thus avoiding needless levels of cooperation. A Composite Application Framework will provide enterprises with the capability to develop new service-oriented functions together with the possibility of combining them with existing functions into a Composite Application.

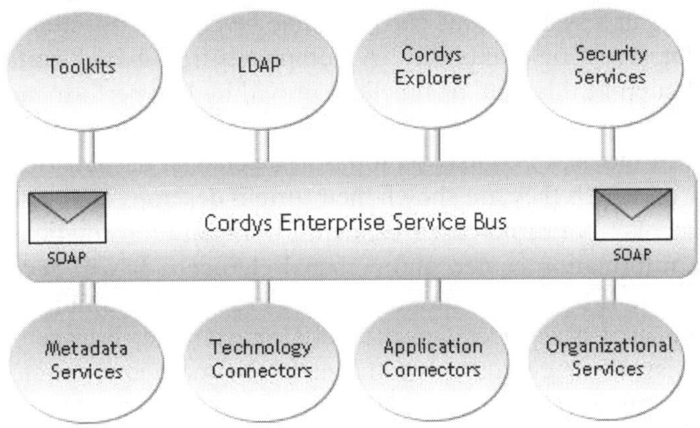

Fig 5.1 Cordys provides an Enterprise Service Bus as the foundation for their Composite Application Framework

Seamless Collaboration between People, Systems and Organizations

Especially in Smart Business Networks, enterprises feel the need to provide flexible multidisciplinary project groups. The people in these groups are no longer located in the same organization, and not even in the same enterprise, but are really transcending the boundaries between enterprises. Characteristic of such collaboration between people are the non-formal and less structured relations compared to collaboration between systems. When they collaborate, people are less bound by fixed interfaces and technologies. They share information in different ways, for example, via E-mail, formal and informal documents, meetings, or discussion panels. Obviously, this less or non-structured information needs to be supported by an environment that provides seamless collaboration between people.

As people tend to move about in an organization and do not know everybody, there is always the challenge of how to find the right person with the right skills. By capturing the personal and skill-related information on persons in the system, other users are enabled to locate a particular person or skill the moment they need them. This is extremely beneficial in larger enterprises and in a chain of enterprises working in a Smart Business Network

Another aspect of the collaboration between people and systems is the way they interact; for example, a user who must react the moment a certain event occurs in a system. This can of course be done in different ways and at different levels of granularity. A completely role-based portal framework will support this kind of function, providing key performance indicators, layered reports, business graphics and alerts to a user or a group of users. All of this is, of course, on top of the personal dashboard offered to the users, on which they are shown their virtual desktop. That virtual desktop will display both role-based elements, company information from the corporate information center, and personal elements. It will become even more effective if the virtual desktop can be expanded to multiple channels so that the user can select the channel (for example, browser, personal digital assistant, or cellular phone) that is the most appropriate for that moment and time.

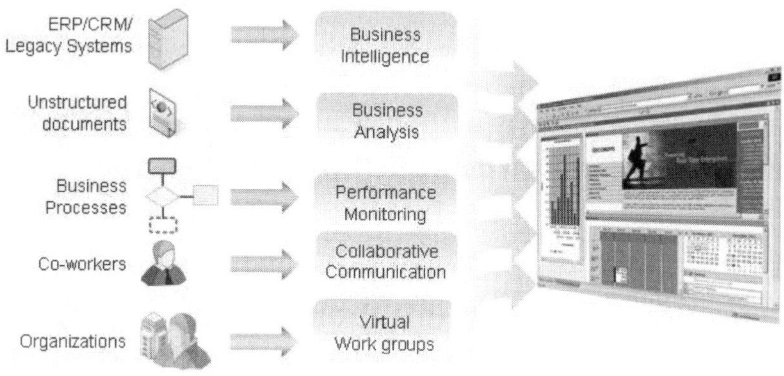

Fig 5.2 The Virtual Desktop as part of the collaboration between people, systems and organizations

Process-Driven Applications Bring the Needed Flexibility

To become really flexible, enterprises are tending to step away from the hardcore functions that need to be created by IT specialists. In general, there is always a kind of Babylonian misunderstanding between Business Analysts and IT people. They live in their own worlds and speak their own languages. And the flexibility is not only frustrated by misunderstanding; this is combined with the stratified approach in which Business Analysts describe their business processes. They describe business processes at different granular levels, from highly conceptual to truly operational. At the conceptual level they describe the processes according to a value chain model: the relationships and processes between organizations, enterprises or groups of them, while at the operational level they describe the processes according to a model with a flow of system and/or human activities.

To create flexible process-driven applications, the Business Analyst must be capable of creating stratified models of business processes that can be published, executed and monitored immediately in their environment. This is the field of Business Process Management, and in a full-fledged Business Process Management environment, the IT specialists must describe the functions offered by the underlying applications in such a way that the Business Analyst can understand them. Using an easy modeling tool, the Business Analyst can, by dragging and dropping the needed function, design the needed flow of activities in the process model. The moment the business changes the analyst can easily adjust the business processes and republish them in their environment. A tremendous flexibility is created by bridging the design and implementation time. In many environments, the business processes are created in an improved drawing tool and thrown over the fence to the IT specialist to implement the process in the system, an extremely cumbersome and ineffective way of working.

In the majority of cases, the real business benefits are not brought about by the common business processes that are executed automatically but by the capability of an enterprise to respond really quickly to exceptional situations in their enterprise or business. What makes the difference is that you must be aware of changes in your market and that you're capable of changing your business according to these changes earlier than the competition. This is the area of Business Activity Monitoring (McCoy and Natis 2003), where all the activities in your enterprise are monitored, filtered and appropriate alerts, events or activities are started the moment that exceptional situations occur.

Cordys, the Composite Application Framework

Cordys provides an enterprise-class and yet lightweight Composite Application Framework to help companies capitalize on new opportunities at acceptable cost and at their own pace. Cordys can make your existing systems web services enabled and plug them into their Enterprise Service Bus. In this way, we truly respect your existing systems and smartly combine them with new functionality.

Cordys, the Composite Application Framework consists of the Cordys Business Collaboration Platform, the technological base, and the Cordys Component Gallery to really accelerate the creation of composite applications with predefined functional building blocks.

The Cordys Business Collaboration Platform is a comprehensive, open and flexible Enterprise Service Bus environment allowing organizations to easily connect, develop, deploy and manage web-services based solutions. The Cordys Business Collaboration Platform contains the following functionality in one product all using the same architecture:

- Cordys Integrator to integrate your existing investments as part of a Service Oriented Architecture by using the enterprise-class and yet lightweight Cordys Enterprise Service Bus,
- Cordys Orchestrator for the execution of process-driven and event-driven business activities by using an XML business object cache, with mapping, transactions, business rules and business flows,
- Cordys Portal as a virtual desktop providing the ability to provide, measure, monitor and improve business processes from multiple sources and on multiple channels,
- Cordys Studio offers customers a solution for business modeling at different levels of granularity, from conceptual to operational. It hides the complexity of the IT specialists and provides the Business Analyst with easy design functionality to create business models at these various levels. The models can be published and executed in the Cordys Orchestrator,
- Cordys Business Application Connectors provide access to various packaged applications, platforms and databases.

Of course, technology is not the only answer. By providing a set of functional components, which can be accessed as services, the creation of a composite application becomes more of a compilation effort than a complete creation from scratch. In this way, the available components can be reused in different solutions, and newly created functions can be offered as components to be used in other solutions. Building new composite applications becomes in such a way mass customization by simply configuring the right components.

By means of this ever growing Components Gallery of predefined functional building blocks, all members of the Smart Enterprise Network can accelerate the compilation of composite applications.

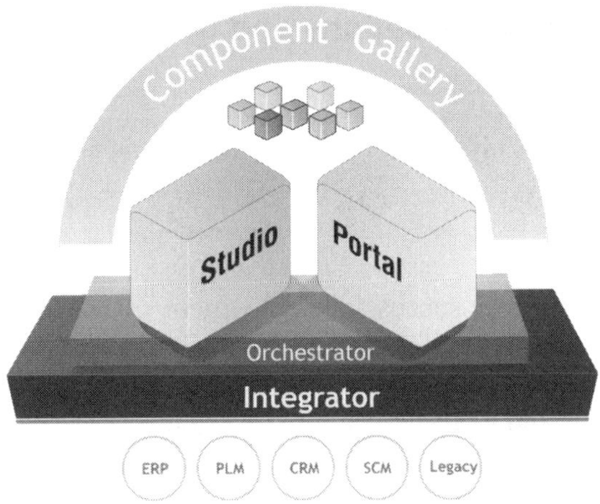

Fig 5.3 Cordys, the composite application framework

References

Abrams C., February 2004, Gartner, Article Top View, AV-22-1413, "Service-Oriented Business Applications Break Down Barriers"

Bloomberg J., June 2004, ZapThink, Presentation, ZTP-0154 "Why Should You Care About SOA?"

McCoy D. W., and Y.V. Natis, April 2003, Gartner, Letter from the Editor, LE-19-7652, "Service-Oriented Architecture: Mainstream Straight Ahead"

Pezzini M., October 2003, Article Top View, AV-21-1772, "Composite Applications Head Toward the Mainstream"

Pezzini M., October 2003, Tutorials, TU-20-9595, "Composite Applications Help Turn Legacies into Assets"

Schulte R., December 2003, Gartner, Research Note, Strategic Planning, SPA-21-7617, "Predicts 2004: Enterprise Service Buses Are Taking Off"

5.2 Composite Applications and the Kaleidoscope Concept

Eeuwe Kamsteeg[2], Winfried van Holland[2] and Vivekanand Sangle[2]

Abstract

The most powerful and successful deployment of web-services seems to finds its application in the upcoming theme: Composite Applications. This theme has emerged strongly in recent feature stories from respected research companies and analysts.

A Composite Application is an application that can be made up of functions drawn from several different existing applications, possibly supplemented by a set of new web-services based business components. The components may be individual web-services, selected functions from other applications, or entire systems whose outputs have been packaged as web-services (often legacy systems). The way these components are used and configured together into a composite application determines the way in which the components support specific business functions and processes. This makes one think of a kaleidoscope, where the ultimate result of configuring and reshaping is highly flexible and of great beauty.

Other articles, such as will elaborate on the concept of Composite Applications and their architectural beauty. In this article, the author introduces the development and deployment of web-services based business components as true Composite Application enablement and highlights the main benefits of deploying the kaleidoscope concept in Composite Applications.

Introduction

These days, enterprises are constantly searching for new ways to meet challenges and capitalize on new opportunities. The world of doing business is changing daily. Customers get more demanding and new business opportunities come and go at a higher rate then ever before. Enterprises are therefore in urgent need of improving their responsiveness, flexibility and efficiency. At the same time, the operational goals are becoming more

[2] Product Marketing, Cordys R&D, Putten, The Netherlands, Hyberabad, India, WvHolland@cordys.com, EKamstegg@cordys.com, VSangle@cordys.com, phone +31 341 37555

challenging – cost reduction, higher throughput, return on investment and improved productivity – measuring rods that mark success or failure.

Even though enterprises cannot do much about this rapidly changing business climate, they can improve their ability to respond. So as to be able to respond better and faster, they are increasingly in need of new adaptable solutions to support their ever-changing business processes while leveraging their currently installed systems. They are looking for new ways to support their growing opportunities through business-to-business collaboration and the development of smart business networks.

For a long time, companies have been trying to achieve this through laborious upgrades, painful customizations and never-ending back-end integration projects. People have been building new applications out of old applications for some time, but they have been doing it via back-end integration, hooking up to the data store and then making changes to the application. The business logic is not decoupled. The interface is probably proprietary and it is inflexible, costly and time-consuming.

"Now a better method is emerging, which uses standardization and web-services to make Composite Applications easier to connect and configure", says Gartner analyst Massimo Pezzini, who was one of the first to use the term.

A Composite Application is an application that can be made up of functions drawn from several different existing applications, supplemented by a set of new individual web-services based business components. The components may be individual web-services, selected functions from other applications, or entire systems whose outputs have been packaged as web-services (often legacy systems).

Web-services fits very well with Composite Applications. Web-services allow you to encapsulate existing applications or their functions in business components. Their interfaces are then published using the Web Services Definition Language (WSDL), which can be invoked via the Simple Object Access Protocol (SOAP) from multiple services consuming front end applications. This is what we call truly Service Oriented Architecture (SOA).

Process-centric configuration will bring the application into existence. The way components are used and configured together into a Composite Application determines the way in which the application will support specific business functions and processes. This makes one think of a kaleidoscope where, based on fixed back-end elements, the ultimate result of configuring and reshaping is highly flexible and of great beauty.

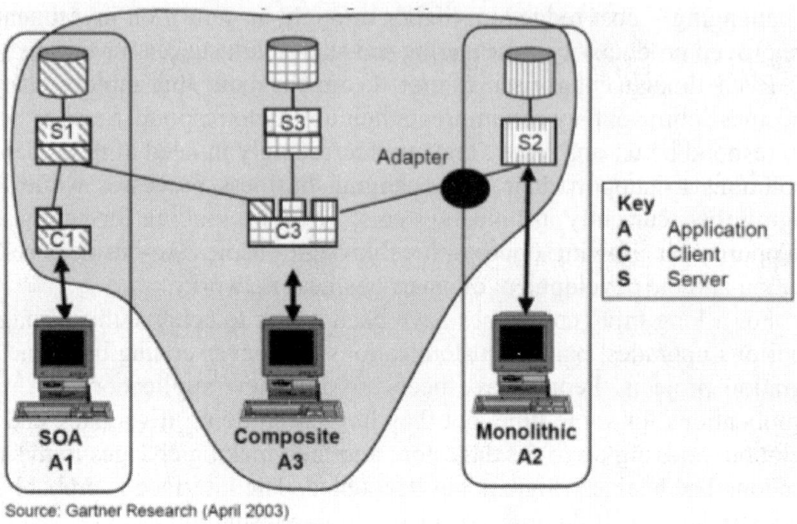

Fig 5.4 Composite Applications consist of functions drawn from several different existing applications, supplemented by new web-services based components

Benefits of the Kaleidoscope Concept in Compo-Site Applications

More than just architectural beauty, the kaleidoscope concept of Composite Applications brings significant benefits to those who adopt it. We will look at three main areas in which this concept manifests its power and gives the enterprise the increased responsiveness it so desperately needs:

- Fast development and deployment,
- Increased flexibility and responsiveness,
- Empowering business process experts in application development.

Fast Development and Deployment

For companies looking to break the expensive and time-consuming technical cycle of traditional application development and integration, adopting the Composite Applications concept may well be the answer.
New applications can be implemented much faster if developers can reuse existing application logic. With Cordys, the new application can be developed in a modern, full-featured studio environment. There is no need to develop complex extraction and reconciliation routines or recode applica-

tion logic to access data if existing data and business logic is shared. In "well-behaved" Composite Applications, the composition logic is separated out and may be organized into a service-oriented architecture. This composition logic provides an access interface to a given application and can be reused across many projects. This reduces costs, and makes application development much faster and more flexible.

The time needed for a new application to become available to its users to support existing or newly defined business processes will improve dramatically. This will bring a competitive advantage to any enterprise doing business in today's rapidly changing marketplace.

Increased Flexibility and Responsiveness

In this new era of doing business and with the rise of Composite Applications, customers should no longer focus on what it takes to build an application, but on what it takes to change it. Composite Applications do not only enable fast development of new applications but also give companies the flexibility to respond quickly to new business opportunities by allowing rapid reconfiguration of the application to accommodate new business structures, processes, and customer or partner requirements.

A Composite Application consists of web-services, either being wrapped functions or newly built application components, all working together to support certain business processes. Reconfiguring the business process model and web-services accordingly, would mean a change in behavior of the end-user application. With this completely new way of process-centric, flexible application development and configuration, solutions will become highly flexible and adaptable to the enterprise's needs. This will improve one's ability to respond to change enormously and will finally give enterprises the agility to capitalize on opportunities.

Empowering Business Process Experts in Application Development

Composite Application Frameworks will increasingly provide tools that can be used by less technically skilled and more business-oriented developers for building new applications. Business Process Managers (BPMs), rules engines and programmatic integration services will all empower process-centric configuration of Composite Applications by business process experts, while driving complex orchestration of large numbers of basic components into a Composite Application.

In its Composite Application Framework, Cordys provides a rich, multi-tier application development environment to develop new process-centric, web-services based Composite Applications. This will enable the business analyst to visually model both business processes within the enterprise and the processes of business-to-business collaboration. These models can then be published to the runtime environment where they can be executed. The people that are familiar with the processes and understand the business are not only capable of creating new applications but are also able to introduce the necessary changes into existing Composite Applications.

Leveraging the Kaleidoscope Concept of Composite Applications

We have just discovered that shaping new Composite Applications is done by configuring different components into new process-centric applications. This new way of building solutions will bring about a faster time-to-market, increased flexibility and improved responsiveness in any enterprise adopting this concept.

Still, the strength of Composite Applications will only attain a real peak with the availability of an extensive library of generic web-services based components that can easily be deployed in a wide variety of Composite Applications.

Clearly, the availability of an extensive library of new web-services based components will truly accelerate the development and deployment of a Composite Application. Development can be turned into a non-coding configuration of new applications. Based on business process models, the new application can be created by both reusing wrapped functions of existing systems and calling on web-services components that are available.

Cordys is building such a library, called the "*Cordys Component Gallery*". This is a continuously expanding set of reusable solution components. It contains individual generic web-services based components like the:

- *Cordys Object Life Cycle Manager (OLCM)* and some directly related functional components, to generate and manage life cycle information on objects,
- *Cordys Multi-Dimensional Hierarchic Modeler (MDHM)* for automatic generation, modeling (tree structure), filtering and smart searches on objects,
- *Cordys Label Generator* for automatic generation, design and printing of labels and work instruction sheets (supporting barcodes and industry standards).

In line with this methodology, Cordys offers not only individual generic business components but also pre-packaged sets of application components that, together, will accelerate the development and deployment of a Composite Application in specific business domains and verticals.

Good examples of these Packaged Composite Applications are the:

- *Cordys Service Manager* - This provides all needed application components to build a comprehensive service solution that supports performance-based (field) Service Management. It provides a flexible, comprehensive suite of functions designed specifically for enterprises engaged in post-sales maintenance and product services,
- *Cordys Kanban Manager* - This provides all the needed application components to fully support the design, maintenance, daily management and execution of an electronic "pull based" Kanban Management System.

Both the *Cordys Service Manager* and the *Cordys Kanban Manager* deploy a number of the same generic individual web-services based components from the Cordys Component Gallery, like the ones mentioned above. In both cases, these are supplemented by a number of more specific functional components and pre-packaged as a solution set. Assembled together with existing functions from applications like ERP at a customer's site, these Composite Applications will fully support the business functions concerned within the enterprise.

The Packaged Composite Applications are Based on Cordys, the Composite Application Framework

Both the *Cordys Service Manager* and the *Cordys Kanban Manager* are based on *Cordys*, the Composite Application Framework. *Cordys* provides an enterprise-class and yet lightweight Composite Application Framework to help companies build Composite Applications to capitalize on new opportunities.

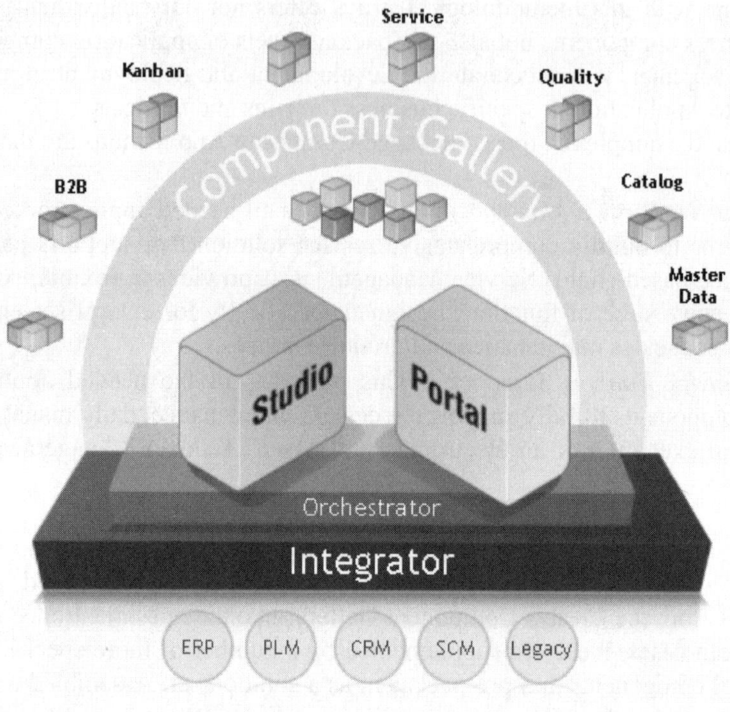

Fig 5.5 Cordys Packaged Composite Applications, like the Cordys Service Manager, are based on Cordys, the Composite Application Framework reusing individual components from the Component Gallery

Cordys contains the *Cordys Business Collaboration Platform*, a comprehensive, open and flexible Enterprise Service Bus environment allowing organizations to easily connect, develop, deploy and manage web-services based solutions. The Cordys Business Collaboration Platform consists of the:

- *Cordys Integrator* to integrate existing systems as part of a Service Oriented Architecture,
- *Cordys Orchestrator* for the execution of process-driven and event-driven business activities, with mapping, transactions, business rules and business flow engines,
- *Cordys Portal* as a virtual desktop creating the ability to provide, measure, monitor and improve business processes from multiple sources and on multiple channels,

- *Cordys Studio* offering the Business Analyst an easy design tool to create business models at various levels. The models can then be published and will be executed by the Cordys Orchestrator,
- *Cordys Business Application Connectors* providing access to various packaged applications, technologies and databases.

On top of the *Cordys Business Collaboration Platform*, Cordys developed the *Cordys Component Gallery* which contains an extensive set of individual, reusable web-services based components. As described above, these components are deployed in several Packaged Composite Applications, like *Cordys Service Manager* and *Cordys Kanban Manager*.

References

Schulte R., 16 April 2003, Gartner Research Note, DF-19-5531, "Use SOA for Composite Application Integration"

Abrams C., Smith D., 9 October 2003, Gartner Research Note, SPA-20-7295, "Service-Oriented Business Applications Show Their Potential"

5.3 Panel Discussion

"Defining the long term without short term details leads nowhere. Defining implementation details without a long term view leads everywhere, hence nowhere." Kenneth Preiss' observation gave a perspective for discussing the Cordys view on the development of smart business networking. In doing so, Cordys must act in the details of the present and the immediate future while being prepared to capture the long term potential of smart business networks.

The question and answer discussions began with the seminar participants guided by a panel of Kenneth Preiss (chair) and Benn Konsynski with Winfried van Holland and Hans de Visser of Cordys.

This part of chapter summarises the key themes of the session rather than providing a detailed record of the actual discussions. As a result, many specific questions and comments are anonymous, but this anonymity is not intended to detract from the incisive questions and valuable comments of those individual participants.

The Participants' Reactions

Two comments captured the participants' positive response to the Cordys story: "This is about retiring useless IT assets instead of integrating them. That is very powerful", *Arun Rai* and "Over the past days we have had fruitful discussions on smart business networks; now we have an industry perspective on the tools that make those ideas reality", *Amit Basu*. The legacy perspective stimulated discussion on the retirement of "old assets" but was preceded by the question:

What Is Cordys' Business Perspective With Respect to Smart Business Networks?

We must take a pragmatic approach to the smart business network and what it is. Both external and internal factors will influence such smartness. It may be found in the way non-core activities are outsourced. For example, a manufacturing company facing strong competition and low margins can be forced to redesign their core capabilities and specialise on one single part of the value chain. Today this requires very tight and rigid agreements with partners; rigid supply chain governance. Organisations seek to maintain and/or build their market share and/or improve their margins. Smart Business Networks enable a company to move from the defensive strategy of bottom line savings by integrating processes across static supply chains, to the offensive strategy of top line revenue from new forms of competition, being agile, quickly connecting and disconnecting from different partners for different and fleeting business opportunities.

The Question of Legacy

Companies seek alternatives that allow them to extend the life cycle of their current infrastructures. They need to escape from the high costs of the upgrade traps of large incumbent software systems. The retirement of IT assets has been viewed as a question of Return on Investment (ROI). In general decisions are made on a rational evaluation of the costs of maintaining the current infrastructure against those of implementing a new infrastructure. "Often this is not a rational decision, rather it is a political decision. We have seen the dominance of the CFO in IT asset decisions", *Benn Konsynski.*

In the present economic downturn many companies invest only if convincing ROI arguments are there. But we do see different approaches. For example a manufacturing company is using Cordys to turn its own internal hub into a supply chain hub for its industry; a bank is using the Cordys platform to run industry payments. This involves more than a straightforward ROI argument.

Retiring legacy systems is more than an ROI decision, it is driven by changing environment and the gradual loss of people. There are now smaller numbers of people who understand how to sustain existing systems.

Kenneth Preiss concluded, "Smart is not an absolute measure. The smart business network is smarter than that of the competitor. Like a smart athlete you only need to be faster than your competitor. The decision to outsource certain activities should not be made purely on the basis of cost cutting. Companies should not outsource their core capabilities. There is a danger that, in off-loading personnel, the smartness of the organisation can be degraded. We tend to forget that the systems are not the assets. The real assets are the data, the longest living thing we have in the systems". *Louis Pau* responded, "Do not forget the people. The people make the money for you".

How Do You Persuade Your Customers of the Value of Cordys?

While the Cordys platform is broad, often customers approach us with a very specific, narrow problem. This is usually a symptom of a much broader problem. By providing one unified view to the end user with the ability to synchronise data between different systems we can unlock opportunities beyond the resolution of a narrow problem. The initial discussions often focus on bottom line cost savings rather than on top line revenue opportunities that can be realised over time.

In fact there is not a single answer to this question. The answers change over time and situations. Consider the example of a retail chain. They intended to embark on a major ERP implementation to combine 17 legacy systems. In reality, with the ERP implementation, the result would be 18 systems. Their basic problems would remain unsolved with future complications and new costs introduced. They really need to master data management across multiple systems to give each user a single experience across the various processes. In doing so they would reduce immediate and future costs, avoid lock-in and, most importantly lay the foundations for future opportunities.

Generally, the first driver is to fix a problem and save money. The first discussions center on "integration" but they do lead to "development". The customer sees the value in the first step rather than in consideration of the true value that can be unveiled in the subsequent developments.

Roger Nagel concluded, "When a new technology emerges the usual driver is to do existing things better and smarter. The next step is to then do things that you could not do before".

Rapporteur's comment: this discussion stimulated questions and issues that have been absorbed into the research questions, below. Pragmatism must dominate Cordys' immediate thinking – winning business with today's customers. However, the potential of their formula for applying lightweight solutions to release intra- and inter-organisational processes from the entrapment of legacy systems provides the basis for pragmatic analysis of building the "operating system" component of the smart business network and, importantly, to shift Cordys' discussions with individual customers to business network benefits.

Assuming that Cordys Can Establish Itself as the "Business Operating System" of Choice, Will it Become the Next Legacy Infrastructure?

Every software provider claims to be "open" but reality has shown that this is rarely the case. The real question is "how easily can our platform interwork with others? Are we simply integrating integration technologies?" We believe not. We are moving to a higher level – the process – and, as a result, to the business network. Technology becomes legacy because it cannot adapt and move forward. By capturing business processes into a reusable, reconfigurable, shared family of business network resources we enable a process engine that is independent to the technologies, interfaces, individual business activities, and the structure of the network itself.

Louis Pau concluded, "business networks need to act in uncertainty. The beauty of "software" should be its ability to handle unexpected shocks. The robustness of the network must be a key characteristic, one of the network metrics".

What, Are for You, the Most Important Research Questions Around Smart Business Networks?

1. Knowledge Management

The response from Cordys was slow in coming. Not because of a difficult question but rather, because the research-oriented participants in the seminar challenged current understanding and directions to ask "what do you really need to understand?"

The first response from *Theodore van Dongen*, Cordys, was, perhaps, unexpected: "How do people learn in a business network?" Knowledge management is the weakest point in business network collaboration. Do we really understand how people learn? What are the tools (simulation, multiplayer games, forums, discussion boards) that support individual and collective learning? How do and can we "share" what we know and what we can do as a result? How can the knowledge and ideas from the various distributed people be linked, acted upon and applied to the business network?

Key question: how is "thinking" enabled in the smart business network? What is "network-based learning? How do we capture and correlate knowledge?

2. Value Creation and the Business Network Models

"In 2015, profitable competition will include that between business networks rather than between individual companies", *Kenneth Preiss.* The concept of the smart business network will change the understanding of the definition and distribution of value between the participants in that network. "We are moving from one-actor sales situation to a network of actors – how do you convince people to facilitate development of this potential network?", *Eric van Heck.*

We are, perhaps, dividing the existing "pie" rather than trying to increase it for each individual. This "breaks existing conceptual frameworks: create the pie then divide it, automatically rather than by coercion", *Otto Koppius.*

How do smart business networks uncover new ways to make money? What is the top line potential? How are smart business networks exploited collectively for customer and competitive advantage? What are the arguments that move organisations into new directions? There is a need to determine new criteria and metrics to measure the degree of success, or "smartness" of a business network. Does the network topology, combined with its dynamics, determine the smartness of a business network? How do you classify and characterise a business network and determine precise metrics to compare "success"? Key question: how is the economic model for the smart business network constructed and translated into effective business argumentation?

3. Transforming Business Understanding of the Networked World

How can we convince a potential network of organisations that competition and value should be viewed at the business network level rather than only at the level of the individual participants? What are the drivers for business network evolution? How can we overcome such barriers as the instinct for people to shield information from others?
Cordys views the network as "virtualised software with market being defined by the "network architect". But we do not ask "Who is this network

architect?", *Henk de Ruiter*. Who will trigger and lead the formation of the smart business network: an individual, a collective? "We are too oriented on the supply chain. We speak of robustness, management and governance, the process...but where is the *discovery* of the business network capabilities? Look at the understanding that can be gained from elsewhere, for example genetic engineering...", *Louis Pau*.
Key questions: Is there empirical evidence and research that can determine the route map for the evolution to smart business networks and provide the business argumentation for this evolution? Is there a role for the "network architect"?

4. Customer Readiness Assessment

"Can we define a "readiness assessment" for the customer's propensity to initiate smart business networks?", *Roger Nagel*. Is there a "customer will to be smarter"? *Eric van Heck*.

We see the failure in implementation projects such as CRM, MRP, and ERP. This is more than qualifying a sales target. When we look at the potential of smart business networks we need to determine and assess the topologies of these networks. *Peter Vervest* commented that Erasmus has worked on Ex Ante Assessment Tools that could be an engine in the Cordys approach. Rather than assessing "more of the same" and "speeding up the mess" we should absorb Dan Braha's paper suggesting that we could be very different, rather than assuming an extrapolation of current approaches. We should seek out recurring interaction structures in business networks that are today perceived as smart and find how to take advantage of these.

Key questions: can we determine the "readiness assessment" based not only on a single participant but also on the ability of other participants to participate in the smart business network? What are the attributes and capabilities needed to find the partners in the network?

Conclusions by the Moderator

This has been a wide ranging discussion. It is difficult to determine the important question that we might have missed. However, I might assume that many organisations and their business networks will start using platforms such as provided by Cordys; initially for data integration but, as their eyes open, as a platform for the business operating system and a basis for enabling smart business networks. I could foresee that, worldwide, many business networks may begin using such solutions. The corollary is that they can then only operate their business applications if they use a single business operating system. What then? How will companies connect across different Business Operating Systems?

I am reminded of the analysis in the book by the economists Shapiro and Varian describing how first movers can become the dominant controller of software in the networked marketplace. In our understanding of the Cordys tools, we could foresee the application of the business operating system in the realisation of smart business networks. The tools are in place…but is the marketplace ready? Our scientific research will help determine possible shapes of the future while organisations like yours prepare and implement the building blocks.

I thank everyone for their inputs, opinions and questions. I close with a goal for our hosts and friends from Cordys "be the business operating system for smart business networks and command the world of business".

References

Shapiro C. S. and Varian H. R. (1998). *Information Rules: A Strategic Guide to the Network Economy,* Harvard Business School Publishing.

Section 1

Outcomes of Smart Business Networks

6 Spontaneous Collaborative Networks

Benn Konsynski[1] and Amrit Tiwana[1]

Introduction

Smart Business Networks (SBNs) reflect an ability of trading partners to establish a unique pattern of practice that serves the participating member firms in a unique and positive fashion. Trading partners establish a discipline of processes and decision rights that serve the community of collaborators. This involves both a business practice element and a technical infrastructure element. The term "smart" merely distinguishes the mundane form of these networks from the interesting forms that create a differentiation in the market of competitors. We expect to see attributes of agility, collaboration, self-organization, responsiveness, and other characteristics of cooperation in volatile markets.

The majority of such networks are planned and executed by trading partners along a fixed program of buyer and seller processes that serve the network membership. Some of the market processes and protocols are consensually defined, while others are imposed by the influence of buyer-side directives that impose a discipline on the seller communities. Such "programmed" arrangements are of great interest as they dominate the scene of current smart business networks.

For our purpose, we will focus on the form of SBN that are highly dynamic and even spontaneous in formation. We focus on the architecture that supports such networks and the governance of their operating environment. Rapid formation of partnering entities into a high performance network is no small challenge. It is only with the employment of effective business governance policies and information technology architecture that we are able to have confidence in our ability to handle the complexity that attends such a pursuit.

Principles of Spontaneous Collaborative Networks

The utopia of the modern market involves a business and technical network that is proactive, dynamically flexible, yet efficient. It is not bound by static form or function in exploiting emerging market opportunities. At

[1] Emory University, Goizueta Business School, Atlanta, Georgia 30322, USA, benn.konsynski@bus.emory.edu, atiwana@bus.emory.edu

the core of this environment lies knowledge—about market processes, competitive practice, and cooperative opportunities. The pathways for this knowledge are etched in information systems through which this knowledge flows intra-organizationally and inter-organizationally.

From an enterprise view, the idea of seamless connectivity has been pursued in perfecting the concept of the extended enterprise (Hitt, 2002). A firm, or market participant, makes decisions on resources, rights and authorities as an extension of the legal boundaries of the firm. The goals and objectives of the firm are projected into the external environment and patterns of influence are brought to bear to influence behavior of entities that extend beyond ownership – usually buyers creating "discipline" among seller communities.

Consider for a moment where the realization of a perfect extended enterprise—if there is one—brings a firm. The epitome of a well-oiled extended enterprise machine is efficiency and near-zero transaction costs. And transaction costs are increasingly growing as solo firms increasingly morph into networks of collaborators and co-conspirators—business partners, suppliers, complementors, and customers. Excessive attention to the boundary where one firm ends and another begins in a collaborative network can undermine the efficiency of the entire enterprise. Paradoxically, volatile markets reward efficiency *and* flexibility.

It is this market agility that demands an operational efficiency while tolerating a high degree of complexity. Volatile, unpredictable, and complex customer needs coupled with exogenous factors that vary unpredictably puts inflexible firms at the grave risk of becoming unnecessary in the marketplace (Ciborra, 1996). Achieving efficiency has now become the prime vulnerability of the contemporary enterprise and the architectures on which it is built. Why? Because it has often come at the cost the ability to be adaptive and spontaneous.

In this paper, we consider how the guiding logic of contemporary interfirm network architectures introduces strategic handicaps by maximizing efficiency but undermining flexibility. We consider how these organizing logics can be refined into adaptive business networks that maintain the capacity to explore new opportunities while exploiting existing ones. Six structural attributes and two governance attributes are key to realizing such spontaneous collaborative networks. These are discussed next. We later describe how these characteristics translate into some of the defining characteristics of the architecture of such networks.

Structural Attributes

Both the business environment and the technical environment define the limits of the possibility for formation of spontaneous community and sustainable partnership. In this section we enumerate a number of attributes and considerations that characterize the environment of business policy and technical capability that are needed to support the formation and adaptation of spontaneous networks that remain improvisational. These reflect observations of environments conducive to ready adaptation in response to, or in advance of, market shifts. Many of the attributes are structural, reflected in both the business governance practice and in the technical capabilities of the participating entities.

Effective market practice includes attention to loose coupling and relevant modularization, a separation of knowledge sharing from process roles, increased visibility of operations across partnering organization, heterogeneity retention, and a self organizing swarm architecture. We observe a continuous alignment of near and long term objectives reflecting the different views of the participants, accommodation of heterogeneous interface, and active relational governance that frequently reviews roles and contributions to adjust behaviors. We consider each of these shifts in behavior as indicators of readiness to participate in spontaneous collaborative networks.

Loose-coupling and Modularization

The relationships between firms in an inter-organizational network define its inter-organizational coupling (Orton and Weick, 1990). Coupling refers to how events in one member firm of the network affect the internal practice of another firm in the same network. Contemporary tightly-coupled networks are built around partnering firms that have made complementary, dedicated investments that facilitate integration of information and business processes. However, dedication to a given network can reduce flexibility in each participating organization as well as in the collaborative network. Improvisational networks require room to maneuver more freely. Consider a clothing manufacturer that can identify an emerging fashion trend and be the first to exploit it, irrespective of whether it currently has the capabilities to do so. This requires both an ability to draw in new organizations with the necessary capabilities that do not already exist in a network.

Clearly, this requires modularization of the inter-firm collaborative process itself. Modularity refers to the attribute of a system to shift interdependence between components to the interfaces between those components (Schilling, 2000; Djelic and Ainamo, 1999). The key principle is that all interdependence between firms or entities in the SCN must be moved to the inter-entity interfaces and complete independence must simultaneously be maintained within each entity[2].

Separation of Knowledge Partitioning from Process Partitioning

Business processes such as manufacturing, maintenance, and delivery are often partitioned among partner firms in business networks. For example, a focal firm might assemble a product, different parts of the product might be manufactured by various partners, another partner might market it, and yet another partner might provide after-sales support. A problematic assumption embedded in this approach is that firms confound the partitioning of business processes with the partitioning of the expertise that is needed to perform the tasks (Takeishi, 2002). An improvisational approach requires firms to treat the two as separate but interdependent approaches to specialization. On one hand, firms in improvisational networks must maintain deep specialization in the process domain but despecialize in their knowledge domain. Deeper specialization means that specialist firms will develop deeper expertise beyond their specialized process and task domains and are therefore are more likely to be attuned to technical advances and environmental shifts in those domains (Powell et. al, 1996). In other words, it is useful for firms to have some understanding of their partners' domains for planning and execution of collaborative processes to converge. This distinction allows a network to reduce coordination complexities without compromising the benefits of specialization inside individual member firms[3].

Interdependence Visibility

The third shift is to enhance management of changing interdependencies among business partners. Information visibility in smart business networks is a useful mechanism for enhancing coordination, but only when inter-

---

[2] For example, a printer parts manufacturer can have exact variable specifications that its components must meet but all of the interdependence with other parts should be exclusively moved to this interface. The manufacturer must have complete independence for how the individual component accomplishes the specified functions. Such process modularization requires both technological as well as governance considerations.

[3] Some early evidence of the value of this distinction is visible in recent studies of interfirm collaboration in the software development (Tiwana, 2003) and automobile industries (Takeishi, 2002).

organizational interdependencies are relatively stable (Konsynski and McFarlan, 1990). As information access migrates, so does the interest in allocation of decision rights and decision authorities. With *Glasnost* comes *Perestroika*.

Continuous Alignability

Strategic alignment of business and technology strategy is often treated as a one-time activity. A well conceived IT architecture that supports the business strategy of member firms in a network might help in the short run, but the two must remain aligned over time. When shifts in markets, partner portfolios, and products cannot be anticipated, inflexibility rears its head again: The existing inter-organization coordination technology becomes *the* bottleneck in adapting business strategy. Smart business networks therefore must allow business and technology strategy to be continuously realigned. The structure of interorganizational relationships and their underlying information architecture must be separated to allow the two to be continuously aligned.

Heterogeneity Retention

Most new knowledge—new product ideas, creative process innovations, new technologies, and recognitions of emerging markets—is likely to be generated outside any given firm. The enterprise challenge is to recognize, appreciate, and exploit such shifts. But some of these shifts might be so removed from existing organizational capabilities that a firm in a traditional business network will be under-equipped to do so. Heterogeneity then is a valuable attribute for flexibility although it *appears*—on the surface—to reduce efficiency. The trend towards relying on partner organizations to perform part of the value-creation function allows individual firms to squeeze more flexibility from their specialized expertise for one simple reason: it widens the repertoire of experiences and possible solutions beyond the routines, worldviews, and mental models of similar specialist member firms. In other words, retention of heterogeneity in the collaborative network broadens the locus of search for potential responses to yet-to-occur changes that remain elusive and unpredictable.

But, this organizing logic relies on islands of seamless coordination in a sea of heterogeneity. A firm with a loosely-coupled approach to inter-organizational collaboration can organize to partner on the fly with other firms that have the complementary expertise, specialized assets, and complementary resources required exploit an emerging opportunity. The problem of being caught short of sufficient resource portfolios appears particularly pronounced in industries faced with turbulent technologies or markets. Case in point: Apple Music's move to position itself as an orchestrator for digital music sales in collaboration with five of the largest record companies. Nike's shoe business is another example of a product line fraught with uncertainties such as changing fashions, international laws, and global markets. Nike has retained the flexibility to reduce the idea-to-shelf time for introducing new shoe designs by encouraging its many suppliers to become more competent in *some* product design activities. However, by retaining the core design innovation activities in-house, it has both managed to make itself indispensable without homogenizing its collaborative network.

Self-Organizing and Swarming

Unlike the hierarchical logic of organizing collaborative networks, partners in a smart business network are deeply specialized in a narrow domain. Increased task specialization and simultaneous disaggregation of the locus of coordination means that each firm in the network narrows its internal focus by deepening its expertise in a few selected areas while relying on network partners to invest in and develop specialization in complementary functional and technical areas. At the same time, higher levels of interdependence demand greater coordination using malleable rules for coordination. In effect, this reduces the capacity of each firm in the network to relate to the knowledge domain of its network peers. The key to compensating for these tensions lies in differentiating yet appreciating task partitioning from knowledge partitioning across firms in the network. Therefore mechanisms are needed to summarize, synthesize, and apply the knowledge flows across the network. Much of the weight of this task falls on the self-organizing ability of IT architectures. Self-organization refers to the organizing logic where activities are neither centrally controlled nor locally supervised (Bonabeau and Meyer, 2001). The capability for self-organizing through network-level knowledge management is embodied in two features of the IT architecture: (1) shared meaning and (2) swarm intelligence. Shared meaning refers to agreed upon "vocabulary" to describe specialized concepts. There capture the subtle ambiguities that are not fully definable in, say, XML extensions. The challenge is not unlike EDI systems except that such vocabularies evolve over time.

Swarm intelligence requires that IT architectures that support improvisation must be intelligent, but based on simple rules. Intelligence in a SBN is not merely in the nodes themselves. Indeed, the effect of a collaborative environment involves a "forming" of a proper community of decision makers and decision influencers. Spontaneous networks bring together (virtually) those that have information and opinions and those that have decision rights and authorities. Thus even the most primitive of nodes (as low as RFID tagged objects) cooperate and communicate with each other. It is the "swarming" or "flocking" of information and expertise that may define the success or failure of the spontaneity of the network. Swarming through such embedded dumb tags allows cognitive reapportionment i.e., cognitive responsibilities can be allocated to a human or humans, or to a system or systems.[4]

Governance Mechanisms

Essential to the success of spontaneous collaborative networks are the governance mechanisms that establish protocols for attainment and severance of participation. In addition, the means by which participants make decisions on allocation of decision rights define the limits of the cooperation as a network system. Both the business policy environment and the IT architecture need to be "readied" for effective participation in spontaneous collaborative networks. Two elements of governance are germane to the de-

---

[4] Most early automation efforts focused on taking thinking responsibilities from individual workers and putting them into information systems. The creation of the massive policy transaction systems that formed the back office of most life insurance companies saw tremendous substitution of computing power for human clerical work. Much of the early history of computerization was logged in accounting and finance--the factories of financial services. This automation was also largely static--that is, the dialogue between the system and the human cognitor was static. Regardless of the skill of the person interacting with the system, the machine always performed the same repertoire of cognitive acts. In cognitive reapportionment there is a conscious design decision focused on the dynamic allocation of thinking responsibilities. The best analogy is the idea of delegation from superior to subordinate. When a superior delegates a decision, he or she gives up direct decision control, but reserves the right to re-take control. In cognitive reapportionment the design consciously takes into account the ability to allocate decisions to people and/or systems with the ability to dynamically share, or even take back control. Thus, in certain situations the expert may be more interested in taking on cognitive responsibilities that might otherwise by handled by the system. In this sort of environment, the human being acts as a co-cognitor or computer as colleague. As computer support environments are more able to support this form of situational movement of decision capabilities from systems to humans, we will become more accustomed to sharing decision-making responsibilities in these human/system dialogues. Moreover, more of these human/system dialogues and more of their important details, will be available for manipulation and design.

sign of such networks: (1) relational approaches to governance and (2) reallocation of selective decision rights across entity boundaries.

Relational Governance

Smart business networks reap the flexibility benefits of specialization while distributing the locus of coordination across multiple partners. However, the absence of dedicated investments by member firms reduces the level of lock-ins to the network (Bensaou, 1997, 1999), thereby creating threats of opportunistic behavior by individual firms in the network. Successful realization of such networks therefore demands higher levels of quasi-relational governance mechanisms based on mutual trust, market reputation, and strong relational norms (Kale et. al, 2000). The information architecture used to build improvisational networks should help reinforce such governance mechanisms. [5]

Decision Rights Reallocation

Decision rights allocation deals with location of authority that are associated with judgment and decision-making (Jensen and Meckling, 1990). At the core of the rights apportionment concept is the idea that decision responsibilities can be allocated to one or more participants in a smart business network. Most early automation efforts focused on taking decision responsibilities from individual organizations and putting them into the SBN for allocation to the proper entity. Every day, retailers move critical merchandising decisions from their organization to their suppliers – offering decision rights for stocking and allocation that might historically have been perceived as an essential right of the retailer.

A useful framework for analyzing decision rights is the classification developed by Fama and Jensen (1995): decision control rights and decision management rights. Decision control rights refer to the authority to set controls such as pricing, timing and schedules, and quality expectations for which each member firm will be held accountable. Decision management rights refer to the authority for deciding on how to implement actions that lead to those outcomes. It is instructive to separate the two types of decision rights and treat them differently in considering how to distribute the two types of decision rights in SBNs.

---

[5] For example, eBay's use of buyer/seller reputations creates a visibility of behavior and experience that is shared by the community to effect decisions that may influence decisions on interaction and participation.

The classic challenge in organizing is that the expertise needed to make or "exercise" a decision right might be located elsewhere from the decision right itself. The architecture of SBNs allows migration of information for decision rights exercise to the location of those decision rights in a fashion that is much more pervasive than extended enterprise networks. For example, swarming technologies such as RFID tagging devices, "smart dust" transmitters, and global positioning technologies facilitate moving information from its locus directly to where decision rights *ought to be* located. In contrast, traditional disciplined enterprise architectures required that decision rights be located where information (rather than expertise or incentives) for those decisions resided. This creates fundamental rethinking and flexibility in redistributing the allocation of decision control rights and decision management rights in SBNs. We believe that organizations must begin by reconsidering reallocation of decision management rights before they reallocate decision control rights. This shift will allow entities with strong incentives for ensuring effective exercise of implementation aspects of decision rights (e.g., to suppliers and contractors) while retaining control in the locus firm.

Architectures Accommodating Spontaneity

Historically, enterprise architectures have focused on the growth of hierarchies. In contrast, spontaneous collaborative networks add market-like attributes on top of hierarchy-reinforcing architectures. This allows firms in the network to engage in dynamic partnering of the nature that is typically found in spot markets, but without losing the efficiencies associated with hierarchical configurations. This shift is illustrated beginning with siloed architectures that preceded the more disciplined enterprise architectures in Figure 6.1.

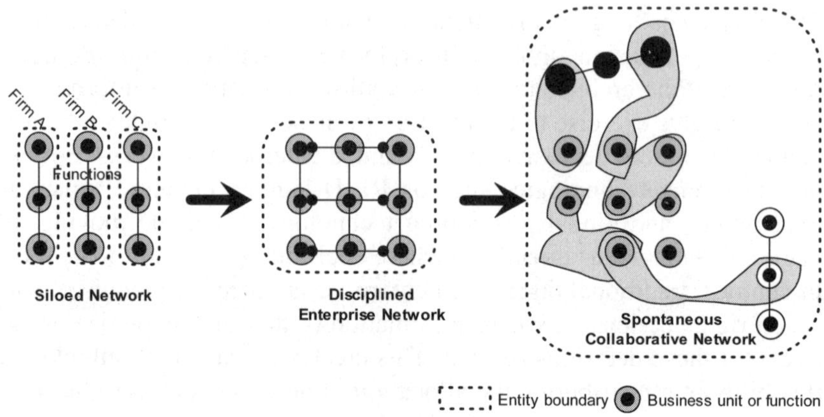

Fig 6.1 From Siloed Networks to Spontaneous Collaborative Networks

The move from traditional organizational architectures to spontaneous collaborative networks requires an organizing logic in which the boundaries of the collaborative network are malleable. Malleability requires that firms that do not belong to the network at a given point in time and be brought in without the cost of dedicated technology investments by such prospective network participants. This form of network approach to partnering thus requires an inherently reconfigurable architecture. The enabling inter-organizational technology architecture must reflect this loose-coupling. Loose-coupling is not synonymous with decentralized processes. It is quite the opposite, where the processes are more tightly coordinated because the rigidity of the IT architecture is no longer a constraint. Four defining attributes of the inter-organizational information architecture enable this shift: (1) loose-coupling, (2) swarming, (3) use of open standards, and (4) staged investments that create strategic real options.

Loose-coupling

Loosely-coupled IT architectures are the building blocks of spontaneous collaborative networks. The looser the coupling in the inter-organizational architecture, the higher is the burden on the information technology architecture that is used to coordinate activities across a network. A viable loosely-coupled architecture must be modular, which means that the interfaces among member firms in the network must be plug-and-play. Merely adopting open standards does not ensure such modularity. The design issue must be approached from a 1,000 foot altitude systemic view. If implemented well, the payoffs of such architectures can be manifold. They allow member firms in a collaborative network to interconnect their existing systems both robustly and without the hurdle of dedicated investments in common systems. The resulting connections are inherently flexible, which allows any underperforming firms to be easily dropped from a product value chain or from the network and be replaced by a different one on an as-needed basis. Such flexibility is rarely possible in contemporary enterprise architectures because of the time lags and expense associated with rapidly integrating a new participant into an existing collaborative network. If glitches surface at any node in a complex collaborative network, a loosely-coupled network can swap one firm for another on the fly. Such architectures therefore lend robustness to the collaborative network, wherein one underperforming participant does not bring down the entire network process.

Swarm Intelligence

With embedded information technologies becoming inexpensive, the feasibility of pervasive tagging of objects is growing. This allows discrete objects to communicate with each other following simple rules; collectively, they create powerful swarming behavior that can be surprisingly "smart." We believe that this is one of the key technological architectural elements of SBNs.

Open Standards

Collectively agreed-upon standards tend to shrink the size of collaborative networks because each member must make dedicated investments in coordination technologies. Many of these investments are network-specific and carry limited redeployability outside a given network. EDI systems are a classic example of this tradeoff: partnering firms made dedicated investments in developing protocols, implementing systems, and increasing connectivity with a focal firm in the EDI network. A widely-cited example is Wal-Mart's supply chain that uses deep, Wal-Mart-specific connectivity into its suppliers' systems. Emerging Web standards and protocols hold promise to change that. Open standards for business collaboration work in the same way as other open standards such as rail-track widths, USB interfaces, and electrical power outlet shapes. The most immediate benefits of open standards lie in their ability to further exploit existing applications and extract more value from them. The trick to making myriad existing systems, databases, and applications communicate using open standards is in using more recently Web-driven innovations such as eXtended Markup Language (XML), Web services and e-utilities (which we discuss later). The move towards complying with open standards does not necessarily involve accepting some kind of one-size-fits-all tradeoff. Industry-specific extensions to XML for example are being developed in the public domain by industry groups led by early adopters such as Dell, General Motors, and Merrill Lynch. As a result, variants of the base XML-type standards are further refined to meet the type of coordination requirements in specific industries. The same trends hold in related emerging technologies including IBM's computing-on-demand architectures. Their collective power lies in allows trading partners to interact in unprecedented ways, but without imposing the rigid precondition of having to make irrecoverable dedicated investments or scrapping existing systems. Together, open-standards and loose coupling enhance the modularity of the collaborative network architecture.

Stageability

The third attribute of improvisational IT architectures is the ability to stage investments. Stageability refers to the ability to partition a larger IT investment into standalone increments that build on the preceding ones. This creates opportunities for embedding real options at each step of the way; such real options are by definition more valuable when they are surrounded by considerable uncertainty and unpredictability. In contrast, traditional IT investments follow a "big-bang" approach: A new system is developed, tested, implemented, and finally turned on. The inherent risk in this approach is that the benefits of the investment begin only after the project in completed. If the business environment, markets, or technology change during the implementation trajectory, this approach cannot easily adapt to accommodate them. Moreover, if a project has to be abandoned halfway through implementation for any reason, there are almost no residual benefits from the sunk investments. This is illustrated in Figure 6.2(a). On the other hand, stageable architectures mitigate this risk by delivering incremental, standalone benefits at each milestone (Panayi and Trigerois, 1998). Stageability therefore creates future option value and the total value of this option can be manipulated by choosing the sequence of staging investments in the architectural elements. Perhaps more importantly, stageability allows flexibility during the implementation process. At each stage, the plan for the following stages can be revisited ands refined. At the level of the entire collaborative network, this attribute reduces the risk of creating prisoners' dilemmas among investing firms.

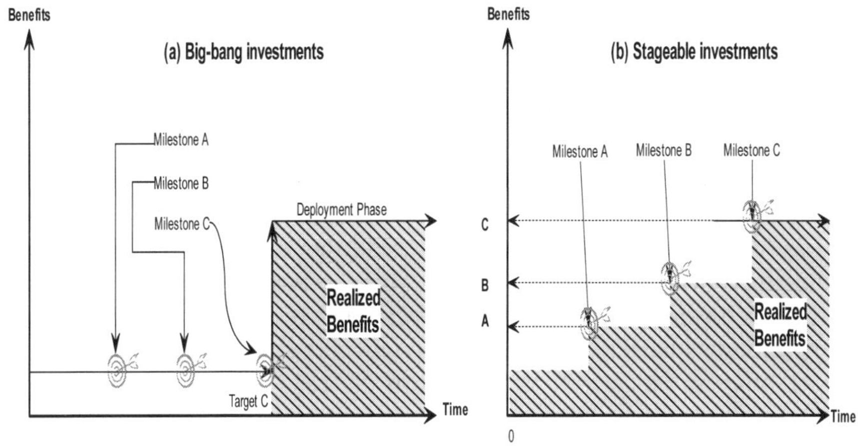

Fig 6.2 Big-bang investments versus stageable investments

Viability of Spontaneous Collaborative Networks

Smart Business Networks exist in many forms. We have considered the particular class of SBNs that encourage fluid membership and active collaboration on roles, rights and responsibilities. Decisions for participation in spontaneous collaborative networks require careful consideration as the risks and rewards are both significant. Managers considering such participation require the proper control environment and collaborative practice. Among the considerations:

1. Need to shift thinking from know-how to know-why,
2. Systemic view, not piecemeal view of the role of the firm in a network,
3. Alignment between business network architecture and IT architecture,
4. Decomposition of strategic intent into a portfolio of capabilities,
5. Development of a shared language in the vocabulary of the market,
6. Linking of distributed knowledge and decision rights through swarming architectures and decision rights reallocation.

Clearly, caveats exist. Enterprises preparing for participation in spontaneous collaborative networks must ask themselves three fundamental questions:

1. Can they rely on network partners without diluting their ability to implement their own competitive strategies?

2. To what extent can they err on the side of overspecialization while trusting their partners to supply the complementary capabilities that can make or break their firm?
3. Can they honor governance contracts and the associated penalties that together are the bloodstream of spontaneous SBNs?

To summarize, this chapter developed the concept of one type of SBN that is spontaneously adaptive. We discussed the key IT capabilities governance mechanisms that are simultaneously required to realize this form of SBN. With inexpensive emerging technologies such as RFID tags, novel opportunities have arisen for firms to reconceptualize how they collaborate with other firms as well as trillions of discrete entities and objects in the extended network. Firms seeking to nurture such capabilities must be cautious that the technology without governance restructuring is a hollow silver bullet.

References

Anand, K., H. Mendelson, (1997). "Information and Organization for Horizontal Multimarket Coordination", *Management Science*, 43(12), pp.1609-1627.

Bensaou, M. (1997). "Interorganizational Cooperation: The role of Information Technology - An Empirical Comparison of US and Japanese Supplier Relations", *Information Systems Research*, 8 (2), pp.107-124.

Bensaou, M., E. Anderson, (1999). "Buyer-Supplier Relations in Industrial Markets: When Do Buyers Risk Making Idiosyncratic Investments?", *Organization Science*, 10 (4), pp. 460-481.

Bonabeau, E., Chr. Meyer, (2001). "Swarm Intelligence: A Whole New Way to Think About Business", *Harvard Business Review*, (May), pp.106-114.

Ciborra, C. (1996). "The Platform Organization: Recombining Strategies, Structures, and Surprises", *Organization Science*, 7 (2), pp. 103-118.

Djelic, M.L., A. Ainamo, (1999). "The Coevolution of New Organizational Forms in the Fashion Industry: A Historical and Comparative Study of France, Italy, and the United States", *Organization Science*, 10 (5), pp. 622-637.

Fama E., M. Jensen, (1983). "Separation of Ownership and Control", *Journal of Law and Economics*, 26 (June), pp. 301-325.

Kale, P., H. Singh, and H. Perlmutter, (2000). "Learning and Protection of Proprietary Assets in Strategic Alliances: Building Relational Capital", *Strategic Management Journal*, 21, pp. 217-237.

Konsynski B., W. McFarlan, (1990). "Information Partnerships: Shared Data, Shared Scale", *Harvard Business Review.*

Orton, J., K. Weick, (1990). "Loosely Coupled Systems: A Reconceptualization", *Academy of Management Review*, 15 (2), pp. 203-223.

Panayi, S., L. Trigeorgis, (1998). "Multi-Stage Real Options: The Cases of Information Technology Infrastructure and International Bank Expansion", *Quarterly Review of Economics and Finance*, 38, pp. 675-692.
Powell, W., K. Koput, and L. Smith-Doerr, (1996). "Interorganizational Collaboration and the Locus of Innovation: Networks of Learning in Biotechnology", *Administrative Science Quarterly*, 41, pp. 116-145.
Schilling, M. (2000). "Toward a General Modular Systems Theory and Its Application to Interfirm Product Modularity", *Academy of Management Review*, 25 (2), pp. 312-334.
Takeishi, A. (2002). "Knowledge Partitioning in the Interfirm Division of Labor: The Case of Automotive Product Development", *Organization Science*, 13 (3), pp. 321-338.
Tiwana, A. (2003). "Knowledge Partitioning in Outsourced Software Development: A Field Study", *Proceedings of International Conference on Information Systems,* Seattle, Washington, pp. 259-270.

7 Where Are the Smarts Located in a Smart Business Network?

Kenneth Preiss[1]

Introduction

Weizenbaum (1977) wrote: "Tools shape man's imaginative reconstruction of reality". That has always been so. The creations of the visual and performing arts follow not only from the tools, but also from the concepts of technology. The defining technologies of the 20th century were mechanical; everyday conversation, news reports and talk shows use mechanical metaphors, such as to "push the gas pedal", to "overhaul", to "mesh with" and so on. The defining technology of this decade is communication technology. Management systems of the 20th century focused on making the company seen as a machine, efficient. Management systems of this and the next decade focus on the company as part of a communicating network. Economic and management structures follow not only from requirements of lowered costs, faster work and higher quality, but more deeply from the images and concepts which we all absorb unconsciously from the environment, and which are changing from the images of mechanical machines to the images of a globally-connected fluid network of interacting nodes. The network provides much more than a tool for enhanced business practice; it provides a conceptual framework that changes perceptions of organizations and of business strategy and operation.

The title of this book, "Smart Business Networks" is taken to mean businesses using electronic networks. An "old boy network" or a social network in which individuals do business based on social interaction, is not within the context of this paper. In the network referred to here a node is a business unit, and a link carries information, goods and services, and money, between such nodes.

This paper deals with a question that initially sounds banal, and that is to trace the meaning, location, and business purpose of smartness in a "Smart Business Network". Elucidation of these words is not an abstract exercise in semantics; it provides a scaffolding upon which we construct our strategic and operational business concepts.

What is considered to be technical smartness today, may very well be considered to be run-of-the-mill tomorrow. When a technology becomes

[1] Ben Gurion University of the Negev, School of Management and Faculty of Engineering, Beer Sheva, Israel, preiss@bgu.ac.il

mature it enters the fabric of society and is not any more considered as technology. When telephones were introduced lessons were given on how to use the telephone, and grandparents asked grandchildren to make calls for them, just as today the younger generation helps the older to use a computer. In the developed world no one would dream of giving lessons on how to use a telephone. Such understanding has become part of the culture and natural understanding of everyone. Smartness is in the end a term with an emotive meaning, indicating creative novelty.

The development of smart business networks is within a competitive business environment that is becoming increasingly agile. Agility is (Goldman, Nagel & Preiss, 1995) a comprehensive response to the business challenges of profiting from rapidly changing, continually fragmenting, global markets for high-quality, high-performance, customer-configured goods and services. It is dynamic, context-specific, aggressively change-embracing, and growth-oriented. Agility is a comprehensive response to new competitive forces that have undermined the dominance of the mass-production system.

The paper will follow the traditional method of scientific analysis of a system, by dividing the system into components, then analyzing each component, and then analyzing the actions of components working together. This division into components and then combinations of components will follow the seminal work of Mackworth (1977) who provided the optimal ordering of algorithms to analyze a constraint network, namely first individual nodes, then links between pairs of nodes, then paths of many connected links. This paper will deal with the network in that order, first discussing smart nodes, then smart links, a chain of links, then a network as a whole. For each categorization, technical smartness and business smartness will be discussed, as well as smartness that derives from the union of technology and business.

The Smart Node

A node in the network is considered to be a business unit or profit center. The unit may of course use technical networks within itself, but this fact does not invalidate this definition of a node, because payments are not made within the node, not even transfer payments if the nodal units are within one corporation. The list of technical smartness at a node (a business unit) would today include programs that give rapid analysis. An example is the credit card company Capital One that has 11,000 employees and 17 million customers. It can predict with reasonable accuracy what the customer is calling about before the customer utters a word. After a telephone caller punches the last digit of the phone number, and before the caller hears the first ring, data analysis at Capital One, enabled by analyses of background information on all the accounts, has identified the customer from the calling phone number, gathered the data of that person's account, correlated the data to what previous customers had asked for, and predicted what the customer is likely to be calling about. The call is then passed on to the appropriate recording or person. The computer also predicts what service the caller is likely to want to buy and passes that to the computer screen of the person taking the call. Capital One has pushed personalized and rapid service to new levels, greatly increasing the value of the company in doing so. This is just one example of rapid analysis that leads to increased efficiency. Other examples are financial portfolio management, improved inventory management, ERP systems, customer relationship management systems, and many other systems that use rapidly improving available computational ability.

In addition to increased efficiency of a node due to improved computational capability, sensors and RFID devices create smartness at a node. The size and cost of sensors has been steadily coming down over the years even while the capabilities have been improving. Today small sensors available include those that sample light energy, such as TV cameras, that sample physical data such as pressure and temperature, or location data such as GPS and active RFID or passive printed barcodes. In addition, the algorithms and computing capability to interpret the data have improved remarkably. Sensors as well as computational capability have led to new nodal capabilities.

If this paper were written 20 years ago, than the business advantages deriving from the items referred to above would have appeared to lie in the future and would have been discussed in detail. Today, the year 2004, such discussion of business advantages is superfluous.

The Smart Link

Attention will now be focused on the relationship between two business units, which are links in the supply chain. Such a link can behave anywhere on the spectrum from networked communication between disjoint business processes, to intense interaction between highly integrated processes of different businesses. The word "interprise", made up of "interacting enterprise", has been coined for this latter relationship.

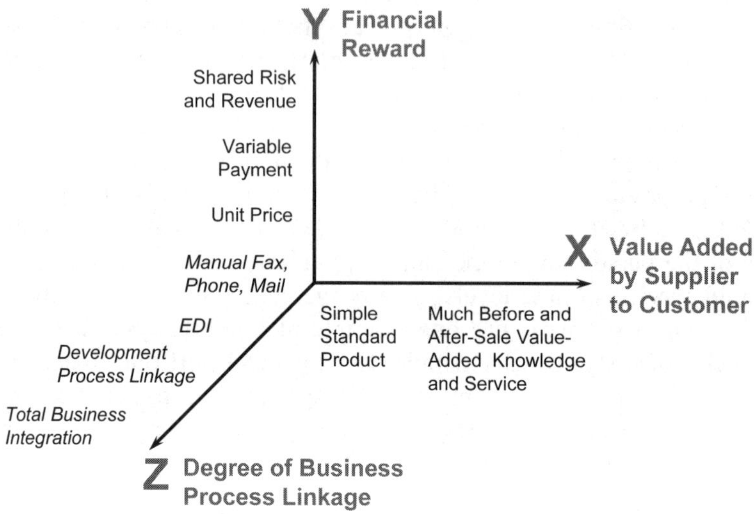

Fig 7.1 The interprise relationship model

This interprise relationship model - shown in Figure 7.1 - is based upon the primary variables in a relationship between a pair of companies (Goldman, Nagel & Preiss 1995; Preiss, Nagel & Goldman 1996). When modeling a system, it is desirable that the variables for the model cover the situation to be modeled, are independent, and are a minimal set. The three variables of this model are such a set.

The X-axis represents the added value conferred on a customer by a supplier. This can be any combination of hardware, software, service, or knowledge over the entire lifespan of a project or product. These can include special services, customized product design, customized delivery, upgrades, maintenance, decommissioning, recycling, and more.

- The Y-axis represents the reward or payment made by the customer, from fixed price through variable payments to shared risk and reward,
- The Z-axis represents the degree of business linkage between companies, starting with disconnected processes, using technologies such as mail, fax, and telephone, through electronic data interchange, to a complete integration of operations.

In short:

- The horizontal, X-axis represents what the *supplier* gives the *customer*,
- The vertical, Y-axis represents what the *customer* gives the *supplier*,
- The third, Z-axis represents how they *work together*.

These three factors define a space within which a relationship between two companies is located. Figure 7.2 shows the same values using parallel arrows, and is a generalization of this model to many serial links between companies, for example as a path in a tree structure.

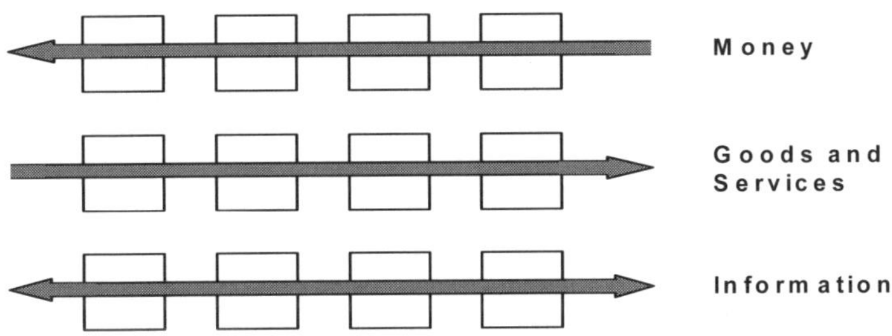

Fig 7.2 The primary flows in a chain of links in the demand chain

Mass production and product-focused trade, where a predefined product is exchanged for a price, and where cost is the only decision variable, is at the origin of the axes in Figure 7.2. As real time interactions between companies increase in intensity, the relationship moves out into the volume of the three-space.

It is interesting to note how efforts made in any one of the three axes must be balanced by efforts in thc other two. Movement has to be coordinated along all three axes in order to achieve a higher value in one of them. Using the three dimensional space of Figure 7.1 allows one to discern an optimal region for an inter-company relationship, in the region of the 45 degree diagonal in space. This can be understood as follows. Imagine a relationship being located at a low value of Y and a high value of X. Here a supplier is required to provide much variable support to the customer while paid on the basis of unit price of product. Such a relationship creates an intolerable strain on the supplier and inevitably leads to friction and possible divorce. It is an untenable region of that diagram. Now imagine a relationship at a high value of Y and a low value of X. Here the customer takes standard product but pays based on shared risk and reward. This creates an intolerable strain on the customer as it is detrimental to his success. Similarly, viewing the Z-axis, the effort and expense of integrating business processes can be justified only for high values of X, where the supplier constantly provides much value-adding service and information. At low values of X the supplier sends standard product with little or no added knowledge. For this case of low X, if one wanted (theoretically) to reach a high value of Z, the expense and effort of establishing business process integration would be both unnecessary and wasteful. Low values of X and high values of Z are hence impractical. Similarly, for high values of X where the supplier supplies much value-adding service and information over the life of the product, it would be impractical to work at low values of Z, where the communication is by mail, phone and fax in disjoint business processes. It is therefore desirable to operate in the region of the 3D space diagonal.

The biggest barrier to the emergence of the interprise today is alignment between the three major flows of Figure 7.2. In practice these flows are choked, discontinuous and misaligned. Overcoming barriers to the flows provides opportunities for research, consulting and for new software products.

This model gives a mechanism for relating use of technology (on the Z-axis), with the business implications (the X- and Y-axes). It is intuitively clear that a culture of trust is increasingly needed as one moves up the axes from the origin outward. Shunk et al (1998) have investigated this on seven intercompany customer-supplier projects in a variety of companies, and provide a gradation of seven categories of cultural alignment that move up the Z-axis and are necessary preconditions that the installed technology for inter-corporate interaction should in fact yield successful business results.

The discussion above referred to information, money, and goods and services. These are linked. The information flow governs the flow of goods and also the flow of money, by including instructions to banks to transfer money. Also, the product or service may be pure information, as for instance a legal opinion or a financial report or recommendation. Even if the product is a physical entity, it includes a significant quantity of information within it. For example, Proctor and Gamble found that to make and sell their products, 65% of their expenses were to gain and disseminate knowledge, while 35% were for raw material, buildings and machines (Stewart 2001).

A Serial Chain of Links

A chain or even a network is composed of many single links tied together. Any one company will be both a supplier to many customers and a customer to many suppliers, and is located on many supply chains. For each link in the network (or chain, which is a subset of the network) the model of the previous section is applicable. In this context it is interesting to note the considerable number of companies that do not subscribe to the tenet "do to your suppliers as you would have your customers do unto you".

The flows of information, goods and services, and money, between each pair of links influence each other. The flow of information between each pair of companies influences the flows of goods and services between them, which in turn influence the flows of money. For any single response to a customer requirement, information and money will flow down a subset of the network that will have the topology of a tree. From the customer's perspective this is a tree; when viewed from the supplier's perspective up to his supplier and beyond, the flow of goods and services is as a chain. Such a serial chain of links is often termed a "supply chain". The supply chain has systemic properties that do not exist in any individual link, and are not extrapolations of the properties of a single link. The best-known such property is the "bullwhip effect" (Lee et al 1997, Fine 1998). This is an oscillation in flow rates of goods and services along the chain, and is a cause of tangible expense since extra inventory is needed to cover the valleys of the oscillation. The reasons for the oscillation include inaccurate forecasting, possibly due to intentional error by "gaming", or over-ordering to ensure supplies, then later reducing or canceling the order. However, Vekstein and Preiss (2002) showed that even when making to order under ideal conditions, oscillation can occur due to time delays in information transfer.

For example, companies such as Proctor and Gamble find that if they generate a small increase in an order, that change shows an amplified oscillation as it is propagated down the supply chain, and the lowest tier suppliers may experience a great increase or decrease in the quantity ordered by their direct customer. This may be understood by considering the analogous system of interacting automobiles. Imagine that the first car in a long line increases speed by 10 kilometers per hour. The second car first experiences a time delay, then also accelerates, and so on. Because of the accumulated time delays, any one car may see a large space suddenly open up to the next car, over-accelerate then need to decelerate so as not to collide with the car ahead. At any instant then, as a helicopter pilot views the whole system, he will see a wave, with some cars accelerating and some decelerating. Similarly, because of time delays in the ordering processes of the supply chain, at any instant some suppliers will see decreases in orders and will see some increases, even though at that instant the first customer up the line ordered an increased quantity of goods.

In a serial supply chain the information seen by each supplier is local, from the company each side of it, and action at each supplier is triggered by an order from its local customer. When producing to order, a company in the chain is sent an order, then in turn sends an order for raw materials to its local supplier. Vekstein and Preiss (2002) showed that there is a critical value of time delay, which becomes shorter as one goes from the customer down the supply chain. If information is delayed more than that critical value at even one supplier, the chain will oscillate. The critical delay time for a low-level supplier is so short as to be impossible to achieve in practice. However, in a parallel information flow topology the critical delay time is the same for all suppliers, and is long enough to be achievable. In this topology all suppliers in the supply chain read information in parallel from a central or global depository, for example a web site. The material goods of course flow in series from one supplier to the next; it is the information that flows in parallel. As soon as an order from the end customer is noted, work begins without waiting for an order from the local customer, who is the next link in the chain. To be competitive in today's business world requires damping of oscillations in the supply chain. One way of doing so would be to revert to disconnected processes along individual links, in other words taking the chain apart. That would not be smart because it would increase response time as well as inventory requirements and expense. Today's smart business establishes processes that maintain a tightly integrated supply chain or network, while damping the oscillations. It is easier to install the technicalities of this than to successfully introduce the change of culture and work procedures that would be needed.

Note that the delay time for information transfer is never zero. Information quality considerations require in practice that a human approve significant information before sending it, but even if the information were checked and dispatched automatically, the transfer time would never be zero. The more integrated the supply chain, the shorter is the critical delay time, the more rapidly must information be sent and the greater the tendency for bullwhip oscillations to occur.

The Smart Network

Up to this point the paper has discussed "smartness", both technical and business-wise at a node, at a link, and along a serial chain of links, in a network. Consideration is now given to the network as a whole.

Just as a serial chain of links has properties that cannot be inferred from the properties of a single link, a network as a whole has properties that cannot be inferred from a single link or single chain. It is only in recent years that such properties have been observed and are being researched. Barabasi (2002) quotes experimental measurements of the number of links from nodes on the world-wide-web on the Internet. This number is given by equation (1), where N(k) is the number of web pages with k outgoing links and A is a constant.

$$N(k) = A * k^{-2.5} \quad (1)$$

The implication of this observation is that on the continuum of the degree of the nodes in the world-wide-web, there will be few high-degree nodes (such as Google or Amazon) and many low-degree nodes. Barabasi also shows that the degree of a given node on the world-wide-web, which is the number of other nodes connected to it, changes dynamically. The reasons for this dynamism are both technology and business acumen. Technological improvement in the processes and data available at a node, as well as increased access speed, can increase the links to that node. In addition, business acumen can create business incentives to connect to a node and can therefore increase the degree of a node in a network.

Braha and Bar-Yam (2004) expand on the results reported by Barabasi (2002). They also showed that problem-solving networks have properties (sparseness, small world, scaling regimes) that are like those displayed by information, biological, and technological networks. Their work also uncovered other characteristics of task-related networks.

The Interprise Relationship Model above separated the flows of money, goods and services, and information. Shunk et al (1998) expanded this model and showed the cultural alignment necessary between companies, in order to effectively use the information network infrastructure. The network can be considered as a set of many links, and so the Interprise Relationship Model with the expansion of Shunk et al, constitutes a suitable representation for analyzing a network as a whole.

Pau and Vervest (2004) point out that when considering information flow, control information should be considered separately from content information flow. It is likely that time delays in the control information will have a very significant effect of the business behavior of a network, since we know that to be so from general considerations of control systems, and as the results of Vekstein and Preiss (2002) show. This question has not been adequately investigated in the literature of businesses and networks. What is clear is that when businesses (nodes) are loosely connected, with buffers of information or goods between them, there is less oscillation. But the demand for customized and speedy response to a market opportunity requires that businesses be tightly coupled, the whole supply chain operating functionally as one operational unit. In such a system smartness is required to minimize or otherwise deal with oscillations of goods and information along the supply chain.

Van Asseldonk (1998) suggested the approach of Kaufman (1993) for biological systems to compute thermodynamic information properties of networks such as network entropy, which is a measure of connectivity and concentration.

The digital network infrastructure has reduced the time and cost for companies to rapidly set up a temporary networks of business connections. These can be thought of as virtual private networks of business connections within a global network. They are known as a virtual organization, since to the customer each appears as a single, tangible, organization, even though such a single legal entity or organization does not exist. Innovativeness in finding the correct partners or nodes with which to connect is a source of competitive advantage (Fine 1998). The ability to do so requires pre-planning. Experience in setting up Virtual Organizations (Preiss, Nagel & Goldman, 1996) has shown that one needs to pre-organize a collection of suitable companies that have agreed to common rules and ethics, with matching technologies and cultures. These are potential participants in a virtual organization, ready to spring to action within the pre-agreed framework when a market opportunity arises. They can be thought of as companies "sitting on the bench", who know the rules of the game and are capable and ready to run onto the playing field when needed. Modularity of processes within companies and plug compatibility to rapidly make and break connections are necessary requirements for setting up a virtual organization. A key decision here is the design of the granularity of the process modules. Too coarse a modularity inhibits flexibility and increases inertia when joining or separating processes; too fine a modularity may lead to increased overhead cost when joining or separating processes and can increase the tendency for oscillatory behavior in the flow of information and goods. Smartness is required in designing and implementing the preconditions necessary for competitive capability in organizing and managing a virtual organization.

Looking ahead especially to the influence of ubiquitous sensors on networks, it appears that networks will develop that dynamically reconfigure, contract and grow. At the level of the dynamic total network a number of interesting questions arise. One such question is whether in fact an equilibrium efficiency point exists for use of resources in the network. As Simon (1981) points out, and is known from theories of operations research, in such a dynamic system an equilibrium point may not exist and rather than searching for an optimum operational point, one should be content with a "satisficing" solution.

When the automobile was first developed and traveled very slowly by today's standards, a paper in the journal of the American Medical Association published a prescient prediction. The paper made the point that above the speed of 80 mph (130 kph) a human would not be able to control the vehicle safely. Today there is no technical barrier to producing a car that can travel hundreds of kilometers per hour, but indeed a car is uncontrollable and dangerous at this speed. The speed of the automobile is limited by human capabilities, not by technology.

By analogy, with regard to properties of the network as a whole, it is gradually becoming very clear that the contribution of a network to business may in the end be limited not by technical considerations such as speed of communication, but by human behavior. The e-mail system is tangibly disrupted and made less efficient by spam, hackers, wreckers, and other anti-social activities and individuals. Throughout the history of commerce, human behavior has led to decreased transaction efficiencies. Since anti-social activists have access to the same technologies as does business, we may expect that the competition between commerce governed by national and international law will constantly be challenged by improving capabilities of persons or groups of people who disregard, or try to outwit, the law.

Conclusions

This paper discussed "smartness", which can be technological or business smartness, or a combination of both. The smartness is located at a node, on a single link, on a chain of links or in the whole network. Choosing strategic directions for a company, and designing and implementing its business processes, should be influenced by knowledge of what kind of smartness is invoked and where it is.

The strategy chosen for a company, and the processes needed to implement the strategy, should be informed by understanding of network properties and the core capabilities of the company relative to those properties. Misunderstanding of these issues can lead a company into serious loss of direction. For example presume that a company works to increase the degree of integration of its supply chain operations, but neglects to dampen the oscillations. This can result in severe operational problems: periods of shortage of raw material followed by periods with excess material for which there is insufficient storage space. In companies that do not understand the characteristics of an integrated chain of links the management method of dealing with oscillations is by expediting, which is not a systematic business approach.

Or imagine that following modern thinking, a manufacturing company that has worked within a defined industry sector, selling its products to an established list of customers, wishes to provide customized total solutions to new customers via the Internet. Achieving this would require fast and comprehensive computation capability within the company (the node on the network) to analyze information for individual customers as well as to identify general trends in requirements, and to locate reusable information and components within the company. It also would need to implement intense interaction with an individual customer on the one hand and with the supply chain on the other, as well as maintaining control of information and material so that items in the company or the supply chain are in fact available when needed, all the while retaining control of its core competencies and ensuring that cooperation with suppliers and customers does not lead to them cutting the company out of the work flow by detouring around the company. Furthermore, the phrase "total solution" may mean that the company retains contact with the supplied product to provide service and upgrades using networked sensors. Successful implementation of the systems needed to implement this strategy while being profitable would require an understanding of the behavior of chains of links in the network, as well as understanding how new customers can be contacted and kept. Successful companies will assimilate the knowledge of how networks work and will undergo significant internal change so as to take advantage of this knowledge. Naïve companies will conceive of this implementation as an extrapolation of old business practice and will in most likelihood suffer inefficiencies and unnecessary expense, as well as being unable to provide good response and service to customers.

We are in a transition period where the last century's mechanical methods, imagery and metaphors for management concepts, are being replaced by the methods, imagery and metaphors of networks. This book is a stage along that transition path.

References

Barabasi, A. L. (2002). *Linked: The New Science of Networks*, Perseus.

Braha D., Y. Bar-Yam, (2004). "The Topology of Large-Scale Engineering Problem-Solving Networks", *Physical Review E.*, Vol. 69, 016113.

Fine, C.H. (1998). *Clock Speed: Winning Industry Control in the Age of Temporary Advantage*, Perseus Books, Massachusetts - New York.

Goldman, S.L., R.N. Nagel, and K. Preiss, (1995). *Agile Competitors and Virtual Organizations: Strategies for Enriching the Customer*, Van Nostrand Reinhold, New York.

Kaufman S. A. (1993). *The Origins of Order: Self Organization and Selection in Evolution*, Oxford University Press.

Lee, H. L., V. Padmanabhan, and S. Whang, (1997). "The Bullwhip Effect in Supply Chains", *Sloan Management Review*, Vol. 38, No. 3, pp. 93-102.

Mackworth, A. (1977). "Consistency in Constraint Propagation", *Artificial Intelligence*, Vol. 8, No. 1, pp. 99 - 118.

Pau L-F, P.H.M. Vervest, (2004). "Embedding Business Logic Inside Communication Networks: A Network-Based Business Process Management", paper presented at the *Smart Business Networks* Science Seminar, The Vanenburg, The Netherlands, 26-28 May 2004. See this book.

Preiss, K, R.N. Nagel, and S.L. Goldman S, (1996*). Cooperate to Compete: Building Agile Business Relationships*, Van Nostrand Reinhold.

Shunk, D., J. Ames, S. Moehring, T. Brumett, and B. Ward, (1998). "Establishing the Enterprise Integration Logical Progression: Technology and Culture", *Agility and Global Competition*, Vol. 2, No. 3, pp. 23-36.

Simon, H.A. (1981). *The Sciences of the Artificial*, MIT Press, Cambridge, Second Edition.

Stewart, T.A. (2001). *The Wealth of Knowledge*, Doubleday.

Van Asseldonk, T.G.M. (1998). *Mass Individualization*, Ph.D thesis, Catholic University Brabant.

Vekstein, D., K. Preiss, (2002). "The Effect of Time Delays in Make-To-Order Information on the Dynamics of Supply Chains", *International Journal of Manufacturing Technology and Management*.

Weizenbaum, J. (1977). *Computer Power and Human Reason; From Judgment to Calculation*, W.H. Freeman & Company.

8 Information Flow Structure in Large-Scale Product Development Organizational Networks

Dan Braha[1,2] and Yaneer Bar-Yam[2,3]

Introduction

On February 1, 1997, a major fire swept through one of Aisin Seiki's plants supplying brake fluid proportioning valves (or P-valves) to all Toyota vehicles manufactured by Toyota-group plants in Japan (Reitman,1997; Nishiguchi and Beaudet, 1998). The sole reliance of Toyota on Aisin Seiki's supply and the low inventory levels of the P-valves inventory due to a just-in-time (JIT) operating environment threatened to shut down Toyota's 20 auto plants in Japan for weeks and damage local economies. Surprisingly, Toyota's car factories succeeded to recover their operations in only five days after the fire. The admirable Toyota's quick recovery can be attributed to the cohesive network structure of suppliers working with Toyota directly and indirectly. This enabled Toyota to rapidly reconfigure the supply chain network and pull together 36 suppliers, supported by more than 150 subcontractors, who produced small batches of P-valves on nearly 50 separate improvised tooling systems and production lines Reitman (1997). The above supply chain disaster recovery illustrates the importance of coordination and collaboration among supply chain partners (e.g., manufacturers, suppliers, and retailers) as a means for achieving greater strategic and operational value to the organization. Today, supply chain integration is further realized by complex business-to-business interactions via information technology, most importantly the Internet (Kambil and van Heck, 2002). In such supply chain networks partners are involved in an intricate web of information transfer such as demand data, inventory status, and shipment schedules.

The usefulness of understanding organizational network structure as a tool for assessing the effects of decisions on organizational performance

[1] Faculty of Engineering Sciences, Ben-Gurion University, P.O.Box 653, eer-Sheva 84105, Israel, brahad@bgumail.bgu.ac.il, braha@necsi.org

[2] New England Complex Systems Institute, Cambridge, Massachusetts 02138, USA, yaneer@necsi.org

[3] Department of Molecular and Cellular Biology, Harvard University, Cambridge, MA 02138, U.S.A.

has been illustrated in the social science and management literatures (Cross et al., 2002). There it has been shown that informal networks of relationships (e.g., communication, information, and problem-solving networks) -- rather than formal organizational charts -- determine to a large extent the patterns of coordination and work processes embedded in the organization (Cross et al., 2002). In recent years, networks have also become the foundation for the understanding of numerous and disparate complex systems outside the field of social sciences (e.g., biology, ecology, engineering, and internet technology, see Albert and Barabási (2002) and Newman (2003). The goal of the this paper is to examine, for the first time, the statistical properties of an important large-scale information network -- new product development – and discuss their significance in providing insight into ways of improving the strategic and operational decision-making of the organization. In general, information networks constitute the infrastructure for exchanging knowledge that is important to the achievement of work by individual agents. We believe that our results will also be relevant to other information-based networks.

Distributed product development (abbreviated as "PD'), which often involves an intricate network of interconnected tasks carried out by hundreds of designers, is fundamental to the creation of complex manmade systems (Alexander, 1964). The interdependence between the various tasks makes system development fundamentally iterative (Braha and Maimon, 1998). This process is driven by the repetition (rework) of tasks due to the availability of new information (generated by other tasks) such as changes in input, updates of shared assumptions or the discovery of errors. In such an intricate network of interactions, iterations occur when some development tasks are attempted even though the complete predecessor information is not available or known with certainty (Yassine and Braha, 2003). As this missing or uncertain information becomes available, the tasks are repeated to either verify an initial estimate/guess or to come closer to the design specifications. This iterative process proceeds until convergence occurs (Yassine and Braha, 2003; Klein et al., 2003; Yassine et al.)

Design iterations, which are the result of the PD network structure, might slow down the PD convergence or have a destabilizing effect on the system's behavior. This will delay the time required for product development, and thus compromise the effectiveness and efficiency of the PD process. For example, it is estimated that iteration costs about one-third of the whole PD time (Osborne, 1993) while lost profits result when new products are delayed in development and shipped late (Clark, 1989). Characterizing the *real-world* structure, and eventually the dynamics of complex PD networks, may lead to the development of guidelines for coping

with complexity. It would also suggest ways for improving the decision making process, and the search for innovative design solutions.
The last few years have witnessed substantial and dramatic new advances in understanding the large-scale structural properties of many real-world complex networks (Strogatz, 2001; Albert and Barabási, 2002; Newman, 2003). The availability of large-scale empirical data on one hand and the advances in computing power and theoretical understanding have led to a series of discoveries that have uncovered statistical properties that are common to a variety of diverse real-world social, information, biological and technological networks including the world-wide web (Albert et al., 1999), the internet (Faloutsos et al., 1999), power grids (Watts and Strogatz, 1998), metabolic and protein networks (Jeong et al., 2000; Jeong et al., 2001), food webs (Montoya and Solé, 2002), scientific collaboration networks (Amaral et al., 2000; Newman, 2001a; Newman, 2001b; Newman, 2001c), citation networks (Price, 1965), electronic circuits (Ferrer et al., 2001), and software architecture (Valverde et al., 2002). These studies have shown that many complex networks exhibit the "small-world" property of short average path lengths between any two nodes despite being highly clustered. They also have found that complex networks are characterized by an inhomogeneous distribution of nodal degrees (the number of nodes a particular node is connected to) with this distribution often following a power law (termed "scale free" networks in Barabási and Albert (1999)). Scale-free networks have been shown to be robust to random failures of nodes, but vulnerable to failure of the highly connected nodes (Albert et al., 2000). A variety of network growth processes that might occur on real networks, and that lead to scale-free and small-world networks have been proposed by Albert and Barabási (2002) and Newman (2003). The dynamics of networks can be understood to be due to processes propagating through the network of connections; the range of dynamical processes include disease spreading and diffusion, search and random walks, synchronization, games, Boolean networks and cellular automata, and rumor propagation. Indeed, the raison d'être of complex network studies might be said to be the finding that topology provides direct information about the characteristics of network dynamics. In this paper, we study network topologies in the context of large-scale product development and discuss their relationship to the functional utility of the system (a more detailed model of PD dynamics is presented elsewhere in Braha and Bar-Yam (2004)).

Planning techniques and analytical models that view the PD process as a network of interacting components have been proposed before (Yassine and Braha, 2003; Eppinger et al., 1994; Steward, 1981). However, others have not yet addressed the large-scale statistical properties of real-world

PD task networks. In the research we report here, we study such networks. We show that task networks have properties (sparseness, small world, scaling regimes) that are like those of other biological, social and technological networks. We also demonstrate a previously unreported asymmetry in the cutoffs between the distribution of incoming and outgoing links.

The paper is organized as follows: In Sec. II, we review the basic structural properties of real-world complex networks. In Sec. III, we describe the data on PD tasks. In Sec. IV, we present an analysis of the PD task networks, their small-world property and node connectivity distributions. We demonstrate the distinct roles of incoming and outgoing information flows in distributed PD processes by analyzing the corresponding in-degree and out-degree link distributions. In Sec. V we present our conclusions.

Structural Properties of Complex Networks

Complex networks can be defined formally in terms of a graph G, which is a pair $G=(V,E)$ consisting of two sets: a set of nodes $V=\{1,2,...,N\}$, and a set of lines $E=\{e_1,e_2,...,e_L\}$ between pairs of nodes. If the line between two nodes is non-directional, then the network is called *undirected*; otherwise, the network is called *directed*. A network is usually represented by a diagram, where nodes are drawn as small points, undirected lines are drawn as edges and directed lines as arcs connecting the corresponding two nodes. Three major characteristics have been identified to play a major role in the understanding of "real-world' complex networks (Albert and Barabási, 2002; Newman, 2003). The first characteristic is the average distance (geodesic) between two nodes, where the distance $d(i,j)$ between nodes i and j is defined as the number of edges along the shortest path connecting them. The characteristic path length ℓ is the average distance between any two vertices:

$$\ell = \frac{1}{N(N-1)}\sum_{i\neq j} d_{ij} \quad (1)$$

The second characteristic measures the tendency of vertices to cluster in densely interconnected modules. The clustering coefficient C_i of a vertex i is defined as follows. Let vertex i be connected to k_i neighbors. The total number of edges between these neighbors is at most $k_i(k_i-1)/2$. If the actual number of edges between these k_i neighbors is n_i, then the clustering coefficient C_i of the vertex i is the ratio

$$C_i = \frac{2n_i}{k_i(k_i - 1)} \quad (2)$$

The clustering coefficient of the graph, which is a measure of the network's potential modularity, is the average over all vertices,

$$C = \frac{1}{N}\sum_{i=1}^{N} C_i \quad (3)$$

The third characteristic is the degree of a vertex, denoted by k_i, which is the number of nodes adjacent to it. The mean nodal degree is the average degree of the nodes in the network,

$$\bar{k} = \frac{\sum_{i=1}^{N} k_i}{N} \quad (4)$$

If the network is directed, a distinction is made between the *in-degree* of a node and its *out-degree*. The in-degree of a node, $k_{in}(i)$, is the number of nodes that are *adjacent to* i. The out-degree of a node, $k_{out}(i)$, is the number of nodes *adjacent from* i.

Regular networks, where all the degrees of all the nodes are equal (such as circles, grids, and fully connected graphs) have been traditionally employed in modeling physical systems of atoms Strogatz (2001). On the other hand, many "real-world' social, biological and technological networks appear more random than regular (Strogatz, 2001; Albert and Barabási, 2002; Newman, 2003). With the scarcity of large-scale empirical data on one hand and the lack of computing power on the other hand scientists have been led to model real-world networks as completely random graphs using the probabilistic graph models of Erdös and Rényi (1959).

In their seminal paper on random graphs, Erdös and Rényi have considered a model where N nodes are randomly connected with probability p. In this model, the average degree of the nodes in the network is $\bar{k} \cong pN$, and a Poisson distribution approximates the distribution of the nodal degree. In a Poisson random graph, the probability of nodes with at least k edges decays rapidly for large values of k. Consequently, a typical Poisson graph is rather homogenous, where most of the nodal degrees are concentrated around the mean. The average distance between any pair of nodes in a Poisson random graph is the smallest among all connected graphs with the same number of nodes and edges. In particular, the average distance between any pair of nodes ℓ_{random} scales with the number of nodes as $\ell_{\text{random}} \sim \ln(N)/\ln(\langle k \rangle)$. This feature of having a relatively short path between any two nodes, despite the often large graph size, is known as the *small-world* effect. In a Poisson random graph, the clustering coefficient is $C_{\text{random}} = p \cong \bar{k}/N$. Thus, while the average distance between any pair of nodes grows only logarithmically with N the Poisson random graph is poorly clustered.

Regular networks and random graphs serve as useful models for complex systems; yet, many real networks are neither completely ordered nor completely random. Watts and Strogatz (1998) found that social, technological, and biological networks are much more highly clustered than a random graph with the same number of nodes and edges (i.e., $C_{\text{real}} \gg C_{\text{random}}$), while the characteristic path length ℓ_{real} is close to the theoretically minimum distance obtained for a random graph with the same average connectivity. Small-World Networks are a class of graphs that are highly clustered like regular graphs ($C_{\text{real}} \gg C_{\text{random}}$), but with a small characteristic path length like a random graph ($\ell_{\text{real}} \approx \ell_{\text{random}}$). Many real-world complex systems have been shown to be small-world networks, including power-line grids (Watts and Strogatz, 1998), neuronal networks (Watts and Strogatz, 1998), social networks (Amaral et al., 2000; Newman, 2001a; Newman, 2001b; Newman, 2001c), the World-Wide Web (Albert et al., 1999), the Internet (Albert et al., 2000), food webs (Montoya and Solé, 2002), and chemical-reaction networks (Jeong et al., 2000).

Another important characteristic of real-world networks is related to their nodal degree distribution. Unlike the bell-shaped Poisson distribution of random graphs, the degree distribution of many real-world networks have been documented to have power-law degree distribution,

$$p(k) \sim k^{-\gamma} \quad (5)$$

where $p(k)$ is the probability that a node has k edges. Networks with power-law distributions are often referred to as *scale-free networks*

(Barabási and Albert, 1999). The power-law distribution implies that there are a few nodes with many edges; in other words, the distribution of nodal degrees has a long right tail of values that are far above the mean (as opposed to the fast decaying tail of a Poisson distribution). Power-law distributions of both the in-degree and out-degree of a node have been also observed in a variety of directed real-world networks (Albert and Barabási, 2002; and Newman, 2003) including the World-Wide Web, metabolic networks, networks of citations of scientific papers, and telephone call graphs. Although scale-free networks are prevalent, the power-law distribution is not universal. Empirical work shows that the total node degree distribution of a variety of real networks has a scale-free regime with an exponential cutoff, i.e. $p(k) \sim k^{-\gamma} f(k/k^*)$ where k^* is the cutoff (Strogatz, 2001; Amaral et al., 2000). The existence of a cutoff has been attributed to physical costs of adding links or limited capacity of a vertex (Amaral et al., 2000). In some networks, the power-law regime is not even present and the nodal degree distribution is characterized by a distribution with a fast decaying tail (Strogatz, 2001; Amaral et al., 2000).

The goal of the present paper is to investigate the statistical properties of large-scale distributed product development networks. We show that large-scale PD networks, although of a different nature, have general properties that are shared by other social, information, technological, and biological networks.

Data

We analyzed distributed product development data of different large-scale organizations in the United States and England involved in vehicle design (Cividanes, 2002), operating software design (Denker[4]), pharmaceutical facility design, and a sixteen story hospital facility design (Newton and Austin[5], pers. comm.). A PD distributed network can be considered as a directed graph with N nodes and L arcs, where there is an arc from task v_i to task v_j if task v_i *feeds information to* task v_j. The information flow forming the directed links between the tasks has been based on structured interviews with experienced engineers and design documentation data (design process models).

---

4 Denker, S., private communication; Available at http://necsi.org/projects/braha/largescaleengineering.html

5 Newton A., and S. Austin, private communication; Available at http://necsi.org/projects/braha/largescaleengineering.html

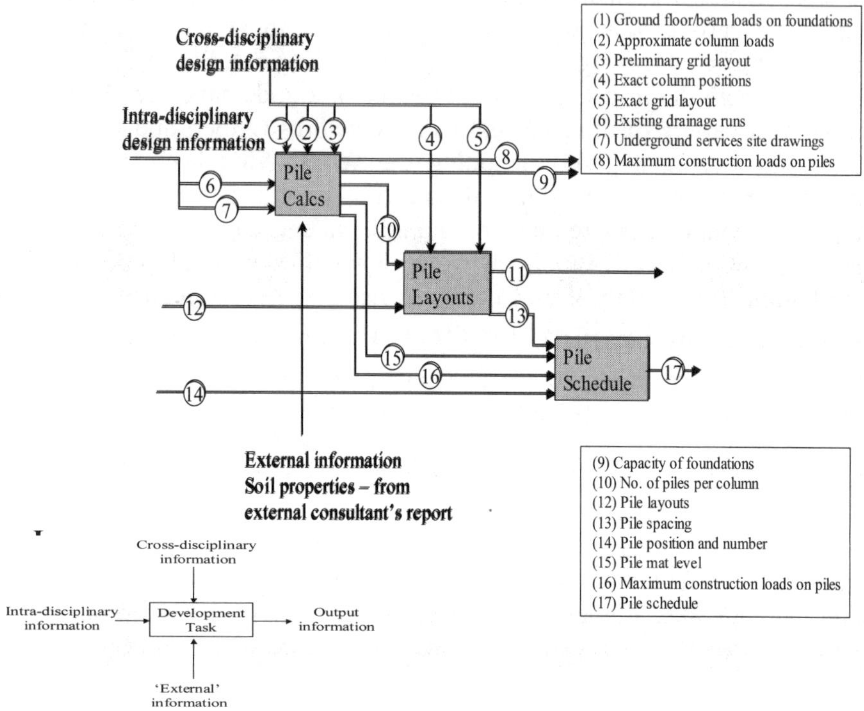

Fig 8.1 Example of a diagram from a design process model used to construct the pharmaceutical facility and the sixteen-story hospital facility networks (adapted from Austin et al. (2000))

In all cases, the repeated nature of the product development projects and the knowledgeable people involved in eliciting the information flow dependencies reduce the risk of error in the construction of the product development networks. More specifically, Cividanes (2002) obtained the vehicle development network by *directly* questioning at least one engineer from each task "where do the inputs for the task come from (e.g., another task)?" and "where do the outputs generated by the task go to (e.g., another task)?"[6] The answers to these questions were used by him to construct the

6 Cividanes, A., private communication. See also A. Cividanes, MSc. Thesis, Mechanical Engineering Department, Massachusetts Institute of Technology, 2002. A complete description of the tasks, the list of interviewees, and the result of the survey are available at http://necsi.org/projects/braha/largescale-

network of information flows (Cividanes, 2002). The operating software development network was obtained from module/subsystems dependency diagrams compiled by Denker; and both the pharmaceutical facility development and the hospital facility development networks were compiled by Newton and Austin[7] from data flow diagrams and design-process model diagrams Austin and Baldwin (1999) deployed by the organizations. An example of a diagram from the pharmaceutical facility and sixteen-story hospital facility process models is shown in Figure 8.1.

Results

Small World Properties

An example of one of these distributed PD networks (operating software development) is shown in Figure 8.2. Here we consider the undirected version of the network, where there is an edge between two tasks if they exchange information between them (not necessarily reciprocal). We see that this network is sparse ($2L/N(N-1) = 0.0114911$) with the average total degree of each node only 5.34, which is small compared to the number of possible edges $N-1 = 465$. A clear deviation from a purely random graph is observed.

We see that most of the nodes have low degree while a few nodes have a very large degree. This is in contrast to the nodal degree homogeneity of purely random graphs, where most of the nodal degrees are concentrated around the mean. The software development network also illustrates the "small-world' property (see Section 2), which can be detected by measuring two basic statistical characteristics: 1) the average distance (geodesic) between two nodes; and 2) the clustering coefficient of the graph. Small-world networks are a class of graphs that are highly clustered like regular graphs ($C_{\text{real}} \gg C_{\text{random}}$), but with small characteristic path length like a random graph ($\ell_{\text{real}} \approx \ell_{\text{random}}$). For the software development network, the network is highly clustered as measured by the clustering coefficient of the graph ($C_{\text{software}} = 0.327$) compared to a random graph with the same num-

engineering.html. For further details regarding the data collection process at GM's Research & Development Center see Cividanes's thesis.

[7] For a detailed description of data flow and design-process model diagrams see S. Austin, A. Baldwin, B. Li and P. Waskett, "Analytical Design Planning Technique: A Model of the Detailed Building Design Process," *Design Studies* 20 (3), 279–296 (1999).

ber of nodes and edges ($C_{random} = 0.021$) but with small characteristic path length like a random graph ($\ell_{software} = 3.700 \approx \ell_{random} = 3.448$).

In Table 8.1, we present the characteristic path length and clustering coefficient for the four distributed PD networks examined in this paper, and compare their values with random graphs having the same number of nodes and edges. In all cases, the empirical results display the small-world property ($C_{real} \gg C_{random}$ and $\ell_{real} \approx \ell_{random}$).

We restrict attention to the largest connected component of the graphs, which includes ~82% of all tasks for the Operating Software network, and ~92% of all tasks for the Sixteen story Hospital Facility network.

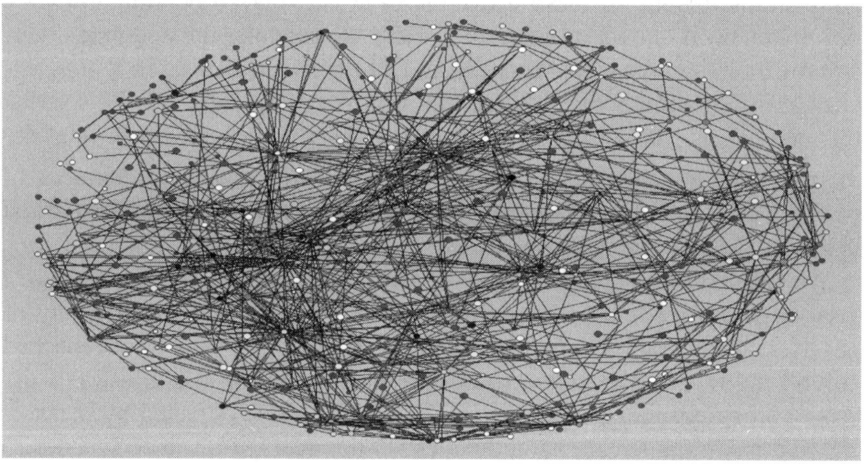

Fig 8.2 Network of information flows between tasks of an operating system development process. This PD task network consists of 1245 directed information flows between 466 development tasks. Each task is assigned to one or more actors ("design teams" or "engineers") who are responsible for it. Nodes with the same degree are colored the same

An interpretation of the functional significance of the architecture of PD networks must be based upon a recognition of the factors that such systems are optimizing. Shorter development times, improved product quality, and lower development costs are the key factors for successful complex PD processes. The existence of cycles in the PD networks, readily noted in the network architectures investigated, points to the seemingly undeniable truth that there is an inherent, iterative nature to the design process (Braha and Maimon, 1998). Each iteration results in changes that must propagate through the PD network requiring the rework of other reachable tasks. Consequently, late feedback and excessive rework should be minimized if shorter development time is required.

Table 8.1 Empirical Statistics of the four large-scale PD Networks

Network	N	L	C	ℓ	C_{random}	ℓ_{random}
Vehicle	120	417	0.205	2.878	0.070	2.698
Operating Software*	466	1245	0.327	3.700	0.021	3.448
Pharmaceutical Facility	582	4123	0.449	2.628	0.023	2.771
Sixteen story Hospital Facility*	889	8178	0.274	3.118	0.024	2.583

The functional significance of the small-world property can be attributed to the fast information transfer throughout the network, which results in immediate response to the rework created by other tasks in the network. The high clustering coefficient of PD networks suggests an inherently modular organization of PD processes; i.e., the organization of the PD process in clusters that contain most, if not all, of the interactions internally and the interactions or links between separate clusters is eliminated or minimized, see Alexander (1964), Braha and Maimon (1998), Yassine and Braha (2003). The dynamic models developed in Yassine et al., Braha and Bar-Yam (2004) show that a speed up of the PD convergence to the design solution is obtained by reducing or "ignoring' some of the task dependencies (e.g. eliminating some of the arcs in the corresponding PD network). A modular architecture of the PD process is aligned with this strategy.In-degree and Out-degree Distributions

We compared the cumulative probability distributions $P_{in}(k)$ and $P_{out}(k)$ that a task has more than k incoming and outgoing links, respectively (see Figure 8.3)[8]. For all four networks, we find that the in-degree and out-

[8] Note that a power-law distribution of the in-degree distribution (respectively, the out-degree distribution) $p_{in}(k) \sim k^{-\gamma_{in}}$ with exponent γ_{in} translates into a power-law distribution of the cumulative probability distribution $P_{in}(k) \sim \sum_{k'=k}^{\infty} k'^{-\gamma_{in}} \sim k^{-(\gamma_{in}-1)}$ with exponent $\gamma_{in} - 1$.

degree distributions can be described by power-laws ("scale-free" property) with cutoffs introduced at some characteristic scale k^*; $k^{-\gamma} f(k/k^*)$ (typically the function f corresponds to exponential or Gaussian distributions). More specifically, we find scaling regimes (i.e., straight-line regimes) for both $P_{in}(k)$ and $P_{out}(k)$; however, the cutoff k^* occurs lower (by more than a factor of two) for $P_{in}(k)$ than for $P_{out}(k)$. The "scale-free" property suggests that complex PD task networks are dominated by a few *highly central* tasks. This is in contrast to the bell-shaped Poisson distribution of random graphs, where each node has approximately the same number of links (in such a homogeneous network each node *equally* affects the network behavior). The "failure' (e.g., excessive rework, lack of integration ability, or delays) of central PD tasks will likely affect the *vulnerability* of the *overall* PD process. Focusing engineering efforts and resources (e.g., funding and technology support) as well as developing appropriate control and management strategies for central PD tasks will likely maintain the sustainability and improve the performance of the PD process.

The edge directedness of the task networks enables us to study the relationships between the in-degrees and out-degrees of tasks. Thus, for example, we are interested in questions such as "Do tasks with high in-degree also have high out-degree?" or "Do tasks with high in-degree have small out-degree?" We address these questions by analyzing the functional relationship between the in-degree and out-degree of tasks.

Interestingly enough it turns out that to a large extent, when considering product development networks, the results reveal almost no correlation between the in-degrees of tasks and their out-degrees; i.e. there are tasks that have a small in-degree but yet have a large out-degree, and vice-versa. To illustrate this finding, we listed the top 10 tasks of the vehicle development network at General Motors' Research & Development Center ranked according to their in-degree and out-degree centrality measures. We have noticed that only 2 out of the 10 tasks appear both in the in-degree ranking and in the out-degree ranking. This finding implies that, generally, there is a clear distinction between large-scale generators of information (i.e. with high out-degree) and large-scale consumers (i.e. with high in-degree); a high generator of information could be a low consumer and vice versa. This further suggests that a distinction has to be made between in- and out-centrality as far as control and management strategies are concerned. Moreover, those tasks that have both high in- and out-centrality (e.g., "track total vehicle issues' at General Motors' vehicle design) should be carefully protected and maintained against uncertain disturbances during the PD process.

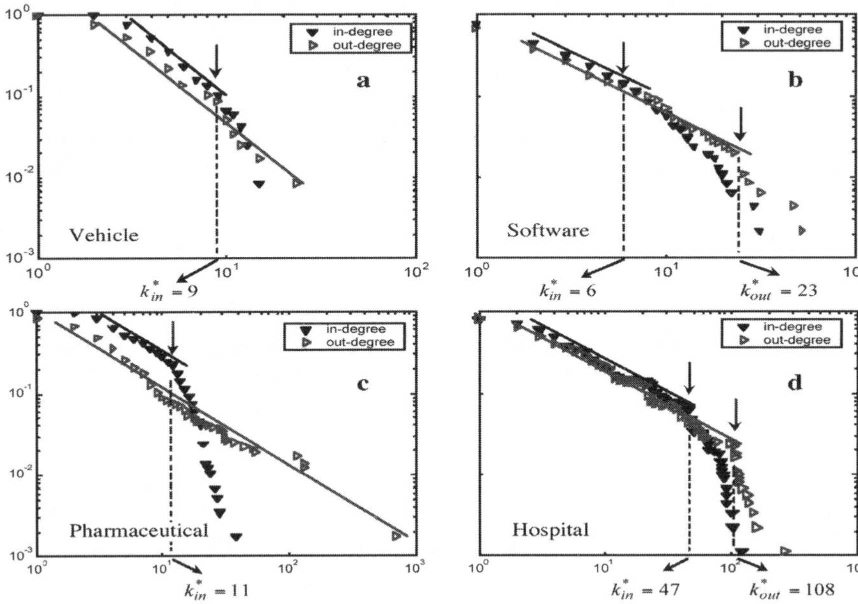

Fig 8.3 Degree distributions for four distributed problem solving networks. - log plots of the cumulative distributions of incoming and outgoing links show a power law regime (Pearson $R > 0{,}98$, $p < 0{,}001$) with or without a fast decaying tail in all cases. - degree distribution has lower best visual fit k_{in}* in each case. **a.**Vehicle t with 120 tasks and 417 arcs. exponents of the cumulative distributions $\gamma_{vehicle}{}^{in} -1$ and $\gamma_{vehicle}{}^{out} -1$, where $\gamma_{vehicle}{}^{in} \approx 2{,}82 \pm 0{,}25$ and $\gamma_{vehicle}{}^{out} \approx 2{,}97 \pm 0{,}24$ denote the exponents of the associated probability density ions. **b,** Software development with 466 tasks and 1245 arcs, $\gamma_{software}{}^{in} \approx 2{,}08 \pm 0{,}13$ and $\gamma_{software}{}^{out} \approx 2{,}25 \pm 0{,}15$. **c,** Pharmaceutical facility development with 582 tasks and 4123 arcs, $\gamma_{pharmaceutical}{}^{in} \approx 1{,}92 \pm 0{,}07$ and $\gamma_{pharmaceutical}{}^{out} \approx 1{,}96 \pm 0{,}07$ **d,** Hospital facility development with tasks and 8178 arcs, $\gamma_{hospitall}{}^{in} \approx 1{,}8 \pm 0{,}03$ and $\gamma_{hospital}{}^{out} \approx 1{,}95 \pm 0{,}03$

The presence of cutoffs in the in-degree and out-degree distributions is consistent with a conjecture by Amaral et al. (2000) that physical costs of adding links and limited capacity of a node should lead to a power-law regime followed by a sharp cutoff (this conjecture has been tested for undirected networks). Our empirical results are also consistent with Mossa et al. (2002) who suggest that making decisions on new Internet links, based on filtered information, leads to an exponential cutoff of the in-degree distribution for networks growing under conditions of preferential attachment. Both Amaral et al. (2000) and Mossa et al. (2002) comment that, in the context of network growth, the presence of costly connections, limited capacity of a node, or limited information-processing capability of a node are not unlike the so-called "bounded rationality" concept of Simon (1998). Our findings suggest that although the cutoff may be attributed to constraints on the information-processing capacities of the actors carrying out the development process (in accordance with the "bounded rationality" concept), there is an *asymmetry* between the distributions of incoming and outgoing information flows. The narrower power law regime for $P_{in}(k)$ suggests that the costs of adding incoming links and limited in-degree capacity of a task are higher than their counterpart out-degree links. We note that this is consistent with the realization that bounded rationality applies to incoming information, and to outgoing information only when it is different for each recipient, not when it is duplicated. This naturally leads to a weaker restriction on the out-degree distribution.

An additional functional significance of the asymmetric topology can be attributed to the distinct roles of incoming and outgoing links in distributed PD processes. The narrow scaling regime governing the information flowing into a task implies that tasks with large incoming connectivity are practically absent. This indicates that distributed PD networks strive to limit conflicts by reducing the multiplicity of interactions that affect a single task, as reflected in the incoming links. This characteristic reduces the amount and range of potential revisions that occur in the dynamic PD process, and thus increases the likelihood of converging to a successful solution. This empirical observation is found to be consistent with the dynamic PD model (using *linear systems theory*) developed in Yassine et al. There it was shown that additional rework might slow down the PD convergence or have a destabilizing effect on the system's behavior. As a general rule, the rate of problem solving has to be measured and controlled such that the total number of design problems being created is smaller than the total number of design problems being solved.

The scale-free nature of the outgoing communication links means that some tasks communicate their outcomes to many more tasks than others do, and may play the role of coordinators (or product integrators see Yassine et al.). Unlike the case of large numbers of incoming links, this may improve the integration and consistency of the problem solving process; thus reducing the number of potential conflicts. Product integrators put the separate development tasks together to ensure fit and functionality. Since late changes in product design are highly expensive, product integrators continuously check unfinished component designs and provide feedback to a large number of tasks accordingly.

Conclusions

The study of complex network topologies across many fields of science and technology has become a rapidly advancing area of research in the last few years, see Strogatz (2001) Albert and Barabási (2002), Newman (2003). One of the key areas of research is understanding the network properties that are optimized by specific network architectures (Amaral et al., 2000; Valverde et al., 2002; Cancho and Solé, 2001; Mossa et al., 2002; Shargel et al., 2003). Here we analyzed the statistical properties of real-world networks of people engaged in product development activities. We show that complex PD networks display similar statistical patterns to other real-world networks of different origins. In the context of product development, what is the meaning of these patterns? How do they come to be what they are? We propose several explanations for these patterns.

Successful PD processes in competitive environments are often characterized by short time-to-market, high product performance, and low development costs (Clark, 1989). An important tradeoff exists in many high technology industries between minimizing time-to-market and development costs and maximizing the product performance. Considering the PD task network, accelerating the PD process can be achieved by "cutting out" some of the links between the tasks Yassine et al. Although the elimination of some arcs should result in a speed up of the PD convergence, this might worsen the performance of the end system. Consequently, a tradeoff exists between the elimination of task dependencies (speeding up the process) and the desire to improve the system's performance through the incorporation of additional task dependencies. PD networks are likely to be highly optimized when both PD completion time and product performance are accounted for. Recent studies have shown that an evolutionary algorithm involving *minimization of link density and average distance* between any pair of nodes can lead to non-trivial types of networks including truncated scale-free networks, i.e. $p(k) - k^{-\gamma} f(k/k^*)$ (Valverde et al., 2002; Cancho and Solé, 2001). This might suggest that an evolutionary process that incorporates similar generic optimization mechanisms (e.g., minimizing a weighted sum of development time and product quality losses) might lead to the formation of a PD network structure with the small-world and truncated scale-free properties.

Another explanation for the characteristic patterns of PD networks might be related to the close interplay between the design structure (product architecture) and the related organization of tasks involved in the design process. It has been observed that in many technical systems design tasks are commonly organized around the architecture of the product (Eppinger et al., 1994). Consequently, there is a strong association between the information flows underlying the PD task network and the design network composed of the physical (or logical) components of the product and the interfaces between them. If the task network is a "mirror image" of the related design network, it is reasonable that their large-scale statistical properties might be similar. Evidence for this can be found in recent empirical studies that show some design networks (electronic circuits by Ferrer et al. (2001) and software architectures by Valverde et al. (2002)) exhibit small-world and scaling properties. The scale-free structure of design networks, in turn, might reflect the strategy adopted by many firms of reusing existing modules together with newly developed modules in future product architectures (Braha and Maimon, 1998). Thus, the highly connected nodes of the scale-free design network tend to be the most reusable modules. Reusing modules at the product architecture level has also a direct effect on the task level of product development; it allows firms to reduce the complexity and scope of the product development project by exploiting the knowledge embedded in reused modules, and thus significantly reduce the product development time.

Of greatest significance for the analysis of generic network architectures, we demonstrated a previously unreported difference between the distribution of incoming and outgoing links in a complex network. Specifically, we find that the distribution of incoming communication links always has a cutoff, while outgoing communication links is scale-free with or without a cutoff. When both distributions have cutoffs the incoming distribution has a cutoff that is significantly lower, in the cases studied by more than a factor of two. From a product development viewpoint, the functional significance of this asymmetric topology has been explained by considering a bounded-rationality argument originally put forward by Simon in the context of human interactions Simon (1998). Accordingly, this asymmetry could be interpreted as indicating a limitation on the actor's capacity to process information provided by others rather than the ability to transmit information over the network. In the latter case, boundedness is less apparent since the capacity required to transmit information over a network is often less constrained, especially when it is replicated (e.g., many actors can receive the same information from a single actor by broadcast). In light of this observation, we expect a distinct cut-off distribution for in-degree as opposed to out-degree distributions when the network reflects communication of information between human beings as a natural and direct outcome of Simon's bounded rationality argument. It would be interesting to see whether this property can be found more generally in other directed human or non-human networks. It seems reasonable to propose that the asymmetric link distribution is likely to hold for such networks when nodes represent information processing/using elements.

Acknowledgements

This paper is an extension of Braha and Bar-Yam (2004). The bulk of the work has been conducted while DB was with the Massachusetts Institute of Technology, Center for Innovation of Product Development. The authors would like to thank Alberto Cividanes of the Massachusetts Institute of Technology for providing the vehicle data at General Motors' Research & Development Center, Stephen Denker of The Business Process Architects for providing the operating software data at a major telecommunication company, and to Simon Austin and Andy Newton of Loughborough University and ADePT Management Limited for providing the pharmaceutical facility, and the sixteen story hospital facility data.

References

Albert, R., A-L. Barabási, (2002). "Statistical Mechanics of Complex Networks", *Reviews of Modern Physics*, 74, pp. 47-97.

Albert, R., H. Jeong, and A.-L. Barabási, (1999). "Diameter of the World Wide Web", *Nature*, 401, pp. 130-131.

Albert, R., H. Jeong, and A.-L. Barabási, (2000). "Error and Attack Tolerance in Complex Networks", *Nature*, 406, pp. 378-382.

Alexander C., (1964). *Notes on the Synthesis of Form,* Harvard University Press, Cambridge, MA.

Amaral, L.A.N., A. Scala, M. Barthélémy, and H. E. Stanley, (2000). "Classes of Small-World Networks", *Proc. Nat. Ac. Sci USA* 97, pp. 11149-11152.

Austin, S., A. Baldwin, B. Li, and P. Waskett, (2000). "Integrating Design in the Project Process", *Proceedings of the Institution of Civil Engineers,* 138 (4), pp.177–182.

Barabási, A-L., R. Albert, (1999). "Emergence of Scaling in Random Networks", *Science*, 286, pp. 509-512.

Braha, D., Y. Bar-Yam, (2004). "The Statistical Mechanics of Product Development", Technical Report, *NECSI.*

Braha, D., Y. Bar-Yam, (2004). "Topology of Large-Scale Engineering Problem-Solving Networks", *Physical Review E.*, Vol. 69, 016113 (January).

Braha, D., O. Maimon, (1998). *A Mathematical Theory of Design: Foundations, Algorithms, and Applications,* Kluwer Academic Publishers, Boston, Mass.

Cancho, R.F., R.V. Solé, (2001). *SFI* working paper, 01-11-068.

Clark, K.B. (1989). "Project scope and Project Performance: The Effect of Parts Strategy and Supplier Involvement on Product Development", *Management Science* 35 (10), pp.1247–1263.

Cross, R., S.P. Borgatti, and A. Parker (2002). "Making Invisible Work Visible: Using Social Network Analysis to Support Strategic Collaboration", *California Management Review*, 44, 2 (Winter), pp. 25-46.

Eppinger, S.D., D.E. Whitney, R.P. Smith, and D.A. Gebala, (1994). "A Model-Based Method for Organizing Tasks in Product Development", *Research in Engineering Design*, 6 (1), pp. 1-13.

Erdös, P. and Rényi, A. (1959). "On random graphs", *Publicationes Mathematicae*, 6, pp.290–297.

Faloutsos, M., P. Faloutsos, and C. Faloutsos, (1999). "On Power-Law Relationships of the Internet Topology", *Comp. Comm. Rev.*, 29, pp. 251-262.

Ferrer, R., C. Janssen, and R.V. Solé, (2001). "Topology of Technology Graphs: Small World Patterns in Electronic Circuits", *Phys. Rev. E*, 63, 32767.

Jeong, H., S. Mason, A.-L. Barabási, and Z.N. Oltvai, (2001). "Lethality and Centrality in Protein Networks", *Nature*, 411, pp. 41-42.

Jeong, H., B. Tombor, R. Albert, Z.N. Oltavi, and A.-L. Barabási, (2000). "The Large-Scale Organization of Metabolic Networks", *Nature*, 407, pp. 651-654.

Kambil, A., E. van Heck, (2002). *Making Markets: How Firms Can Design and Profit from Online Auctions and Exchanges*, Harvard Business School Press.

Klein, M., H. Sayama, P. Faratin, and Y. Bar-Yam, (2003). "The Dynamics of Collaborative Design: Insights from Complex Systems and Negotiation Research", *Concurrent Engineering*, (September), Vol. 11, No. 3, pp. 201-209.

Montoya, J.M., R.V. Solé, (2002). "Small World patterns in Food Webs", *J. Theor. Bio.*, 214, pp. 405-412.

Mossa, S., M. Barthélémy, H.E. Stanley, and L.A.N. Amaral, (2002). "Truncation of Power Law Behavior in 'Scale-Free' Network Models Due to Information Filtering", *Phys. Rev. Lett.*, 88, 138701.

Newman, M.E.J. (2001a). "Scientific Collaboration Networks I. Network Construction and Fundamental Results", *Phys. Rev. E*, 64, 016131.

Newman, M.E.J. (2001b). "Scientific Collaboration Networks II. Shortest Paths, Weighted Networks, and Centrality", *Phys. Rev. E*, 64, 016132.

Newman, M.E.J. (2001c). "The Structure of Scientific Collaboration Networks", *Proc. Nat. Ac. Sci USA*, 98, pp. 404-409.

Newman, M.E.J. (2003). "The Structure and Function of Complex Networks", *SIAM Review*, 45, pp. 167-256.

Nishiguchi, T., A. Beaudet, (1998). "The Toyota Group and the Aisin Fire", *Sloan Management Review*, (Fall).

Osborne, S.M. (1993). *Product Development Cycle Time Characterization Through Modeling of Process Iteration*, MSc. Thesis, Massachusetts Institute of Technology.

Price, S. (1965). "Networks of Scientific Papers", *Science*, 149, pp. 510-515.

Reitman, V. (1997). "Toyota's Fast Rebound", *Wall Street Journal*, May 8.

Shargel, B., H. Sayama, I.R. Epstein, and Y. Bar-Yam, (2003). "Optimization of Robustness and Connectivity in Complex Networks", *Phys. Rev. Lett.*, 90 (6), 068701.

Simon, H.A. (1998). *The Sciences of the Artificial,* MIT Press, Cambridge, Mass..

Steward, D.V. (1981). "The Design Structure System: A Method for Managing the Design of Complex Systems", *IEEE Transactions on Engineering Management*, 28, pp. 71-74.
Strogatz, S.H. (2001). "Exploring Complex Networks", *Nature*, 410, pp. 268-276.
Valverde, S., R.F. Cancho, and R.V. Solé, (2002). "Scale Free Networks from Optimal Design", *Europhys. Lett.*, 60, pp. 512-517.
Watts, D.J., S.H. Strogatz, (1998). "Collective Dynamics of 'Small-World' Networks", *Nature*, 393, pp. 440-442.
Yassine, A., D. Braha, (2003). "Complex Concurrent Engineering and the Design Structure Matrix Method", *Concurrent Engineering*, (September), Vol. 11, No. 3, pp. 165-176.
Yassine, A., N. Joglekar, D. Braha, S. Eppinger, and D. Whitney, (2003). "Information Hiding in Product Development: The Design Churn Effect", *Research in Engineering Design,* Vol. 14 (3), pp.131-144.

Review Comments

Reviewer: Falk Graser
Rapporteur: Hong Chen

One of the key issues of this paper is understanding the network properties that are realized by specific network architectures. This paper analyzes the statistical properties of real-world networks of people engaged in product development (PD) activities. The authors show that complex PD networks display similar statistical patterns to other real-world networks of different origins. In particular:

- PD complex networks exhibit the *"small-world"* property, which means that they react rapidly to changes in design status,
- PD complex networks are characterized by an *inhomogeneous distribution* of nodal centrality measures,
- PD task networks are *dominated* by a *few highly central* tasks,
- Focusing engineering and management efforts on central PD tasks will likely improve the *performance* of the overall PD process,
- PD tasks can be classified into three major categories: "Information-Receivers," "Information-Generators," or "Information-Brokers",
- "Failure" of central PD tasks affects the *vulnerability* of the overall PD process, and7) PD Networks have inherent *nested modularity*, where many highly integrated small modules group into a few larger modules, which in turn can be integrated into even larger modules.

The paper analyzes an *intra-organizational* network (where PD tasks are nodes) whereas Smart Business Networks (SBN) should be analyzed at the inter-organizational level (where enterprises form the nodes). It would be interesting to see if the statistical patterns uncovered for intra-organizational networks remain invariant when moving to the level of SBN. The authors believe, though, that the level of abstraction will not significantly change the qualitative structure of the network's topology; but may change the embedded parameters underlying the network's characteristics (e.g., coefficients and cut-offs of the power-law distributions).

The main finding of this paper is that topology provides direct information about the characteristics of network dynamics. As a further step, it is instructive to detail the managerial implications of the theory as well as develop some guidelines for managers to follow. For example, in the context of a SBN, what are the network design and operational principles that will render a SBN more resilient to unanticipated crises (such as supplier's delays, lost delivery, server failure)?

The authors conclude that the cut-offs observed in the in-degree and out-degree distributions (see Figure 8.3) reflect Herbert Simon's notion of bounded rationality, and its extension to group-level information processing. It would be interesting to see (by direct observations) if the group-level information-processing capacity can be extended; e.g., by redesigning the structure or topology of the network or by incorporating sophisticated information technologies and transaction protocols.

The authors identify three generic categories of network nodes: "Information-Receivers," "Information-Generators," and "Information-Brokers." It is suggested to expand this set by considering two further types of nodes: "Control" and "Decision-based". The authors believe that this further categorization can be achieved by at least two methods: 1) analyzing the structure of sub-graphs ("building blocks") embedded in the networks; 2) assigning richer data structures that more naturally describe a SBN; e.g., adding characteristics to each node or adding information bandwidth (weights) to links. The authors remarked that for some networks (e.g., citation networks) the qualitative properties remain unchanged even when link weights are incorporated.

The paper focuses on network topology as a means to obtain direct information about the characteristics of network dynamics. It is recommended to explore the effect of richer data structures (e.g., bandwidth assigned to links or information-processing capabilities assigned to nodes) on the dynamical properties of SBN.

The authors have created the network of information flows between tasks, where each task is assigned to one or more actors ("design teams" or "engineers") who are responsible for it. It is also suggested to create the network at the level of individuals involved in the system. This can be achieved by mapping the task network to the corresponding human network.

The authors mentioned Toyota's 1997 quick recovery from a major operational crisis as a prototypical example of the benefits that can be obtained from a "well-designed" network of enterprises (e.g., suppliers and manufacturers) working directly and indirectly. The review concludes that this case study should be further expanded by analysis of additional large-scale supply chain networks. This would be a valuable contribution to understanding the effect of network structure on SBN behavior.

9 Smart Business Networks Enable Strategic Opportunities Not Found in Traditional Business Networking

Roger N. Nagel[1], Jason P. Walters[1], Greg Gurevich[1],
and Patrick D. Schmid[1]

Introduction

Almost ten years ago, Xerox executives began to worry about a network phenomenon they saw as an inevitable and critical challenge to their major printing systems business. Their large web printers were used in the publishing industry whose operations were characterized as "print and then distribute" information. They saw a time in the not too distant future when the use of networks would make a simple reversal in that business to "distribute and then print" information. The Xerox executives were very worried, not only because it would disrupt the demand for large-scale web printers, but also because they envisioned the reversal of the two words "print and distribute" to "distribute and print" as reinventing their industry. To survive, they perceived a need to partner with a network of firms in a virtual organization, and create totally new strategies. Xerox therefore assembled their own key executives, and invited senior executives from potential partners including Adobe, Kinko's, AT&T, IBM, Apple, Ernst and Young and a small number of other potential partners for a two-day brainstorming retreat. Gary Hammel (re-engineering) and Roger Nagel (virtual organization) were asked to facilitate the brainstorming sessions. The group quickly concluded that the reversal of the two words "print and distribute" to "distribute and print" had massive strategic implications for them all.

Today, we would suggest that Xerox understood implicitly the need to form a smart business network in order to reinvent the way business is done. The company had realized that the market of the future could not be served by its traditional business network, especially because it was lacking key partners in the areas of network communications, information integration and cooperation across traditional business lines. Xerox thus

[1] Lehigh University, 200 West Packer Ave., Bethlehem, PA, USA, 18015,
rna-gel@lehigh.edu

transformed itself into a network business operating as a node in a smart business network.

There is no doubt that smart business networks are currently emerging and transforming many industries at an ever increasing pace. In the future, business networks instead of individual business organizations will be the competitors (Preiss et al., 1996). Those networks need to *look smart* through the goods, products, services and experiences they provide and *be smart* in terms of how the individual members coordinate, collaborate, innovate and organize themselves. However, even though they are facilitating new strategies and business everywhere around us, we do not have a good understanding of their concept. What we do know is that smart business networks are information fueled, networked enabled, and operate across the traditional boundaries of individual organizations. We also know that technology is a key enabler of new and changing business strategies and relationships. Furthermore, we have observed that technologically enhanced smart business networks enable the development of new or altered strategic advantages across and between traditional businesses, simply not found in traditional business networks. Finally, we know it is critical to integrate technological and business expertise to create benefit from these new strategies.

Information is at the heart of every smart business network. Information is a necessary, but not sufficient qualifier of a smart business network, which means that the existence of information in itself in a business network does not render it any "smarter". The key factor is how this information is used, or, in other words, how the information is integrated into the business network. The concept of *information integration* is therefore central to understanding smart business networks. We present in this paper an overview of our research of this fundamental concept.

The term *information integration* has been the source of confusion because it is used in many different ways. For some people, it deals with the technological aspects of integrating information systems, e.g. integrating a CRM into an ERP system. For others, the term might refer to the organizational challenges of the integration process. We believe that information integrates humans and machines enabling them to collaborate and to function in a way that empowers the creation of value and the achievement of goals. Some of these goals were previously not feasible or even possible without the exchange of information in smart business networks. We introduce a classification system that we define as *levels of information integration* and define six levels of information integration for smart business networks. It is important to understand that this is not an absolute classification system. The smartness of a network is defined only relative to other networks, or sometimes only to its competitors. The levels are not mutually exclusive, nor are they strictly hierarchically inclusive. We define six consecutive levels, but they really have to be regarded as two groups of three levels each.

The first three levels – Access, Transaction and Digitization – are about what a business network can do to be perceived as smart. The network appears smart to the outside, because it assimilates and integrates the information dispersed in it to create value through innovative products, services, solutions and experiences as explained below. In this context, the business network itself is a node that is part of a larger network, namely its marketplace. We dedicated most of this paper to the discussion of these three levels, because we believe that a smart business network which acts smart, but is not seen as smart, is not viable. Therefore it is crucial to any smart business networks to understand the first three levels of information integration.

The second three levels – Virtual Organization, Collaboration Network and Innovation Network – are about what a business network can to do to act smart in the way its partners coordinate, collaborate, innovate and organize themselves. This is achieved through the integration of information with the people, cultural and organizational issues that could otherwise prevent the network from being smart. Although these levels are not covered in detail here, the transition from one level to the next requires a major paradigm shift that should not be taken for granted. They are summarized below to provide the reader with a perspective on what is possible.

Information Integration in Smart Business Networks

Information integration is a term that has been used to represent many different levels of integration. We define six levels and indicate key strategic benefits which can accrue at each level. Even the simplest integration, which allows for information access, can create new strategic advantage, by offering "convenience" to clients who find it valuable. At each level we define several value based factors similar to convenience and provide a brief example of a company that used the value proposition to redefine or significantly change the way business is done in its industry. In addition, each level sees the emergence of some unique value creation mechanisms. In many cases, this value proposition is further enhanced at subsequent levels as is done with convenience. For ease of understanding, many of the examples deal with consumers, but the value propositions clearly extend to business to business relationships as well. Further, as with any emerging concept, the pioneers who intuitively find, invent or create new value propositions do not always use the terms we give them in retrospect. Thus while what we describe below takes place in a Smart Business Network (SBN), the participants in the SBN frequently do not know the term, and do not use it in describing how they are operating. This section introduces the six levels, followed by an in-depth discussion of the first three.

Access

Access is the ability to look-up or request information in one or more "sessions." Strategic value is created by introducing *convenience* (Amazon), *transparency* (FedEx), and by *performing introductions or referrals* (Google). In all three examples, the information access provided by the company changed the way business is conducted in its industry. All three factors – convenience, transparency, and introductions – are achieved through SBN enhancements to traditional business concepts. At the "access" level, transactions also take place. However, we place these value propositions in access, because the new value created is based on information access innovations, not transaction innovations.

Transaction

Transaction refers to the setting of the structure for actual business transactions, or, more generally, for the exchange of goods, services and money. Information access is used to set a context for defining and executing transaction. Dell redefined the way business is done in its industry by using a SBN to offer customers the ability to configure Dell's products in real time and provide "customized products" for each customer (Dell and Margretta, 2001). Cisco uses their SBN "customization" strategy with its partners and eliminates the need to own its manufacturing capability, while "partnering" with clients who order and configure their products (Cisco, 1998; Nolan et al., 2001). In other cases a SBN is used to create a virtual marketplace or transaction hub as was done by Covisint, Dupont and many others. eBay uses the virtual transaction space to facilitate new markets extending the referral and introduction based value propositions of the access level. FreeMarkets.com creates a new form of transaction by introducing and facilitating a virtual market place for reverse auctions (Rangan, 1999). In addition by integrating and automating simple transactions stock brokers redefine their industry adding convenience as a transaction based value proposition. Transaction based convenience is migrated and copied by transportation networks who now provide "transaction convenience" to clients through E-ZPass (windshield based transponder) for consumers passing through toll booths.

Digitization

Digitization is the process of using information technology to replace, enhance or substitute for physical processes, resources and delivery systems. Digitization can redefine an industry or distribution mechanism by providing for digital delivery of music (Apple iTunes), the delivery of printed material through a "distribute and print" mechanism (E-Stamps, Kinkos and others). Digitization can also create value by facilitating virtual interactions as is done by WebEX for business meetings and N-Gage for multiplayer games. In many emerging applications digitization provides self sufficiency for the client in the smart business network, e.g. empowering purchasing agents, business travelers, etc.

Virtual Organization

A virtual organization is a dynamic set of companies that come together for a time based and opportunity driven goal. Relationships vary from formal to informal, and typically include only moderate interaction and a limited scope of activities. Many fail over trust issues, but some succeed such as the One World airline alliance, the groups of organizations working on standards, e.g. Rosetta Net, and many franchise operations, such as hotel networks, etc.

Collaboration Network

A collaboration network is a set of companies who share a short and long term roadmap or vision and focus significant resources on value-producing intensive interaction. Companies are typically committed and each is involved in the goals and success of the other collaborators. An integrated infrastructure facilitates both people and information sharing in a proactive SBN environment. It can provide value in many ways such as through the swarm effect, which enables the VISA network to compete effectively with American Express. Collaboration networks are also used to create a distributed location and authority governance model for a smart network, as evidenced by CNN.

Innovation Network

This is a network that evolves to build and deliver value through products & services, solutions & experiences, e.g. by creating & managing networks of suppliers. An agile network of partners in innovative seamless relationships, using a variety of infrastructures to optimize for each client. It can redefine an industry and provide value in many ways. Li & Fung, e.g., creates and manages a unique supplier network for each client (Warren and McFarlan, 2002), whereas the Agile Web of PA organizes itself differently for each client project. This last level of information integration is only now emerging and still evolving.

Value Propositions

The following value propositions for each of the integration levels could be distinguished, see Table 9.1.

Table 9.1 Integration Levels and Associated Value Propositions in SBNs

Level	Value Proposition Enabled	Simple Example
Access	Convenience	Amazon
	Transparency	FedEx
	Introduction	Google
Transaction	Customization	Dell, Cisco
	Facilitate market	Covisint, EBAY
	Transaction convenience	EZPass
Digitization	Digital delivery	ITunes
	"Distribute and print"	E-Stamps, Kinkos
	Facilitate interactivity	WebEX, N-Gage
	Provide self-sufficiency	Airline check in
Virtual Organization	Standards	Rosetta Net
	Global Alliance	One World,
	Franchise	Holiday Inn, Hertz
Collaboration Network	Collaboration hub	DuPont
	Node and network charisma	Cisco
	Swarm effect	VISA, MasterCard
Innovation Network	Dynamic teams	Agile Web of PA
	Network economy	Li & Fung Enterprise
	Virtual Reality worlds	Asheron's call

Access

A SBN can use relationship and experience-based results to redefine the way industries operate and introduce new ways of doing business even with simple information access. For example, Amazon used the strategic value of convenience made possible in a SBN environment to reinvent the way books are sold. The strategy used by Amazon is not new in concept, rather it is a network communication and information enhanced version of the killer category strategy used by Toys R Us and others. While traditional business networks have been able to copy the killer category strategy over time, the networked and information enhanced version used by Amazon has grown at network speed, and changed not only the book industry, but a host of others as well.

Convenience

Convenience has different meanings to different people. It might be the ability to easily locate and find what you want, regardless of whether you know exactly what you want, or just have an idea. Another form of convenience includes the ability to look at something in detail before you buy it. Thus the ability to find and then sample a chapter or excerpt out of a book at Amazon, hearing a sound clip of a song at Apple's iTunes store, or taking a virtual tour of a suppliers plant, offers convenience which changes the value proposition of how those industries operate. Convenience can result from suppliers offering access to information, including virtual visits, which allow customers to make better, more informed decision with the same or less effort. It can offer less complicated steps in acquiring a product, a service, or a solution, or it can simply be the ability to complete a process in a timely and self-sufficient way. Convenience is created via the use of information based tools such as large distributed databases, intelligent agents, Customer Relationship Management (CRM), Supply Chain Management (SCM) and other software systems and tools. These software systems enhance and create value using information access to offer buyers and sellers ways which stretch the concept of convenience far beyond the ones originally introduced by the killer category stores. A SBN offers a variety of new and enhanced strategies for using convenience as summarized in Table 9.2.

Table 9.2 Convenience through information access in a SBN

- **Savings:** Information saves resources – a combination of time, money, or effort.
- **Empowering**: Information makes complex things simple and/or possible.
- **Fewer steps**: Fewer interactions provide the information needed rapidly.
- **Mistakes**: Prevents one from making an uninformed or bad decision.
- **Self Service**: Reduces reliance on other people, organizations or processes.
- **Full Service Solution**: Details are handled in the customer's context, creating a solution.
- **Knowledge**: Information arms executives with the ability to enhance decisions and their value.
- **Trust**: Information provides peace of mind.

Transparency

The ability for members of a SBN to see information not under their control is related to transparency. In its simplest form, as introduced by FedEx, transparency is the ability to track an order in another organization's computer system. It was used first to build trust. People would believe the data they see in FedEx's computer. Later, the tracking systems provided the ability to integrate information access in one organization with another and provide for the support of some simple SBN capabilities (Goldman et al., 1999). For example the ability to find out if suppliers have certain parts or subsystems in their product line, or to gather the descriptions, functional specifications, price, lead time and availability are critical factors in the creation of third party proposals, scheduling production and a wide variety of other decisions. Transparency, which in this case refers to the ability to have access to the data in the SBN, regardless of its location can and does enhance the ability of a SBN to create and offer value. The value of transparency raises the issue of timeliness and accuracy of the information one is accessing. We introduce the concepts of static and dynamic information systems, and discuss at length the impact of this in a longer version of this paper (Nagel at al., 2004). For example, a common clock speed in a dynamic information system enhances the value and reliability of real time scheduling decisions across partner SBN organizations.

Introductions and referrals

Search engines like Google are now so popular that "Google" has become a verb, like its predecessor "Xerox" did years ago. It is worth noting that search engines refer the user who is seeking information to other locations which may have it. The value is in the introduction and directly related to the relevance of the material at the location referred to. Referrals and introductions operate in three modes to create value. We call these modes the context, and have found a *generic, focused, and customized context* capability. In the *generic* case the referral is based strictly on the inquiry, with no knowledge of the context of the user. In the *focused* case, the referral is based on focused categories, e.g. the user is a doctor, lawyer, or shoe company with a request for information. In the *customized context* significant information about the request and or requestor is used to enhance the value of the referral. This is perhaps easiest to understand in the operation of the e-harmony online dating service which uses over 500 questions to learn about each prospect, before introducing them to someone they might be compatible with. We see the use of context as a significant advantage for a SBN that is trying to leverage resources in creating and executing business using a network of resources. Furthermore, referrals and introductions are now proven to be of value as demonstrated by the fact that businesses and individuals now routinely pay for them. Again, in the longer version of this paper we provide information on the value propositions of current search engines, in the *generic and focused* domains (Nagel et al., 2004). We leave the topic of introductions and referrals with the suggestion that the value of this form of information is only emerging. We see it as a valuable network phenomenon which will be the focus of significant attention in future SBN operations and their strategic evaluations.

In closing our discussion of information access, we raise the concept of solution versus service. In most uses of information access users and information access providers attempt to get the information to the requestor so that the requestor can then use it to his or her advantage. The Apple Sherlock system instead tries to infer what problem the user has and provide a solution rather than arming the user to achieve a solution. For example, when looking up the phone number of a restaurant, Sherlock provides the number, address, directions from one's location and a map. Similarly when finding out what is playing in the movies, Sherlock shows the film names, where they are playing in the neighborhood, the show time, a description of the film, and the movie trailer can be played. The challenge we see for a SBN is to use information access and the subsequent levels of information integration to create and enhance smart solutions for themselves and their customer's ala Sherlock. This means, to try and focus on what problem is being solved and use the information to solve it, not just to arm the user with the ability to solve it.

Transactions

When we speak of *transactions,* what we mean are the innovation and value creation concepts that can be introduced via transactions. The value created by a transaction is more than just the ability to organize and store information. It is the types of business solutions and experiences that are made possible by the transaction. We show that transactions create value through customization, facilitation of markets, and through smart convenience.

Customization

Dell Computers began its operation as a traditional maker of computers using forecasts to pre-build computers it predicted would be wanted by its customers. Only when their predictions were so wrong that the cost of "build and then sell" almost drove them out of business did they invent the concept of "sell and then build" (Dell and Margretta, 2001). The fact that a make to order company would be more profitable than a make to stock company was of course well known and part of every business 101 strategy course. What was not well known is that one can, in fact, reverse the order and sell before one builds, if one lets the customers configure or *"customize"* the products. Customers appreciate this, because they get what they want and control their decisions and cost/time implications. What Dell invented is the use of a network of companies electronically integrated at the transaction level to offer customized configuration of modular products. Like Xerox before them, the reversal of two words implied the need for business partners in a network, operating for mutual benefit to reorganize and reinvent the way computers are sold. The companies throughout Dell's SBN see the whipsaw effect in the supply chain eliminated, and no longer stockpile obsolete parts. The Dell SBN eliminates the traditional ramifications of poor information communication found in a typical business supplier network. Dell also uses the networked based ordering capability to target more sophisticated business customers and consumers who order expensive upscale products.

Facilitate Markets

Transactions facilitate the creation of new markets which operate in cyber or virtual space, but conduct real business. The role of a SBN is again in the enabling and facilitation of the new market space. In most industries the manufacturers, distributors, or possibly buyers exercise control over the way business takes place in their industry. For example, in the automobile industry the manufacturers are in control, in the entertainment industry the distributors have the power, and in the construction industry the builders exercise industry wide power. The concept of using a SBN to facilitate a market goes beyond the idea of enhancing the standard way of doing business. It offers changes in the control of industry wide decisions and norms of operation. When first introduced, the concept of digital markets or transaction hubs was considered to be a major breakthrough. The basic concept is that a network of companies can get together and create efficiency in either transaction cost or market price in order to create value for the network members (Cisco, 1998). The reasons why some fail and some succeed are in understanding the details of how to facilitate transactions, and the benefits that can accrue from them. This is covered in many long papers and beyond our scope here. Nonetheless, we offer the reader simple lessons from two organizations that created virtual markets to facilitate transactions in cyber space. Both required a cooperating network of participants, a SBN.

The simpler example is Freemarkets.com who conceived the idea of organizing a network of suppliers who would bid in a reverse auction for the right to manufacture parts for a client customer. Freemarkets.com created value by organizing the bidding process, and assembling a qualified network of suppliers who could produce the parts. The reverse auction was found to be a useful tool in some cases, but often the process destroyed relationships and created negative long term effects. We are convinced that a SBN requires a belief in a common destiny and assurance that each of the partners receives his desired benefits. The creation of a network of companies to bid against each other and whose success results in lower profits for the bidder is not a good concept for a SBN. The real value in digital marketplaces lays in the facilitation of transactions which could not otherwise take place, or which generate benefit for all players. eBay has introduced such a model. eBay uses the principle of introduction and referral to facilitate markets without borders. eBay uses a network of formal and informal partners to make this possible, and to grow its impact. We believe a SBN can learn a lot from the eBay model, specifically in its organization and the marketing possibilities it offers.

Transaction Convenience

The use of information as a substitute for time, or other valued resources, is not new. However, the creation of a network of businesses that share information to create more convenient transactions can create strategic value. Consider the transportation network of toll collectors, who now share in the E-ZPass system. In the Eastern United States, five state governments and more than a dozen toll authorities partner in a network with credit card companies, police and many others to offer and utilize digital toll collection. All players see a benefit though information integration and transaction automation. In a similar fashion transaction convenience is now offered by a network of organizations called third and/or fourth party logistics providers who routinely organize and facilitate the completion of transactions which require physical movements of goods and or services.

The idea is to use information integration to create value in the real world through the use of transducers, transponders, or even logistic networks to allow for the automation and completion of transactions which can be global in scope. The key concept for a SBN is to understand that information integration begins with simple information sharing or access. However, when transactions take place, they may not be limited to information based transactions, e.g. database updates. In fact, frequently transactions take us into the physical domain for completion, and require the use of various services or devices to be completed. In the case of E-ZPass a smart card based transducer is needed, in other cases we begin to take advantage of the myriad of devices which now can provide closure to transactions. Airlines ask customers to use printers to print a boarding pass; theaters do the same with tickets. As we add photo printers, music players, disk writers, and digital analog interfaces for cars, etc, we enter the domain of what we call "digitization".

Transactions have the capability to align several differing parties and allow them to interact in a focused manner. The value created by a transaction is not just the ability to organize and store information. It is the types of business solutions and experiences that are made possible by their very existence. Transactions are important in today's business, not because they exist, but rather what they are capable of enabling.

Digitization

Digitization enables something more than just the convenience of self-service. Its value is in taking a task not previously possible before and making it possible and profitable to "distribute and then print." We can do more than just "distribute and print". We can generalize it to digital delivery, e.g. of music. We can also use digitization to facilitate interactivity as is done by WebEX and others who facilitate virtual meetings and collaboration space or by N-gage with multiplayer interactive games. We can also provide for self-sufficiency by enabling people to do on their own what used to require trained professionals. Consider for example making travel reservations, printing and sharing photographs, editing movies, etc. We see self-sufficiency in the business world through the empowerment of people throughout an organization to purchase materials and parts, make rapid prototypes, conduct research, automate testing, create publishable materials, etc.

The topic of digitization is an incredibly important emerging phenomenon. We are only just beginning to see its use become widespread. In what we articulate below we hope to stimulate the thinking of the readers. This topic is covered extensively in a longer paper (Nagel et al., 2004) and is the subject of brainstorming efforts in many executive board rooms. The creation of strategic value, the reinvention of the way business is done, and the shift of power from traditional business networks to SBNs using digitization has only just begun.

Distribute and then Print

We now distribute airline boarding passes, tickets to concerts and shows, and stamps to self-print. Email, instant messages, pictures, and a variety of other information is now distributed and then printed, and in some cases not even printed anymore. The digital archive is searchable, indexable, and provides a legal and useful record of what was previously a collection of information in books, papers, memos, mail, etc. This is such a valuable concept that significant research is being invested in developing and completing digital libraries for enhanced business and research usage.

Digital Delivery

The digital delivery of music, by iTunes and others which is changing the power of traditional music distributors, and is putting the power in the organizers of digital distribution, is only one example of things being delivered digitally. Beyond the obvious extension to videos, books, and electronic media, consider also the digital delivery of directions, driving instructions, and medical advice based on one's own history.

Facilitate Interactivity

Digitization is not just surfing the Internet. It is enabling people and systems to interact to create value and build relationships beyond transactions. Consider for example the information system integrated into a modern car or airplane. The driver/pilot uses GPS, and many sophisticated digitization based systems to operate the car or plane. The concept of fly-by-wire introduced years ago has been extended many fold and reached into consumer based products. SBNs need to ask how they can facilitate interaction in ways which will create value for them and their customers and suppliers.

Provide Self-sufficiency

Digitization can empower the user to accomplish tasks which previously required the expertise of professionals: For example, to arm purchasing agents with shopping bots, doctors with automated diagnostic tools and or diagnosis; to provide tools to allow the distribution of authority for purchasing goods and services, etc.; 3D CAD systems, automated process planning systems. The myriad of computerized enhancements to individual professionals are now the subject of possible integrated digitization processes used to create new and enhanced system wide value, e.g. dynamic scheduling, the development and use of global sourcing, and selling in global markets.

Conclusion

We live in an increasingly digitized and networked world, and the old ways of doing business need to be re-examined in light of smart business networks. We have presented information integration as central to such networks, and discussed six levels of information integration. The purpose of this paper is to stimulate the thinking and imagination of the reader. To assist the reader in evaluating the applicability and value of each level to a particular business situation, we close by presenting two resulting network characteristics.

In Figure 9.1 we show the network of companies associated with the Cisco hub. The companies shown benefit from the SBN's *network charisma*, which also attracted them to it in the first place. They benefit from being

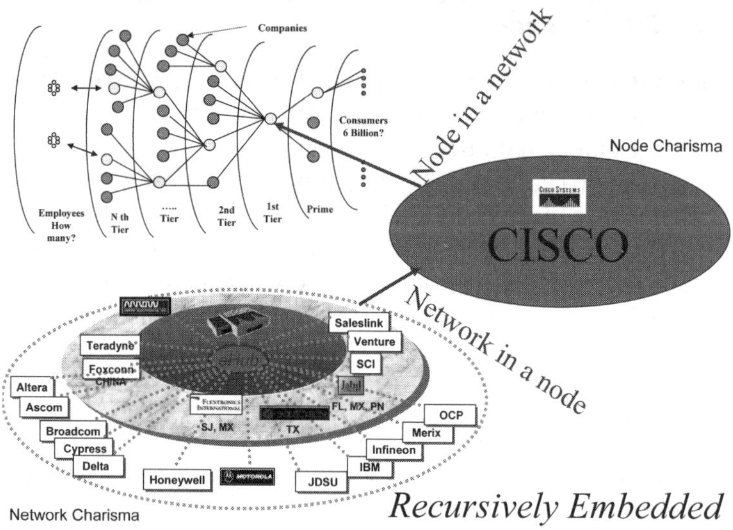

Fig 9.1 Cisco network (Frendo, 2002)

Cisco partners, receive business, and share in the SBN's information which adds to their competitiveness. In a similar manner, Cisco is itself a node in a bigger manufacturing network shown at the top of the figure. Cisco has *node charisma* in that it has a certain reputation and power in its industry.

Organizations deal with and do business with Cisco because of its node charisma. Note that Cisco thus represents both a network and a node. We believe this is not unusual and that networks really are made up of recursively embedded networks of nodes. We further believe that the *charisma* of a node and or a network is but one of the phenomena which SBN's need to think about as they position themselves for success in the global competitive environment emerging in the 21st century. For this, truly smart business networks will not look to find the recipes for success rather they will seek the understanding by which they can craft dynamic information based strategies to meet the evolving challenges they will face and establish their own charisma.

Acknowledgements

We are extremely grateful to Napoleon Devia and Kira Mendez for their contributions to this paper as part of our research group. We would also like to thank the participants of the RSM Workshop on Smart Business Networks for their feedback, especially Rob Peters for serving as repertoire in capturing the discussion and Kenneth Preiss for his ideas and advice. We are also thankful to Peter Vervest and Eric van Heck for organizing the workshop and Jan Baan for its inspiration and sponsorship.

References

Cisco Systems, Inc. (1998). *Creating Competitive Advantage through Internet Commerce: An Over-view of Cisco's Internet Commerce Solution.*

Dell, M., J. Magretta, (2001). "The Power of Virtual Integration: An Interview with Dell Computer's Michael Dell", *Harvard Business Review*, 7907.

Frendo, M. (2002). "Strategic Technology and Marketing Collaboration – Different Ways to Make IT Work", in: *CoDev*, Phoenix, AZ.

Goldman, S.L., R.N. Nagel, and K. Preiss, (1995). *Agile Competitors and Virtual Organizations: Strategies for Enriching the Customer*, Van Nostrand Reinhold, New York.

Nagel, R.N., J.P. Walters, and G. Gurevich, (2004). "Information Integration - Using Information Sharing", *White Paper*, Lehigh University, Bethlehem, PA.

Nolan, R.L., K. Porter, and C. Akers, (2001). "Cisco Systems Architecture: ERP and Web-Enabled IT", *Harvard Business Review*, No. 9-301-099.

Preiss, K, R.N. Nagel, and S.L. Goldman, (1996). *Cooperate to Compete: Building Agile Business Relationships*, Van Nostrand Reinhold.

Rangan, V.K., (1999). "FreeMarkets OnLine", *Harvard Business Review*, No. 9-598-109.

Warren, F., McFarlan , F.Y., (2002). "Li & Fung: Internet Issues (A)", *Harvard Business Review*, No. 9-301-009, p. 20.

Review Comments

Reviewer: Marcus Herzog
Rapporteur: Rob Peters

What interests Roger Nagel is the fact that "smart" is value added by an Agile- solution-experience. It then follows that information complexity follows the same range of complexity as Agility. Smart is Information technology applied to create strategic new business and value propositions and opportunities. This leads to a six level classification of information integration ranging from access to transaction to digitization to virtual organization to collaborative network to innovation network. In consequence this in-depth sharing in a network it is not only a technological issue: It is a challenge of trust: virtual organizations have failed because of lack of trust.

The discussion started with the comment of the reviewer Marcus Herzog pointing out that handling complexity always involved increasing costs. Any classification failing to identify this aspect would leave important drivers. Another remark of the reviewer was made in relation to the added value-for-all perspective: We cannot assume there is equal distribution of value in the network: value for one may mean costs for another, see the automotive industry. Roger Nagel replied that this example illustrates bad networks. One of the keys is to measure IT costs in relation to customer-perceived value, so the perception of core competences and the experiences of the customer (access to new markets, convenience, self sufficiency, multiplayer game environment, etc) govern which costs may be allocated where in the network. The discussion proceeded with the question of innovation as smart in itself: are smart networks innovative networks? One of the first remarks was that innovation is relative and time-related. There seems to be evidence that the most innovative companies are indeed networks. However, innovation may not always be beneficial and smart but it is unavoidable and probably exponentially increasing. Its limitations are set by human characteristics, not technology. The best route map for innovation follows innovative added value for customers. A question raised the issue about description of networks in terms of what they *are* versus what they *do*. The point is to illustrate a relationship between information exchange and value networks. With respect to the power in a network it is clear that much is unknown, because we still have to learn how to collaborative effectively. Most organizations in this field started only 10 years ago, for example university research teams. Some promising developments like the Game industry will affect organizations. It is also clear that discussing classification helps understand what "smart" is about. A number of models of this aspect have to be tested. The graphical representation is useful but different graphs have different meaning for different science domains. If a graph does not include a cycle, then in some domains it is not considered a network. The best way of division between hubs and nodes in the smart network is also a factor yet unknown, but with time we are getting closer.

10 Unlocking Smart Business Networks

Al Dunn[1]

Introduction

A smart business network emerges when organisations combine to amplify their cooperative capabilities to deliver specific value to a specific customer. The arguments for the "smart business network" are compelling. By enabling different organisations to combine and collaborate in close-to real-time they can improve the ability to determine and deliver an agreed service to a customer while improving resource usage and reducing costs. By improving performance for the customer and releasing the capabilities of the joint business network their joint competitive position can be improved.

Smart business networks ensure performance improvement by streamlining and aligning activities to ensure accurate and profitable fulfilment and to attack organisational waste. Speed and accuracy can ensure that unnecessary delays, resources and uncertainties and can be removed from the "supply chain". This brings not only significant cost savings but also, more importantly, customer retention and growth of customer profitability through recognised performance improvements. Yet, despite these opportunities and the available capabilities, there are few organisations that can claim to act in a smart business network.

Evolving Towards Smart Business Networks

The "business network" must be as old as business itself. Organisations have always called on the skills of external organisations. In 1980, Wassenberg wrote on the "structure of mutual relations among independent organisations". In 1986, Thorelli viewed business networks as two or more organisations involved in long-term relationships. In 1992, Miles and Snow discussed the dynamic network where numerous firms operated at each of the points on the value chain ready to be pulled together for a given run (i.e. a particular customer order) and then disassembled to become part of another temporary alignment. This was reflected by Österle et al. (2000) in observing an organisational form of a "temporary network of independent companies – suppliers, customers and rivals – linked by IT to

[1] D-Age, 17 Berks Hill, Chorleywood, Herts, WD3 5AG, UK, dunn@d-age.com

share skills, costs and access to one another's markets". In 2000, Klüber et al. wrote of the move from "vertically integrated hierarchies towards flexible network organisations and the ability to quickly and efficiently set-up, maintain, develop and dissolve partnerships with business partners". Barrett and Konsynski (1982) analysed inter-organisational information systems. Porter (1984) emphasised the pervasive role of "information systems technology" in the value chain enabling competitive differentiation by acting on the linkage between units inside and outside of the organisation. Cash and O'Callaghan (1985) concluded that the "most dramatic and influential uses - of information technology - involve systems that transcend company boundaries".

The concept of the information system as a competitive weapon gained intense attention during the 1980s as computing and, increasingly, communication capabilities pervaded business. The view developed that ICT could create competitive advantage rather than merely automating existing behaviour. It could redefine the boundaries of markets (Keen, 1991; Scott Morton, 1991). Rather than simply facilitating operations, information services were bringing a promise of effecting the competitive position of the firm or the structure of its industry (Porter, 1984; Keen, 1986).

In reality most businesses were not realising this potential. In 1990 Benjamin et al. (1990) voiced a growing concern that "the reality of developing and maintaining electronic linkages between companies is not as easy or profitable as the optimistic preaching of IOS advocates would lead us to believe". The technology platforms and tools were limited. The business network benefits were restricted to larger organisations and between adjacent participants in the supply chain. They certainly did not reach out to the end-customer. As a result ICT acted on the existing supply chain to reinforce the *stable network*, Miles and Snow (1992): "one core organisation maintaining tight relationships with a limited set of outside suppliers and distributors that also serve organisations outside the network".

Breaking the Chain

Vervest (1995) proposed that "effective communications can result in value chains being organised in a flexible and even an ad-hoc way" to begin and end with the "ultimate customer". The value defined at the point of customer contact signals the start of the relay race in the chain. The chain is linked together rapidly to deliver to the customer. This reflects the *dynamic network* as proposed by Miles and Snow (1992): "numerous firms (or units of firms) are operating at each of the points on the value chain, ready to be pulled together for a given run (i.e. a particular customer order) and then disassembled to become part of another temporary alignment"

The dynamic network enables coordinated action to facilitate clearly defined objectives from a family of potential business network participants – the customer specific supply chain. The network acts to deliver to the specific agreed requirements of a "customer". In the mid-90s technology could not deliver the dynamic network. It was an inflexible inhibitor forcing business networks to retain their historic and deeply embedded functional and hierarchical structures. Smart stable networks were improving performance but reinforcing the status quo.

Breaking the Frame

In May 1994, CERN organised the First International World Wide Web Conference. The subsequent emergence of the Internet combined with pervasive digital business technologies and digital consumer technologies redefined how information systems could act. One result is a confrontation between customer expectations and business capabilities. Having become web and technology confident, the consumer now expects and demands with near-immediate gratification, clear time-defined delivery or, at minimum, no surprises. The majority of organisations, restricted by their technologies and organics, struggle to react.

Organisations struggle with the collision between the new outside world and the old inside world. Meeting the increased demands and bandwidth of the customer requirement and delivering to its completion conditions challenges the capabilities of current business networks with their propensity for failure: transaction integrity can be broken; transaction informational can be decoupled.

Digital consumer technologies provide a high definition lens on organisational activities. They show capabilities but reveal inabilities or incompetence. Many customers feel they suffer from technology abuse as walls of automation (such as call centres) have been erected to ensure that the business process cannot be interrupted. More than ever before those organisations able to act with immediacy or guaranteed timeliness will gain a competitive premium.

There is an increasing mismatch between the expectations and requirements of the customer and the ability of organisations to deliver to these requirements. This performance gap can and will widen as digital consumer technologies pervade. It will drive organisations to lay the foundations of "smarter" business networks.

Discovering Smartness

Today I can log in to expedia.co.uk to organise a holiday or to arrange specific business travel. Is this a smart business network? The user interface (web page) allows the combination of available travel components to meet my needs by constructing a solution from their portfolio of travel capabilities according to various parameters (type of holiday, price, location, date). This is a "smart" stable network. It provides structured access to the product database of the pre-determined business partners acting in a stable network. Other travel sites have equivalent capabilities. "Smartness" is exhibited in the ability to manage the customer requirement to suggest and act on pre-determined solutions. These smart stable networks converge the bandwidth of the customer requirement (holiday, flights, hotels) to the narrower bandwidth of the capabilities of the existing business network (these holiday choices, these flights, these hotels), see Figure 10.1. They are putting their smartness at the customer edge and echoing it in their business network.

Business network smartness can be exhibited at the edge in the ways in which it acts to ensure that the customer requirement can be defined and met. It can also be embedded in the business network itself to organise the value web to react and deliver to the customer requirement.

An effective business network must:

1. *match* the requirements bandwidth of the customer and the portfolio bandwidth (made up of internal and external capabilities) of the organisation by acting - negotiating - with the customer to ensure an agreed fit from the bandwidth of the portfolio (service/product components) together with the conditions of delivery,
2. *organise* production from the portfolio. Ensure that the portfolio participants (production partners) can combine to deliver the agreed portfolio fit to the delivery conditions,
3. *fulfil* to the agreed customer requirements with necessary informing of the customer.

Smartness can lie in the nature of the customer interaction. A simple narrow bandwidth transaction (a book, CD, flight, hotel) can be enabled and completed by strings of automated business processes. However, as the customer requirement bandwidth increases so does the complexity of the matching process and, more importantly, the complexity of the portfolio. This creates a greater propensity for failure in matching and in fulfilment resulting in a greater number of business network partners and the concomitant need for rigorous coordination of the internal and external network participants.

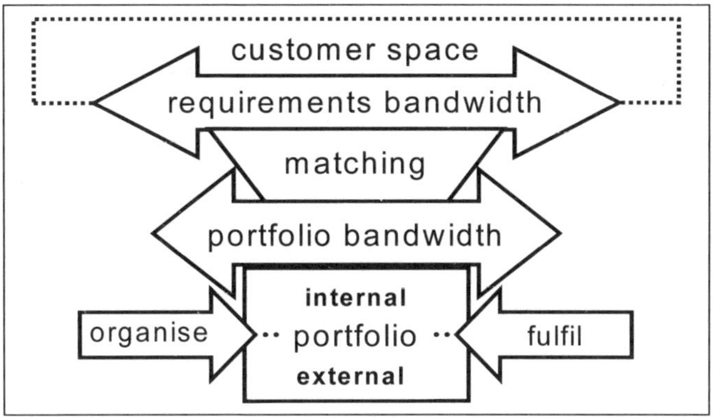

Fig 10.1 Key functions of the business network

The Characteristics of the Smart Business Network

"Smart" is subjective and comparative. The essence of "smart" is that the business network applies intelligence to outperform other competitive business networks. The performance advantage may be perceived by the customer in terms of the business network's ability to act effectively according to that customer's benchmarks thus being a customer attractor or it may be achieved with imbedded intelligence (the structuring of the organics) to realise internal advantages (such as cost performance).

"Smartness" emerges with *amplification* of the participants' capabilities. This amplification is delivered by the network's combined ability to enable and coordinate matching (determine the specific value) and fulfilment (deliver the specific value) to provide improved performance that is recognisably "better" than that of other providers to the end-consumer or to a business customer.

The main functions of a smart business network include:

1. *match*: determine and agree the specific customer value (the desired product/service) including the conditions for delivering,
2. *configure*: definition, execution and management of the appropriate "supply chain" selected from the business network according to the network's "fulfilment rules"),
3. *fulfil:* organise and coordinate activities between the selected chain participants to deliver according to the fulfilment rules, and

4. *monitor:* continual reporting of the fulfilment activities in the selected chain with the ability to reconfigure the chain on failure (or on redefinition of the customer requirement).

These characteristics seem beyond those of today's stable business networks. Breaking the frame of current business and business network organics seems to restrict the ability to combine matching and fulfilment into a more dynamic network. The requirement that the business network is configured with a flexibility to meet the customer requirement and, on agreement, configured according to the organisation's or business network's fulfilment (business) rules present a significant challenge as does the close-to-real-time monitoring of the different participants to ensure corrective actions on the failure of a participant

Building the Smart Business Network

The smart business network cannot be enabled in isolation from the dynamics of the participating organisations. The complexity and, in many cases, the inertia of organisation behaviour can cause theory or vision to dissolve. Organisations exhibit great difficulty in absorbing substantive change. Continual change or adjustment is essential but breaking the logic of the status quo is difficult. Many reasons are given for failure – the wrong idea, time, reasons, or leader.

There is a digital dilemma: the conflict between "traditional" organising the way we were and are – and acting in the "smart digital world" - the way we could, or must, be.

Resolving the Digital Dilemma

In "Total Action", Vervest and Dunn (2000) formulated a business template for organisations and their business networks to address this dilemma. The approach was derived from experiences with larger business clients and academic research. Its key proposition was that the company or the business network must ensure that every action is an action for the individual customer so removing unnecessary activities and centring on the matching and fulfilment of customer requirements, see Figure 10.2. Total Action recommends three fundamentals to ensure that the business network acts to make every action an action for the individual customer:

1. make the customer the locus of decision making,
2. ensure that customer information drives the organisation, and

3. enable excellence in fulfilment.

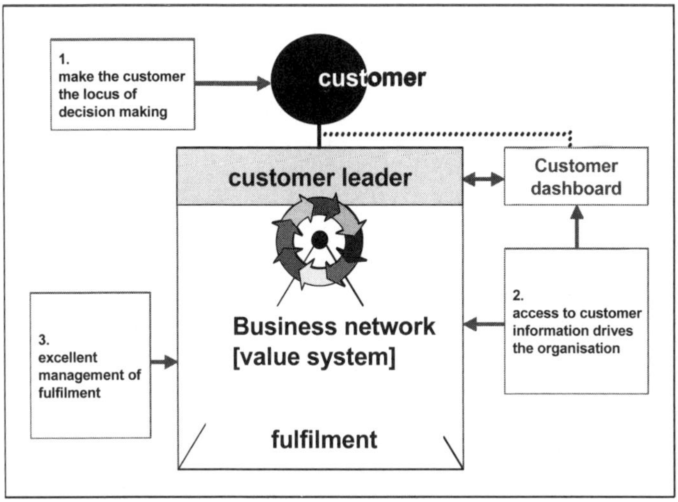

Fig 10.2 The Total Action framework

Total Action centres on a "customer leader" being the point of business network coordination, see Figure 10.3. The "customer dashboard" is the information and activity monitoring resource. The customer leader is responsible for directing the relationship with the customer, agreeing the customer solution and triggering fulfilment. The customer leader captures and acts on knowledge of the customer and the organisation's performance for that customer. The role is much more than taking the order and triggering the order process. The customer leader acts as the coordination point for the smart business network to ensuring the completion of the customer service cycle: from seduce through deliver to renew. Augmented by appropriate informational support (the customer dashboard), the customer leader can be aware of and can act on the service cycle.

The customer leader may be permanent for a particular customer, as in account management, or temporary as in, for example, a customer call centre. The customer leader may be a person, supported by a customer dashboard, or captured in software. This may be a Web Page that serves as a customer leadership window to manage the relationship with the customer, trigger fulfilment and ensure the subsequent fulfilment process (as exhibited by Amazon, Dell Computer, and many other customer-web interfaces). In each case the principles of customer leadership are the same. With temporary or permanent responsibility for the customer there is the

clearly defined ability to determine the customer's portfolio solution, invoke fulfilment, and then monitor its completion.
The customer, or activity, dashboard is the information window between the customer and the business network and within the business network itself. It allows the customer leader to act on the necessary information on the customer and on the portfolio participants to define and invoke fulfilment of the customer solution.

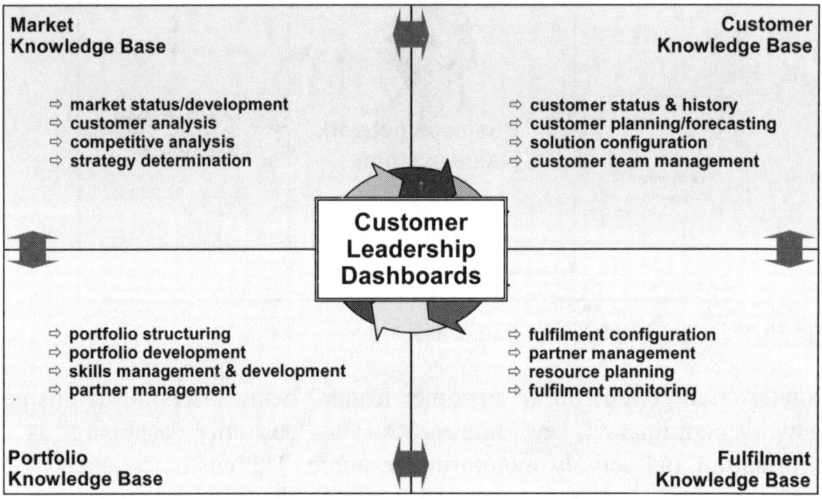

Fig 10.3 Framework for the customer dashboard

In addition, it can support management by providing information on the organisation's performance for the customer and the customer's contribution to profitability.

The customer dashboard is not a single point. In fact it is a family of dashboards presenting information according to the specific situation and requirements of the business network participants. It is, however, the point of coordination for matching and fulfilment by the business network. The customer leader works with a customer dashboard providing relevant information on the individual customer and that customer's context. It must also work with fulfilment to configure the "solutions" and monitor their realisation. This does not mean that the customer leader (in whatever form she, he, or it will take) continuously monitors every activity on the fulfilment chain but rather is informed of variances (current and potential failures) and is able to negotiate the changes with the business network and the customer.

To be effective each interaction between the participants on the chain demands unambiguous clarity during the commitment phase (matching) combined with the orderly and timed execution of the fulfilment phase. Effective collaboration and interaction between the participants is needed for integral management of the network to:

1. define all activities that must be undertaken according to the customer agreement,
2. find and commit the parties (the smart business network participants) that can undertake these activities within the agreed metrics of time, cost, etc, and
3. manage its sequenced execution.

Modular network design, e.g. Hoogeweegen (1997), provides a useful approach to enact such capabilities. It concentrates on the translation (matching) of the service elements required for the specific customer solution into the organisation of the production elements (the participants in the smart business network) to deliver them, see Figure 10.4. Modular networks can provide indicators for structuring and identifying the participants on a smart business network, in particular the matching (service elements) and the fulfilment (production elements) coordinated by a customer leader. However, there are questions of the relationship between the degree of modularisation and concomitant coordination costs.

Modular network design proposes more than "product modularity":

1. *service modularity*: determining the elements that are combined to provide the desired outcome for the customer (enabling matching),
2. *production modularity*: the individual elements of production that must be combined to deliver the required service combinations,
3. *process modularity*: defining a "library" of the processes (between participants) that are called on and combined to enable matching and fulfilment.

In particular the "process module network" determines the enactment of the smart business network. By capturing business logic and business rules within and between the participants they can begin to provide the "business operating systems" that determine the operating rules for the business networks and allow the differing organics of the participants to combine. However, organics are much more than the technologies, the process and the business rules. They reach across all components of organisational behaviour and its effective structuring.

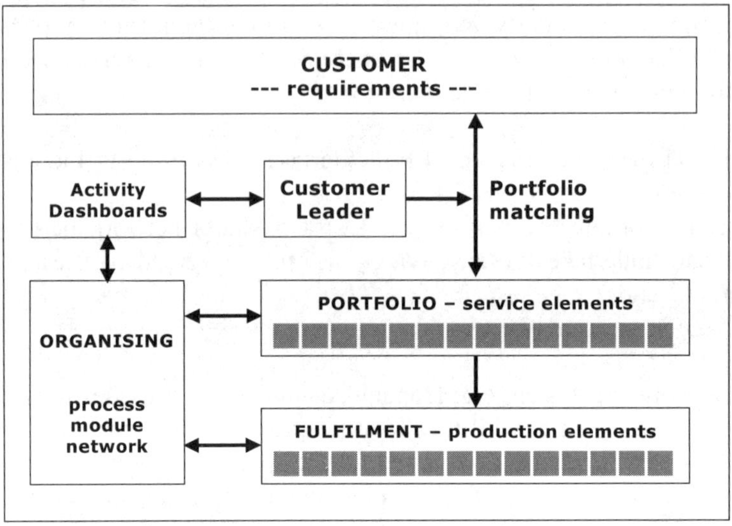

Fig 10.4 Structuring for modularity

Smart business networks cannot be enabled in isolation from the dynamics of the individual and collective participants in the business network. To enable smart characteristics, the business network must ensure the combination and coordination of the "people" and the "technology" factors Vervest and Dunn (2000):

1. *engagement* – ensure that the business network goal is preserved - the ability of the network participants (as organisations and people) to combine and act for and with the network customer according to agreed goals and business rules. This requires communication,
2. *completeness of communication* – ensure the availability of full relevant information (the dashboards) to all participants in the business network - the ability to give all participants clear and relevant information. *Complete communication* is achieved when the business network knows exactly what is happening with and for the specific customer at all times. The business network is customer aware and is able to take corrective action on fulfilment failures.

Even with a single organisation (acting in a stable network) such synchrony is essential for success. Experience reveals that asynchrony between four key inter-linked components: people, processes, (information) platforms, and the portfolio of capabilities are a major barrier to realising smartness.

- *people:* the human skills acting in and supporting the matching and fulfilment activities. These skills can be "automated" or made available by applying smart processes (decision-making capabilities that are embedded in business process automation tools). Key requirement – people engagement and knowledge exploitation,
- *process*: the structuring and coordination of goal-based activities: "the specific ordering of work activities across time and place, with a beginning, an end, and clearly identified inputs and outputs. Key requirement: automation of key business processes with future proofing,
- *platforms*: information technology platforms – the infrastructures across which the necessary information is gathered, managed and provided to the participants in the business networks. Key requirement: legacy migration and destruction – emphasis on intelligence building,
- *portfolio*: the combination of products and services combining into the capabilities that deliver value to the customer. Key requirement: move away from "product management" to modular structuring with the match/fulfil model.

With an understanding of a five-to-ten year vision of the smart business network (agile, self-organising, contextually aware, temporary but always available) it is important to consider the struggle of organisations as they seek to overcome the present and move into "smart" capabilities that are, indeed, available today. In reality they are trapped in disparate technology solutions from powerful suppliers to effect a sub-optimal compromise between their legacy systems and an unsure instinct for the future information platform technologies.

Larger organisations have a propensity for maintaining their stability by applying gradual, well-justified and non-disruptive evolution. There are many experiences reflecting the dangers of tampering with one or more of the 4Ps according to some grand intent resulting in a decrease in synchrony. Usually only severe crisis will break this evolution. However, many organisations are faced with a creeping, almost invisible, crisis. There may be compelling arguments for investigating and initiating smart business networks but many organisations will concentrate on immediate optimisation. As a result, there may be only few organisations ready to combine into a smart business network.

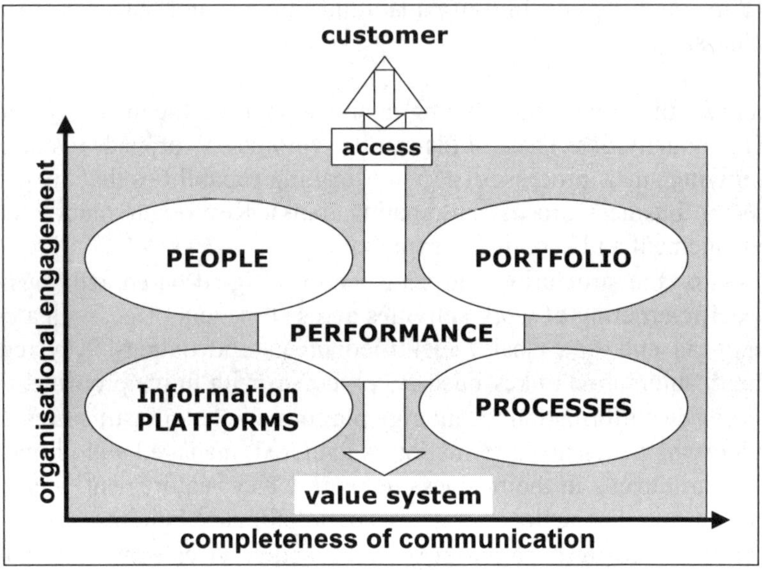

Fig 10.5 Enabling synchrony

Incumbent (bricks and mortar) smart business networks will be triggered by internal rather than inter-organisational networking. Smart business networks will evolve as sub-networks of existing stable networks as the "smartness" extends from a core organisation and its immediate partners to a wider range of participants. Today one sees examples of this evolution as the stable network hubs seek to smarten the links with the fulfilment partners to improve performance in the full customer service cycle.

In addition organisations are concentrated on new models for organising and managing their product/service portfolio working closing with partner organisations included in their portfolio production and delivery. As they break from the more rigid product management forms to seek a more modular approach (service and production module combinations) and embed increased process automation capabilities, the core of their future smart business networks will be formed.

Concluding Remarks

There are compelling arguments for the smart business network. Understanding of the organisation and structuring of ICT-enabled inter-organisational networks has developed over many years. However only in recent years have technology tools emerged to realise the *dynamic* rather *smart stable* network. In particular, the emergence of business process automation tools that allow the capture, enactment and sharing of business processes are creating the possibility of enabling cooperation and collaboration between a web of business network partners. There are barriers to understanding and creating smart business networks. Understanding will be determined by academic and empirical research and by increasing visibility of the benefits and advantages that smart business networks can provide. The barriers lie in the capabilities of the core constituents of an organisation – the people – to absorb and act on the possibilities.

There is one key driver: the competitive imperative to optimise the customer experience – to ensure that any organisation within its business network can deliver effectively and efficiently to its customers' requirements and act to the benefit of all participants in the network As organisations seek to meet the requirements of their individual customers they must ensure their internal synchrony and ensure the organics – people, processes, platforms and portfolio – to be the agile and externally-aware organisations that smartness demands. To achieve this they must extend their smartness to their immediate business partners, their co-participants in an effective business network.

References

Barrett, S., Konsynski, B., (1982). "Inter-Organizational Information Sharing", *MIS Quarterly*, (December), 00 93-105.

Benjamin, R. I., D.W. De Long, M.S. Scott Morton, (1990). "Electronic Data Interchange: How Much Competitive Advantage?", *Long Range Planning*, 23:1, pp. 29-40

Cash, J., R. O'Callaghan, (1985). "The Impact of Computers and Communications on Competitive Strategy - The Case of the Inter-organisational System", unpublished working paper, *Harvard University*, (May).

Hoogeweegen, M. R. (1997). *Modular Network Design: Assessing the Impact of EDI*, Doctoral Dissertation, Erasmus University Rotterdam.

Keen, P.G.W. (1986). *Competing in Time – Using Telecommunications for Competitive Advantage*, Ballinger Publishing Company.

Keen, P.G.W. (1991). *Shaping the Future: Business Design through Information Technology*, Harvard Business School Press, Boston MA.

Klüber, R., R. Alt, and H. Österle, (2000). "Implementing Virtual Organizing in Business Networks - A Method for Inter-Business Networking - Theories, Practices, Technologies and Methods", in: Malhotra, Y. (Eds.), *Knowledge Management and Virtual Organizations: Theories, Practices, Technologies and Methods,* Idea Group Publishing.

Miles, R.E., C.C. Snow, (1992). "Causes of failure in Network Organizations", *California Network Review*, (Summer), pp 53-72

Österle, H., E. Fleisch, and R. Alt, (2000). *Business Networking, Shaping EnterpriseRrelationships on the Internet,* Springer.

Porter, M., E., (1984). *Competitive Advantage: Creating and Sustaining Superior Performance*, The Free Press, New York.

Scott Morton, M.S. (ed.) (1991). *The Corporation of the 1990s: Information Technology and Organizational Transformation*, Oxford University Press, New York.

Thorelli, H.B. (1986). "Networks: Between Markets and Hierarchies", *Strategic Management Journal*, Volume 7, pp 37-51.

Vervest, P.H.M., (1994). *Communication Not Information: An Ad Hoc Organisation of the Value Chain*, inaugural speech, Erasmus University Rotterdam.

Vervest, PH.M., A.F. Dunn, (2000). *How to Win Customers in the Digital World: Total Action or Fatal Inaction?*, Springer.

Wassenberg, A.F.P. (Ed) (1980). *Netwerken: Organisatie en Strategie, Boom, Peppel*, (in Dutch).

11 Smart and Sustainable Supply Chains

Jo A.E.E. van Nunen[1], Rob A. Zuidwijk[1], Hans M. Moonen[1]

Introduction

Over the last decades, companies have utilized supply chain management principles and practices as instruments to gain advantage in competition between business networks. In this chapter, we explore the use of Information and Communication Technologies to make supply chains smart and sustainable.

It is customary to refer to the supply chain instead of the supply network, and we shall adhere to this convention. According to the definition of the Council for Logistics Management, Supply Chain Management encompasses the planning and management of all activities involved in sourcing and procurement, conversion, and logistics. It involves the planning and control of the forward and reverse flows and storage of goods, services and related information within the supply chain in order to meet customer requirements. Importantly, it also includes coordination and collaboration with channel partners, such as suppliers, intermediaries, third-party service providers, and customers. In essence, Supply Chain Management integrates supply and demand management within and across companies (www.clm1.org).

Recently, an increased focus on sustainable supply chain management practices has been evident. This is due to external drivers such as environmental legislation and customer requirements, as well as internal drivers, such as business economics.

In sustainable supply chains, the creation of economic value is based on efficient processes that minimize consumption of scarce resources. For example, waste materials during production, distribution and use are collected, sorted, and recycled. Products and service packages are designed in such a way that repair and maintenance, updates, and returns of products are synchronized with value recovery processes, such as remanufacturing and refurbishing. These processes extend the life of products and parts to several use cycles. Customer relationships that support the use of the prod-

---

[1] RSM, Erasmus University Rotterdam, PO Box 1738, 3000 DR Rotterdam, The Netherlands: jnunen@fbk.eur.nl, rzuidwijk@fbk.eur.nl, hmoonen@fbk.eur.nl

uct instead of ownership are also extended through the provision of customized services such as proactive maintenance and repair, updates based on user profiles, and profitable take-back options (Van Nunen and Zuidwijk, 2004). Sustainable supply chains are henceforth characterized by three P's:

Profit — Creation of economic value through efficient use of scarce resources and design of innovative packages of products and services that create opportunities both for suppliers and customers.

People — Creation of customer value through the offering of profitable service packages while taking social responsibilities of environmental impact due to sourcing, making, delivering, and returning products.

Planet — Minimizing the consumption of natural resources through efficient use of materials and energy, and reducing the environmental impact of hazardous waste.

As indicated above, some sustainable supply chains are characterized by the fact that value is being recovered from product returns. Figure 11.1 represents the basic processes in these so-called closed loop supply chains. The forward supply chain processes are source, make, deliver, and use of the products by the end customers. After the initial delivery of the product to the end customer, additional deliveries of parts may be required to repair or upgrade the products installed in the market. Customer returns consist of e.g. products at the end of their life or parts that have been replaced during repair. During the manufacturing process, returns are generated that consist of e.g. raw materials surplus, quality test returns and production leftovers. Returns can also be initiated by an actor in the distribution channel and include product recalls due to safety or health problems with the product, commercial returns induced by agreed take back options, collection of perished goods or redistribution of goods. Returns are collected via the forward distribution channels or via special reverse channels. The quantity, quality and timing of returns can be anticipated using monitoring data, but in quite a few present day cases, test data is obtained only after arrival at the collection facility. Based on the quality assessment and demand, returns are either disposed or forwarded to recovery options. Recovery processes such as recycling recover value on the material level, while remanufacturing and refurbishing restore products to as good as new state and upgraded state, respectively. In some cases, products are simply returned to the market after repackaging. As indicated in Figure 11.1 the recovered materials, parts and products are fed into the forward supply chain.

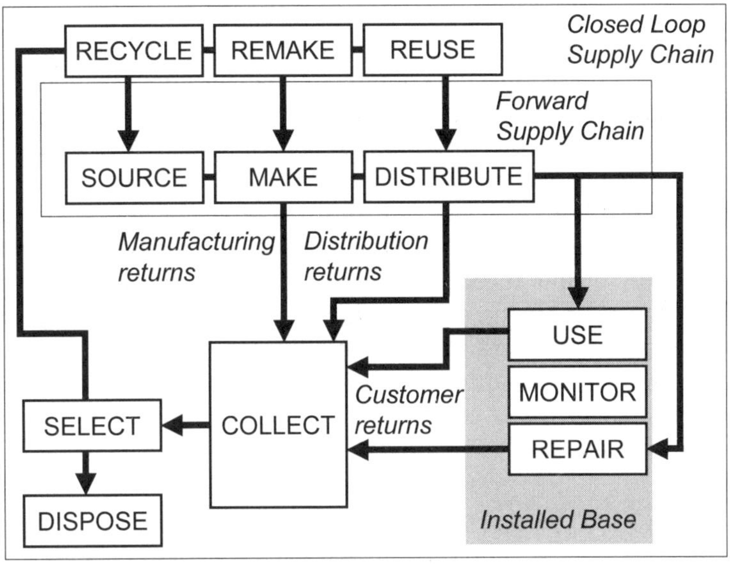

Fig 11.1 Closed Loop Supply Chain

Among others, costs of resources, governmental policies and regulations, and customer markets, are important drivers for the geographic positioning of facilities and resources that support the processes and flows in Figure 11.1. As a result, they are dispersed across continents. The management of supply chains that span the globe is confronted with additional challenges in terms of coordination and collaboration. Global transport systems, for example, involve several transport modes, such as aircraft, sea vessel, train, truck and barge, transshipment hubs at air- and sea ports, and a diversity of organizations that are involved directly or indirectly in the logistics processes. Logistics service providers add value by coordinating these transport chains while using Information and Communication Technology as an enabler.

The European project RevLog (Reverse Logistics), which focused on the management of closed loop supply chains and logistics in particular, resulted in the development of quantitative methods for optimizing closed loop supply chains (Dekker et al., 2004) and applications in practical environments reported in case studies (Flapper et al., 2004).

Monitoring and Controlling Supply Chains

Monitoring and control of supply chain operations and flows has always been aimed at mitigating uncertainty through information retrieval and process interventions. Information and Communication Technology now acts as an enabler by lowering the costs for these activities through automation. Computational power as well as embedded sensors and chips, available against low costs, help create smart products and smart processes through the entire global supply chain. The application of new technology enables supply chains to become more responsive and proactive, with a large role for autonomous decision making- and event-handling technology, and henceforth utilizing human intelligence only where it is truly required. In the case of maritime transport of fruits and vegetables, the development of smart reefer containers is under development as can be seen in the exposition below.

Monitoring the global food supply chain of maritime reefer containers.

Reefer containers deploy climate control in order to minimize deterioration of product quality. Transport of reefer containers is still characterized by high energy costs and use of harmful chemicals. Moreover, short interruptions in the control of the so-called cold chain may result in immediate deterioration of product quality. Design principles for new types of reefer containers include the use of embedded monitoring and control devices enabling remote climate control in order to arrive at sustainable supply chain processes characterized by more efficient use of energy and less use of hazardous chemicals. In this manner, a reefer container should be used as a smart container, in which sensors can monitor cargo status, and recognize when certain parameters, such as levels of ethanol, acetaldehyde, carbon dioxide and oxygen, lead to e.g. fermentation or respiration. Remote monitoring may induce appropriate action to maintain the quality of the cargo through e.g. an injection system for chemicals. The sensor devices need to have certain characteristics, like robustness, low energy usage, accuracy, sensitivity, low-costs, precision, employability, and appropriate size and shape. A supervisory control strategy is to maintain the best product quality at all times through continuously determining the best condition strategy for the cargo. The control strategy's target is to optimize transport through leverage between energy savings, quality and logistics, while taking into account external influences such as weather conditions.

New monitoring technologies that enable remote identification, diagnosis and maintenance are used in supply chains in which customers, products and processes are monitored worldwide. For example, recovery processes are commonly associated with uncertain yields. Monitoring these processes provides immediate yield information and may even help improve yields. Customers have their own requirements, usage patterns, and budget. Monitoring usage profiles together with preferences may enhance customer relationships while respecting customer autonomy and privacy.

In order to manage products, processes and customers, information on the following attributes is required: The state of the product, such as usage and repair history, and configuration, product preferences of the customer including user requirements and budget, and recovery options for a product. The recovered value of the product can be measured in terms of market price for the recovered item minus costs of the chosen recovery option. Therefore, the value of the recovered product depends on the product state, the customer preferences and the available recovery processes. Since the value of recovered products like computers deteriorates in time due to technical and market properties, information needs to be provided in a timely fashion so that product returns and recovery processes do not suffer from serious lead times. Maintenance and repair of business machines installed at customers using smart product technology is the issue of the exposition below.

Monitoring and controlling copiers and printers at customers

CopyMagic assembles copiers and printers, but actually sells document handling services to its customers. The customers will buy the function of these business machines that enable a smooth flow of information and documentation through their offices. In particular, smart copiers and printers contain sensors and processors that measure, analyse and report on machine status to enable pro-active maintenance planning, remote usage control, and even self-maintenance to enhance the operational readiness of the installed machinery. Moreover, comparing actual usage profiles with product and service capabilities may result in beneficial upgrade proposals to the customer. These upgrades can be offered against sharp prices when synchronized with demand and supply of recovered parts and products elsewhere in the market. The customer experiences a copying and printing function that is not only very reliable, but also matches his requirements throughout the development of his business. On the other hand, CopyMagic can offer these enhanced services in a sustainable way by monitoring the products installed in the market, and controlling forward and reverse flows of parts and products. Although the technology has become available, the integration of product and services development, customer relationships management, and marketing remains challenging.

From Tracking and Tracing to Sensing and Pacing

In today's supply chains, data and information is available in every node and link in the chain. Processes are monitored and controlled automatically, as well as products which get a certain amount of intelligence built in through the application of embedded chips, sensors and software. Smart Products are capable of sensing their own technical status through e.g. temperature or movement sensors, register usage patterns, perform diagnosis and even conduct self-repair, such as image enhancement in a copier when image quality has degraded. These products either flow through the supply chain or are involved in adding value processes, such as production or distribution.

Software developments play a large role in this trend. From the functions of data storage and basic financial transaction-processing in the 1960s, enterprise software today provides the backbone systems for almost all companies. Enterprise Resource Planning (ERP), Advanced Planning Systems (APS), Customer Relationships Management (CRM), Supplier Relationships Management (SRM), and Product Lifecycle Management (PLM) systems are widely deployed in large multi-nationals, as well as in SME's.

Having focused on island-automation, such systems still do not truly support the core supply chain management concepts, despite the success of tools such as Enterprise Application Integration (EAI). However, with the appearance and rise of new generations of technology such as Web Services, the Semantic Web, Grid Computing, Ubiquitous Computing, Business Intelligence, Electronic Auction mechanisms, and Agent Technology we may expect smart business networks to become a reality soon; see for example (Fleisch, 2001) and (Hagel, 2002). An important example related to smart products is Agent technology, which consists of software behaving autonomous, proactive, goal-oriented, and truly focused on communication and interaction with other agents to arrive at solutions.

Dynamic planning and control of road logistics through a Multi-Agent System

Agents are a powerful, natural metaphor for conceptualizing, designing and implementing complex, distributed applications (Scholz-Reiter and Höhns, 2002). The nature of intelligent agents enables decentralized control of (processes of) the enterprise, which is desirable in a dynamic and flexible environment. Wooldridge & Jennings (1995) define the four main characteristics of an agent: (1) autonomy, (2) social ability, (3) reactivity, and (4) pro-activeness. Erasmus University Rotterdam participates in a large Dutch government funded research project titled DEAL, which stands for Distributed Engine for Advanced Logistics (DEAL project proposal, 2002). This project aims at creating an agent-based-system to support a network based truck-scheduling system. In the DEAL architecture, each truck, shipment, truck-company and customer is represented by an agent. An agent representing a truck resides on the truck's board computer and is aware of its location, speed and planned route. An agent that represents cargo is aware of its planned destination, penalties for late delivery, specific transportation requirements etc. As cargo is presented to the DEAL network, agents are created that represent the cargo. These agents then start negotiating with nearby trucks. Based on the negotiation rules, goals and constraints, a successful 'Deal' is made. Trucks of different truck companies can collaborate by exchanging cargo whenever this is in their mutual benefit. As multiple customers and suppliers are connected through DEAL, this agent system is an example of a true supply network-wide inter-organizational information system. Future generations of the platform are likely to link tightly with all kinds of external monitoring and control systems, to make the planning and execution of road-transportation even more dynamic, and cost-optimal. Examples include a strong integration with traffic technologies (such as traffic-congestion information systems), dynamic cargo functionalities (when cargo is tagged with an RFID+ chip, it is no longer passive when transported), and cost-saving-leveraging technology (like links with information on dynamic fuel pricing, toll, et cetera). The DEAL project demonstrates that the use of this new generation of technologies (encapsulating all three categories of technology as shown in), can provide good help in actually achieving dynamic control in supply chains, in order to achieve true Sustainable Smart Networks.

Other important developments are the advances made in mobile telephony and data-communication. Technologies such as 3G telecom make it possible to submit large data streams in real-time from anywhere in the network. The exchange of data in global supply chains is a prerequisite for coordination and collaboration. Moreover, combined with location-determination technologies such as GPS or the European alternative to GPS, Galileo, which is to be integrated with GPS by 2008, supply chains are no longer bounded to fixed tracking and tracing points, but can be controlled and optimized in real-time, all around the globe, resulting in sensing and pacing the supply chain; see Figure 11.2.

Micro technology and its application in supply chains and products are a third important technological development. Products can be quipped with smart sensors, (RFID) chips, or small computers. Furthermore we see an increasing utilization of micro technology in resources such as trucks (e.g. board computers), warehouses, and even on shelves in the shop.

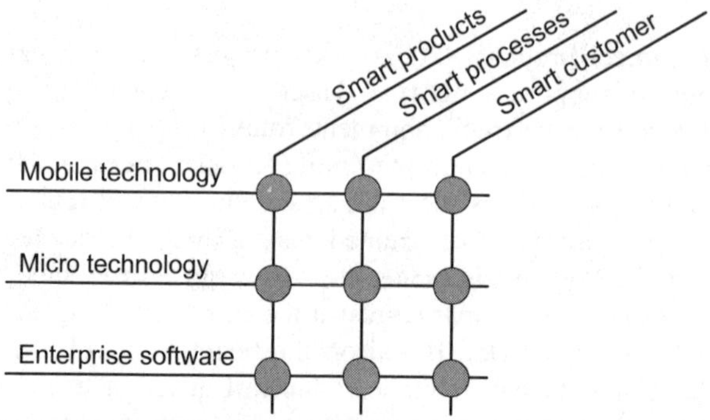

Fig 11.2 Technological developments enable smart products, processes and custome

Conclusions

The coordination of global supply chain activities through collaboration with customers and suppliers enhances performance in supply chains. Enabling technologies support data exchange, automated control mechanisms, and integrated planning involving smart processes and products. The benefits are not only in terms of profit, but also in terms of planet and people, so that these technologies may contribute to the sustainability of supply chains.

The aforementioned technological developments contribute to the availability of a vast amount of data and processing power in the supply chain. The challenges are in utilizing these capabilities as information and intelligence. Some of today's most innovative companies do pioneer in their supply chains already, and achieve promising results. However, the best is yet to come.

References

DEAL *project proposal* (2002). Written by the consortium partners: Almende, Vos Logistics, Post Kogeko, Groeneveld, VU, CWI and EUR.

Dekker, R., M. Fleischmann, K. Inderfurth, and L.N. Van Wassenhove, (eds.), (2004). *Reverse Logistics: Quantitative Models for Closed-Loop Supply Chains*, Springer-Verlag, Berlin.

Flapper, S.D.P., J.A.E.E. Van Nunen, L.N. Van Wassenhove, (eds.), (2004). *Managing Closed Loop Supply Chains,* Springer-Verlag, Berlin.

Fleisch, E., (2001). Business perspectives on Ubiquitous Computing, M-Lab Working Paper No. 4, Institute of Information Management – University of St. Gallen, Switzerland, pp. 1 – 20.

Hagel III, J., (2002). *Out of the Box - Strategies for achieving profits today and growth tomorrow through Web Services*, Harvard Business School Press, Boston, Massachusetts, ISBN 1-57851-680-3.

Nunen, J. Van, R. Zuidwijk, (2004). E-enabled closed-loop supply chains, *California Management Review* 46(2), pp. 40-54.

Scholz-Reiter, B., H. Höhns, (2002). Agent-based collaborative supply net management, pp. 3-19 in *Collaborative Systems for Production Management,* Proceedings of the IFIP WG 5.7 Eight International Conference on Advances in Production Management Systems (APMS 2002), September 8-13, 2002, Eindhoven, The Netherlands, Jagdev, H.S., Wortmann, J.C. and Pels, H.J. (eds.), Kluwer Academic Publishers, Boston, ISBN 1-4020-7542-1.

Thierry, M., M. Salomon, J.A.E.E. Van Nunen, L.N. Van Wassenhove, (1995). Strategic Issues in product Recovery Management, *California Management Review* 37(2), pp. 114-135.

Wooldridge, M., N.R. Jennings, (1995). Intelligent agents: theory and practice, *Knowledge management review* 1995 (January), pp. 1-62.

Section 2

Execution of Smart Business Networks

12 Marketing Translation Services Internationally: Exploiting IT to Achieve a Smart Network

Christopher P. Holland[1], Duncan R. Shaw[1], J.B. Westwood[1], and Ian Harris[2]

Introduction

The global market for translation services is extremely fragmented. There are a small number of large companies including Bowne global solutions and Lionbridge, but the largest five companies account for less than 5% of the worldwide market and there are literally thousands of extremely small companies and individuals offering different types of translation services around the world, often in a very limited geographic range. Large companies rarely co-ordinate their global requirements and consequently use different translation services suppliers in different divisions and geographic regions. "Thebigword' company (www.thebigword.com) recognised that in order to escape severe local price competition and commoditization of its own translation services it needed to differentiate its services and offer them on a global scale to international customers. This paper describes how it is implementing its strategy in terms of distinctive product offerings based on the innovative use of IT and the re-design of business relationships with customers to create smart translation networks.

Thebigword's customers are typically international organisations in a wide variety of industries including financial services, technology, manufacturing, travel and retailing. These organisations need to adapt their products for local markets, and as part of this adaptation process must use their customers' preferred languages and cultural concepts. In order to deliver translation services that take into account the technical requirements of language translation and also satisfy the local cultural needs, thebigword employs approximately 4,500 "mother tongue' linguists, often based in the target translation country. These linguists translate content and must also take into account specific local cultural dimensions of language translation. All translators must have translation qualifications and where relevant must also have qualifications and training for specific markets such as

[1] Manchester Business School, Booth Street West, University of Manchester, Manchester M15 6PB U.K., chris.holland@mbs.ac.uk

[2] Thebigword, 59 Charlotte Street, London W1T 4PE, UK: www.thebigword.com

technical engineering or medicine. The organisation of the company is complicated because its customers are based worldwide, its translators are located in its own offices and also include a large number of home workers, and there is a wide variety of language translation permutations. Their strategy is based on the innovative use of technology to support every aspect of its operations including relationship management with customers, product design and delivery, allocation of resources and monitoring of service quality. An example of a large client is given to illustrate the problem.

Marketing Problem

British Airways operates in 93 countries, uses five operating languages and wants to standardize brand messages on sites that contain several hundred pages of ever-changing content. BA's customers come from cultures all over the world and in recent years BA has endeavoured to portray itself as a global organisation rather than as a purely British company. This is a marketing technique designed to make itself more attractive to a wider segment of air travellers. In addition to this BA wishes to realise the benefits of strategic procurement by moving from many suppliers to fewer partnerships negotiated around scale and scope economy-based deals. BA's procurement strategy is to work with a very small number of preferred suppliers and this strategy has been applied to its global translation services procurement requirements.

Thebigword has chosen to standardise its services around four key products that are targeted at specific market segments. All of the products employ what the company terms "translation memory' as an integral part of its definition. Translation memory is a record of previous work done for the client. Many translation requests are revisions of previous work whether this is a revised technical document or an update to a website. It is therefore very inefficient if the whole document is translated from scratch. The translation memory works by cross-checking the revised document with the database of previously translated phrases and documents. The benefits are to improve the quality and consistency, to reduce costs, and offer a faster service. In the case of BA, the content management system of BA's website is linked to thebigword so that a change on BA's website triggers a request for new translation which is passed to a dedicated team of translators who are already familiar with the client's specific requirements and are supported by the translation memory and automatic document management and web services technology. Translation memory was the company's first effort at moving away from a commoditized market

characterized by one-off transactions to longer-term relationships where it could add more value to the client and improve its own profitability.
The four translation services are collectively termed "TranzManagement Suite', and individually the products are called Portal, PC, Content and e-procurement. All of these products offer translation services but vary along key dimensions: target market; strategy; business processes; IT architecture and systems; and network intelligence which are shown in Figure 12.1.

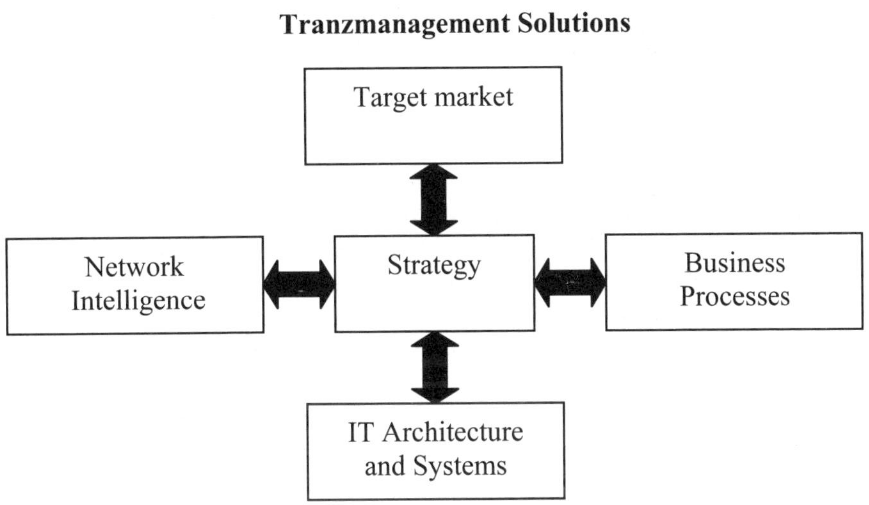

Fig 12.1 The product dimensions of the "Tranzmanagement' suite of translation services

Strategy is at the centre of the model because it drives the development and implementation of different product offerings. For all products, from the simplest portal to the e-procurement service, the overall strategy is to create a differentiated service that creates customer value, and one that creates a reciprocally strong business relationship between thebigword and its customers based on shared systems, and shared business processes. Over time, as the customer uses the services, thebigword is able to use its systems to create a memory of previous transactions and adapt or personalize the offering.

The target markets are defined primarily by size: individual/SME; mid-sized corporate; and multinational. All of these companies may start with the simplest portal translation service and the marketing objective is to move larger customers with more complex requirements onto longer-term relationships based on PC, content and e-procurement systems, depending on individual circumstances and requirements.

Business processes define the nature of the interaction. For example in the portal service, the business processes create a simple workflow system that manages the exchange of files that is initiated by the client, typically on an ad-hoc basis. The content management system is very different because the work is initiated automatically when the client's web content is changed, and the resulting translation requirements are carried out and posted back to the client's website.

IT architecture and systems are the information systems that connect thebigword to individual clients. Again, they vary in complexity from the relatively simple file exchange system in the portal service, through to the sophisticated content management system and e-procurement product. The technology used is standard web technology to support data exchange in the case of the portal, and fully shared systems in the content management system. The actual deployment of different technology is dependent on the service. Standard technology is used to differentiate the service by using IT to support shared business processes that over time create a smart organisational translation network with thebigword as the hub.

Network intelligence is the knowledge that thebigword gains about individual customers that is then built into the service offerings and evolves over time. This is another facet to the company's differentiation strategy. To give an overview of the "tranzmanagement' solutions, each individual product is described in Table 12.1 using the product dimensions detailed in Figure 12.1.

"Tranzmanagement' Solutions

The four distinctive services represent an emergent strategy based on the broad principles of product differentiation and market focus. The portal service uses the basic capabilities of the internet to attract new customers and deliver a secure, reliable translation service either on an ad-hoc basis, or on a continual request basis by customers. Marketing to new large customers is managed through a field-based sales force. As new customers use the service more frequently, thebigword builds up a history of usage and is able to offer value-added information in areas such as budget control, management information and customer defined access control.

Table 12.1 An overview of thebigword's TranzManagement Translation Solutions

Product dimensions	Target market	Strategy	Business processes	IT architecture and systems	Network Intelligence
TranzManagement Solutions					
Portal	Wide range of customers ranging from occasional users, ad-hoc requests from within a large corporate organisation, and potential large customers exploring the site	Offer web-based service for ad-hoc users that can be branded and easily distributed in target organisations. Offers multi-user support with access control, budgeting and user management.	Secure logon to support file exchange and workflow management. The initiation of work demands is from the client and when the work is completed the client is informed by email.	Users from within customer organisations use a standard HTTPS connection with 128-bit SSL and firewall security. Access to the portal is through a standard web browser.	Customer behaviour is tracked over time and this enables management information to be shared with customers and new marketing initiatives offered based on current behaviour.
PC	Large organisations with frequent use of language translation services linked to PC based documents.	Make it as easy as possible for individual users to access the translation services by providing an automatic service linked to individual PCs. The objective is to offer more consistent services.	Easy installation of service that links the PC to thebigword's server using secure technology. Users submit files automatically where they are tracked and returned to the user when completed.	Email requests generated from within a PC desktop application during its use. Encryption ensures security.	Thebigword can track the uptake of translation services from individual users and aggregate the information to give full budget, workflow, outstanding documents and control access information for the client.

Table 12.1 (continued)

Product dimensions **TranzManagement Solutions**	**Target market**	**Strategy**	**Business processes**	**IT architecture and systems**	**Network Intelligence**
Content Management Systems	Large organisations, often multinational, that require sophisticated content management services for intranets and internet servers	The strategy is to hook into client's internet and intranet servers so that any changes made are automatically notified to thebigword. An individual client can therefore change their site in one language and all of their other language based sites are updated within an agreed timeframe	Large clients operate sophisticated client management systems to organise web content on their sites. Thebigword connects to these through a web service that integrates a translation service directly with the client's web site.	This is a web services product. Simple Object Access Protocol (SOAP) is used to direct the CMS requests to thebigword with originator information. Content is written in an XML standard agreed with the customer.	Thebigword uses a loosely coupled architecture that makes use of SOAP and the XML standard that models content type. By using a web service to deliver the translation, the client's systems and thebigword's systems become closely connected. Depending on the particular service level agreements, changes made on a client's web site can be changed automatically into whatever other language sites are used by the client. This automatically keeps web pages up to date and avoids errors introduced by web authors or administrators using cut and paste. It also provides a mechanism for accurate version control, change detection and ensures consistency across all web sites.
E-procurement	Large organisations that employ sophisticated e-procurement systems.	Act as single source translation service that is controlled through large organisations' e-procurement systems.	E-procurement systems are not designed to buy non-standard services such as translation. To overcome this problem, thebigword links directly to e-procurement systems and automatically places the quote for a particular piece of work in the client's e-procurement system as a single line itme.	Connects to e-procurement system using cXML. An accepted quotation is placed directly in the client's systems so that it an individual, unique piece of translation can then be purchased as if it were a simple product item.	

The PC connection offers similar translation services but it links directly with PCs in the customer workplace for organisations that use translation services on a regular basis and wish to have an easy and automatic way of sending documents directly from individual PCs. The effect is to increase the level of integration between thebigword at the level of data sharing capability.

The content management system takes this a stage further by sharing applications with customers' information systems. In this way the business processes and IT systems become shared across organisational boundaries and thebigword is able to respond dynamically to changes in an individual customer's web content that often needs to be replicated in different languages very quickly. This is an example of the web services concept.

Most large organisations are now moving towards consolidated and formal procurement systems based on company-wide enterprise systems, and thebigword has set up the e-procurement system so that it slots directly into the main IS vendors' purchasing applications such as those found in SAP and Oracle. A limitation of standard e-procurement systems is that they only work for standard product items that can be described and priced on a standard basis. For translation services this is very difficult to achieve in a manner that is fair and transparent to both the customer and the translation services company. For example if a translation service is priced on a per document basis then the client gains at the expense of the supplier for a long document and vice-versa for short documents. If the work is priced on a per word basis the client may be paying too much for a slightly revised document that has already been translated in the recent past, and too little for a brand new document that requires extensive translation work. Thebigword uses a concept called "punchout'. A request for translation is made directly from the e-procurement system and this generates a quotation for a particular piece of work that takes into account the difficulty, scale and complexity of the work. If the quotation is accepted, it is then automatically placed onto the client's e-procurement system so that the administrative processes for ordering and payment are tied into the business relationship between the client and thebigword. In this way a unique translation requirement is fitted into a global e-procurement system that achieves the administrative benefits of standardization of systems, whilst retaining the unique translation services needs. The web services concept for a sophisticated content management system is described in more detail below.

Content Management and Web Services

The most sophisticated of all the translation services is the content management system that exploits web services technology. A diagram of the service is shown in Figure 12.2.

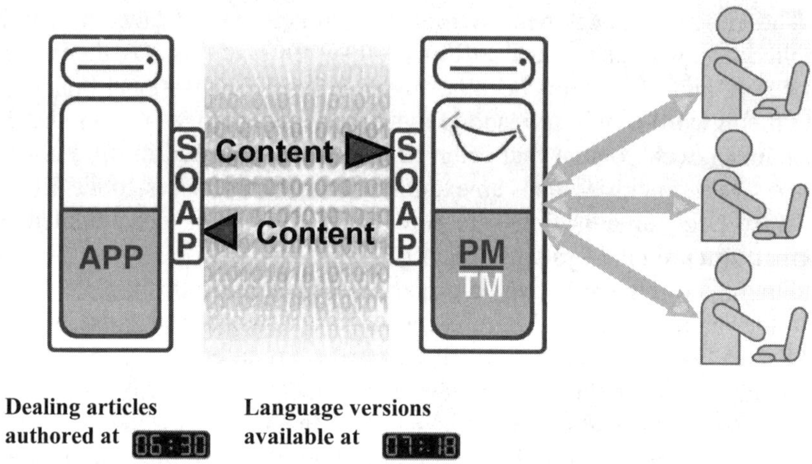

Fig 12.2 Web services in the translation market

The example shown is that of an international bank that creates new documents on its web site at 6.30a.m. The content management system of thebigword is alerted of the change and the content of the changed documents is transferred to thebigword through a SOAP link. The work is distributed to specialist translators who must complete the translation in a specified time frame. In this case the whole process must be completed in less than 48 minutes in order to be able to distribute the information worldwide to different national audiences simultaneously. The translation memory contains a record of previous jobs so that translators are able to familiarize themselves with the type of problems that were tackled in the past, and also with possible mistakes that were made regarding conventions, styles or use of language. This improves the quality and consistency of the service, and with experienced translators, reduces the amount of time required. The concept is similar to what Simon (1969) proposed when he referred to problem solving being more efficient when it was carried out in the context of previous similar problems and knowledge of established solutions because there is inevitably an element of re-use in the new solution based on past efforts on similar problems.

Case Analysis

The description of services in Table 12.1 demonstrates that thebigword connects with customers using web-based technology to differentiate the translation services that it offers. The main methods of differentiation are to exploit the translation memory to add intelligence about individual clients' specific requirements based on previous experiences and the use of technology to connect customers' systems and business processes to those of thebigword. The connection between thebigword and customers organisations at the multiple levels of strategy, business process and IT infrastructure and systems is shown in diagrammatic form in Figure 12.3.

The description of services in Table 12.1 demonstrates that thebigword connects with customers using web-based technology to differentiate the translation services that it offers. The main methods of differentiation are to exploit the translation memory to add intelligence about individual clients' specific requirements based on previous experiences and the use of technology to connect customers' systems and business processes to those of thebigword. The connection between thebigword and customers organisations at the multiple levels of strategy, business process and IT infrastructure and systems is shown in diagrammatic form in Figure 12.3.

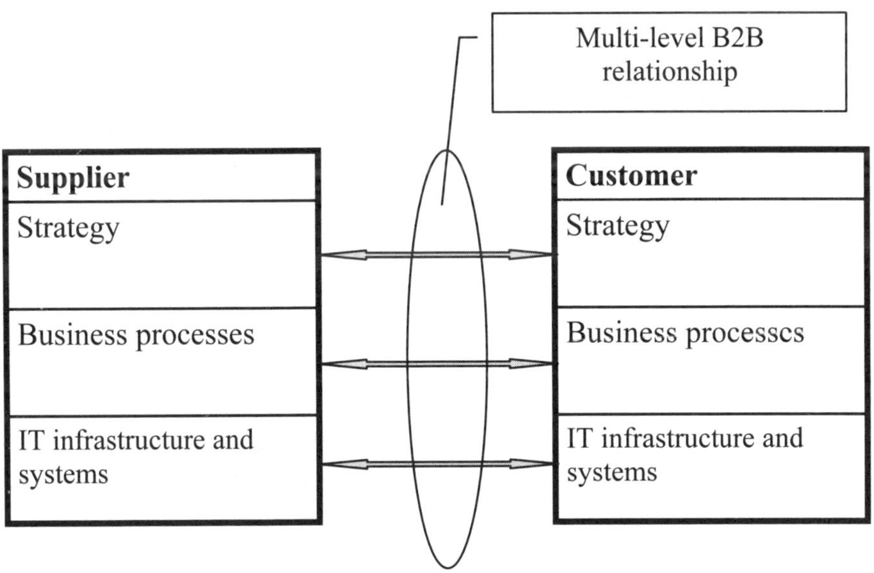

Fig 12.3 Schematic model of B2B relationships showing multiple levels of interaction

The simple model shown in Figure 12.3 illustrates that B2B relationships occur at multiple levels. Early examples of EDI were focused on connecting disparate IT infrastructures and systems across organisational boundaries. EDI systems implicitly changed some business processes, but most of the effort was technical in nature and focused on data standards. More recent efforts to exploit web technologies, particularly XML, takes the early ideas from the EDI innovators into the internet age and standards bodies and commercial organisations such as RosettaNet and Covisint now explicitly focus their efforts on standard *business processes* that in turn determine *data standards*. The web services model exploited by thebigword

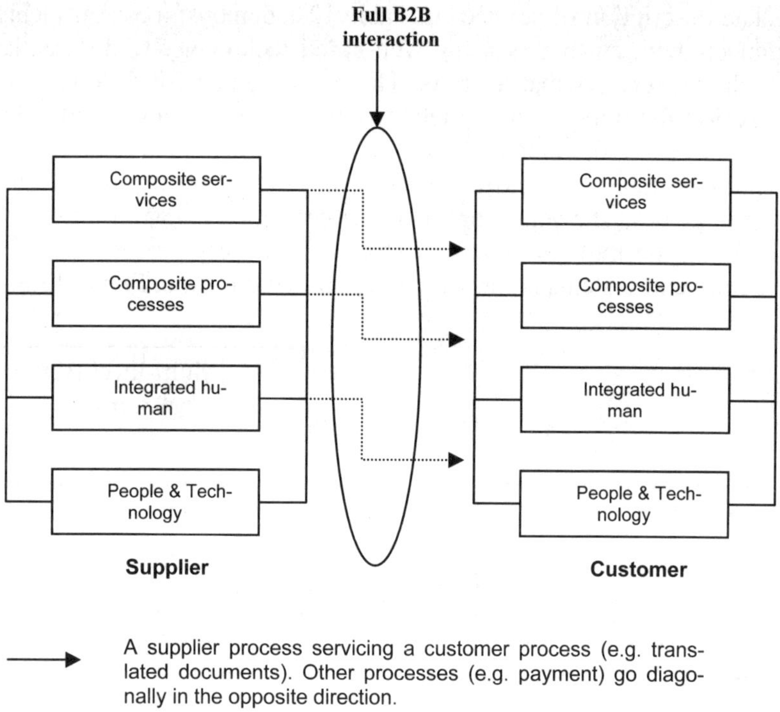

Fig 12.4 Business processes producing services for the different levels of a B2B partner's own processes (partly based upon Kalakota and Robinson (2003))

supports the B2B relationship at multiple levels. Web services connect the IT infrastructure and systems and links the applications in customers' sites directly to the translation services of thebigword. Web services also integrates the business processes of both companies because it defines the roles and activities required to happen whenever a change is made to the customer's web content. The business process element of Figure 12.3 is expanded to show more conceptual detail in Figure 12.4 above.

The central idea contained in Figure 12.4 is that the service offered by a supplier (in the case of thebigword, the translation service) is an input to the composite processes of a customer. The overall purpose is to achieve a sophisticated workflow system with guaranteed service level agreements in the context of a contractual agreement. The shared systems make this possible and also add new possibilities to share information about the translation process with customers. In this way thebigword gains intelligence about customers prior behaviour, new requests, and overall usage of the system, and customers gain better service and support because they are provided with the translation service itself and all of the tools and information to manage the associated workflows.

Information Technology

The information systems that makes the connections work is based upon the following technologies:

1. A model of possible services that gives flexibility of language type.
2. Internet and WWW technology that enable data sharing capability.
3. XML language carrying messages about the model that enables systems integration.
4. A SOAP addressing protocol to ensure messages go to the correct destination.

Intelligence is embedded within the architecture of thebigword's delivery channel. It has enough flexibility to "fully overlay" other non-Smart Networks – i.e. it is a smart overlay whose function is to process one natural language and set of cultural concepts into another, on demand.

Conclusions

Thebigword's smart distribution architecture connects into a customer's information systems in such a way as to meet highly diverse language type, structural and volume requirements. It does this by decoupling back-office processing from front-office interaction; by the smart design of its front office systems architecture and by the use of internet technologies. The case study is an illustration of a smart network that is controlled by a single organisation, which uses intelligence encapsulated within distributed business process models and loosely coupled information systems to solve a global translation services problem.

The core service of translation appears to a casual onlooker as a straightforward product offering. However this is not the case when the translation service is placed in the context of a global company that is managing intellectual assets expressed as information in whatever format (printed documents, technical papers, web site content, printed or e-mail communication with economic partners) that needs to be managed in a dynamic and timely fashion. The marketing of thebigword is based on an event driven system where changes or requests from clients are managed through a smart business network that connects clients with thebigword on multiple levels: data systems; business processes and strategy. XML and web technologies enable the sharing of data from the clients' systems to the translation engine of thebigword. The automatic workflow systems that overlay each of the product offerings of portal, PC, content management system and e-procurement, co-ordinate the business processes from the initiation of a new request through to the final payment. The strategy link exists because thebigword is arguably helping its clients manage their global identities and brands through the consistent management of their information assets and communication channels. In terms of potential future development, thebigword may only have exploited a fraction of what is possible in the translation services market, especially when one considers the rate of change in just the past couple of years and the development of new mobile technologies.

The value of the translation service is obviously much higher when the client and the translation services company work together using advanced information systems that enable the loose coupling of the translation service with whatever internal systems and processes the client wishes to use. The case illustrates the strategic value of translation services and also identifies the potential of web services in other sectors and business contexts.

Acknowledgements

The authors acknowledge the support of the Engineering and Physical Sciences Research Council (EPSRC) in funding this piece of research as part of the MBS research project into flexible business integration. The paper has also benefited from the extensive and insightful feedback received at the Cordys/RSM workshop on smart business networks held at De Vanenburg, Holland, May 2004. A large number of delegates contributed and particular thanks go to Benn Konsynski for his response to the paper and Uladzimir Radkevitch for documenting the feedback. Any mistakes or omissions in the paper are the sole responsibility of the authors.

References

Anderson, P. (1999). "Complexity Theory And Organization Science", *Organization Science*,10(3).
Kalakota, R., M. Robinson (2003). *Services Blueprint: Roadmap For Execution*, (p. 132), Addison-Wesley, London.
Simon, H. A. (1969). *The Sciences of the Artificial*, MIT Press, Cambridge, Mass.
Vogt, S. (2003). "Going Native to Get Global", *vnunet.com* (www.vnunet.com/Features/1140733) (accessed 28th February 2004).

Review Comments

Reviewer: Benn Konsynski
Rapporteur: Ulad Radkevitch

The paper by Christopher Holland, Duncan Shaw, J.B. Westwood, and Ian Harris presented an example of a smart business network implemented between a leading provider of translation services, a company called Thebigword, and its customers and service providers. This smart business network involves several levels of IT-enabled integration of business processes between service provider community and its customer community. Services range from support for one-off projects to full integration with the procurement systems of the client. On the highest levels of business process integration, translation services are performed in a mode similar to the concept of web services. Also, translation services leverage a customer-specific knowledge base labeled "translation memory" that serves to establish a record of the vocabulary, grammar and style preferred by the client.

Participants of the discussion were unanimous in acknowledging that the case study presented an excellent example of a smart business network. A few comments made explicit what features of the network developed by Thebigword contributed to its "smartness". The company's approach to organizing collaboration with its customers is new and highly innovative. This business model has been noticed by the competition and produces considerable impact on the structure of translation services industry. The accumulation of "translation memory" allows network intelligence to develop as time goes by. High degree of integration between customer and service provider enables the latter to provide more value to the former and also makes it more difficult for the customer to switch to another service provider.

Several comments were elaborated on the mechanisms underlying the smartness of Thebigword's approach. Flexible integration achieved through the use of web services enables customized response to customer's requests. At the same time, the network operates in a plug-and-play mode that makes it possible to connect new customers to the service provider in a timely and efficient manner. A high proportion of value created by the service provider is achieved due to the knowledge of the customer's context. For example, translation consistency empowered by "translation memory" helps customers preserve its brand identity across different markets. The knowledge transfer from customer to service provider is gradual and does not incur additional costs for the former. The knowledge transfer is empowered by IT support for the learning process. However, technology is not the single factor contributing to service excellence; communication on the level of individuals is still important as development of relationships of Thebigword with its customers benefits from contributions of individual translators.

In the course of the discussion, development of a teaching case on the basis of the presented material was discussed. This work is already under way; video interviews with Thebigword's employees and, possibly, its customers will be carried out. The participants of the discussion were also interested to learn about the structure of Thebigword's model of margins and profitability to gain more insight into generation of customer value.

13 Node to Network: Partnerships in the Second-Hand Book Trade

William Golden[1], Martin Hughes[1], and Helen Burke[2]

Introduction

For the last number of years the Internet, electronic commerce and electronic business have being offering exciting new competitive opportunities for SMEs to extend their customer base into the global marketplace and broaden their involvement into new international markets. Web based business can be an extremely attractive option for SMEs to create a global presence without vast expense when compared to other media and the emergence of internationally active SMEs is a worldwide trend (Fellenstein & Wood, 1999).

One area where the Internet can help lessen the impact of geographical distance is in enabling the restructuring of supply chains with a view to enhancing alliances and promoting the efficient and timely exchange of information between business partners. The integration of advanced technology and partnership sourcing offer SMEs unprecedented opportunities within the global marketplace (McGloin & Grant, 1998). Through partnerships, SMEs can increase business on their web site; conduct low risk business experiments; gain access to information technology competencies; and serve foreign markets through the use of local partners (De Man et al. 2002).

Establishing e-business partnerships has therefore become a strategic means for retailing SME firms to gain access to new markets, new channels to serve customers and enhance the value of their offering through an infinite array of complementary products and sophisticated value-added services without losing autonomy and at lower levels of investment and risk (Rahman & Raisinghani, 2000). Partnerships help to bridge the gap between the firm's present resources and its expected future requirements (Hoffman & Schlosser, 2001). The network nature of the electronic medium makes it easier for online retailers to develop their unique competencies and bring together or borrow resources and expertise from a wide

---

[1] Department of Accountancy and Finance, National University of Ireland, Galway, Ireland, willie.golden@nuigalway.ie

[2] Kenny's Bookshop & Art Galleries Ltd, High St., Galway, Ireland, www.kennys.ie

range of alliance partners (Chatterjee, 2002). Alliances improve the competitiveness of firms by providing access to external resources, by providing synergies and by fostering rapid learning and change (Hoffman & Schlosser, 2001). The Internet provides SME's with opportunities to create their own business network by adding partners virtually where appropriate. By taking a proactive approach to establishing such partnerships the SME has the capability of creating a smart business network with the SME as the node that organises the network.

These alliances provide the possibility for SME's to divorce information about the product from the actual physical product and thus create virtual value chains (Rayport & Sviokla, 1994). Such virtual value chains can then be exploited via virtual marketplaces which capitalise on the separation of the physical and informational processes associated with the sale of the product (Kambil & van Heck, 1998).

This paper presents the case of an SME that has proactively managed the creation of a smart business network in the second-hand book trade. The case details how the SME succeeded in creating a virtual network, in which the SME remains central, by utilising the separation of the physical and informational processes. The case also illustrates how the SME established its own virtual value chain to achieve scale and scope benefits inhibited by the economics of a physical value chain alone.

Case Study

Kenny's Bookshop & Art Gallery Ltd. is a family run small business, based in Galway, Ireland. Currently the business employs just over 40 people and have an annual turnover of approximately €5 million. The bookshop side of the business sells both new and second-hand books. The business was established in 1940 and during the initial years of the business the focus was on serving customers who came into the bookshop. However, in the 1970's in order to expand its business the bookshop started selling books internationally by mailing paper catalogues of the books they had in stock to libraries in the US. This focus on export became a central component of the business and by the 1990's the company had become the leading supplier of books of Irish interest to U.S. libraries. In addition, it also started to grow its personal book club –"Kennys Irish Book Parcels" through which Kenny's supply Irish books to over 1,500 customers in 45 countries. In the mid 1990's new export markets were identified and the company commenced selling books to the Asian market, especially Japan.

The sourcing of second-hand books for re-sale is predominantly done on the basis of buying a full library or consignment of books. Out of each consignment approximately 20% of the books can be quickly resold by Kenny's to previously identified customers. However, the remaining 80%, while still very valuable stock, needs to be displayed in the bookshop so that it is accessible for customers to browse. In a period of rapid growth in the late 1990's the company bought a large numbers of second-hand book consignments, which resulted in them accumulating over 900,000 second-hand books. Only 10% of these can be displayed in the retail store while the rest had to be put in to storage.

Concurrent with the expansion in second-hand stock within the company was a growing use of the Internet by the company. Their initial web site (www.kennys.ie) went on-line in 1994 and provided little more than a brochure-ware presence to the company. However, as web site traffic grew the company became increasingly aware that the web held the potential to radically transform the business. The web was identified as a strategic tool that could be used to better manage current export markets, enhance the book-parcels service, explore emerging markets in a cost effective manner and as a means of making the in storage stock visible and saleable.

Early experiences of the company with using the Internet were very positive. One of the early benefits was the use of e-mail to gain efficiencies. Prior to using the Internet the company sent libraries in the U.S.A. monthly lists of all new Irish publications and a list of some of the high value second-hand books that were available for sale. Initially these lists were typed, copied or printed, envelopes addressed, stamped, and the information inserted into them. By 1998 the paper-based process had been replaced by email, which reduced communication costs and increased efficiency benefits. The number of mailing lists has grown to over 50 with over 5,000 registered customers. Kenny's now supply in excess of 150 U.S. academic and research libraries and have clients in other countries including the U.K., France, Germany, Australia, Russia and Japan.

The success in being able to cost effectively reach existing customers via the Internet and in particular by using electronic book catalogues, (word-processed or Pdf documents) distributed via e-mail provided an impetus to expand the company. In order to better service the export market for second-hand books and to provide space to store the burgeoning stock of second-hand books in an accessible manner a major business decision was made in 1999 to build a new custom-built book warehouse and electronic cataloguing facility on the outskirts of Galway city.

The decision to setup the book warehouse was primarily based on the success the company had achieved in selling books via the Internet and the belief that this sales avenue possessed substantial growth potential. Information on the books available in the warehouse was only available via electronic book catalogues. As such the warehouse was not open to the public and existed as a pick-and-select location for books that existing customers had opted to buy as a result of seeing them in the electronic catalogues that had been e-mailed to them. The sales being achieved via electronic catalogues continued to increase steadily, but the communication of the catalogues was only reaching those who had subscribed to the company mailing lists. To expand the reach of the electronic catalogues Kenny's designed a second web site www.kennyscollections.com for their Japanese clients so they could view all Kenny's catalogues and prices. This site provided a cost efficient and effective way for Asian clients to view Kenny's catalogues with emails arriving daily with orders from these clients.

In a further effort to expand access to their stock of second-hand books Kenny's began to list their stock on second-hand book marketplaces, which were appearing. The company realised that the marketplaces could provide both extended geographic and customer reach. E-partnerships were formed with Alibris, Abe, Amazon.com, Bibliodirect, Bibliology, Tomfolio, Ilab-Lila and other marketplaces. These marketplaces act as an intermediary, to facilitate booksellers to list and sell online and for buyers to find and purchase books. They do not take title to any books; they simply facilitate the transaction between buyer and seller to make the transaction as seamless and easy as possible. In Kenny's web orders arrive daily from customers worldwide through these e-marketplaces. By 2002 over 150 orders for books coming from these sites were being shipped each week accounting for 25% of export sales.

By 2002, Kenny's were enjoying considerable success on the Internet. However, the technological infrastructure underlying the Internet presence was quickly becoming inadequate and was resulting in a number of problems for the company.

The first issue was that the book marketplaces require that booksellers such as Kenny's who use their site have a high fulfilment rate – i.e. be able to find and send with 24 hours of receiving the order 95-98% of the books selected. As the number of books that Kenny's were cataloguing increased the ability to quickly and efficiently find a particular book in the warehouse became problematic. To alleviate this problem an ERP system was purchased and implemented in 2003 to enable each catalogued book to be tracked and located.

A second problem was that cataloguing each book for sale was a slow and expensive process. A more efficient cataloguing system was needed if the company was going to catalogue the 900,000 remaining items in a reasonable timeframe. While the ERP system provided logistic and financial functionality it did not possess the ability to catalogue books. Having built up considerable experience of using technology the company sought out a way that it could use the Internet to reduce it cataloguing costs while also making it more efficient. It entered negotiations with the largest database of bibliographical records in the world - the Online Computer Library Centre (OCLC). The OCLC is a not-for-profit organization, which provides bibliographical records to public libraries. Kenny's were the first commercial organization to negotiate a deal with the OCLC for the supply of bibliographical records – which would be delivered electronically via the Internet.

Once agreement with the OCLC had been reached software specifically designed for cataloguing – a Library Management System was purchased in 2003. This software supports the OCLC cataloguing standard and enables bibliographical records to be purchased from OCLC and seamlessly inserted into Kenny's database which enables much more efficient cataloguing. Prior to the agreement with OCLC a cataloguer in Kenny's had to complete the entire bibliographical information for each book, which included entering data in approximately 20 separate data fields. Now rather than typing in all the bibliographic information for each of the book, they simply submit certain information about the book to the OCLC database and the OCLC returns, if they have it, a full bibliographic record.

The cataloguing of a book is central to the business model and is reflected in the fact that for accounting purposes un-catalogued item are nominally valued at a cost price of €1. When the item comes back from OCLC with its complete bibliographical record it is given a cost price on the internal system of €4. The intent behind this cost price evaluation is twofold, first to highlight the fact that the book is not a salable item until it is catalogued and secondly to reflect the actual cost of cataloguing an individual book.

A third problem the company faced was the incompatibility of the data formats required by each of the book e-marketplaces. Due to these incompatibilities the daily additions and deletions that had occurred to Kenny's stock had to be individually uploaded manually to each e-marketplace. To solve this problem Kenny's started using the services of BookRouter.com. What this service does is "automates the task of uploading database files to various book indexing services. It is as fast and easy to send data to ten services as it is to only one, once you've signed up with them. You send your list once to BookRouter, which will then automatically configure it in the format each indexing service requires. BookRouter offers convenience and saves time. Indexing services may come and go, or change procedures, but you will never need to change yours -- BookRouter takes care of the behind-the-scenes hassles" (www.bookrouter.com/routerFAQ.html)

Using bookrouter.com has enabled Kenny's to fulfill one of their strategic initiatives, which is to get their books listed on as many book marketplaces as possible.

As a result of all of the changes made by the company the Internet has become the main sales channel with approximately 75% of all books now being sold are via the Internet. According to Conor Kenny, Managing Director these changes have dramatically impacted the business to the extent that:

"We are not booksellers any more. We are information providers".

Discussion

The advent of the Internet has dramatically changed the second-hand books industry. In particular the advent of e-marketplaces such as ABE.com provide an extensive database of second-hand books. ABE.com operates both as a B2C and B2B site. Booksellers use it to procure books for their own stock and a standard book-traders discount of 10% is given on the retail price. Due to the convenience of such sites more and more B2B book sales are happening through these marketplaces. A consequence of this is that if a small bookshop is to survive and prosper it needs to be able to cost effectively find ways of publishing it stock of books to such sites.

For Kenny's effectively distributing information about books to potential customers has long been a successful sales strategy. As illustrated by Figure 13.1, the initial strategy was to leverage the capabilities of a company website. While providing another listing for second hand books available at Kenny's the site was limited by the number of active users. Achieving multiple listings and attracting increased customers was achieved by extending the business network to include e-partners. The ability of the company to take advantage of the new developments offered by e-business was the result of a cumulative learning experience with the Internet. Over time the use of the Internet increased within the company and the expertise gained enabled them to make strategic decisions with respect to enhancing the internal IT infrastructure of the company by acquiring an ERP and a library management system. At each stage in the development of the IT infrastructure the cost escalated and soon the company was making substantial investments in new technologies. While such investments are high they have provided the company with an infrastructure, which provides them with the capability to operate as a central node in the emerging smart business network of second-hand books. In particular, their alliance with OCLC provides them with a cost advantage in cataloguing books. At the customer end their ability to send information electronically to bookrouter.com enables them to obtain extensive reach on the Internet through multiple marketplaces in a timely and cost effective manner.

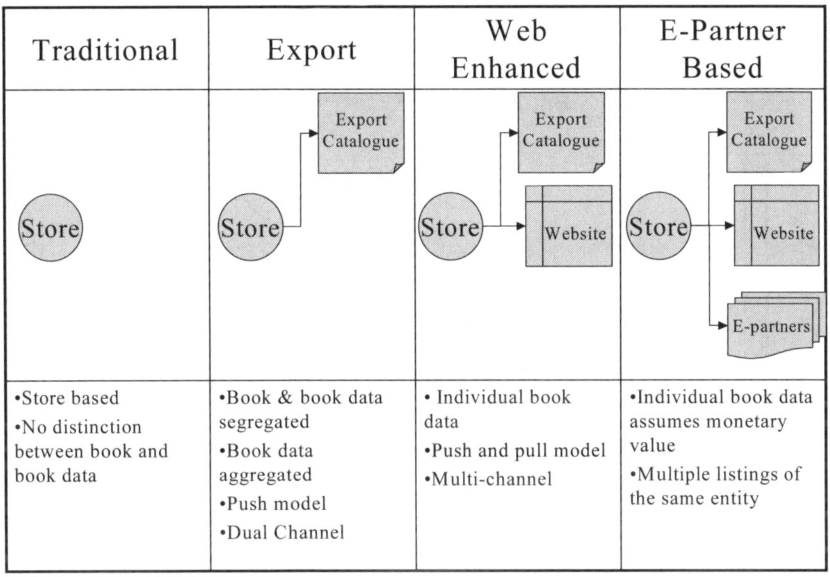

Fig 13.1 Evolving Value Chain

The advent of book e-marketplaces has greatly facilitated the complete separation of the physical and the information value chains for the stock of second-hand books. Figure 13.2 illustrates the increasing importance of the virtual value chain for Kenny's. The virtual value chain incorporates the e-business system, the multiple information distribution channels and the customer interface. By exploiting the virtual value chain the company has achieved multiple virtual copies of the bibliographical record for the same book and greatly increased the number of potential sales opportunities.

Indeed the bibliographical record has become a product in its own right with such records being purchased by Kenny's from OCLC. Kenny's also sell such bibliographical records in instances where the record does not exist on the OCLC database. When this occurs, Kenny's catalogue the book to OCLC standards and send the record to OCLC, and receive payment on a record-by-record basis.

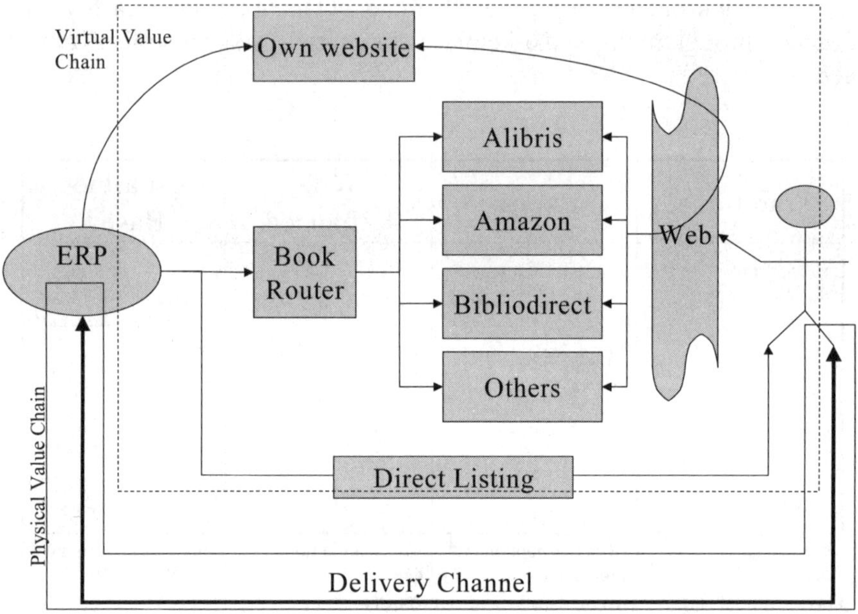

Fig 13.2 Virtual and Physical Value Chains

The decision to use the intermediary bookrouter.com has greatly facilitated the virtual value chain by creating a seamless smart network for the transfer of bibliographical records to multiple e-marketplaces. The cost effectiveness of this technological solution provides a single access point through which all data is routed and batch updated on a daily basis.

However, the move to a more sophisticated e-business network has produced one unanticipated consequence. While the use of bookrouter.com facilitate a daily update, it is still in batch format and thus the individual e-marketplaces do not immediately register the deletion of an item from Kenny's stock on the basis of a sale. As the sales orders have increased so also have the incidents of "already sold' problems as two or more customers attempt to purchase the same book before the network can be updated. Further iterations of the network will require the movement to a smarter, real-time update mechanism.

Conclusions

The Internet has dramatically changed the second-hand book trade – information about a book in the form of a bibliographical record has become more important as an Internet sales tool than the physical book. This change has provided the possibility for companies providing specific expertise to be combined together through alliances to create a loosely coupled smart network based on information exchange.

In this case study the company has created a smart business network by combining components from separate virtual partners. The two main virtual partners of note are OCLC, which is used for the cost effective electronic downloading of bibliographical records and bookrouter.com, which is used as a single point for publishing their stock of second-hand books on multiple internet sites specialising in the sale of such items. The ability of the company to create such a smart virtual business network is predicated on the fact that they have put in place an internal IT infrastructure, which enables them to connect electronically relatively seamlessly to these virtual partners. As such any company wishing to emulate this companies strategy will first have to build equivalent internal systems and then negotiate the virtual partnerships that Kenny's have negotiated. While their competitors are doing this Kenny's – if past experience is anything to go by - will be using the time to refine the virtual business network they have already created – thus remaining ahead of the competition by continually innovating at a business network level.

References

Chatterjee, P. (2002). "Interfirm Alliances in Online Retailing", *Journal of Business Research*, (5752), pp. 1-10.

De Man, A., M. Stienstra, and H. Volberda, (2002). "E-Partnering Moving Bricks and Mortar Online", *European Management Journal*, 20 (4), pp. 329-339.

Fellenstein, C., R. Wood, (1999). *E-commerce, Global E-business, and E-societies*, Prentice-Hall, Inc.

Hoffman, W., R. Schlosser, (2001). "Success Factors of Strategic Alliances in Small and Medium Sized Enterprises - An Empirical Survey", *Long Range Planning*, 34 (3), pp. 357-381.

Kambil, A., E. van Heck, (1998). "Reengineering the Dutch Flower Auctions: A Framework for Analyzing Exchange Organizations", *Information Systems Research*, 9 (1), pp. 1-19.

McGloin, E., C. Grant, (1998). "Supporting Partnership Sourcing in Northern Ireland Through Advanced Technology", *Technovation*, 18 (2), pp. 91-99.

Rahman, S. M., M. S. Raisinghani, (2000). *Electronic Commerce: Opportunities and Challenges*. Idea Group Publishing.

Rayport, J.F., J.J. Sviokla, (1994). "Managing in the Marketspace", *Harvard Business Review*, 72 (6), pp. 141-150.

Review Comments

Reviewer: Lorike Hagdorn
Rapporteur: Otto Koppius

The audience quickly agreed that the Kenny's case is a fascinating example of the industry changes taking place through the possibilities that e-business offers, although some argued that the fundamental smartness of the network may actually reside more in Bookrouter.com than Kenny's itself, since Bookrouter.com is what enables the interoperability between customers on one hand and the network players in the second-hand book trade on the other hand. This turned into an interesting discussion of several conceptual issues surrounding smart business networks and as the discussion challenged several preconceptions of various participants, the issues are formulated as three tensions:

- Tension 1: short-term adaptation vs. long-term adaptability. A focus on the end-customer may overemphasize adaptation to current customer wishes at the expense of adaptability to future market changes, thus jeopardizing the long-term viability of the network,
- Tension 2: effectiveness vs. efficiency. Within the same market, different types of customers exist with different priorities. Some care mostly about the effectiveness of the network, i.e. getting the product in the first place and are relatively insensitive to delivery time and pricing issues, i.e. the efficiency of the network, whereas other customers may have a different tradeoff. A network focused on effectiveness will most likely have different organizations involved and a different network structure than a network focused on efficiency, yet a smart business network needs to deliver on both counts, necessarily resulting in slack in the network,
- Tension 3: organizational goals vs. network goals. Profit-maximization behavior of individual organizations in the network may impede the co-operation between organizations that is necessary to create value for the end-customer at the network level and maximum value creation at the network level may result in sub-optimal profits for individual organizations. Alignment of incentives, goals and expectations within the network becomes a crucial issue here.

Obviously, these tensions were not resolved within the time frame available, but highlighting them here will hopefully sensitize readers to them and analyze how smart business network manage these tensions in practice.

14 Towards Smarter Supply and Demand Chain Collaboration Practices Enabled by RFID Technology

Katerina Pramatari[1], Georgios I. Doukidis[1], and Panos Kourouthanassis[1]

Collaboration in the Supply and Demand Chain

The advent of e-business has created several challenges and opportunities in the supply chain environment. The Internet has made it easier to share information among supply chain partners and the current trend is to try to leverage the benefits obtained through information sharing (also called visibility) across the supply chain to improve operational performance, customer service, and solution development (Swaminathan and Tayur, 2003).

Since the early 1990s, there has been a growing understanding that supply chain management should be built around the integration of trading partners (Barratt and Oliveira, 2001). Bowersox et al. (2000) state that firms collaborate in the sense of "leveraging benefits to achieve common goals". Anthony (2000) suggests that supply chain collaboration occurs when "two or more companies share the responsibility of exchanging common planning, management, execution, and performance measurement information". He goes further suggesting that "collaborative relationships transform how information is shared between companies and drive change to the underlying business processes". Research carried out by Andersen Consulting, Stanford University, Northwestern University, and INSEAD, as reported in Anderson and Lee (1999), recommends that industry participants "collaborate on planning and execution" of supply chain strategy to achieve a "synchronised supply chain".

Some scholars suggest using the term demand chain management (DCM) instead of supply-chain management (SCM) (Vollmann et al., 2000; Vollmann and Cordon, 1998). This puts emphasis on the needs of the market and designing the chain to satisfy these needs, instead of starting with the supplier/manufacturer and working forward. The main stimulus behind this has been the shift in power away from the supplier towards the customer (Soliman and Youssef, 2001).

---

1 ELTRUN, Athens University of Economics & Business, Department of Management Science and Technology, www.eltrun.aueb.gr, k.pramatari@aueb.gr, gjd@aueb.gr, pkour@aueb.gr

In retailing, supply-chain collaboration has taken the form of practices such as Continuous Replenishment Program (CRP), Vendor Managed Inventory (VMI) and Collaborative Planning, Forecasting and Replenishment (CPFR). VMI is a technique developed in the mid 1980s, whereby the manufacturer (supplier) has the sole responsibility for managing the customer's inventory policy, including the replenishment process, based on the variation of stock level in the customer's main warehouse or distribution centre (Cooke, 1998; Frantz, 1999). VMI is probably the first trust-based business link between suppliers and customers (Barratt and Oliveira, 2001). CRP moves one step ahead of VMI and reveals demand from the retailers' stores. The inventory policy is then based on the sales forecast, built from historical demand data and no longer purely based on the variations of inventory levels at the customers' main stock-holding facility (Andraski 1994).

Collaborative Planning, Forecasting and Replenishment (CPFR) can be seen as an evolution from VMI and CRP, addressing not only replenishment but also joint demand forecasting and promotions planning, focusing on promotions and special-line items. CPFR is based on extended information sharing between retailer and supplier, including point-of-sales (POS) data, forecasts and promotion plans. Pramatari et al. (2002) further suggest a new form of CPFR, which they name Process of Collaborative Store Ordering (PCSO), addressing the daily store replenishment process. This process is supported by special IT infrastructure (collaborative platform) allowing the daily online sharing of store-level information (e.g. POS sales data, store assortments, stock-level in the store, promotion activities, out-of-shelf alerts, etc), the sales forecasting and order generation, the online collaboration of the trading partners, and finally the order exchange and order status tracking. Any user connects to this collaborative platform through a secure Internet connection using a simple Web-browser interface.

Based on these short descriptions, VMI and CRP are more about supply-chain collaboration, whereas CPFR puts more emphasis on the demand side. What makes the distinction in the evolution path followed by these collaboration practices is the amount of information exchanged between the trading partners and the process(es) enabled by this information sharing. In this paper we discuss the next generation of supply and demand chain collaboration practices empowered by the additional information that becomes available when the technology of Radio Frequency Identification (RFID) is used to identify product delivery units (e.g. pallets, cases) and/or individual items.

In the following section we discuss the technology infrastructure that has enabled collaborative practices up-to-now and what are the current trends in this area. We then discuss the technology of Radio Frequency Identification and the processes that are enhanced by the new information that becomes available in this “smarter” context. In the fourth section we describe the underlying infrastructure required to support RFID-enabled collaborative practices in the demand and supply side and conclude with some closing remarks and future directions in this area.

Enabling Collaboration Between Trading Partners

Efficient information and data exchange is the most essential requirement for implementing the collaborative practices referred to above. In the traditional ordering process, retailers provided manufacturers with only data on quantities of goods required once a week (through ordering). VMI/CRP and CPFR dramatically increase the total volume of information transmitted between retailers and suppliers.

Table 14.1 summarises the evolution in information exchange from pure ordering to CPFR and the underlying technology supporting the exchange of information and collaboration between the trading partners.

As we move from VMI/CRP to more advanced forms of collaboration, such as CPFR, and the amount of exchanged information increases, so do the requirements towards the underlying technology infrastructure.

Electronic data interchange (EDI) (Doukidis et al., 1994) has been a key enabling technology for efficient replenishment and supply chain coordination (Hill and Scudder, 2002). Without EDI, CRP wouldn't have been economically viable, as the amount of daily information processed and transmitted in the channel is too large to handle manually. Information technology is a necessary condition for the CRP innovation, thus serving as an enabler of this new form of interorganisational relationships and joint channel process redesign (Lee et al., 2003).

However, EDI is also expensive and too complicated compared to the alternatives that have emerged lately for secure and reliable communication over the Internet and for information exchange in XML format (Stefansson, 2002). Furthermore, EDI confines the exchanged information to certain types, as defined by the respective standard EDI messages (e.g. Inventory Report (INVRPT) message supporting CRP) whereas new forms of supply-chain collaboration require a lot more types of information to be exchanged between the trading partners and these types may vary significantly in different occasions.

Table 14.1 Information exchanged and underlying technology from traditional ordering to CPFR

Supply-Chain Collaboration Practice

	Traditional ordering process	VMI/CRP	CPFR	PCSO: Daily, storelevel CPFR
Information Exchanged	Orders Dispatch advices	Orders Suggestive orders Inventory report (including store orders and ware-house shipments in CRP)	Orders Inventory reports Aggregated POS data Sales forecasts Promotion plans	Orders Store inventory Daily POS data Store product assortment Store promotion activities Dispatch advices
Collaborative Business Processes	Replenishment	Central Warehouse (CWH) Replen-ishment	CWH Replen-ishment Store Replenishment Promotion planning	Store Replenishment
Technology sup-porting informa-tion exchange	Paper EDI EDI over Internet	EDI (mainly) EDI over Internet (lately)	XML/ ASCII files over Internet	XML/ ASCII files over Internet
Technology sup-porting collaboration	Internal ERP systems	Internal application (mainly) Collaborative platform – retail exchange (lately)	Collaborative platform – retail exchange	Collaborative platform – retail exchange

In order to cope with this increasing need for extended information exchange, the retail sector has started moving away from EDI to new ways of information exchange, mainly enabled by Internet-based communication platforms and retail exchanges (Sparks and Wagner, 2003), also referred to as electronic marketplaces (e-marketplaces). Such exchanges are characterised by the retailers' direct access to distributors and suppliers, enabling businesses to interact via a neutral intermediary (the exchange) to conduct either one-to-one or multiple transactions. Thus, suppliers gain access to more buyers, and buyers can contact many suppliers. Such exchanges also hold out the hope of a more efficient supply system, through better and more rapid communications facilitating improvements in planning, deployment of transport fleets, warehouse management and procurement procedures (WWRE 2000). Pramatari et al. (2004) specifically discuss the requirements of an Internet-based platform supporting information sharing and collaboration with the objective to streamline the store replenishment process.

A recent investigation by Eng and Spickett-Jones (2002) reported that current Internet exchanges are more suitable for commodity-based products and services, and that key issues concerning collaborative planning, forecasting and replenishment have been impeded by short-term focus of transaction-based activities in e-marketplaces. Furthermore, the Internet so far has been confined to internal processes and not yet been used to exploit opportunities beyond the traditional ownership of supply chains or involved collaboration with external firms to reach new markets and synchronise product planning and promotional activities (Eng and Spickett-Jones, 2002). Retail exchanges are intuitively compelling, but it is still not really clear how they are going to affect retail industry competitiveness and their influence on the supply base (Sparks and Wagner, 2003).

However, the third-party operated e-marketplace is not the only option for operating an Internet-based collaboration platform. Sparks and Wagner (2003) report that suppliers are wary of further involvement in e-marketplaces. Disillusioned by pricing and other concessions, they are still waiting to see the promised volume and liquidity levels. On the other hand, they see the emergence of private exchanges, namely invitation only networks that connect a single company to its customers, suppliers or both. A few retailers e.g. Wal-Mart, have had the will and the finance to create priority supply chain information systems and the power to force suppliers to adopt them.

Eng (2003) further identifies two main barriers to implementing strategic collaborative supply chain processes:

1. Technical uncertainty on reliability of e-marketplaces in that migration from EDI to an e-marketplace system requires technical support and integration of various supply chain activities in a company,
2. Sharing of strategic information with other participant organisations is not a common practice. This hinders the extent of the types of collaborative and strategic supply-chain management activities that can be carried out in the e-marketplace.

These points raise several discussions as to what form will supply chain collaboration take, especially when considering new types of information exchanged and new forms of collaboration among supply chain partners, such as those enabled by RFID, as will be discussed in the following section.

Enhancing Retail Business Practices Using RFID Technology

Radio-Frequency Identification Technology (RFID) falls under the umbrella of Automatic Identification (Auto-ID) technologies along with technologies such as magnetic stripe, smart cards, voice data entry, touch memory and so on (Agarwal, 2001). RFID technology has been extensively used for a diversity of applications ranging from access control systems to airport baggage handling, livestock management systems, automated toll collection systems, theft-prevention systems, electronic payment systems, and automated production systems (Agarwal, 2001; Smith et al., 2003; Tierney, 2002; Wilson, 2001). Nevertheless, recent advances have made possible the identification of consumer products using RFID.

Traditionally, the retail sector uses barcodes as the main identifier for cases, pallets and products. Today, over 5 billion products are scanned everyday in 141 countries. Whilst it is clear to retailers and manufacturers that the barcode's relevance and importance to the industry will remain for years ahead, many in the industry are now looking to the business case of RFID as the "next generation of barcode".

The technology uses radio waves to automatically identify individual items. In effect, RFID technology comprises of two main parts:

- The *RF-tag* consisting of a small, versatile, and cheap (predicted to eventually cost less than five cents by 2006) microchip attached to an antenna, which can be easily and invisibly embedded in most products packaging, clothing or parts. Tags can be characterised as active, semi-passive, and passive depending on whether they incorporate a power source (battery) or draw power from the reader. Moreover, RF-tags can either be read/write or read-only. Read/write tags are useful in some specialised applications, but since they are more expensive than the read-only ones, they are impractical for identifying low-value items,
- *RF-Tag readers* are able to scan tags when they reach their range. Readers are usually connected to a computer, which in turn communicates with a back-end information system (e.g. a warehouse management system, a management information system, and so on). The antenna on the tag enables the microchip to transmit the identification information to the reader.

The prospects of RFID have attracted the attention of large retailers and suppliers. Over the past few years, we have witnessed several initiatives in the retail sector that have tried to field-test RFID in different application areas; Metro has launched the "store-of-the-future' initiative in Rheinberg,

Germany, a converted traditional supermarket that uses RFID technology as a means to enhance the shoppers' experience during their visit to the retail outlet (Wolfram et al., 2004). Moreover, Metro has installed RF-Readers at their distribution centre at Essen (Wolfram et al., 2004). By attaching RF-tags in boxes and pallets and integrating the RFID infrastructure with its existing Warehouse Management System, Metro is able to accurately and automatically monitor which products arrive and exit the distribution centre, reducing significantly labour costs and receiving additional benefits such as automated proof-of-delivery.

MyGROCER, a European project in which Procter & Gamble and the Greek supermarket chain ATLANTIC participated, also investigated the potential of RFID to the downstream environment and in particular its effect to the traditional shopping experience (Kourouthanassis et al., 2002a). This was supported through an intelligent shopping cart equipped with a display device and an RFID sensor capable of scanning the contents of the cart. Shoppers could use their loyalty card to log in the system and receive the following facilitating services:

- continuous monitoring of the products that are currently in their shopping cart along with their cumulative value,
- a reminding list of products they wish to purchase during their shopping visit,
- a list of all available promotions,
- fully personalised based on their shopping behaviour and past consumption patterns,
- display of valuable information for each product (such as nutritional value, recipes and so on) complementing or even extending the information available on the product packaging,
- and advanced navigation capabilities (Kourouthanassis et al., 2002a).

Finally, Gillette investigated the potential of RFID in store management focusing on the elimination of out-of-shelf conditions (Cantwell, 2003). In particular, Gillette in collaboration with the MIT Auto-ID Centre and Metro implemented a "smart-shelf" where RF-Readers were able to monitor RF-tagged razor blades and initiate replenishment and theft alerts, and proceed even to automatic re-ordering. The increased interest of the retail sector in the RFID technology can also be depicted from Wal-Mart's decision to have its top 100 suppliers to begin shipping tagged pallets and cases by January 2005 (Roberti, 2004).

RFID can thus enhance core supply and demand chain management operations, ranging from the upstream to the downstream side. Figure 14.1 illustrates the different classes of RFID-enhanced applications.

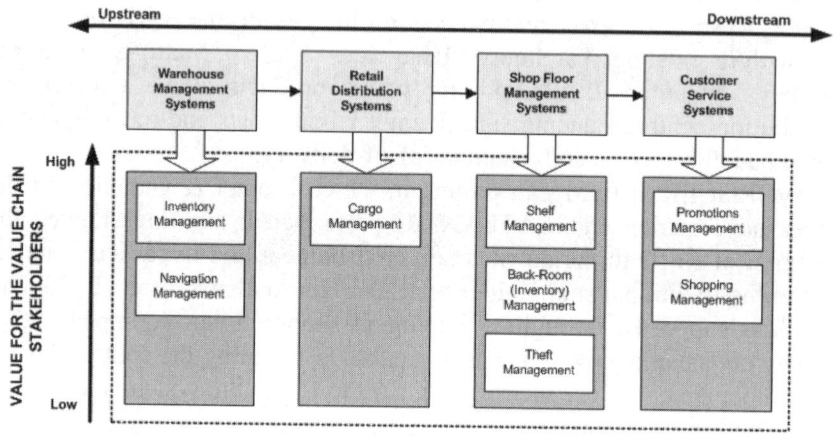

Fig 14.1 A taxonomy of different classes of RFID-enhanced applications

The prospective RFID-enhanced applications are classified across two axes: The first axis spans across the value chain, from the upstream side (referring to applications targeted to the supplier and intermediate distribution centres), down to the retail outlet, and finally, the end consumer. The second axis refers to the perceived value of the individual application for the interested stakeholder. This value derives from the nature of the application and its perceived benefits; high value applications introduce totally new means to operate a particular process resulting, in most cases, to increased business effectiveness; low value applications simply automate or provide an alternative means to conduct a particular operation.

Smith et al. (2003) characterise the integration of RFID technology to supply chain management operations as "an internet for physical objects", implying that the new technology will introduce significant changes in the way that companies conduct business. RFID does not simply embed new hardware and software in the retail arena. On the contrary, it is a major business undertaking focused to and driven by the retail sector. It is all about delivering innovation through enhanced business processes. Different forms of business collaborations will emerge mainly in order to benefit from the rich information availability that will exist in the retail sector. The following section discusses an approach that tries to integrate the existing collaborative schemes that have been discussed in the beginning of this paper with the underlying RFID infrastructure.

Supporting RFID-enabled Collaboration

The previous section presented a brief overview of the capabilities and potential application areas of RFID technology for the retail sector. Most of these applications refer to internal information systems operating either in the retailer or the supplier in order to streamline and automate internal business processes. However, RFID solutions need be integrated with the existing back-end infrastructures of retailers and suppliers and this requires significant overhead, especially if we take into account that such infrastructures have been developed incrementally over a rather long period of time and thus their current architectures have been evolved rather than designed. Still, this integration represents the initial phase for the retail sector in order to benefit from the rich information provided by RFID. In this phase, companies investing in RFID systems will reap the expected benefits by creating proprietary systems owned and controlled solely by them.

The second phase will require the creation of the necessary infrastructures that support *information sharing and collaboration* among the retail value chain. While the Internet has provided new means for retailers and suppliers to collaborate and share information using dedicated platforms, we argue that RFID will significantly enhance the *depth* and *quality* of the information exchanged over such collaborative platforms, leading to *smarter* forms of collaboration. Indeed, the capability to know on a real-time basis the current stock level at the warehouse or the shelf will lead to gradually eliminating out-of-stock and out-of-shelf situations. Similarly, tracking a product along the supply chain on a real-time basis, even within the retail outlet, will enable suppliers to effectively manage replenishment and product recalls, have better forecasting accuracy and provide more tailor-made promotional plans.

Table 14.2 gives an overview of the extended information that can be exchanged among trading partners in the RFID context and the collaborative processes than are empowered based on this information exchange. We expect that, in this context, information exchange and collaboration will be supported by an intermediate collaborative platform, either e-marketplace or private retail exchange, driven by the high amount of information to be exchanged and sophistication of the collaborative processes.

Table 14.2 Characteristics of RFID-enabled collaboration

	RFID-enabled collaboration
Information Exchanged	• Products shelf position • Out-of-shelf indication • Accurate inventory information (including lot numbers, expiration dates, etc.) • In-store shopping route • Order and place of product selection
Collaborative Business Processes	• Replenishment • Shelf management • Evaluation of promotion effectiveness • Promotion planning
Technology supporting information exchange	• XML/ ASCII files over Internet (expected)
Technology supporting collaboration	• Collaborative platform – retail exchange (expected)

The new collaborative mediator will act as a hub that manages and integrates the information generated from the various sources, process it, and use it for offering value-added smart services to the entire business network. Figure 14.2 provides an integrated map of the applications mentioned in the previous section to the revised smart business network.

The RFID technology can ultimately be embedded in our everyday-lives. Fully aligned with the recent developments pertaining to "smart information appliances' (Roussos, 2003; Roussos et al., 2003b), RFID readers may be embedded in the last mile of the supply chain towards the consumer: the consumer's own household. In this scenario, the consumer can be fully supported by a "ubiquitous commerce' system, which is able to continuously monitor the home inventory and generate "out-of-stock' alerts when a product needs replenishment. Extending this scenario, the shopper can receive in his/her mobile phone (or other wireless device) the automatically generated alerts (accompanied with personalised promotion messages) and proceed, should he/she desires, to replenishment orders.

Alternative scenarios pertaining to the deployment of RFID into our everyday activities have been extensively discussed in (Roussos et al., 2003a). Ultimately, RFID technology can generate "intelligent' supply and demand chains where the product instead of the end user triggers the business process.

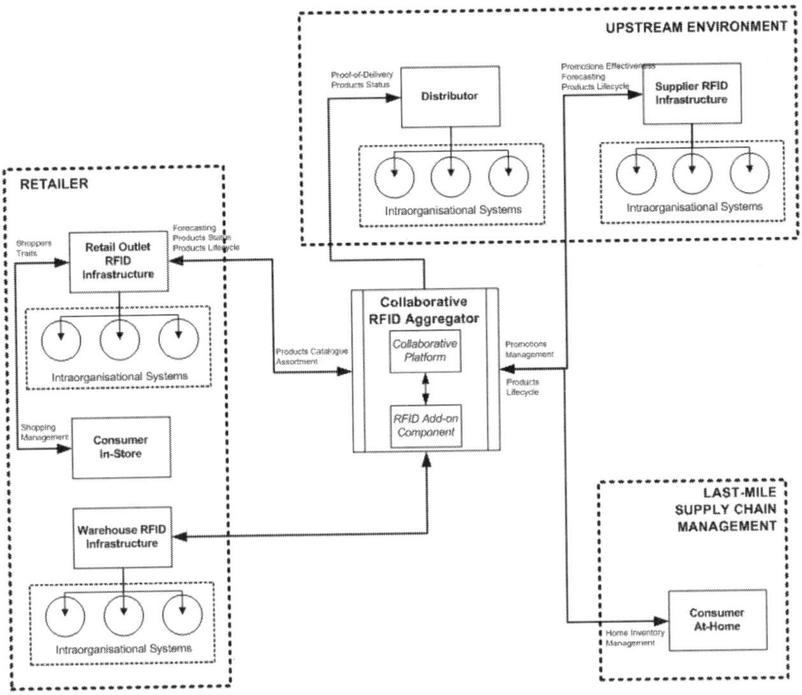

Fig 14.2 RFID-enabled smart business networks

Conclusions

The previous discussion assumes that all the technical barriers regarding the application of RFID have been overcome and that RF-tags have been introduced on all or a big proportion of the consumer goods. However, this assumption is still far from reality, as the technical barriers have not been totally overcome yet, especially when considering great scale implementations, and standards are still evolving to support the wide adoption of RFID technology across the industry.

And while research is progressing fast on the standards and technology front, there is an ever increasing concern about consumer privacy relating to the use of RF-tags on consumer goods, which has recently led companies like Benetton and Wal-Mart to temporarily shirk off RFID-at-consumer-level pilots (McGinity, 2004). Analysts predict that while four or five years will pass before consumers are directly affected by RFID, privacy will be a major problem if it isn't addressed up-front. These concerns, in combination with the lower costs associated with introducing RF-tags on product cases and pallets instead of consumer units, currently lead the industry to implementing warehouse applications at first round. Eventually, privacy concerns will be overcome, as has happened during the initial introduction of barcode technology several decades ago, allowing companies to adopt advanced RFID applications and smarter collaboration practices. This perspective opens up many new directions for research and development in this area, both relating to technology but also to the many different business aspects associated with it. The work presented in this paper is a first attempt towards this direction.

References

Agarwal, V. (2001). "Assessing the Benefits of Auto-ID Technology in the Consumer Goods Industry", Auto-ID Centre. Available online at: *www.epcglobalinc.org*

Anderson, D.L., H. Lee, (1999). "Synchronised Supply Chains: The New Frontier", pp. 112-21, in: *Achieving Supply Chain Excellence Through Technology*, Montgomery Research Inc.

Andraski, J.C. (1994). "Foundations for Successful Continuous Replenishment Programs", *International Journal of Logistics Management*, Vol. 5, No. 1, pp. 1-8.

Anthony, T. (2000). "Supply Chain Collaboration: Success in the New Internet Economy", pp. 241-44, in: *Achieving Supply Chain Excellence Through Technology*, Montgomery Research Inc.

Barratt, M., A. Oliveira, (2001). "Exploring the Experience of Collaborative Planning Initiatives", *International Journal of Physical Distribution and Logistics Management*, Vol. 31, No. 4, pp. 266-289.

Bowersox, D.J., D.J. Closs, and T.P. Stank, (2000). "Ten Mega-Trends That Will Revolutionize Supply Chain Logistics", *Journal of Business Logistics*, Vol. 21, No. 2, pp. 1-16.

Brewer, A., N. Sloan, and T. Landers, (1999). "Intelligent Tracking in Manufacturing", *Journal of Intelligent Manufacturing*, Vol. 10, pp. 245-250.

Cantwell, D. (2003). "RFID Real World Applications: The Case of Gillette", *working paper*, GCI Intelligent Tagging Working Group, Berlin 2003.

Cooke, J.A. (1998). "VMI: Very Mixed Impact?", *Logistics Management Distribution Report*, Vol. 37, (p. 51), No. 12.

Doukidis, G. I., A. Fragopoulou, and S. Smithson, (1994). "EDI in Greece: Rational, Applications, and Benefits, in: *Proceedings of the 2nd European Conference on Information Systems*, Nijenrode University, The Netherlands.

Eng, T.Y. (2003). "The Role of E-Marketplaces in Supply Chain Management", *Industrial Marketing Management*, in press, No: 5567. Available at: *www.sciencedirect.com*

Eng, T.Y., G. Spickett-Jones, (2002). "An Investigation of The Concept of E-Marketplace in Supply Chain", *working paper*, BAM International Conference, London.

Frantz, M. (1999). "CPFR Pace Picks Up Consumer Goods", *www.consumer goods.com/archive/*JanFeb99

Grieger, M. (2003). "Electronic Marketplaces: A Literature Review and a Call For Supply Chain Management Research", *European Journal of Operational Research*, Vol. 14, No. 4, 280-294.

Hill, A.C., G.D. Scudder, (2002). "The Use of Electronic Data Interchange For Supply Chain Coordination in the Food Industry", *Journal of Operations Management*, Vol. 20, pp. 375-387.

Kourouthanassis, P., G. Roussos, (2002a). "Developing Consumer-Friendly Pervasive Retail Systems", *IEEE Pervasive Computing*, Vol. 2, No. 2, pp. 32-39.

Kourouthanassis, P., D. Spinellis, G. Roussos, and G.M. Giaglis, (2002b). "Intelligent Cokes and Diapers: MyGROCER Ubiquitous Computing Environment", *Proceedings of the 1st International Conference on Mobile Business*, Athens, Greece.

Lee, S.C., B.Y. Pak, and H.G. Lee, (2003). "Business Value of B2B Electronic Commerce: The Critical Role of Inter-firm Collaboration", *Electronic Commerce Research and Applications*, in press. Available at: www. Computer-ScienceWeb.com

McGinity, M. (2004). "RFID: Is This Game of Tag Fair Play?", *Communications of the ACM*, Vol. 47, No. 1, pp. 15-18.

Pramatari, K., G.I. Doukidis, and P. Miliotis, (2004). "Streamlining the Replenishment Process Through Extended Information Sharing and Collaboration: Defining the Underlying E-commerce Infrastructure", *Proceedings of IEEE Conference on Electronic Commerce*, (July 6-9), San-Diego, California.

Roberti, M. (2004). "Wal-Mart Begins RFID Rollout", *RFID Journal.*

Roussos, G. (2003). "Appliance Design for Pervasive Computing", *IEEE Pervasive Computing*, Vol. 2, No. 4, pp. 75-77.

Roussos, G., A. Gershman, and P. Kourouthanassis, (2003a). "Ubiquitous Commerce", *UBICOMP 2003*, Seattle, USA.

Roussos, G., P. Kourouthanassis, and T. Moussouri, (2003b). "Appliance Design for Mobile Commerce and Retailtainment", *Personal and Ubiquitous Computing,* Vol. 7, No. 3-4, pp. 203-209.

Smaros, J., J. Holmstrom, (2000). "Viewpoint: Reaching the Consumer Through E-Grocery VMI", *International Journal of Retail and Distribution Management*, Vol. 28, No. 2, pp. 55-61.

Smith, H., B. Konsynski, (2003). "Developments in Practice X: Radio Frequency Identification (RFID) - An Internet for Physical Objects", *Communications of the AIS*, Vol. 12, pp. 301-311.

Soliman, F., M. Youssef, (2001). "The Impact of Some Recent Developments in E-business on the Management of Next Generation Manufacturing", *International Journal of Operations and Production Management*, Vol. 21, pp. 538-564.

Sparks, L., B.A. Wagner, (2003). "Retail Exchanges: A Research Agenda", *Supply Chain Management: An International Journal*, Vol. 8, No. 3, pp. 201-208.

Stefansson, G. (2002). "Business-To-Business Data Sharing: A Source For Integration of Supply Chains", *International Journal of Production Economics*, Vol. 75, pp. 135-146.

Swaminathan, J.M., S.R. Tayur, (2003). "Models For Supply Chains in E-Business", *Management Science*, Vol. 49, No. 10, pp. 1387-1406.

Tierney, S. (2002). "UK Home Office Still Chipping Away at RFID Doubters", in: *Frontline Solutions* (Pan-European edition), Vol. 11, No. 8, p. 24.

Vollmann, T.E., C. Cordon, and J. Heikkila, (2000). "Teaching Supply Chain Management To Business Executives", *Production and Operations Management*, Vol. 9, No. 1, pp. 81-90.

Vollmann, T.E., Cordon, C. (1998). Building successful customer-supplier alliances. *Long Range Planning,* Vol. 31, No. 5, pp. 684-694.

Wilson, J.R. (2001). RFID Offers Inside Track for Baggage Security. *Air Transport World* Vol. 38, No. 10, p. 7.

Wolfram, G., Scharr, U., and Kammerer, K. (2004). RFID: Can we realise its full potential?. *The ECR Journal*, Vol. 3, No. 2, pp. 17-29.

WWRE (2000). *Information Pack for Potential Members*. WWRE, Washington, DC.

15 Building Networks In-Sync

Matthijs J.J. Wolters[1], Peter H.M. Vervest[2], and Eric van Heck[2]

Introduction

This paper discusses the smartness of networks in the Dutch building industry. A recent trend in this industry is the mass-customization of newly built houses. Due to increased demand for customized houses and changed governmental regulations, the Dutch housing industry tries to shift to more customer participation. This brings many new problems and challenges for the building organizations.

Recently, in the Dutch city of Almere an experimental project has been carried out to explore these organizational and technical difficulties evolving from a mass-customization strategy. This project was called "Gewild Wonen', which may be translated as Sought-After Housing. The *Gewild Wonen* project was analyzed to see which of the participating networks were "the smartest'. That is, which of the networks outperformed the other ones, in terms of degree of customization, financial measures and customer satisfaction.

The starting hypothesis for this investigation was that networks that were designed "in-sync' would outsmart networks that were "out-of-sync'. Whether a network is designed in-sync or not, depends on the degree of modularity it uses in its design of the product, the business processes and the business network itself. When these dimensions are all three equally modular or equally integral (the opposite of modular), the network is labeled "in-sync'. On the other hand, when for example one dimension is highly modular and the other two are integral, the network is labeled "out-of-sync'.

In the project the in-sync hypothesis was confirmed. The houses designed for *Gewild* Wonen were, in general, more modular than houses built in regular housing projects. The building networks that also increased the modularity of their production processes and the structure of the network itself outsmarted the networks that did not do this. However, the more

[1] Vrije Universiteit Amsterdam, Faculty of Economics and Business Administration, De Boelelaan 1105, 1081 HV Amsterdam, The Netherlands, mwolters@feweb.vu.nl

[2] RSM, Erasmus University Rotterdam, PO Box 1738, 3000 DR Rotterdam, The Netherlands, vervest@d-age.com, eheck@fbk.eur.nl

modular these dimensions are, the more difficult it becomes. In these cases effective use of ICT is really needed to manage the increased complexity of product, process and network design as well as the interaction and dialogue with the customer. It was also found that increasing the modularity of all dimensions is only fruitful when the end-customers, the buyers of the houses, are both willing and able to participate in the design.

Being Smart = Being In-sync

Whether a network is designed in-sync or not, depends on the degree of modularity it uses in its design of the product, the business processes and the business network itself. When these dimensions are all three highly modular or highly integral (the opposite of modular), the network is labeled "in-sync'. On the other hand, when for example one dimension is highly modular and the other two are integral, the network is labeled "out-of-sync'. The hypothesis that in-sync-networks will outsmart networks which are out-of-sync, when it comes to mass-customization, finds it origin in the work of Fine (1998). He claims that product and supply chain architectures tend to be aligned along the integrality-modularity spectrum. That is, integral products tend to be developed and built by integral processes and supply chains, whereas modular products tend to be designed and built by modular processes and supply chains. They tend to be mutually reinforcing and conducive to each other. It is hypothesized by Fine that a synchronous, concurrent design in these three dimensions leads to better results and performance than a more asynchronous approach. The synchronicity between processes and supply chains is also addressed by Feitzinger & Lee (1997) who state that manufacturing processes should be designed such that they, too, consist of independent modules that can be moved or rearranged easily to support different distribution-network designs.

For effective mass-customization modularity is suggested by many authors as the key-factor. Therefore, we expect to find strong proof for the in-sync hypothesis in networks that specialize in mass-customization. The concept of modularity is further explained below.

Modularity

Several different perspectives and definitions of modularity (and its opposite, integrality) exist. Although these perspectives and definitions mutually differ, a number of key characteristics and features of modularity in general and modular systems in particular can be distinguished.

- Distinctiveness/autonomy of components,
- Loose coupling between modules; tight coupling within modules,
- Clarity of mapping between functions and components,
- Standardization of interfaces,
- Low levels of coordination (self-organization; coordination embedded in the architecture).

The first issue is distinctiveness of components, originating from the work of Weick (1976) on loosely coupled systems. We combined distinctiveness with autonomy while Orton & Weick (1990) argue that responsiveness of the system's components is just an important feature of loose coupling and we believe that autonomy is a very good indicator of this variable. Especially for processes and supply chains, autonomy is a better indicator than distinctiveness. In the case of products, distinctiveness will be used.

The second feature is the loose coupling between modules whereas the modules are tightly coupled within themselves. This feature builds forth upon the previous feature, with the addition that the modules themselves can be seen as black boxes, i.e. we do not need to know the inner structure or functioning of the modules in order to be able to use the modules.

Third, a modular design is characterized by a clear mapping between the components and their functions. Ulrich and Eppinger (1995) introduced this feature and argued that a 1:1 mapping is most clear and typifies a modular architecture while a more complex mapping, say n:m, denotes integrality. In the latter case many (n) functions are performed by many (m) components; their exact allocation (an n:m mapping) is unclear however.

Such a clear mapping of functions and components is often combined with standard and well defined interfaces between the modules. That is, the way the modules interact or come together is predefined and clear (to all module designers). Standardization of interfaces also enables the easy interchange of modules that make use of the same interface. It further enables easy separation and recombination of the modules. In the case of process and supply chain modularity, these interfaces could refer to contracts, transaction protocols, operating procedures and input/output agreements.

Finally, modular architectures exhibit low levels of coordination, thus enabling self-organizing of the modules. Coordination is, in other words, embedded within the architecture. In this respect, coordination of product modules may be somewhat ill-defined. What exactly is meant by coordinating product modules? In product development literature this often refers to the process of developing a new product, i.e. the process of specifying design rules, initial design, fabrication, prototype testing, final design etc. (Baldwin & Clark 2000). In management literature, Sanchez (1999), Schilling (2000), Worren et al. (2000) and O'Grady (2000), focus on the end-result of this process: the product offered to the customer. Coordination in this respect simply refers to "managing dependencies", as defined by Crowston (1997). Combining these features into one single definition leads to:

A system is modular when it consists of distinct (autonomous) components, which are loosely coupled with each other, with a clear relationship between each component and its function(s) and well-defined, standardized interfaces connecting the components, which require low levels of coordination.

With this definition we are able to determine the degree of modularity of different levels (or dimensions) of a "business system', i.e. products, processes or networks.

The in-sync hypothesis is moderated by two other variables. The first is Customer's Disposition to Participate, the second Information Technology. Both variables are explained below.

Customer's Disposition to Participate

The essence of (mass-)customization is that customers should be allowed to customize their products or even more, be involved in the design of the production processes and supply chains. The degree of customization or personalization should be as high as possible (or necessary), without the loss of efficiency and effectiveness. As an organization, one should however wonder whether their customers actually care about this type of service (Hart 1996). Do they want to spend time on choosing between all the different options offered and are they sophisticated enough to make these decisions at all? If customers do not care about variety and do not want to participate in the design process, chances are high that mass-customization is not the right strategic choice for an organization.

Huffman & Kahn (1998) also note the limitations of unlimited variety by arguing that the optimal amount of variety to be offered depends on the competition and customer values in a particular industry. The mere consideration of the question how much variety to offer suggests that there may be such a point where there is *too* much variety. Large assortments can be perceived as negative by consumers, if instead of offering possibilities and choice, they seem monumental and frustrating. Although consumers nowadays have become much more autonomous and individualistic, a recent study by Schwartz (2000), published in the American Psychologist, shows that there is another side to this. Schwartz claims that our contemporary culture has gone too far in stressing freedom and autonomy. Consumers are given too much freedom of choice, which makes them unhappy and depressed. Experiments show that if people only need to choose from a few alternatives, they are more satisfied with their choice. For most people in the world, Schwartz argues, individual choice is neither expected nor desired.

Furthermore, if it is difficult for a customer to choose appropriate components, or to assemble those components into the product configuration, then a non-modular product may offer additional functionality by eliminating the selection and assembly responsibilities of the customer. In order for a customer to choose components of a modular system, the customer must be able and willing to distinguish among the performance, quality and value attributes of different components (Schilling 2000). This frequently means that a customer must have understanding of how the components function individually as well as how they work together and interact. When products are very complex this may be more difficult for customers.

Hart (1996) calls this customization sensitivity, Larsson & Bowen (1989) denote this as the customer's disposition to participate in the design. We will use the latter definition.

Technological Feasibility: Use of ICT

Applying modularity is often a complicated and complex task. Developing the individual modules and assembling them requires knowledge and information about the individual modules and the way they interact with other modules. Baldwin & Clark (2000) stress that modular systems are much more difficult to design than comparable interconnected or integral systems. An organization must be technologically capable to manage this increased (informational) complexity. If not, using modularity will not lead to the desired effects, such as innovation and customization, but instead will increase costs or decrease quality of the product or process. A less modular design is in this case preferable.

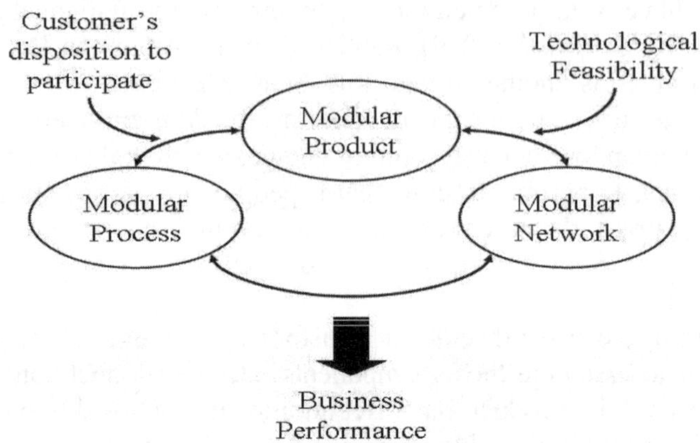

Fig 15.1 The in-sync hypothesis

In traditional business models mass-customization, even in combination with modularity, is always more expensive or less profitable than fewer customization with integral designs. The advent of information technology has made it much more cost-effective to address individual customers' needs. It is hypothesized that only by using ICT in an efficient manner can one remove the cost-flexibility paradox. ICT can be used to link the different modules (being either product, process or network modules), coordinate their development and execution or automate the modules themselves (Pine 1993). One could think of the use of multi-media systems to enable clients to build their car in the showroom and for forwarding the order for the car to the distribution centers. Information technology and extensive databases allow the marketer to understand how likely a consumer is to buy in a new category, given his or her current purchases from the firm. Implementation of intelligent datasystems, such as point-of-sale datasystems and customer information systems are other options (van Hoek & Weken 1998). Furthermore, Nadler et al. (1992) point out that the creation of effective architecture hinges on the use of structural materials capable of implementing the architecture and stress ICT's power in creating future organizational architecture.

The in-sync hypothesis, together with the two moderated variables, is illustrated in Figure 15.1.

The "Gewild Wonen' Project

To explore the organizational and technical difficulties belonging to more mass-customization in the housing industry, the city of Almere, a 25-year-old town in one of the Dutch polders, decided to initiate an experimental project in early 1999: *Gewild Wonen.* The *Gewild Wonen* project originates from the ideas of Carel Weeber, a professor in architecture and a well-known architect in the Netherlands (Weeber 1998). In 1997 he introduced the concept of "*Het Wilde Wonen*' (in English: Building Wildly or Spontaneous Housing). *Het Wilde Wonen* disputes the governmental influence on and interference with the architecture and urban design in the Netherlands. It resists the rigid way of urban planning, the uniformity and the lack of variation within the housing industry. Houses should be built in lower densities, avoiding the compact housing areas dictated by the government. Weeber argues for more informal types of living, where no central direction or control is present. The customer should get freedom in choosing the shape, the building method and the exterior of the house. Building companies need to reorganize their processes to be ready for more customer-oriented development and building, according to Weeber.

The city of Almere decided to initiate an exposition around the theme of *Het Wilde Wonen.* However, the "wildness' of the project could not be as large as Weeber originally had in mind. Almere felt the market (both the customer as well as the supplier side) was not ready for this. It was decided to invite a number of professional property developers to come up with architectural designs, based on the theme. Therefore, because there is still no direct interference of the buyer with the architect and builder, the project was renamed into *Gewild Wonen*[3]. The project in its entirety had to display the image of housing in the 21st century according to the initiators. The objective was to design and build houses with such a variety that on the one hand no house would look the same, while on the other hand the advantages of project-wise (mass-produced) building were preserved.

The initiative of the project was taken in early 1999. Almere invited 11 property developers to participate in the projects. Later on, three public housing corporations were invited to participate as well, just as Carel Weeber himself. Each property developer was asked to invite two architects, which they could select from a list offered by the city of Almere or search for themselves, to come up with a house design. Subsequently, the city of Almere chose, based on a number of criteria, one of the two designs of each of the property developers.

[3] The transition from *Wild* to *Gewild* is, in Dutch, both in meaning as linguistic a nice find.

The initiators of the project came up with only a minimum set of rules. The exact position of the house on the plot should be free to choose for the buyers, as long as the privacy of the adjoining dwellings was not hampered. The appearance of the houses was bounded by only a minimum of rules. Only the building height was limited to three floors. Flat roofs or topped roofs, both were allowed. Furthermore, the shape of the roof was free, as well as its slope and its direction. Complete freedom also existed with respect to the materials and the colours. The houses could be built as detached houses, semi-detached or three in a row at most. Most houses were low-rise houses, complemented with five urban villas along the central canal. Four of these villas were built with seven floors (plus a penthouse). The fifth urban villa could be built higher than the other ones, because of its different position in the neighbourhood, on a crossroad between two canals.

The project was located in a part of Almere-Buiten, the Eilandenbuurt (Island neighbourhood). The total number of houses to be built was approximately 600. The area in which the exposition took place consisted of a dry and a wet part. The wet part has been developed as a series of islands. The dry part consisted of one large island surrounded by canals.

Research Protocol

A three-step approach has been followed in the *Gewild Wonen* case study. In the preparation phase of the project, semi-structured interviews with the stakeholders (architects, property developers, builders, public housing corporations, estate agents, employees of the city of Almere etc.) were held to gain more background knowledge about the project and the viewpoints and experiences of the participants. The content of each of the questionnaires was appropriated for the participant being interviewed, either focusing on the design phase or focusing on (the preparation of) the execution phase. Questions about the design phase were mainly posed to the architects and property developers. Questions about the execution phase were posed to the builders and again, the developers.

After most of the stakeholders were interviewed once, we were able to come up with a global impression of all projects, the problems they were facing and the solutions they had found. At the end of the sales period, the stakeholders were approached once again and they were asked to fill in a more structured survey. This enabled us to further validate our initial conclusions and to confront the stakeholders with each other's remarks. After the sales process an investigation was held among the buyers of the houses to assess their perceptions and experiences in the project. The opinions of the customers, together with financial data, were used to obtain a measure of the success of the individual sub-projects within *Gewild Wonen*.

Building Networks In-sync?

In general, the houses designed in *Gewild Wonen* were more modular than houses built in regular housing projects, although the difference was not that big in a significant number of sub-projects. Regular houses in the Netherlands are most often integral designs, without much possibility for switching and/or separation of the modules. Most of the *Gewild Wonen* houses did possess this feature: they needed to be expandable or changeable in the future and customers were able to select from a (sometimes small) catalogue of modules in order to design their own house. Most of the architects decided to introduce modularity on the level of the exterior, that is the most rigid level of house design, which determines the size and shape of the house. Flexible house systems were designed instead of more integral fixed hulls and floor plans, where the customers could only decide about the accessories of the house. The architects did not go as far as designing already predetermined – and prefabricated – bedroom – or living room-modules[4]. The mapping between function and modules therefore was certainly not 1:1. Neither was the standardization of interfaces – the scheme by which the modules are connected. The building industry has not developed such standardization yet. As a consequence, the architects had to design every specific interface in detail.

Most of the *Gewild Wonen* houses were designed as follows: a core module containing all necessary facilities, such as entrance, staircase, storage rooms and the "wet cells' (bathroom, toilet, pipes etc.), which could be further extended by the customer with other modules, selected from some sort of catalogue. Still however, the customer was limited in two ways: he could not choose anything that was not in the catalogue and he could not decide about the design of the core. Even when the fixed core was omitted, the customers were limited in choosing only from a fixed catalogue of options. The granularity of the product modules was thus quite low.

Although the degree of product modularity was only a little higher than "normal", manufacturing processes still became more modular as well. That is, builders needed to use production techniques that actually allowed

[4] In the USA many "modular homes" are built. They consist of three-dimensional, volume-enclosing units that are shipped as complete components from a factory and assembled on site. Essentially, a modular unit is thought of as a "box", with all the internal or external features and finished completed in the factory, and only the connection to adjoining units and the hook-up of services are completed on site.

for building of these more modular homes. This meant that the more integral techniques, such as concrete building, were replaced by more flexible techniques such as wood frame building, assembly building or the so-called "Open-Building" method (Habraken, 1961). By using the "Open Building" method it is possible to produce different houses, while using the same hull. The hull is fixed, while the infill (inner walls, pipes and installations) can be done in different ways. The idea behind the method is that a hull should last for at least 50 years, while the layout of a house can change many times within this period. This way of designing and building houses not only means that within a fixed hull, mutual different layouts can be made, which are easily replaceable. It also means that the variable building elements need to be manufactured and assembled, such that this easy replacement is indeed possible. All of these techniques allow for late changes in design, while also making use of many prefabricated elements.

The way the stakeholders in most of the fifteen sub-projects cooperated with each other really did not differ much from ordinary practice. Partly, this could have been caused by the new and experimental character of the project, raising many unexpected problems that needed to be solved first. Another explanation however, is the following, related to the synchronicity of the three business dimensions. What we saw most of the times in the sub-projects was that whenever both product and process modularity were low, the building network did not require many changes compared to normal. This was in many cases a successful strategy, at least when the customer's disposition to participate was also low. The participants in these projects relied on well-proven organizational structures and efficient and relatively low-cost building methods. We may say that such a conservative strategy proved its worth, even in such an innovative and ambitious projects like *Gewild Wonen*.

A few sub-projects demonstrated a high degree of modularity in product, process and network design. It turned out that such a design is more difficult to accomplish for building companies than one that has low modularity in the three dimensions. In these cases, ICT is really needed, customers require support and guidance and the entire network must be ready for this. Koopmans, the organization that developed one of these projects, made use of ICT to support their customers and was really looking for multiple suppliers for their key components and use these suppliers' creativity and knowledge wherever they could. They worked with several sub-contractors. At the start of the project, as many agreements as possible were made, also about prices. They tried to use the creativity and knowledge of these external parties as much as possible. In return, they allowed them to produce certain modules. However, they did not want them to produce exclusive modules. If they would outsource the production to one single party, then the competition would disappear and they would limit themselves too much. This is a typical example of using multiple suppliers for key components. No fixed, long-term agreements are made with one particular supplier. For each (set of) module(s) and each new project, one starts looking in the market for suitable sub-contractors and suppliers. The coupling between the network modules is loose, and more distinct parties can be identified. The property developer needs standardized contracts to enable this switching between suppliers, to shorten the process of price setting and making agreements as much as possible. All of these features are synonymous with a more modular design of the building network. They managed to make their project profitable and make their customers, with a high disposition to participate, satisfied.

Summarizing, in the majority of the projects we were able to validate the in-sync hypothesis. Either because successful projects designed the three dimensions in-sync (like described above), or less-successful projects were out-of-sync. For instance, there were projects that had to deal with a relatively low disposition of the customer to participate and solved this with a highly modular product design and a highly modular building method. This was overdone and unnecessary: the projects were loss-making. On the other hand, projects with a high customer's disposition to participate and a highly modular product design, failed to design their processes and network accordingly. To keep these type of houses affordable and feasible for the customer, one surely needs modularly designed network, which make it possible to configure a cut-to-fit process design for each individual house. In this case, if the property developer wants to support the customer in keeping the costs low, he needs to have access to a very modular network of actors. For each individual customer he needs to be able to set up a temporary, loosely coupled network of organizations, willing to participate in the design of this house. The difficulties in setting up such a structure were often underestimated.

Conclusions

In the *Gewild Wonen* project the in-sync hypothesis was generally confirmed. In the building industry a strong linkage exists between the design of the product and the design of the production processes and the accompanying network of participating organizations. The dimensions are closely related to each other. The houses designed in the *Gewild Wonen* project were, in general, more modular than houses built in regular housing projects. The building networks that also increased the modularity of their production processes and the structure of the network itself outsmarted the networks that did not do this, in terms of customer satisfaction and profit.

However, the more modular these dimensions are, the more difficult it becomes. In these cases, effective use of ICT is really needed to manage the increased complexity of product, process and network design as well as the interaction and dialogue with the customer. In addition, it was found that increasing the modularity of all dimensions is only fruitful when the end-customers, the buyers of the houses, are both willing and able to participate in the design. When the so-called customer's disposition to participate is low, it is not "smart" to increase the modularity. An integral design of all three dimensions is then the smartest thing to do.

References

Bakker, D., C. Rapp, (1998). *Het Kant-en-Klaarhuis - Standaard en Karakter in de Woningcatalogus*, Nederlands Architectuurinstituut, Rotterdam, (in Dutch).

Baldwin, C.Y., K.B. Clark, (2000). *Design Rules: The Power of Modularity*, The MIT Press, Cambridge, Mass.

Crowston, K., (1997). "A Coordination Approach to Organizational Process Design", *Organization Science*, 8, 2, pp. 157-175.

Feitzinger, E., H.L. Lee, (1997). "Mass Customization At Hewlett-Packard: The Power of Postponement", *Harvard Business Review*, (Jan-Feb), pp. 69-89.

Fine, C.H., (1998). *Clockspeed - Winning Industry Control in the Age of Temporary Advantage*, Perseus Books, Reading, Mass.

Habraken, H.J., (1961). *De Dragers en de Mensen*, Amsterdam, (in Dutch).

Hart, C.W., (1996). "Made to Order", *Marketing Management*, 5, 2, pp. 10-22.

Huffman, C., B. Kahn, (1998). "Variety for Sale: Mass Customization or Mass Confusion?", *Journal of Retailing*, (Winter), 74, 4, pp. 491-513.

Larsson, R., D.E. Bowen, (1989). "Organization and Customer: Managing Design and Coordination of Services", *Academy of Management Review*, 14, 2, pp. 213-233.

Nadler, D., M. Gerstein, and R. Shaw, (1992). *Organizational Architecture: Designs for changing organizations*, Jossey-Bass, San Francisco.

O'Grady, P., (1999). *The Age of Modularity*, Adams and Steelse Publishers, Iowa City, Iowa.

Orton, J.D., K.E. Weick, (1990). "Loosely Coupled Systems: A Reconceptualization", *Academy of Management Review*, 15, 2, pp. 203-223.

Pine, B.J., (1993). *Mass Customization: The New Frontier in Business Competition*, Harvard Business School Press, Boston, Mass.

Sanchez, R., (1999). "Modular Architectures in the Marketing Process", *Journal of Marketing*, 63, (Special Issue), pp. 92-111.

Schilling, M.A., (2000). "Toward a General Modular Systems Theory And Its Application to Interfirm Product Modularity", *Academy of Management Review*, 25, 2, pp. 312-334.

Schwartz, B., (2000). "Self-Determination: The tyranny of Freedom", *American Psychologist*, 55, millennial issue, pp. 79-88.

Ulrich, K.T., S.D. Eppinger, (1995). *Product Design and Development*, McGraw-Hill, New York, NY.

Van Hoek, R.I., H.A.M. Weken, (1998). "The Impact of Modular Production on the Dynamics of Supply Chains", *The International Journal of Logistics Management*, 9, 2, pp. 35-50.

Weeber, C., (1998). *Het Wilde Wonen*, Uitgeverij 010, Rotterdam, (in Dutch).

Weick, K.E., (1976). "Educational Organizations As Loosely Coupled Systems", *Administrative Science Quarterly*, 21, pp. 1-19.

Worren, N., K. Moore, and P. Cardona, (2000). "Modularity, Strategic Flexibility and Firm Performance: A Study of the Home Appliances Industry", Submitted to *International Journal of Technology Management*, (May).

16 "Off the Shelf" Smart Business Networks

Peter C. Muller[1] and Gerrit Schipper[1]

Introduction

Business process outsourcing firms are often self proclaimed "partners". Telling your customer that you are not a mere supplier but a "partner in business" not only conveys the feeling that your futures are bounded but also that your mutual interests are aligned. Outsourcing business processes indeed guarantees a long-lasting relationship, for better and for worse. Although the supplier dependency is essentially of a contractual nature, changing suppliers is costly and impractical. At the same time, insourcing the activities after the contract period is often impossible, due to the fact that the necessary skills and knowledge have eroded (Alexander and Young, 1996; Aubert et al., 1998).

In essence, supplier dependency and loosing control over quality, timing and service is inherent to outsourcing and should be considered to be part of the game (Quélin and Duhamel, 2003). Moreover, why worry if the outsourcing deal produces the desired results: lower operational costs, focus on core activities and/ or flexibility. In stable business environments this could and should be true, although practice often proves to be cumbersome leading to dismal tales of hidden costs (Alexander and Young, 1996; Aubert et al., 1998; Barthélemy, 2001; Earl 1996; Lacity and Hirshheim, 1993) and non-performing suppliers (Aubert et al., 1998; Earl 1996).

However, in dynamic business environments traditional outsourcing is based on the false premise that the outsourcer's and outsourcee's interests are aligned. Apart from low costs, the outsourcer needs flexibility and responsiveness while the outsourcee strives for stability. The later is quite understandable, given the fact that it usually takes a huge upfront investment to acquire a deal and to implement it. Once the operation has been stabilized it is in the interest of the outsourcee to constantly refine the operation and make use of the learning curve. The outsourcer however does usually not benefit from these efficiency gains produced by the outsourcee. Ultimately, the outsourcer risks to get the worst of both worlds: an inflexible and relatively expensive service.

---

[1] ABZ Nederland BV, P.O. Box 124, 3700 AC Zeist, The Netherlands, pmuller@abz.nl, gschipper@abz.nl

Obviously, outsourcing a business process turns it into a "black box" over which the outsourcer has little control. According to the philosophy of smart business networks, the solution lies in opening the black box by breaking it up in modular pieces and outsourcing the pieces to different suppliers. This approach results in a loosely coupled "chain" of suppliers which is inherently more flexible than the tightly coupled solution of a single outsourcing partner. Moreover, by making the suppliers in the supply chain exchangeable, expensive suppliers can easily be weeded out in favor of less expensive suppliers. The disadvantages of traditional outsourcing have been tackled effectively. Or haven't they?

Managing a network of suppliers requires different control measures than managing a single supplier. Due to the inherent complexity of networks the difficulties and associated costs of coordinating the network may offset the advantages in terms of costs and flexibility. This paper will discuss the requirements for effectively controlling business networks and indicate how business service providers may help companies with standardized solutions for setting up and managing business networks.

Smart Business Networks and Control

Managing a supplier can be seen as a form of control. The systems theory of control defines control as "any form of directed influence" (Kramer, 1978, in Kramer and De Smit, 1982; De Leeuw, 1982). In its most simple form, a control situation is represented by a controlling system, a target system, and an environment. The controlling system exerts goal directed influence over a target system, while the environment affects both part-systems (see Figure 16.1). The control situation central to this paper is that of a company controlling its suppliers. The question is whether and how companies can effectively control their suppliers in such a way that they provide low cost, high quality services while retaining flexibility concerning market needs and the ensuing operational processes. The effectiveness of control constitutes a central issue in the systems theory of control. In order for control to be effective, there needs to be a balance between the amount of control required by the target system (control need) and the amount of control delivered by the controlling system (controlling capacity; Van Kesteren, 1996; De Leeuw, 1982). The amount of control delivered by the controlling system depends on its "controlling capability" and its "controlling effort" (see Figure 16.2). These aspects are well understood from a procurement management perspective. Outsourcing activities to external suppliers often solves problems and creates new ones. The effort required by a company to manage its so called outsourcing "partners" is often substantial. At the same time the capability to manage suppliers is fairly restricted. In theory, instruments like a service level agreement (SLA) should enable companies to exert control, while in practice such legal instruments are often mere "paper tigers".

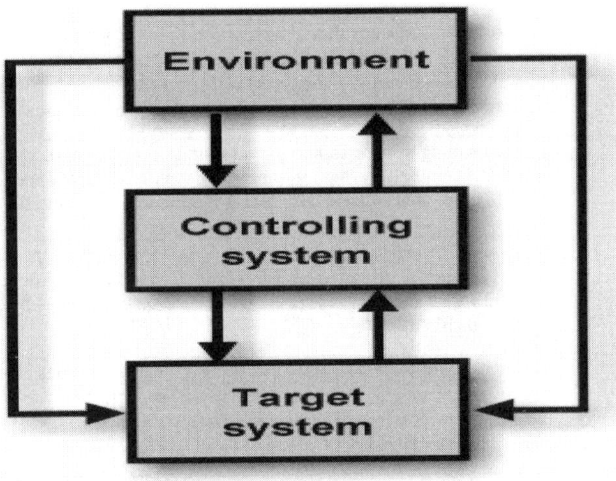

Fig 16.1 Control Situation

The issue is how to increase the "controlling capability" of companies using the concept of smart business networks. The "controlling capability" is determined by a number of attributes that the controlling system should possess in order to achieve effective control. These requirements for effective control are outlined in Table 16.1 (De Leeuw, 1982).

The requirements for effective control bear relevance for controlling suppliers. The current state of procurement management theory and practice makes it abundantly clear that one or more of the requirements is often missing. The goal for the supplier is often specified as part of the negotiating and contracting process. However, this goal is usually not updated during the contract period. Contracts usually incorporate escalation routines, but offer little insight in the internal workings of the supplier and hence provide little certainty with respect of the outcome of escalations. Information is scarce, usually ambiguous and certainly not real time. Service level reports are a small measure of what is really needed. The measures at the disposal of the outsourcer are usually limited to angry letters from the CEO and threats of turning to another supplier.

Table 16.1 Requirements for effective control

Requirement	Description
Goal	The controlling system should specify a goal for the target system, which serves as a guideline when control is exerted. The goals may or may not be constant in time or stated explicitly. The minimum requirement is a mechanism for evaluating the effect of the control measures taken by the controlling system. Without such a mechanism the influence cannot possibly be directed.
Information	The controlling system should have information about the current state of the target system and the influence of the environment. Together with the control measures these determine the future state of the target system. Without this information it is impossible to choose the right control measures.
Information processing capacity	The controlling system should possess the information-processing capacity to turn the incoming information (about the environment and the target system) into effective control measures (using the model and taking the goal into account).
Model	The controlling system should have a model to predict the (possible) effect of control measures, or should at least have a good understanding of the target system. Without such a model the choice for certain control measures cannot possibly be directed.
Measures	The controlling system should have enough control measures at its disposal. In this respect "enough" means that the variety in control measures should equal the variety in possible disturbances. This is called the Law of the Requisite Variety (Ashby 1956).

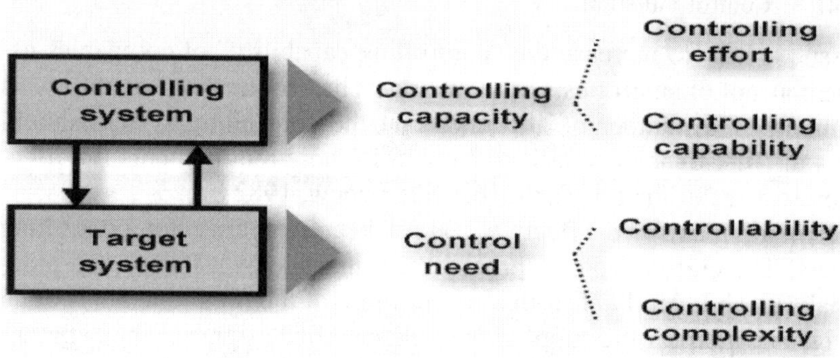

Fig 16.2 Controlling capacity and control need

The next paragraph will show how smart business networks may provide a solution. The associated principles will be illustrated using the case of claims management in the Dutch insurance market.

Networked Claims Management

The Dutch automotive insurance market represents a total premium income of € 4,2 billion (CVS and CBS, 2003). With 135 car insurers (op cit.) it is traditionally a highly competitive market characterized by ultra low margins. The case study will show how Dutch car insurers have dramatically reduced cost by means of networked claims management.

Twenty years ago, insurance companies and body repair shops did not share the same value chain. Body repair shops supplied their services directly to consumers. When confronted with a car damage, consumers turned to a body repair shop, had their car fixed and presented the bill to the insurance company. This way of working was problematic for two reasons. Firstly, a standardized way of determining the repair costs was lacking, which often lead to negotiation between insurance companies (represented by claims adjusters) and body repair shops. Secondly, the communication between insurance company, body repair shop and claims adjuster took place by mail, fax and telephone and was very inefficient. The overall result was: soaring claims costs and severe losses.

In 1981 automotive insurers sought a solution to the first problem by implementing the Audatex calculation standard as an objective instrument to determine the costs of repairs. ABZ was founded in order to maintain the calculation standard and to provide the IT support for making the calculations. Implementing the Audatex model prompted the birth of a new way of working. ABZ developed a claims hub allowing insurance companies, body repair shops and claims adjusters to electronically exchange data regarding claims (see Figure 16.3).

Nowadays, about 80% of all claims is calculated using the Audatex model. The resulting claims information is stored in a central database, which is used to generate valuable management information. Both insurance companies (the outsourcers) and body repair (the outsourcees) use this management information to benchmark their own operation and that of their suppliers. Apart from that about 80% of all claims is processed electronically. About 90% of all insurance companies, 90% of all body shops and 100% of all claims adjusters are linked to the insurance hub and generate more than 4,5 million claims related transactions.

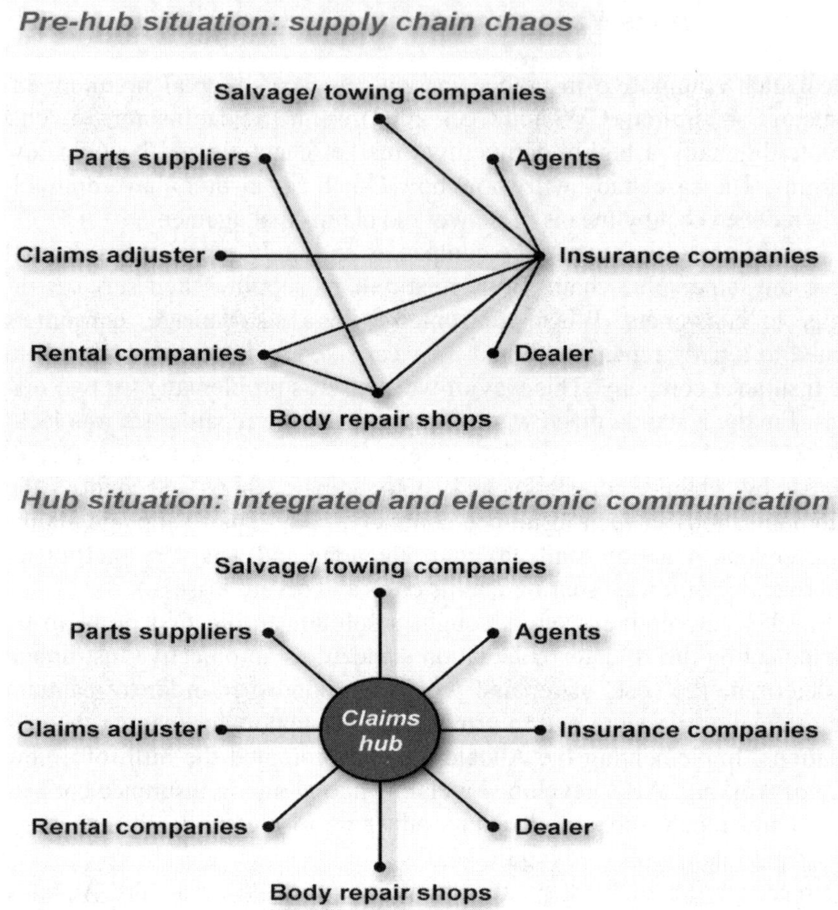

Fig 16.3 ABZ Claims Hub

Obviously, electronic claims processing has generated enormous efficiency gains for all parties involved. Ernst & Young has estimated that the claims hub saves the insurance branch and their business partners about 250 million Euro each year (Ernst & Young, 1999). So, the savings are there, largely due to the existence of an infrastructure that enables electronic exchange of information. The question is to what extent insurance companies have become networked in an organizational sense. Do they have become more agile; switching between suppliers and changing their processes at will? The next paragraph will show how some insurance companies have even gone further in creating networks that are truly smart.

Smart Networks and Supply Chain Coordinators

Building on the existing central infrastructure in the insurance branch and the connectivity it offers, some insurance companies have gone further in their quest for control over their business partners. More specifically, some constellations of insurance companies have created supply chain coordinators. At present the most prominent supply chain coordinator is Schadegarant, a collaboration of 17 intermediary insurance companies.

Schadegarant has been founded with the objective of further reducing claims losses. Schadegarant's approach has been to create a network of Schadegarant body repair shops with whom it has made comprehensive and stringent agreements concerning hourly wages, repair methods and procedures. The unwritten win-win in this scenario is that the insurance companies benefit from advantageous commercial terms and conditions while the body repair shops receive a certain guaranteed workload. Both parties profit from the efficiency gains brought about by an integrated way of working.

There are two important prerequisites for Schadegarant's success as a supply chain coordinator. Firstly, Schadegarant coordinates a substantial volume in the Dutch market. The combined premium income of the insurance companies behind Schadegarant is about 60%. Moreover, these insurance companies have decided that cooperation in the field of claims management will allow them to compete better where it really matters: marketing and sales. Secondly, Schadegarant has been able to get control over the claims intake process, allowing them to direct damaged vehicles to selected body repair shops. Controlling the claims intake process has been made possible by stimulating agents to register new claims in a central system specifically developed for Schadegarant and serviced by ABZ.

The claims process developed by Schadegarant roughly consists of six steps (see Figure 16.4). Firstly, the agent registers a new claim after being contacted by a customer. Secondly, the Schadegarant system automatically verifies whether the claim is covered by an insurance policy. Thirdly, the agent selects a body repair shop that is part of the network. Fourthly, the body repair shop calculates the damage using the Audatex model and sends the calculation including digital pictures of the damage to Schadegarant. Fifthly, the Schadegarant system automatically assess the calculation based on business rules. These business rules have been derived from historical data concerning the average costs of comparable damages with similar types of vehicles. In step six, the Schadegarant system sends the claim to the insurance company advising the insurance company to either pay the claim directly, to assess the damage using the digital pictures or to send a claims adjuster.

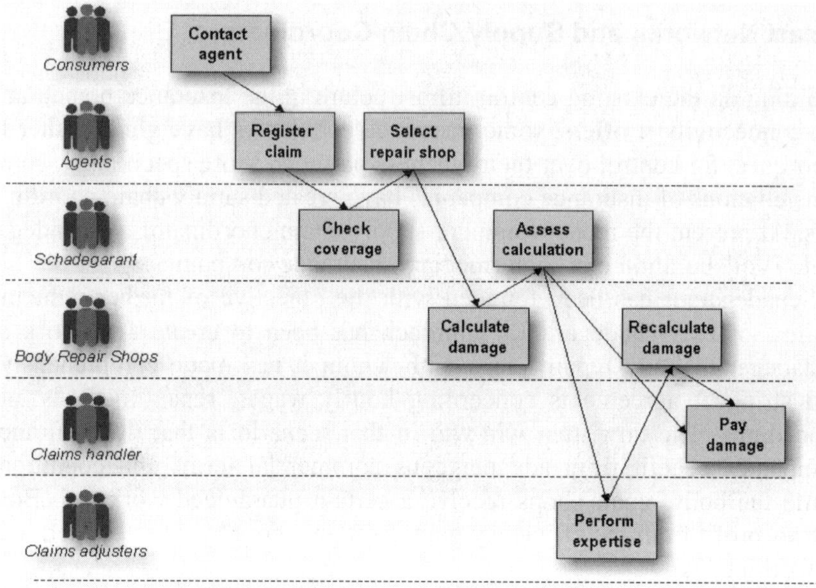

Fig 16.4 Schadegarant process

The partnership between insurance companies and body repair shops is based on trust. Body repair shops in the Schadegarant network (with an A or B status) are for example allowed to start repairing the vehicle before the damage has been assessed and has been approved by the insurance company. In the end this reduces the throughput time of repairs and saves the costs of rental cars, file handling and so on. "Trust", however is combined with a system of checks and balances. An important instrument is the database with historical Audatex calculations. Among other things, Schadegarant uses this database to benchmark its suppliers. Furthermore, Schadegarant audits their body shops once a year. Non conformance with Schadegarant procedures and bad performance in terms of repair costs may lead to a lower classification of the repair shop (and hence less favorable terms of operation) or even exclusion from the Schadegarant network.

The network Schadegarant has created is smart in the sense that it offers real control over the suppliers in the network. Looking at the requirements for effective control it becomes clear how Schadegarant has achieved this (see Table 16.2).

Table 16.2 Schadegarant implementation of requirements for effective control

Requirement	Description
Goal	Schadegarant has clear guidelines concerning the quality of repair (e.g. use of new and original part, use of certain repair methods), throughput time of repairs and the way the damage is calculated.
Information	Schadegarant makes extensive use of management information to benchmark the quality, cost and throughput time of repairs made by body repair shops within the network. Moreover Schadegarant is able to benchmark the average cost of repair between Schadegarant and non-Schadegarant repair shops.
Information processing capacity	Schadegarant uses an expert system to automatically assess quotations from body repair shops. Its cheap, fast and reliable.
Model	Schadegarant has a clear understanding of the entire claims management process and the activities performed therein by body repair shops.
Measures	Schadegarant has the ability to downgrade repair shops or to exclude them form the network.

Clearly, Schadegarant has attained a position where it can control its suppliers and if need be, exchange them for others. However, exchanging suppliers overnight requires a "quick connect" (Sanchez 1995, 1996) of new suppliers to the Schadegarant process. Moreover, also the Schadegarant process is subject to changing market requirements. The ease and flexibility with which Schadegarant is able to change its processes in response to new market needs is subject to the flexibility of its business service provider. The next paragraph will outline how ABZ enables a "quick connect" and how ABZ continues to support Schadegarant's changing processes using the concept of business modularity.

Community Resource Planning and Business Modularity

As previously shown, Schadegarant governs the relations between insurance companies, agents, body repair shops, and claims adjusters at a process level. ABZ in turn supports these processes at a technological level. Contrary to Schadegarant, which defines the processes for part of the insurance branch, ABZ offers its technology based services to all insurance companies and their business partners. As will be shown later this central position is part of ABZ's quick connect capability. Through ABZ companies may employ resources in their external environment (Community Resource Planning) without encountering the usual problems of disconnected processes and systems.

ABZ's Community Resource Planning (CRP) solutions are based on a comprehensive portfolio of centrally hosted, generic hub functions (the XNet suite of services™). These functions consist of four layers (see Figure 16.5). Firstly, a number of generic services which are necessary to turn a software application into a managed business service (services that are housed, hosted, secured, billable, managed, and so on). Secondly, a workflow and central archiving capability which links all parties involved in processing a claim (or any other process). Thirdly, a number of "plug in" business services which provide specialized claims handling functionality. These business services may be based on software applications of third parties. Fourthly, the internet as a medium for secure, anywhere access to the hub functions.

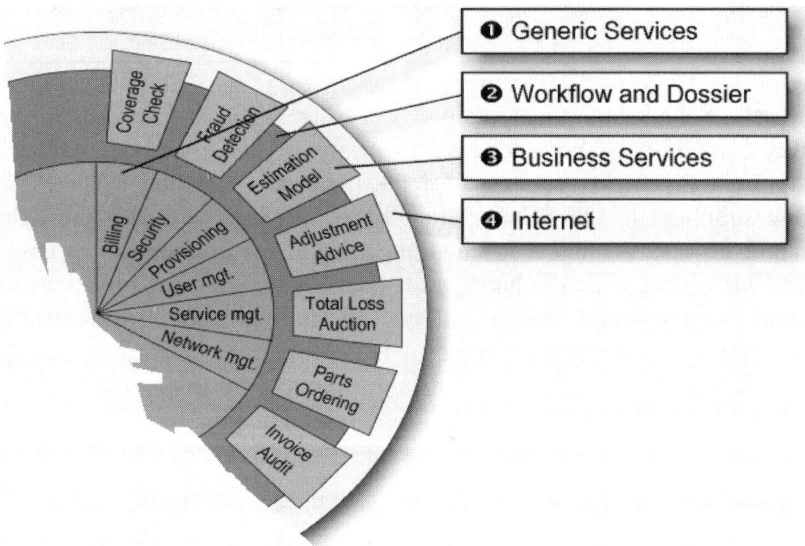

Fig 16.5 Layers XNET Suite of Services

The hub functions offered by ABZ have been developed with the concept op business modularity in mind (Garud and Kumaraswamy, 1995; Sanches and Mahoney, 1996). The hub functions in the XNET suit of services are elementary building blocks which may be combined in any order to construct new CRP solutions or to adapt existing ones. By adopting modularity as a leading principle of doing business, ABZ can offer its customers flexibility and freedom of choice. This is however not enough to make business networks "smart". In order to enable players like Schadegarant to change their network of suppliers on the fly, one needs a "quick connect" to the CRP solution that supports the network in its day to day operation. The quick connect offered by ABZ consists of four elements. Firstly, all CRP solutions are accessible through the public internet. This means that participation in a network does not require the installation of software or network connections. Secondly, all CRP solutions are secured by means of digital certificates which have been issued by ABZ's Trusted Third Party. The wide adoption of these certificates and the underlying Public Key Infrastructure (at present 50% of all agents and 60% of all body repair shops have been issued digital certificates) means that almost all potential suppliers have the technological means to join a network like Schadegarant's. Thirdly, the CRP solutions that require integration with local back offices have standardized interfaces (mostly webservices), the implementation of which is certified by ABZ. This means that suppliers with certified back office systems have instant connectivity with certain CRP solutions. Fourthly, the CRP solutions are based on data dictionaries, developed and maintained by ABZ's standardization institute.

The keyword in the elements mentioned above is "standardization". In a way, smart business networks and the underlying technological support are nothing more than a set of rules based on standards agreed upon by (part of) the industry. The central position of ABZ allows it to develop and maintain these standards in close cooperation with the branch.

Conclusions

Smart business networks constitute a promising and relatively new approach to outsourcing. In dynamic business environments, cost effectiveness and flexibility are the prime advantages over more traditional ways of outsourcing. The advantages are brought about by the fact that the networked approach offers new means of controlling suppliers. The differences have been illustrated using the five requirements for effective control.

The first requirement "goal", has to do with the fact that the outsourcer needs to set clear goals for the supplier in terms of quality, costs and throughput time. Traditionally, goals are made explicit in contracts, service level agreements, and so on. Setting goals in a business network environment differs in two respects. First, the network owner sets goals for homogenic (sub)groups of exchangeable suppliers. The fact that the same goals apply to every supplier in a certain segment, means that suppliers' performance can be compared. In short: the market has become transparent. Secondly, the network owner does not only specify its needs, but in some instances also how it wants the results to be achieved. This approach gives the network owner more control over the delivery process and thus its output.

The second and third requirement "information" and "information processing capacity" have to do with measuring the performance of the supplier(s). Again this is nothing new. Parties usually agree that the outsourcee will regularly produce service level reports. In a business network environment the differences are threefold. Firstly, the information is collected and processed real time. This enables the network owner to intervene speedily if things go awry. Secondly, the information is gathered by the outsourcer instead of the outsourcee, hence increasing the objectivity of the information. Thirdly, the information is collected at a granular level, indicating the performance of every step in the process. This enables the network owner to identify weak spots in the process; the "black box" is effectively made transparent.

The fourth and fifth requirement "model" and "measures" deal with the fact that the outsourcer needs to possess enough instruments for controlling the outsourcee. In traditional outsourcing situations this is covered by escalation procedures and termination clauses. However, this negates the fact that reversing a outsourcing deal or changing outsourcing partners takes a lot of time and effort. A business network offers a solution, which is different in two respects. Firstly, the model which stipulates how the network owner wants the suppliers to act is embedded in workflow software. This makes it easy to predict the effect of a measure (e.g. stopping a work item to go to the next phase). Secondly, network owners can easily switch between suppliers due to the existence of a "quick connect" and the fact that suppliers perform sets of atomic tasks which makes them exchangeable with other suppliers.

Prerequisites for smart business networks are a quick connect and flexible support systems. The quick connect is facilitated by a central infrastructure that gives suppliers and potential suppliers access to the network's support systems. The key ingredient of such an infrastructure are standards with respect to information exchange, network connectivity, and security. The flexibility of the support systems is realized by adopting a services oriented architecture which is based on the principle of business modularity. The huge potential of smart business networks will lead to the creation of new "community builders". Both at a technological level (the business service provider) and at a process and organizational level (the supply chain coordinator). Business service providers and supply chain coordinators will provide complementary services and develop their business in a symbiotic way.

References

Alexander, M., D. Young, (1996). "Strategic Outsourcing", *Long Range Planning*, Vol. 29.

Aubert, B.A., M. Parry, and S. Rivard, (1998). *Assessing the Risk of IT - Outsourcing*, Cirano, Montreal.

Barthélemy, J., (2001). "The Hidden Costs of IT Outsourcing", *Sloan Management Review*, Vol. 42, No. 2.

CVS and CBS, (2003). *Verzekerd van Cijfers*, (in Dutch).

De Leeuw, A.C.J., (1982). *Organisaties: Management, Analyse, Ontwerp en Verandering: Een Systeemvisie*, Van Gorcum, Assen, (in Dutch).

Earl, M., (1996). "The Risks of Outsourcing IT", *Sloan Management Review*.

Garud, R., A. Kumaraswamy, (1995). "Technological and Organizational Designs for Realizing Economies of Substitution", *Strategic Management Journal*, 16 (Special Issue).

Kern, T., L.P. Willcocks, and M.C. Lacity, (2002). "Application Service Provisioning: Risk Assessment and Mitigation", *MIS Quarterly Executive*, Vol. 1 No. 2 (June).

Kramer, N.J.T.A., (1978). *Systeem In Problemen*, Leiden, (in Dutch).

Kramer, N.J.T.A., J. de Smit, (1982). *Systeemdenken*, Stenfert Kroese, Leiden-Antwerpen, (in Dutch).

Lacity, M., R. Hirshheim, (1993). "The Information Systems Outsourcing Bandwagon", *Sloan Management Review*.

Quélin, B., F. Duhamel, (2003). "Bringing Together Strategic Outsourcing and Corporate Strategy: Outsourcing Motives and Risks", *European Management Journal*, Vol. 21, No. 5.

Sanchez, R., (1995). "Strategic Flexibility in Product Competition", *Strategic Management Journal*, Vol. 16, Special Issue: Technological Transformation and the New Competitive Landscape.

Sanchez, R., (1996). "Quick-Connect Technologies for Product Creation: Implications for Competence-Based Competition", in: *Dynamics of Competence-Based Competition*, Sanchez, R., A. Heene, and H. Thomas, (eds.), Oxford: Elsevier Pergamon.

Sanchez, R., T. Mahoney, (1996). "Modularity, Flexibility, and Knowledge Management in Product and Organization Design", *Strategic Management Journal*, 17, (Winter).

Van Kesteren, J.H.M. (1996). *Doorlichten en Herontwerpen Van Organisatie-Complexen*, Doctoral dissertation, Groningen School of Management and Organisation, Van Kesteren Consult, Schoonoord, (in Dutch).

17 Designing Intelligent Service Supply Networks

Arun Rai[1], Jonathan Wareham[1], and V. Sambamurthy[2]

Introduction

Intelligent networks are emerging as a class of supply systems that permit extreme customization and serve-to-order (i.e., minimal inventory) responsiveness by co-integrating product design, process redesign, and network-wide control mechanisms (Rai, Bush et al., 2002; Rai and Sambamurthy , 2002). The airlines in-flight services involve a globally dispersed partnership of suppliers, manufacturers, distributors, caterers, and airlines where tens of thousands of SKUs, including many perishable units, flow through the logistics systems. In fact, a long haul 747 flight requires over 40,000 SKUs.

There are significant interdependencies between core processes in supply networks (Lee , 1996), such as the in-flight services supply network. Changes in service design can create significant oscillations in production and distribution planning. Lack of coordination of service design planning with master production planning can result in huge losses due to perishable inventory. Resource inefficiencies and service pitfalls are very likely to occur if flight cancellations and delays are not detected in real-time and corrective action invoked.

We examine the intelligent networks at eGateMatrix, a venture that was created to streamline supply processes and develop adaptive supply-demand synchronization for AirCo, a major airline. We develop insights about the design features of intelligent supply networks, particularly for service industries. The next section presents the framework used for the case study and its analysis. We then identify the process capabilities enabled by eGatematrix and analyze the digital capabilities used to achieve these process capabilities. We conclude with implications for the design of intelligent service supply networks.

[1] Center for Process Innovation & Department of Computer Information Systems, Robinson College of Business, Georgia State University, Atlanta, GA 30303, arunrai@gsu.edu and wareham@acm.org

[2] Eli Broad College of Business Administration, Michigan State University, East Lansing, MI 48824, smurthy@bus.msu.edu

A Framework for Evaluating Intelligence in Supply Networks

Recent advances in information technologies have promoted thinking about unbundling of physical, information, and financial flows across supply networks in order to enhance speed, flexibility, customer satisfaction, and cost economy (Hagel ,1999; Lee , 2000). Unbundling allows the optimization of individual value chains and development of greater intelligence around key decisions affecting the effectiveness of the supply network.

Services supply networks can be broadly described in terms of design, sourcing, inbound logistics, production, and outbound logistics, and asset management. We take the perspective that intelligence in supply networks for services, including in-flight services, can orchestrate the conduct of these core processes and their interaction to generate behavior that yields superior performance. This intelligence can be embedded in the control systems of the network and its discovery and learning mechanisms (Choi, Dooley et al., 2001).

The network's control system can be described in terms of its predictive control and reactive control (Simon, 1981). Predictive control enables greater accuracy and reliability in forecasts about estimates of the future states of key variables and allocations of resources and capabilities. These control mechanisms observe deviations of outcomes from established goals and feed into the next planning cycle. Reactive control uses feedback about exceptions and asynchronous conditions that have occurred to discover the need for remedial action plans; that is, recovery from an aberrant state once the problems have occurred.

Discovery and learning mechanisms can be used to exploit existing knowledge and competencies or explore new knowledge or opportunities (March , 1991). Exploitation-oriented learning mechanisms focus on refining knowledge and their application in processes, whereas exploration-oriented learning is focused on generating new knowledge and defining opportunities. Firms can potentially fall into "competency traps" with excessive exploitation or into "innovation traps" with excessive exploration. The challenge for firms is to balance exploration with exploitation.

eGateMatrix: Birth of An In-Flight Services Supply Network Orchestrator

AirCo is a big airline company that flies about two and a half thousand flight legs every day from many different airports around the country. Required services included meals, beverages, duty-free items (for international flights), audio and video entertainment, as well as cabin cleaning, equipment loading and supplies provisioning. In a single year, AirCo spends well over 100 million dollars a year on in-flight catering alone. Figure 17.1 shows the nature of its above-the-wing services supply network.

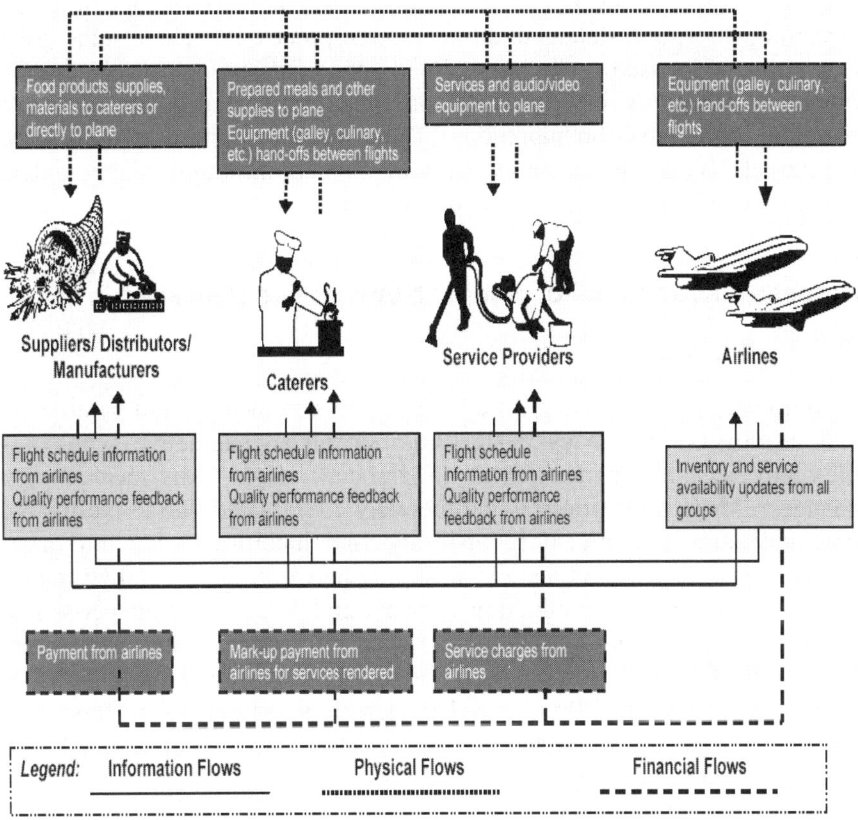

Fig 17.1 Three-Dimensional Features of Above-the-Wing Services Supply Network

Gate Gourmet is one of the leading caterers of the airline industry and a major services provider for AirCo. The two partners were increasingly concerned about the costs, quality, and quality of the in-flight services provisioning network. In 1999, they contracted SupplyTech, a supply network management applications vendor, to conduct a strategic assessment. The study concluded that process redundancies, antiquated procedures and internal inefficiencies of its current supply network were deteriorating in quality and increasing costs of above-the-wing services.

e-Gatematrix is a joint venture between the two partners whose goal is to design, develop, and implement intelligent networks for in-flight services provisioning. e-Gatematrix created new operating processes and paradigms to generate value and allow buyers and sellers to concentrate on their core competencies and brands. They introduced digital collaboration solutions targeted at design, sourcing, procurement, inbound logistics, outbound logistics, and financial administration processes. Their value creation strategy focused on building intelligence for strategic procurement, inventory reduction, inbound and outbound transportation, requirements planning, and transition planning. The solutions platform provides for seamless B2B commerce, supply network collaboration tools and complete visibility to all trading partners within the marketplace.

Process Capabilities for Supply Network Orchestration

Service Design

Traditionally there has been little linkage between meal design parameters and business outputs. Meal design requirements are subjective, with complex pricing making it difficult to associate costs with meal design changes. Menu transition was ineffectively coordinated due to ineffective communication and inventory visibility, and inability to lay out menu changes on a master plan across the supply network. This resulted in significant oscillation of production systems and losses through perishable foods. It was essential to determine a clear set of meal design parameters for design communication between AirCo and its supply network partners. Analytical Hierarchical Process (AHP), which is a structured method, was applied to make subjective parameters objective. This resulted in a set of prioritized, consistent, and agreed upon meal design parameters that could be effectively communicated and managed.

The design management module integrates product lifecycle management tools that focus on transition planning with collaborative forecasting and planning tools. This design management module requires visibility of supply network-wide capacity, inventory status, and master production plans, so as to evaluate the implications of a menu design change and its timing.

To assist in service design planning for retail and impulse sale items, eGate aggregates data concerning retail sales and special services (gourmet meals – sold meals, duty free items). For products and services sold on-demand in-flight, forecasting the exact demand information is impossible.

However, with data aggregation across many airlines, industry trends can be assessed to determine optimal inventory levels as well as pricing promotions.

Sourcing and Procurement

Traditionally, Airco had not defined a process for supply base segmentation and its sourcing practices did not leverage economies of scale. The heuristics used to classify products, and consequently suppliers, were not formulated, nor refined, based on supply risk or market value. Furthermore, service design changes were not synchronized with sourcing and procurement to manage efficiencies.

eGate's sourcing and procurement module maps the supply base into suppliers for strategic or commodity products for food, services, and supplies. Heuristics are defined and applied to re-classify products as strategic or commodity. These heuristics are evaluated and refined based on the procurement savings accrued as a result of the classification. In addition, standardized web-based procurement processes for proposals, bid and auction, and purchase execution are defined and enforced.

Inbound and Outbound Transportation

Airco's catering supply system had many less than full loads and empty return deliveries. Transportation was managed on a load-by-load or contract-by-contract basis and the accounting methods did not provide visibility into overall transportation costs. High levels of inefficiencies were created due to deadhead backhauls from distribution centers and lack of competitive bidding.

eGate developed intelligent planning modules to coordinate the flows of distribution trucks across the supply network, fill backhauls, manage reverse logistics, optimize loading schedules and constrain costs.

Production Planning

The network includes suppliers as diverse as rice wholesalers to toiletries to entertainment providers. E-gatematrix deployed Internet technologies for instant demand information access across the network through three applications:

a. *Flight service schedule* application posts daily updates on flight schedules including menus, provisions and activity codes assigned to each flight,

b. *Passenger load forecast* is a daily update of passenger reservations per flight combined with a forecast of anticipated passenger loads,
c. *Service demand forecast* was perhaps the first of its kind in the industry. It gives a concentrated view of service assignments and forecasts for a given flight based on forecasted passenger loads and scheduled departures. Service forecasts are revised as passenger loads and schedule updates occur.

Asset Management

Airlines own more than 10 times the amount of catering inventory that they require, because it is flown out of the hubs and does not come back on the return flights. There is also inventory shrinkage of assets. For instance, a blanket is used on average of nine times before is disappears. In addition, lack of packaging product standardization increases handling complexity, constrains logistics efficiency, and decreases production efficiency.

eGate has implemented systems to track valuable in-transit and in-stock inventory and optimize it. Since catering assets are now identified and tracked, heuristics have been derived and applied to standardize them. E-gate has derived heuristics and then applied them to standardize packaging products, such as dish and tray sizes, and containers. This results in an increased scope of their use in galleys. These uniform standards have led to global improvements across the supply network.

Each airplane has a different internal structure of the galley. As different physical plane types were used interchangeably on different flights, planning what types of cabinets and galley accessories would be used on specific flights can become complicated. By building a repository of design specifications of plane galley structures and galley loading equipments, integrating flight scheduling systems, and applying intelligent forecasting methods, eGate optimizes galley loading equipment and reduces overall inventory.

Digital Enablers of Intelligence in In-Flight Service Supply Processes

Four digital capabilities enable the process capabilities discussed above. They are visibility, process integration, data mining for knowledge discovery, and measurement and benchmarking (Table 17.1).

Visibility

Demand visibility has been regarded as important in manufacturing supply networks (Seidmann and Sundararajan, 1997; Lee and Whang, 2000). Airco, eGate, and key supply network partners identified key information that needed to be shared for improved planning and execution of operations. These include, but are not limited to:

- Load and service demand estimates,
- Menu rotation plans,
- Master production plans,
- Inventory and service availability status,
- Resource tracing and tracking, and
- Flight schedule change alerts

Traditionally each airline provided demand signals by sending out flight schedules by fax, email, post and EDI to supply network partners fifteen days to three months in advance of flight departure. Airlines hesitated to share their passenger load forecasts because of the inherent risks involved. Thus, the erratically published flight schedules only provided a rudimentary demand signal in the form of a maximum carrying capacity of each scheduled flight.

Sharing passenger load and service demand estimates addresses the problems caused by lack of visibility of demand-related information. In the absence of this shared demand information, caterers and sub-contractors develop production plans based on published flight schedule information, which is the only demand signal available to them. Consequently, the supply network is rippled by the bullwhip effect. As a result, key planning activities - procurement, labor, transportation, and distribution – at each stage are misaligned with each other and eventually with customer requirements.

Though menu rotation policies are popular with frequent, loyal fliers, they cause tremendous waste in the earliest stages of the supply network, as suppliers are not fully able to accommodate the consequences of menu rotation when the information is not relayed to them. eGate complemented the load forecasting information already transmitted through the supply network with the menu rotation planning of each airline. This permits the greatest sense and response abilities to endogenous and exogenous shocks in this fulfillment system. In addition, eGate is able to acquire price data from supplying caterers to combine menu rotation policies with current forecasts of process inputs to constrain catering costs.

Caterers and service organizations are just as vulnerable to flight delays as the airlines. eGate used real time data to signal aberrations in actual

flight data to the personnel scheduling systems of the sub-contractors. This permits caterers and service subcontractors to respond to unanticipated shifts in routing, thereby minimizing overtime costs.
In summary, eGate's approach to visibility includes three facets:

a. Rich demand and supply signals are collected and distributed real-time through the supply network for planning purposes. This enables adaptive planning in place of advanced planning and improves predictive control.
b. Event exceptions are captured and transmitted in real-time, which enables operational workflow coordination through efficient reactive control.
c. Resource stocks and flows are made visible through uniform identification tags, and near real-time tracking of in-stock and in-transit assets.

Process Integration

Process integration is a significant digital lever for agile responses in organizational systems (Sambamurthy, Bharadwaj et al., 2003). eGate developed modular integration across transaction and decision environments to implement a dynamic and global optimization perspective. This integration spans reservation, ERP systems, invoicing, suppliers, and B2B exchanges. Further, eGate couples systems that operated in a standalone fashion for the optimization of local objectives that they were built for. For example, the plane scheduling systems and intelligent forecasting systems have been integrated to optimize asset management. As a result, inflight service assets, such as galley loading equipment, can be dynamically optimized based on near-real time flight schedules. Allocated service resources can be de-committed from flights when schedule changes occur making them available for commitment elsewhere for productive use.

eGate also couples strategic and tactical planning systems to evaluate decisions. For example, the product lifecycle management system is integrated with the sourcing and procurement to evaluate cost implications of contemplated menu design changes. Transition planning of new and old services is integrated with the collaborative forecasting and planning system, which consolidates inventory and capacity status across the supply network. This enables assessment of timing of menu service design changes with a perspective on supply network-wide impacts of a decision.

The process integration initiatives have improved predictive control and reactive control as exception conditions are automatically cascaded through integrated workflow processes and corrective actions focus on system-wide efficiencies.

Benchmarking and Measurement

Benchmarking and measurement are increasingly enabled by automated data collection and analysis (Ravichandran and Rai, 2000). Benchmarking and measurement encompassed regulatory compliance, performance against service level agreements, industry norms and customer feedback, granular cost tracking, resource productivity, and process and event cycle times.

There are many industry standards and regulatory requirements (e.g. FDA, USDA, Customs, FAA, HAACP, and ATA) for the above-the-wing services. E-gate collects compliance information from supply network participants along defined parameters, and feedback control information is generated for external regulators and participant firms. Temporal analysis is conducted to evaluate trends pertaining to compliance. Similar analysis is applied across the thousands of service level agreements with vendors

eGate compiles customer feedback concerning services and aggregates statistics concerning industry norms to manage vendors and suppliers. Programs collect highly granular customer service data to monitor subcontractor performance as perceived by flight passengers. Customer feedback is categorized as: (a) operational impact indicating service failures resulted in the interruption of customer service, and (b) customer impact indicates a product or service failure negatively impacted the end user. This customer feedback can be sorted specific to care provider, station, segment and cause.

Cost structures are measured at a granular level so that the impacts of actions can be evaluated from a bottom-line perspective when appropriate. For instance, service menu design changes are now evaluated in terms of their cost implications by focusing on inventory impacts of perishables associated with the current menu design.

Knowledge Discovery

Advanced analytics are used to discover patterns within and across processes and refine decision heuristics used for strategic, tactical, and operational planning. Data mining of customer satisfaction data is used to discover the implications of service design choices, including menu item substitutions. Dramatic reductions in cost structures have been realized by discovering customer indifference to product variety and product type offerings. Data about supply risk and value are mined to refine heuristics for classifying sourced goods as strategic or commodity. Substantial reductions in cost structures have been realized by re-classifying strategic goods as commodity products and changing their sourcing process. Similarly, intelligent planning modules are used to discover superior transportation choices for inbound and outbound logistics, and to improve overall transportation efficiencies.

Implications for the Design of Intelligent Supply Networks

Intelligence in supply networks is shaped by the digital capabilities that; (a) create and exploit visibility, (b) integrate distributed and fragmented processes, (c) track and measure activities at low levels of granularity, and (d) discover knowledge. Our case analysis suggests that supply networks for services exhibit intelligent behavior when these complementary digital capabilities are applied to the design of their control systems and learning mechanisms.

Design of Control Systems for Intelligent Behavior

Interdependencies between planning for service design, sourcing, and production require significant intelligence at their edges. Control systems designed to feed-forward information from service design to sourcing and to production lead to high imprecision and variability in estimates of future states at all stages of the supply network. Intelligent decision-making pertaining to service design changes must also process feedback pertaining to customer utility, sourcing market conditions, and production and transportation resources. This intelligence is enabled by requisite supply network visibility, customer value and cost measurement, and process integration.

Table 17.1 Summary of Digital Enablers of Intelligence in In-Flight Services Supply Processes

In-Flight Services Supply Processes	Digital Enablers			
	Visibility	**Process Integration**	**Benchmarking & Measurement**	**Knowledge Discovery**
Service Design	Supply network-wide capacity and inventory Master production plans of caterers and sub-contractors Aggregate data across carriers regarding retail sales and special services	Product lifecycle management with collaborative forecasting and planning	Customer feedback on the impact on operations, quality perceptions, and satisfaction. Operational costs Regulatory compliance	Level of customer indifference to elements of service design; identification of cheaper substitutes Heuristics for transition management of service design Heuristics for pricing retail sales and special services
Sourcing and Procurement	Service level agreements	B2B exchanges with ERP systems Product lifecycle management with collaborative forecasting and planning	Supplier trends in cost, quality, and delivery lead times Regulatory compliance	Heuristics for classifying goods as strategic or commodity based on supply risk-value analytics
Inbound / Outbound Logistics	Transportation capacity and pricing	Integrated planning system for inbound and outbound logistics	Transportation cost Quality and lead time Regulatory compliance	Heuristics for improved transportation efficiency across inbound and outbound network

Table 17.1 (continued)

In-Flight Services Supply Processes	**Digital Enablers**			
	Visibility	**Process Integration**	**Benchmarking & Measurement**	**Knowledge Discovery**
Production Planning	Flight schedules Passenger load forecasts Service demand estimates Menu rotation plans Schedule change alerts	Collaborative planning and forecasting and coordinated master production planning Integration of systems for service transition planning with production planning Integration of flight scheduling system with labor planning	Inventory levels Perishable inventory costs during design transitions Production efficiency Regulatory compliance	
Asset Management	In-transit catering asset visibility In-stock catering asset visibility Flight schedule changes	Uniform identification tags for system-to-system communication Flight scheduling system integrated with asset management system	Inventory shrinkage Asset productivity Logistics efficiency	Heuristics for packaging product standardization that improve logistics efficiency with no adverse impacts on value

The timing of service design changes can cause significant volatility in its supply network's operations. Effective evaluation of this timing requires visibility to procurement conditions, production inventory, especially perishables, and production and transportation capacity. Intelligence in transitioning to new service designs requires a total cost perspective enabled by process integration and visibility.

Service design parameters that are subjective, unprioritized, and hard to communicate lead to requirement design errors, and reduce supply network agility. This information crosses boundaries of processes and organizations and significant loses occur in its transfer and translation. Analytical techniques that translate these subjective design parameters into a reliable, consistent, and communicable form, and prioritize them, reduce information distortion in its transfer. This process of knowledge discovery for effective representation of design parameters creates essential visibility for shared cognition on design requirements and planned changes to them.

The case analysis offers insights into the de-centralization of control systems required for intelligent behavior, an issue recognized as critical in the context of manufacturing supply networks (Simchi-Levi.and Kaminsky, 2000). In the context of the in-flight service supply network, federated predictive control systems in generates adaptive supply network behavior. This approach recognizes the importance of global coordination and utilization of local expertise for the planning and execution of specific processes. Global information sharing of demand and supply signals and of master plans provides critical input for local planning, and compressed cycles of planning and execution improve estimates and reduce goal variation. In addition, an integrated event management and exception handling capability enables reactive control systems to identify and recover from exceptions with minimal degradation of performance.

Design of Learning Mechanisms for Intelligent Behavior

Organizational learning can entail exploration of new opportunities and discovery of new knowledge or exploitation of existing knowledge by refining and fine-tuning it to better attain current goals. While we limited our current analysis to focus on digitally-enabled mechanisms for learning, we recognize that other organization design mechanisms, such as cross-functional teams, can be used. Nonetheless, the case illustrates the importance of balancing exploration and exploitation in the design of learning mechanisms. In the context of the in-flight services supply network, several new opportunities were discovered and a granular measurement system enabled continuous improvement of existing processes.

The digital capabilities of measurement, visibility and process integration create a rich repository for the discovery of heuristics. Our case analysis suggests that intelligence in supply networks in enhanced by knowledge discovery processes that explore heuristics for improvements in efficiencies or effectiveness without compromising the other. The analysis revealed specific heuristics discovery areas relevant for service supply networks. Heuristics can be discovered on customer indifference to service design elements and their substitution with cheaper elements. Sourcing heuristics can be discovered to re-classify goods as strategic or commodity based on their risk-value profiles. Asset management heuristics can be discovered for packaging product standardization that improves logistics efficiency with no adverse impacts on value. Logistics-related heuristics can be discovered to improve inbound and outbound logistics efficiency without compromising service levels.

Fine-grained measurement systems that track activities and their performance enable refinement of processes. The case suggests that such a measurement system should at least encompass: (a) customer feedback on operations and their satisfaction, (b) service level agreements and performance of outsourced activities relative to them, (c) total cost tracking of activities, (d) resource productivity, (e) event and process cycle times, and (f) regulatory compliance. Timely and granular measurement of these elements is critical not only for exploitative learning but for effective control.

References

Choi, T. Y., K. J. Dooley, et al., (2001). "Supply Networks and Complex Adaptive Systems: Control Versus Emergence", *Journal of Operations Management*, 19, pp. 351-366.

Hagel, J. (1999). "Net Gain: Expanding Markets Through Virtual Communities", *Journal of Interactive Marketing* 13 (1), pp. 55-65.

Lee, H. (1996). "Effective Inventory and Service Management Through Product and Process Redesign", *Operations Research* 44 (1), pp. 151-159.

Lee, H. L. (2000). "Creating Value Through Supply Chain Integration", *Supply Chain Management Review.*

Lee, H. L., S. Whang, (2000). "Information Sharing in a Supply Chain", *International Journal of Manufacturing Technology and Management*, 1 (1), pp. 79-93.

March, J. G. (1991). "Exploration and Exploitation in Organizational Learning", *Organization Science*, 2 (1), pp. 71-87.

Rai, A., A. Bush, and A. Tiwana, (2002). *Adaptive Planning and Distribution*, SAP Sponsored Thought Leadership Forum on Adaptive Supply Chain Networks: 1-15.

Rai, A., V. Sambamurthy, (2002). *Adaptive Distribution Networks*, SAP Sponsored Thought Leadership Forum on Adaptive Supply Chain Networks:1-15.
Ravichandran, T., A. Rai, (2000). "Quality Management in Systems Development: An Organizational Systems Perspective", *MIS Quarterly*, 24 (3), pp. 381-415.
Sambamurthy, V., A. Bharadwaj, et al. (2003). "Shaping Agility Through Digital Options: Reconceptualizing the Role of Information Technology in Contemporary Firms", *MIS Quarterly*, 27 (2), pp. 237-264.
Seidmann, A., A. Sundararajan, (1997). *Building and Sustaining Interorganizational Information Sharing Relationships: The Competitive Impact of Interfacing Supply Chain Operations with Marketing Strategy*, International Conference on Information Systems, Atlanta, GA..
Simchi-Levi D., P. Kaminsky, et al. (2000). *Designing and Managing the Supply Chain: Concepts, Strategies, and Case Studies*, Irwin/McGraw-Hill, New York.
Simon, H. (1981). *The Sciences of the Artificial*, MIT Press, Cambridge, Mass.

Review

Reviewer: Amit Basu
Rapporteur: Diederik van Liere

Case Summary

This case describes the development of an in-flight service supply network between Airco and its suppliers. The case describes problems in the following five core process areas: 1) service design, 2) sourcing and procurement, 3) inbound and outbound logistics, 4) production planning, and 5) asset management. The case continues describing four fundamental digital capabilities to resolve the problems in the above mentioned core processes, the digital capabilities are: 1) visibility, 2) process integration, 3) benchmarking and measurement and 4) knowledge discovery.

Case Characteristics

The case has the following characteristics:

- it describes complex processes,
- the network constitutes of different organizations with different capabilities and different seizes,
- change is happening at various levels which add to the complexity or resolving the problems in the different process areas.

These factors make the case suitable for smart business network research.

Case Implications

This case has two implications for both academics and business people; these are the various types of change and interdependence in a network.

The case identifies three types of changes: 1) at the actor level, 2) at the relational level and 3) at the network level. Changes at the actor level can be unforeseen, and at the relational level can be incremental. This raises the challenge of *responsiveness* to meet those changing circumstances. Changes at the network level have a more profound impact and require *adaptiveness* of the actor.

Next, the case illustrates increased *interdependence* in a smart business network. This increased interdependence is a result of:

- reaching agreements on network wide performance measurements,
- shift in decision rights from AirCo to the suppliers,
- greater information sharing.

This creates a challenge for management, process problems that you do not own become your problem because of increased interdependence in the network. These process problems cascade throughout the network and effect the operations of every firm involved in that particular process.

Section 3

Governance of Smart Business Networks

18 Embedded Coordination in a Business Network

Diederik W. van Liere[1], Lorike Hagdorn[1], Martijn R. Hoogeweegen[1], and Peter H. M. Vervest[1]

Introduction

The organizational capabilities to interact with others have been greatly improved as a result of modern information and communications technologies (Butler et Al., 1997; Hall et al., 1997): Nowadays a company can maintain more relationships with more companies at much lower costs than before. What impact does this increased interaction capability have on the company's choice to perform tasks itself or to 'outsource' such tasks to others (the trade-off between 'make' or 'buy')? More specifically, how does this influence the choice of business partners? Business network theories (Miles & Snow, 1992) place the company in a 'business network', a web of business partners linked together in a flexible way to produce different outputs depending on the customer requirements (Vervest & Dunn, 2000). Research (Hoogeweegen, 1997; Hoogeweegen et al., 1999; Wolters, 2002) suggests that such business networks require modularization of the products, the processes, as well as the value chain of interconnected business partners in order to be effective. Business networks would be more 'dynamic', i.e. can generate a greater variety of outputs with higher effective value for the participating 'actor' organizations. Actors would develop more links, or ties, with other actor organizations in their network: They are better able to share their core capabilities and therefore can respond faster, and more effective, to different requirements.

Research Problem and Research Question

The business network is increasingly becoming the locus of resources, knowledge (Kogut, 2000) and innovation (Langlois & Robertson, 1992; Li & Williams, 1999). The modularization of processes and products from within the firm boundary into the business network requires the integration of those modular processes and modular products as well. According to

1 RSM, Erasmus University Rotterdam, PO Box 1738, 3000 DR Rotterdam, The Netherlands: dliere@fbk.eur.nl, lhagdorn@fbk.eur.nl, mhoogeweegen@fbk.eur.nl, vervest@d-age.com

Hinterhuber (2002) the main task of the network orchestrator is the integration and coordination of processes, resources and assets. The coordination and integration task of a network orchestrator poses important research questions to practitioners and academics alike. This chapter will focus on interorganizational coordination of activity components. We have formulated the following research question: "How are activity components coordinated in a business network?"

Modularity as Enabler for Business Networks

Garud and Kumaraswamy (1995) define modularity as "modularity allows components to be produced separately and used inter-changeably in different configurations without compromising sys-tem integrity". This allows for the mix and match of components thereby realizing benefits such as economies of substitution (Garud & Kumaraswamy, 1995), increase strategic flexibility (Sanchez, 1995), focused organizational learning (Sanchez & Collins, 2001) and autonomous innovation (Langlois & Robertson, 1992). Modular products tend to favor a modular organization form, because the design and production processes are not sequential but concurrent and autonomous (Sanchez, 1995). Modular components are "components whose interface characteristics are within the range of variations allowed by a modular product architecture" (Sanchez & Mahoney, 1996). In the case of products they are referred to as "modular components", in the case of service they are referred to as "activity components".

Table 18.1 Building Blocks of a Modular Architecture

Building Blocks of a Modular Architecture	Products	Services
Components	Modular components (Sanchez, 1995)	Activity components (Sanchez, 1995)
Interface	Interface modularity such as slot modularity, bus modularity and sectional modularity (Ulrich, 1995) and combinatorial modularity (Salvador, Forza et al., 2002).	Multi layer modularity; a combination of different types of interface modularity to connect two activity components.
Embedded coordination	Information Structure (Sanchez, 1996)	Standards and protocols

The remainder of this chapter will focus on activity components and services because those two have received less attention in comparison with modular components and products.

Embedded Coordination in a Business Network

The information structure (Sanchez & Mahoney, 1996) provides the specifications for the interfaces of the modular components. Modular components, both tangible and intangible, exhibit embedded coordination (Sanchez, 1995). Embedded coordination is not the result of managerial intention but is the result of the information structure. By defining standards and protocols for activity components, it becomes possible to embed the coordination within the activity components. Standards, protocols, agreements and rules, referred to as procedures from hereon, are part of the coordination activities of managers and employees. By embedding procedures within activity components, coordination tasks are partly automated and efficiency is increased. For example, an activity component can automatically verify data input or establish a link with another business process without human input. Embedded coordination is a form of automation at the business process level; IT greatly increases the efficiency of such activity components. Other benefits include the reduction of errors because of less involvement of employees and reduction of activities like data verification.

Connecting two activity components is more than 'plug-and-play' the two interfaces. The same principle applies to activity components, connections have to be established at the network, transport, syntax, and semantic layer. The network and transport layers are covered by the OSI model (Segot et al., 1991) and have reached maturity and interoperability. How-ever, at the syntax and semantic level is the development of standards still in de velopment, especially with the arrival of XML has the number of standards witnessed a dramatic increase (Pentland, 2004). A syntax standard is a standard that determines how a message should be encoded, a semantic standards gives context and meaning to the syntax level. A se-mantic standard defines the entities and attributes to describe a business process. Each industry is developing its own standard that results in in-compatible standards and consortia competing with one and another. When consensus has been reached at the four levels of standardization, including the syntax and semantic level, interoperability of activity components within and across organizational boundaries becomes possible.

The information structure delineates the modular components or activity components and this in turn forces the firm to select which activity components it will offer in its network. Components, whether they are tangible or intangible, are produced by a combination of resources and capabilities. Resources are the material inputs and data required to produce the activity component. We define a capability (Collis, 1994) as the set of routines and skills that transform resources into an (part of an) activity component that is of value to the customer. An activity component describes specific features of the service bought by the customer. Each activity component a firm owns becomes subject to a "make or buy" decision. This means defining the capabilities of the firm and the strategic importance of the capabilities for the overall product or service architecture. Thus, the firm becomes a bundle of capabilities (Grant, 1996) that is embedded in one or more business networks.

Business Network and the Activity Component Network

The building blocks of a business network are the firms and their ties. In this study, a tie exists when the output of one activity component is the input for the other activity component. Encapsulated in the business network is the activity component network, the building blocks are the distinct activity components and their interfaces. The interfaces are the ties that connect the activity components, for the production of a particular service. The make or buy decision at the activity component level alters the boundary of the firm. The resources function as the input for the capabilities that transform them into an activity component. Beneath the activity component network is the capability and resource network. Resources and capabilities are linked whenever the resource can function as the input for a capability. The relationships between the business network, the activity component network, and the capability / resource network are depicted in Figure 18.1. Controlling the resources or having access to these resources is of strategic importance to a firm. Without access to the proper resources, a firm will find itself quickly in the periphery of a network. Thus, the locus of both resources and capabilities will gradually move away from within the firm boundaries and outwards to the business network. Figure 1 illustrates how resources, capabilities, activity components are linked and together form a business network.

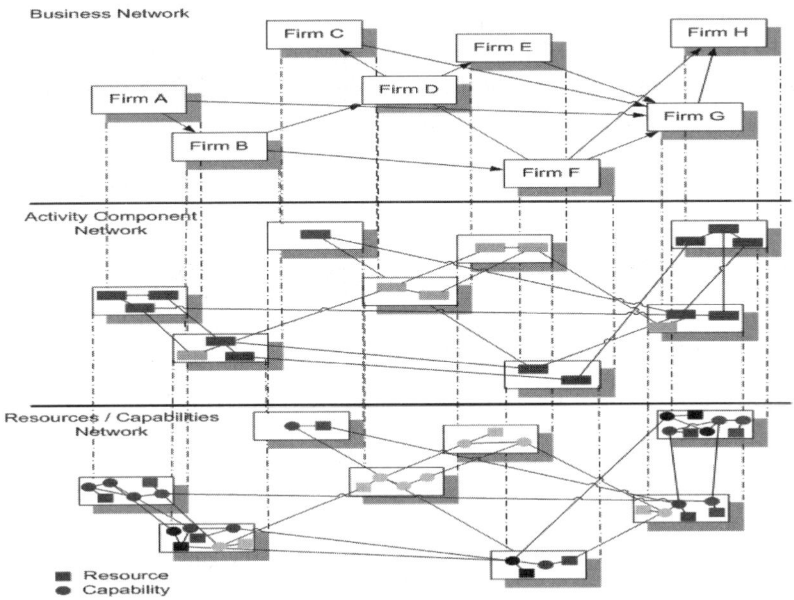

Fig 18.1 Relationship between business network and activity component network

ABZ and the Dutch Insurance Industry

The Dutch Insurance industry consisted in 2001 of 981 non life insurance firms, 261 life insurance firms and 961 pension funds (Verzekeringsstatistiek, 2003). The premium income of the non life insurance firms in 2001 was 15.5 billion Euro and the life insurance firms had a premium income of 25.5 billion Euro (Verzekeringsstatistiek, 2003). In 2002 there were a total of 21,590 intermediaries active in the Dutch insurance industry (Verzekeringsstatistiek, 2003), and 408 underwriting agents. An underwriting agent can accept a customer without prior consent of the insurance firm, an intermediary cannot do this. Of those 21,590 intermediaries, only 25 firms had 100 employees or more and 500 intermediaries had between 10 and 100 employees. The fragmented nature characterizes the intermediary market, of the 21,590 intermediaries 6,070 are one-man businesses (Verzekeringsstatistiek, 2003).

Background of ABZ

ABZ was founded in 1997 and was a merger between the Assurance Data Network, Atriserv, Eurotax, Audalet, Arisco and other firms. The Assurance Data Network, founded in the late eighties, facilitated data communication between intermediaries and insurance firms. Audalet was also founded in the late eighties and its goal was to introduce a national standard for the calculation of future loss of earning capacity because of bodily injury. Eurotax existed for 40 years and was operating in 16 European countries offering damage calculation information for car insurance. Atriserv offered the insurance industry electronic network services to exchange general and administrative information using a general standard. Finally, Arisco offered services and products to optimize damage claims.

These companies merged and since 1997 operate under the brand ABZ, since then ABZ has transformed itself into a trusted Business Service Provisioner (tBSP) who supports, improves, and integrates business processes in the insurance business network. Typical customers of ABZ are insurance firms and the intermediaries who sell insurance products to the customer. The difference between an Application Service Provider (ASP) and a Business Service Provisioner is that an ASP only focuses on the application layer, while a BSP also takes care of the content, business, and presentation layers.

"Our business focuses on improving both efficiency and effectiveness of process governance and business processes. There are two sides to this: first, there is the functional or technological aspect, how could you organize your business? Secondly, is there is the stakeholder aspect, what are the interests of each party involved? How can you cope with both competitive and non-competitive issues? We are trusted and neutral, and we will not interfere with the business of our customers" (source: Chief Technology Officer ABZ).

ABZ vision is that companies will automatically connect their applications and business processes using the Internet to increase jointly the effectiveness and efficiency of business processes. ABZ has chosen to function as a centralized integration hub and it uses the Schiphol, the airport, metaphor to describe itself. They function as the hub that offers the necessary infrastructure to connect business processes across organizational boundaries and are the network developer who develops new standards for interoperability of activity components that allow for further electronic integration.

The Assurance Data Network Case

The Assurance Data Network (ADN) is a communication network for the Dutch insurance industry and was started in the late eighties based on EDI

/ EDIFACT standards. Its goal was to connect electronically insurance firms with their intermediaries and underwriting agents to compete with direct writers. Direct writers are insurance firms who do not use intermediaries and where the customer is in direct contact with the insurance firm. Because of the direct contact between the customer and the direct writers, the direct writers has more up to date and detailed information about the customers and had at the time a higher level of efficiency because it did not faced the challenges of connecting business processes across organizational boundaries. Insurance firms, intermediaries, and underwriting agents communicate electronically at every stage of the insurance product life cycle. Figure 18.2 shows the different stages of the insurance product life cycle in the Dutch insurance industry. All the activity components depicted in Figure 18.2 have their origin at the intermediary, but the insurance firm has to administer at most stages. For example, the "close deal", "prolongation", "mutation", "inform" and "terminate" involve communication between the intermediary and insurance firm and the activity components "close deal", "prolongation" and "inform" take primarily place at the insurance firm, see also Figure 18.3.

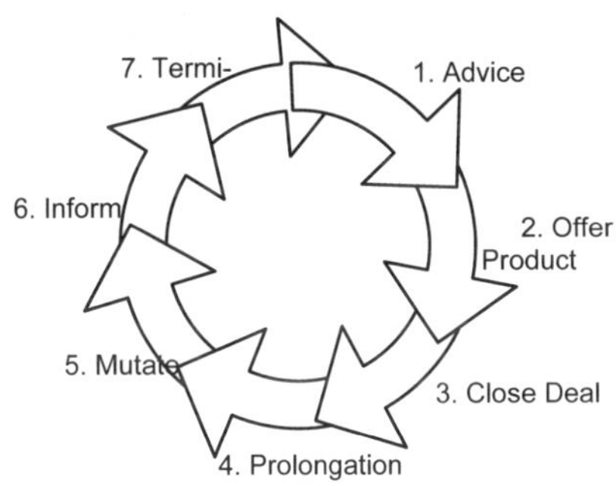

Fig 18.2 Activity Components Needed to Offer an Insurance Product

The cycle starts when a consumer wants to have advice regarding a certain risk he has. This advice is offered by the intermediary who translates those wishes into a specific product. Next, if the product matches the customer wishes the deal is closed and the applicant is being checked in numerous databases whether he committed fraud. During the prolongation phase, the intermediary receives an amount of money for keeping the customer. The execution of the prolongation is on a monthly basis and in 2002 the Assurance Data Network conducted 95,000,000 of these transactions. Mutate refers to changes about the customer data in the intermediary database. During the inform phase the mutations of the previous phase are being communicated with the insurance firm. In 2002, this accounted for 600,000 messages. The final stage of the insurance product life is "Terminate", the customer decides to end his / her insurance and this has to be communicated to the intermediary and insurance firm as well.

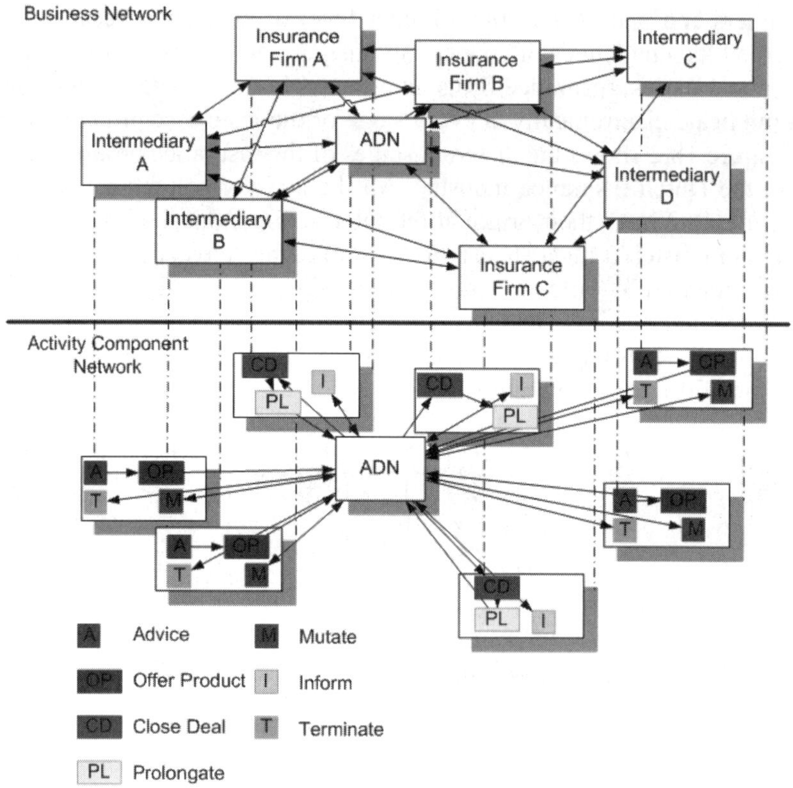

Fig 18.3 The Activity Component Network and Business Network for Non-Life Insurance Products

Figure 18.2 shows the different activity components that are needed in the business network to be able to sell an insurance product. Figure 18.3 illustrates the activity component network and the business network; the capabilities from Figure 18.2 are distributed among the parties that are involved with selling insurance products.

A comparable network was developed for the mortgages business, the Mortgage Data Network (HDN) and for consumer loans business, the Finance Data Network (FDN). Fig. 18.4 shows the situation in 1994. This illustrates only the electronic communication using the AND, FDN and HDN. There are direct ties between the different participants of the each network but they have been left out.

Properties of these networks were that the networks are closed. Especially for the intermediary is this troublesome. An intermediary has to have three different infrastructures, three sets of standards, three sorts of security and has to cope with three different standard setting bodies. Only single products could be communicated electronically, it was not possible to attach more than one product to a customer and this meant redundant data entry. Furthermore, the networks are asynchronous, which means that once a day all the messages (such as offer a product, mutate a product or a prolongation) are sent and received.

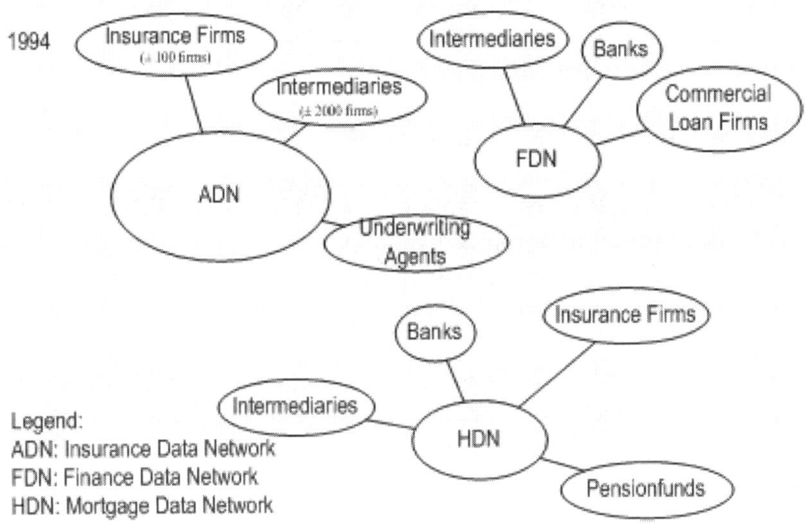

Fig 18.4 The Insurance, Finance, and Mortgage Business Networks

While the communication layer and the syntax layer have been standardized, the level of electronic integration (Malone et al., (1987) is lower than expected. The reason is that intermediaries, insurance firms and the software application providers do not strictly adhere to the standards that lead to the following possible standard conflicts, see Figure 18.5. There are two reasons for software application providers not to adhere to the standards, 1) misinterpretation of the standard, 2) standards are updated twice a year and this requires continuous development efforts of the software firms.

Some are too small and have not enough money to keep in pace with the development of the standards.

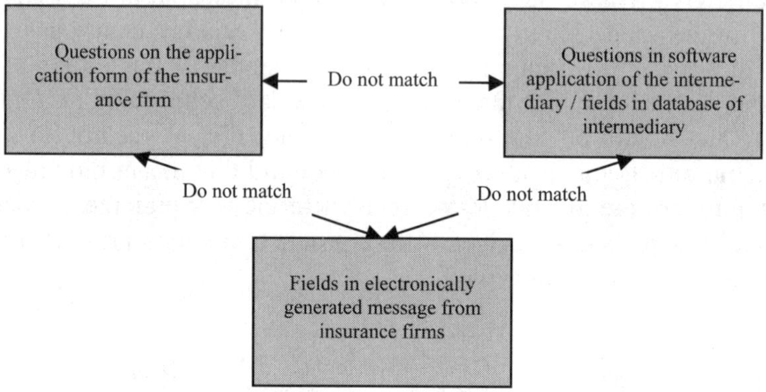

Fig 18.5 Possible sources of standard conflicts

Within each standard conflict, there are three potential errors:

- Entity level: required entities are missing or asking forbidden entities,
- Value level: entering forbidden values,
- Relational level: certain combinations of values and entities are forbidden.

These errors lead to the situation by which some insurance firms stopped using the ADN, and asked their intermediary to fax the mutations, or the errors had to be fixed manually using the telephone.

In theory, the benefits of electronic integration should outweigh the costs and lead to the creation of efficient business relations. Adherence to the standards was not strictly enforced. As result ADN did not fully live up to its mission, i.e. to make insurance firms more competitive vis-à-vis the direct writers. The reason that standards were not enforced was because none of the parties took that responsibility. The large intermediary firms chose software that did adhere to the standards, the very small intermediaries did not participate in ADN, and the other intermediaries were very cautious with any interference from the insurance firms. Moreover, usually one intermediary deals with on average ten different insurance firms: The fact that standards kept evolving and insurance firms customized the standards for themselves made the situation even more complicated.

Another common problem with standardization is that two or more levels are merged into one single standard, for example the syntax and transport layer are merged into one standard. It creates inflexibility of the standard and lock-in effects. This has happened for example with EDI and EDIFACT that became technically separate standards. ABZ recognized this potential problem early on, and was very strict in keeping the semantic and syntax level separate. This has allowed them to migrate quickly to the XML language without having to develop a new semantic standard.

The situation of ADN has changed by 2004 significantly. The three incompatible standards used in 1994 by the Insurance Data Network, the Mortgage Data Network and the Loans Data Network have been integrated in an All Finance Model. The All Finance Model is used to describe a broad range of products in a uniform way: non life insurances, life insurances, various medical insurances, mortgages, universal life (an insurance product with a form of investment), employee benefits (including various insurances, retirement and health care insurances). Over one hundred insurance firms, 25 software application developers, and 5000 intermediaries have adopted the All Finance Model. The Mortgage Data Network has not yet adopted this new standard as of early 2004 but expectations are that this will happen soon (source: Standards and Certification Manager).

To assure the independence of the different standards, a new Standard Body has been established called SIVI, see Figure 18.6. SIVI has taken over the responsibility for standards developing and maintaining tasks of ABZ and is responsible for further development of those standards. Thus, the end-users take responsibility for their business process and the requirements for standards that emerge from that process. ABZ continues its role as a provider of standardization for the Dutch Insurance Industry. Not only at the semantic level have changes taken place, the network infrastructure has changed as well. The current network is an open Internet based one, one that is synchronous, and can handle multiple products simultaneously.

Because of the adoption of more generic standards and the usage of XML, which can check whether messages are valid, the three isolated business networks are becoming more integrated, see Fig. 6. This means for the intermediaries less costs because of one standard, and one infrastructure, but also for the customer a higher level of service. While the old semantic standards still exist, they are being phased out.

Furthermore, three new types of standards have been designed, aimed at the process, transaction, and presentation level. These three standards facilitate the coordination of business processes that cross multiple organizations and applications, or, in terms of Malone et al. (1987), electronic integration. The transaction standard Generic Interface Manager (GIM) aims at the 25 software applications built for the intermediaries and the different extranets being built by the insurance firms. The process atlas describes in depth the activity components of the insurance life cycle (see Fig. 2). GIM establishes the connection between the application running at the intermediary and the extranet, which is the portal to the back office of the insurance firm. Finally, the "Style Guide" aims at a uniform web user interface and uniform data entry for the extranets, the goal is to minimize learning curves for the intermediaries using the different extranets.

Table 18.2 Development of the Dutch Insurance Standards 1994 – 2004

Situation		**Situation**
Standard Body Agreements		Standard Body Agreements
ADN, HDN, FDN data catalogues	**Semantic** - process standard - transaction standard -data standard - presentation standard	Process Atlas Generic Interface Manager (GIM) All Finance Model (AFM), HDN, FDN cat. Style Guide
EDIFACT	**Syntax**	EDIFACT - XML
X400	**Transport**	HTTP(S), SOAP, ebXML, SMTP
TCP / IP	**Network**	TCP / IP

The pressure towards the software application builders and insurance firms to adhere to the agreed standards is increasing with SIVI as an independent party. The penalty for non-compliance with a standard will be higher because other firms will refuse to cooperate with a firm that behaves in a non-compliant way. While at the semantic level the standards are reaching maturity, a new problem has evolved but this time at a lower level, namely the transportation layer due to the wide assortment of transport standards.

"Sometimes the data has been standardized but the transport layer not! So while you and I both talk Dutch, I use the telephone and you use e-mail, and so we still need a connector to connect those two worlds while we do speak the same language. This is a common problem, the language is standardized, but the transport layer is not." Nevertheless, due to the far-reaching efforts of standardization at the four levels of process integration, the three separate business networks are being integrated.

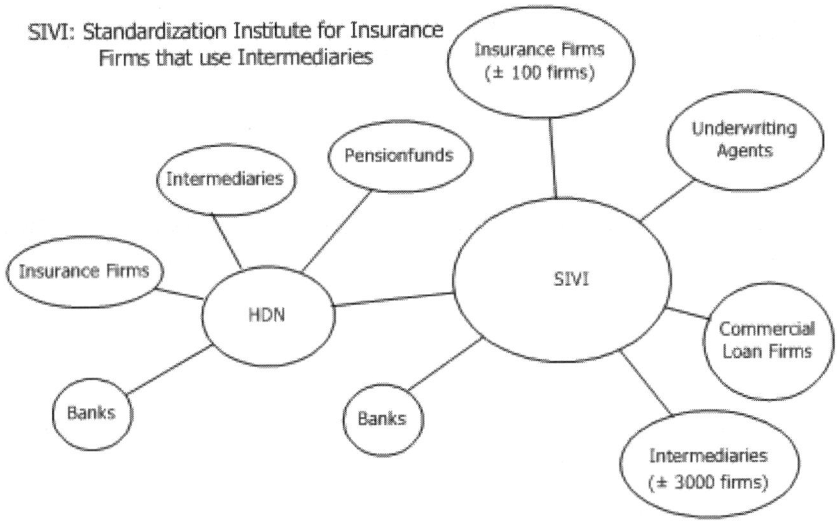

Fig 18.6 Integration of the Insurance, Finance, and Mortgage business networks

Discussion

By embedding coordination in standards at the network, transport, syntax and semantic level, business process interoperability across organizational boundaries becomes a reality. This process interoperability is a first step in developing a "quick-connect capability" (Sanchez, 1995). A quick connect capability is the capability to quickly establish an interorganizational tie that facilitates the exchange of information and transactions. Establishing such interorganizational ties is a complex process both at the technological and at the firm level. Some sort of cooperation or exchange has to be established between two firms before they can implement a quick connect capability. However, even when two firms have a business relationship and see the benefits of electronically connecting, there are the technological hurdles to be taken. Standards and protocols have to be developed at the different levels (network, transport, syntax and semantic), the interfaces of business processes need to be standardized or modularized in order to connect them together, and agreements have to be reached about responsibilities and tasks.

Embedding coordination in the business process results in efficiency gains unless there are invalid interpretations of the standards or standards are not strictly enforced, as was the case in the Dutch insurance industry. Benefits of embedded coordination are 1) business process coordination is automated thereby increasing transaction speed, 2) errors are reduced thereby improving quality and 3) the business network as a whole has the capacity to quickly embrace new firms in the production process of products and services and thereby making the network more agile.

ADN illustrates the advantages of the use of modularity. For example, it gave them the flexibility to quickly adapt to the XML standard while there was no interference with standards at other layers. Furthermore, by connecting the three separate networks it is now possible to offer a wider range of products to the customer while using a limited set of activity components.

Returning to the research question "How are activity components coordinated in a business network?" the ABZ case has illustrated that by embedding coordination in standards and protocols, activity components are electronically coordinated. This is a necessary step to reach activity component interoperability. Interoperability of activity components leads to the creation of new business networks or the integration of existing business networks.

References

Butler, P., Hall T.W., A.M. Hanna, L. Mendonca , B. Auguste, and A. Sahay, (1997). "A Revolution In Interaction", *The McKinsey Quarterly* (1), pp. 4-23.

Collis, D.J. (1994). "Research Note - How Valuable Are Organizational Capabilities", *Strategic Management Journal*, 15, pp.143-152.

Garud, R, A. Kumaraswamy, (1995). "Technological and Organizational Designs For Realizing Economies of Substitution", *Strategic Management Journal*, 16, pp. 93-109.

Grant, R.M. (1996). "Toward a Knowledge-Based Theory of The Firm", *Strategic Management Journal*, 17, pp.109-122.

Hinterhuber, A. (2002). "Value Chain Orchestration in Action and The Case of the Global Agrochemical Industry", *Long Range Planning*, 35 (6), pp. 615-635

Hoogeweegen, M.R. (1997). *Modular Network Design - Assessing the Impact of EDI*, Erasmus University Rotterdam.

Hoogeweegen, M.R., W.J.M. Teunissen, P.H.M. Vervest, and R.W. Wagenaar, (1999). "Modular Network Design: Using Information and Communication Technology to Allocate Production Tasks in a Virtual Organization", *Decision Sciences*, 30 (4), pp.1073-1103.

Kogut, B. (2000). "The Network As Knowledge: Generative Rules and the Emergence of Structure", *Strategic Management Journal*, 21 (3), pp. 405-425.

Langlois, R.N., P.L. Robertson, (1992). "Networks and Innovation in a Modular System - Lessons From the Microcomputer and Stereo Component Industries", *Research Policy*, 21 (4), pp. 297-313.

Li, F., H. Williams, (1999). "Interfirm Collaboration Through Interfirm Networks", *Information Systems Journal*, 9 (2), pp. 103-115.

Malone, T., J. Yates, and R. Benjamin, (1987). "Electronic Markets and Electronic Hierarchies: Effects of Information Technology on Market Structure and Corporate Strategies", *Communications of the ACM*, 30 (6), pp. 484-497.

Miles, R.E., C.C. Snow, (1992). "Causes of Failure in Network Organizations", *California Management Review*, 34 (4), pp. 53-72

Pentland, B.T. (2004). "Towards an Ecology of Inter-Organizational Routines: A Conceptual Framework for the Analysis of Net-Enabled Organizations", *Proceedings of the 37th Hawaii International Conference on System Sciences*.

Salvador, F., C. Forza, and M. Rungtusanatham, (2002). "Modularity, Product Variety, Production Volume, and Component Sourcing: Theorizing Beyond Generic Prescriptions", *Journal of Operations Management*, 20 (5), pp. 549-575.

Sanchez, R., (1995). "Strategic Flexibility in Product Competition", *Strategic Management Journal*, 16, pp. 135-159.

Sanchez, R., (1996). "Strategic Product Creation: Managing New Interactions of Technology, Markets, and Organizations", *European Management Journal*, 14 (2), pp. 121-138.

Sanchez, R., R.P. Collins, (2001). "Competing - and Learning - in Modular Markets", *Long Range Planning*, 34 (6), pp. 645-667.

Sanchez, R., J.T. Mahoney, (1996). "Modularity, Flexibility, and Knowledge Management in Product and Organization Design", *Strategic Management Journal*, 17, pp. 63-76.

Segot, H., C. Lecerf, and P. Joly (1991). "Network Management - State of the Standards", *Annales Des Telecommunications - Annals of Telecommunications*, 46 (7-8), pp. 425-433.

Ulrich, K. (1995). "The Role of Product Architecture in the Manufacturing Firm", *Research Policy*, 24 (3), pp. 419-440.

Vervest, P.H.M., A. Dunn, (2000). *How to Win Customers in the Digital World - Total Action or Fatal Inaction*, Springer-Verlag, Berlin.

Verzekeringsstatistiek Cv. (2003). *Dutch insurance industry figures*, Verbond van Verzekeraars

Wolters, M.J.J. (2002). *The Business of Modularity and the Modularity of Business*, Erasmus University Rotterdam.

19 Supply and Demand Driven Coordination in Smart Business Networks

Otto Koppius[1] and Eric van Heck[1]

Introduction

It has often been noted that an organization faces a difficult task in balancing short-term and long-term requirements (Christensen, 1997; Christensen & Bower, 1996). Similar balancing of seemingly conflicting demands has been noted in many guises for a single organization, e.g. efficiency vs. flexibility (Adler et al., 1999), exploration vs. exploitation (March, 1991), static vs. dynamic (or strategic) flexibility (Sanchez and Mahoney, 1996) or customer-oriented vs. market-oriented (Slater and Narver, 1998). Within the context of a business network, it has received much less attention though, even though it seems equally crucial there. Perhaps the best terminology is the distinction between *adaptation* and *adaptability*. Adaptation is the ability to fit a narrowly defined market segment, whereas adaptability is the ability to respond to market change (cf. Weick, 1979; McKee, Varadajan & Pride, 1989; Lukas, 1999). As the primary focus of a smart business network is that of fulfilling current customer preferences, the emphasis is on adaptation at the expense of adaptability, which potentially jeopardizes the long-term health of the network. So, the central question of this study is: how does a *smart business network* manage adaptation and adaptability?

To answer this question, we focus on a sector that has seemingly been very successful in ensuring adaptability while maintaining adaptation, namely the Dutch Flower Industry. This industry has been the world leader in the flower industry over the last 30 years and thus seems a suitable case for analyzing a successful balance between short-term and long-term goals. We focus on the role of the Dutch Flower Auctions as network orchestrators (Lorenzoni & Baden-Fuller, 1995; Hoogeweegen et al, 1999; Hinterhuber, 2002) of the network of growers and buyers. We show how the flower auctions simultaneously employ both supply-driven and demand-driven market mechanisms and that these each emphasize adaptation and

[1] Erasmus University's Rotterdam School of Management, PO Box 1738, 3000 DR Rotterdam, The Netherlands; o.koppius@fbk.eur.nl, e.heck@ fbk.eur.nl

adaptability to varying degrees, by analyzing in detail the business rules that are embedded in these market mechanisms. Through a study of several electronic market initiatives in the last decade, we show how IT has enabled the introduction of more complex business rules, removed certain business rules altogether and reinforced successful existing business rules, making the problem of adaptability easier to manage by allowing for more varied forms of network coordination.

Theory

Given our focus on network coordination, the question arises: how do network members coordinate activities among themselves? One strategy is decentralized coordination, in which network coordination "emerges" from coordination at the dyadic level. For instance in a standard supply chain setting where the supplier coordinates with the producer, the producer coordinates with the distributor, the distributor coordinates with the retailer and the retailer coordinates with the consumer. However, optimal coordination at the local level will often lead to suboptimal coordination at the global level (Lee and Whang, 1997), making it a somewhat problematic approach. This implies that at least a partial form of centralized coordination is necessary to improve network performance. One form this can take is by establishing a *network orchestrator*. Such a network orchestrator has an overview of the resources and capabilities of the network members on one hand and the demands of the end-customers on the other hand. The network orchestrator is responsible for configuring the network such that customer and network member preferences are satisfied. Examples of this network orchestration role can be found in the role of the *"impannatori"* in the Prato industrial district (Kumar, van Dissel and Bielli, 1998), export agencies (Ellis, 2003) or the lead underwriter in the security issuing process (Podolny, 1994; Pollock, Porac and Wade, 2004).

The examples in these articles highlight that these network orchestrators have to balance the short-term and long-term interests of the network. For instance in an IPO process for a relatively unfavorable deal, the lead underwriter is less likely to engage high-status underwriters in the network (even though this would improve the profitability of that particular deal). This is because the risk of a bad outcome may reduce the chances of being able to involve those high-status underwriters in future deals in which they could be even more useful (Pollock, Porac and Wade, 2004). A description of a similar balancing act is given by Ellis in an interesting analysis of international trade intermediaries (ITIs). ITIs are export agencies that are used by companies seeking to enter new markets with which they are unfamiliar. They thus seek the help of an ITI to connect to the network of customers in the target country. As these ITIs are primarily vehicles for exchange, their focus is on opening new markets and maintaining existing markets for as long as possible. A crucial aspect of the mediated markets created by the ITI is that, from the viewpoint of the ITI, have a limited lifespan. As the supplier organization becomes more experienced with the market in the target country, it will develop a network of customers of its own and thus need to rely less and less on the ITI's network. This will eventually lead to the supplier organization taking over the ITI's role in managing and maintaining the market for their own products. Thus, while an ITI obviously has to pay attention to the problem of adaptation, i.e. it has to ensure that its existing customers and markets are well-served, the problem of adaptability, in this case actively creating new markets for potential customers, is particularly salient for an ITI. It is particularly this task of balancing the short-term and long-term requirements of the network that makes the role of the network orchestrator unique and complex.

Ellis' analysis highlights that the function of the network orchestrator (in his case the ITI) needs to be analyzed in the context of the networks on both sides of the exchange that it is mediating. Wathne and Heide (2004) similarly argue that the analysis of relationship governance needs to shift from the dyadic level of buyer-supplier to the triadic level of supplier-manufacturer-buyer. They show that a manufacturer's ability to adapt in an existing relationship with a downstream customer, is dependent on the relationship the manufacturer has with its upstream supplier. Another way to think about this is that from the manufacturer's perspective, downstream markets are designed differently than upstream markets. Using a transaction cost perspective, Wathne and Heide (2004) outline two approaches to govern the uncertainty of the upstream relationship. The first approach is selection of exchange partners, for instance through qualification and inspection programs. The second approach centers around designing proper incentive structures through mutual relation-specific investments and lock-in situations. They show that both approaches, i.e. more stringent selection of suppliers and better incentive alignment, reduce upstream uncertainty and improve the ability to adapt downstream, but that achieving adaptation by means of aligning incentives is more difficult than by means of selection. This is not to say that incentive alignment is less important for the functioning of a business network, because a study of the European Patent Office shows that incentive (re-)alignment was a key factor in the redesign of the EPO's business network (Delporte-Vermeiren, Vervest & van Heck, 2004).

This underscores the point made earlier that the network orchestrator faces a complex task. For instance, Hinterhuber (2002) outlines the following four functions that a network orchestrator needs to fulfill:

1. *Network Architect*: defining network objectives and selecting network members,
2. *Network Judge*: setting performance standards for network members,
3. *Network Developer*: developing the network's physical and intellectual assets,
4. *Network Leader*: instilling reciprocity, a "network spirit" in network members.

Of these four functions, only the function of network developer (and perhaps the network architect to some degree) is explicitly aimed at the long-term problem of adaptability (see in this respect also Kogut (2000)) as the other function are geared towards the functioning of the current network, i.e. adaptation. Similarly, Ritter and Gemunden's (2003) concept of network competence is defined as the ability to manage the network of relationships effectively. As argued before, this needs to be complemented by an analysis of adaptability.

Some useful lessons in this regard can be drawn from the literature on market orientation and how it is linked to firm innovation, a crucial component of long-term survival. Market orientation consists of three components: customer orientation, competitor orientation and interfunctional coordination (Slater & Narver, 1994). Gatignon and Xuereb (1997) focus on the role of demand uncertainty and show that when demand is uncertain, customer orientation improves the commercial success of a product innovation, but when demand is more certain, it is competitor orientation that improves innovation success. Lukas and Ferrell (2000) find that customer orientation is correlated with more new-to-the-world products and less me-too-products. As this is contrary to Christensen and Bower's (1996) detailed study of the disk drive industry, it is clear that the relationship between adaptation to current consumer wishes and being able to adapt to uncertain future market changes is not straightforward at all.

However, this does not mean that the two are inherently in conflict with each other. For instance, in a study of the Toyota production system, Adler et al. (1999) show that the often-argued paradox between flexibility and efficiency (another variant on the adaptability-adaptation distinction) can be managed or even solved. In particular, they point to the trust that Toyota places in administrative structures, procedures and rules. The positive effect, particularly in dynamic environments, of reliance on explicit guide-

lines and rules has also been noted several researchers in the strategy process literature (Brown & Eisenhardt, 1997; Eisenhardt & Sull, 2001; Grant, 2003; van Fenema & Koppius, 2003), as well as the recent studies on the role of business rules and workflow management in ensuring process agility (Gartner, 2003; Basu & Kumar, 2003; van der Aalst & Kumar, 2003).
It is the starting point of our analysis that the different business rules in an organization affect adaptation and adaptability in different ways. Some evidence for this is provided in Narayandas, Caravella & Deighton's (2002) study of Arrow, a reseller in the electronics industry. The reseller's central business is generating demand for electronics products (not unlike Ellis' (2003) ITIs), but generating demand for commodities (a case of adaptation) is different from generating demand for new technologies (a case of adaptability). In the latter case, the focus is on obtaining a first order for a new technology instead of generating repeat orders. However, obtaining a first order requires more effort from the reseller than generating a repeat order. To compensate for this extra effort, new technology supplier have instituted the business rule of "authorized suppliers'. These are the exclusive reseller channels through which that particular technology can be obtained. For the commodity products, this business rule does not apply because there is no special extra effort required from the reseller and therefore the focus is simply on obtaining as broad a market coverage as possible. The simultaneous integrated presence of these different business rules for different products and markets enables the reseller to handle both types of orders, and this integration creates value for its suppliers and customers (Narayandas, Caravella & Deighton, 2002). On a more general level, this shows that supply-driven approaches (creating demand for a supplied new technology, a case of adaptability) can coexist with demand-driven approaches (satisfying customer demand for existing commodity products, a case of adaptation) within one market and even within one firm, in some sense creating an all-in-one market (Kambil et al, 1999). As we will describe in more detail in the empirical section below, this is precisely what we observe in the Dutch flower industry, where the flower auctions employ multiple market mechanisms with different business rules embedded in them. This in turns enables the flower auctions being able to simultaneously handle both supply-driven and demand-driven network configurations, thus allowing them to manage adaptation and adaptability.

Supply versus Demand Driven Network Coordination

In this paper we focus on the role of electronic markets for business network coordination. We ask ourselves:

- How is business logic embedded in electronic markets for smart business networks?
- Can different types of business logic be distinguished and what is its relationship with network performance?

Business logic is defined as explicit business rules for conducting business with a business network. In our research we focus on the flower industry. We compare two different business logics in that industry:

1. The *supply-driven network configuration* of cut flowers coordinated via spot markets with the help of the traditional and electronic flower auctions,
2. The *demand-driven network configuration* of cut flowers coordinated via forward markets with the help of traditional and electronic flower brokers.

The following differences could be distinguished between the supply-driven and demand-driven network configurations, see Table 1. The theoretical analysis above of the two different types of networks, coupled with the long-term success of the Dutch Flower Industry, leads to our proposition:

Proposition: *A smart business network will ensure adaptation and adaptability by employing both supply-driven as well as demand-driven coordination mechanisms.*

In the analysis of the cases we show how different IT-enabled markets embed different business logics and we analyze how these logics related to different types of network outcomes We are especially interested in how rules of executing and coordinating activities of the business network are embedded in the business operating systems of the participating companies and how these IT driven systems might make the network smarter.

Each of the cases are analyzed and described in depth. We will use the following questions that will guide our analysis of the different cases:

- What are important business rules in the network configuration? Why?
- How are business rules embedded in IT systems?
- Which business logic contributes to the network performance?

Table 19.1 Different aspects of supply and demand driven network configurations

Network Description	**Supply-driven network configuration**	**Demand-driven network configuration**
Coordination Mechanism	Auction	Brokerage
Logistical Stream	From growers, via auction to buyers	Direct from growers to buyers
Information Stream	From grower to buyer	From buyer to grower
Financial Stream	Payment after delivery	Delivery after payment
Network Objectives	**Supply-driven networks**	**Demand-driven networks**
Flexibility	Long-term (adaptability)	Short-term (adaptation)
Expected Network Outcome	Establish price and bring product to end-customer	Satisfy customer demand
Price Transparency	High	Low
Product Quality	Focus on freshness and reputation	Focus on services and delivery time
Competition Among Suppliers	High	Low
Supplier Income	Unpredictable	Predictable
Innovations	Product itself	Services around product

KOA Case: Auction Market, Supply-driven Network

Kopen op Afstand (KOA), or remote purchasing, was initiated by both the Aalsmeer Flower Auction (VBA) and FloraHolland, who both have their own systems. The initiative started in the year 1996. KOA uses the same technique as purchasing via the clock. The difference between both systems is that when buying through KOA it is not necessary to be physically present in the auction room. From behind a company desk buyers have access to all auction clocks. This offers the advance of organizing the purchasing process closer to the wholesaler's own business processes and thereby increases efficiency. It is possible to connect data on purchased batches through their own system immediately, and thus process integration is achieved. When buying through KOA, an electronic purchase agreement is received real-time, if products are bought in front of the clock the purchase agreement has a delay of one minute. Through KAO (Klok Aanbod Online) it is possible to see in advance what products are being put up for auctioning at which clock. This offers the buyer the advantage of knowing when and where to buy. By marking the batches that are interesting, the buyer receives a signal that will be given in due time and indicates that the product is about to be auctioned and the buyer can switch to the correct clock. The technology used for KOA is ISDN direct lines in combination with the Internet. This makes it possible for buyers to log into the system from every place, as long as they are members and thus have access to the system.

In May 2002 the number of subscribers, i.e. buyers, for KOA initiated by the VBA reaches 70. KOA has a firm but controlled grow of 50% in comparison with last year. The KOA system is steadily growing without additional financial sponsoring.

FlowerXL Case: Brokerage Market, Demand-driven Network

FlowerXL is an initiative started by the Aalsmeer Flower Auction. The description of FlowerXL is taken from Blok et al. (2003). FlowerXL is VBA's electronic information and ordering system that connects growers with exporting and importing wholesalers via the Internet. The wholesalers can choose from a wide committed assortment, in large batches at anytime and are ensured that these products will be as fresh as possible (and of a consistent high quality) what will satisfy customer's demand more easily. Using FlowerXL saves the wholesalers time and effort. They still play the same role in the supply chain, only now have the advantage of an efficient buying- and selling tool. The orders are directly electronically given to the exporting wholesaler and grower. These can arrange transport, and do not need to keep products in stock. Furthermore, fewer mistakes will be made because of the efficient exchange of information between the wholesalers and the growers. Currently FlowerXL is evolving into "VBA Handelsplein".

The system started with only one customer, but is growing. It is still operational but far from the intended scale. Its origin is called Floweraccess which was started in 1995. Due to the fact that trade through this channel takes place in large batches, the addition XL (eXtra Large) was given to the word Flower.

Comparing Two Cases

Given the exchange processes the two cases are compared, see Table 2. The main differences are in the search, pricing, and logistics processes.

Table 19.2 Comparison Exchange Processes of KOA and FlowerXL

Exchange Processes	**Case 1: KOA Electronic Auction**	**Case 2: FlowerXL Electronic Brokerage**
Search	Buyers use electronic system to search for auctioned supply	Buyers use electronic system to search potential supply
Pricing	Pricing via Dutch auction mechanism	Pricing via bilateral negotiation between broker and buyer
Logistics	Logistics from grower via auction hall to buyers – hub and spoke system	Logistics directly from grower to buyer – point to point
Payment & Settlement	Within 24 hours via auctioneer	Within specified time frame
Authentication	Products are authenticated by auctioneer	Products are authenticated by broker
Product representation	Physical product representation in auction hall or digital picture online	Digital picture in database
Regulation	Regulated by auctioneer	Regulated by broker
Risk management	Grower risk - not selling – is tackled by analysing auction prices; Buyer risk – not getting what needed – by analysing supply and ordering	Grower risk – needing more flower-growing resources than predicted – is tackled by optimising input resources (energy, light); Buyer risk – not being able to sell what was ordered – is tackled by analysing customer demand
Influence	For grower – sequence of auctioning; For buyer – setting price	For grower – specifying products; For buyer specifying contract
Dispute resolution	By auctioneer.	By broker.

Lessons Learned

The following lessons came out of the analysis. Firstly, we recall our central proposition in this article.

Proposition: *A smart business network will ensure adaptation and adaptability by employing both supply-driven as well as demand-driven coordination mechanisms.*

The two cases show that the combination of supply and demand driven network configurations provide the flower industry with the right balance between adaptation and adaptability and create for a long period of time a profitable network outcome.

Supply-driven Network

In the supply-driven network the Dutch auction model is a rational choice due to the fact that it is supply driven and it assumes bargaining power from the sellers (growers) side. Business network coordination is steered by the (electronic) auction mechanism. It is an excellent allocation mechanism both in terms of finding the best price/buyer but also in terms of speed (time specificity: an asset is time specific if its value is highly dependent on its reaching the user within a specified, relatively limited period of time (Malone et al, p. 486)). Its strength is also that the seller will get immediate market feedback and therefore the auction is a strong impulse for sellers to innovate. Electronic auctions impact the buying behaviour and have some implications for logistics and transport of products. Its weakness is related to the supply orientation.

Important Business Rules

In the supply driven network business rules with regard to pricing by the Dutch auction clock are important and critical. These business rules determine the value of the traded flowers and allocate the supply to the best buyer. It is an efficient mechanism in terms of time; 30,000 transactions are taken place every morning in each of the main auction centres. Secondly, business rules with regard to logistics are critical. These business rules govern the logistical stream of flower and determine how and when flower are distributed to the right buyer.

Embeddedness in IT

Several attempts were developed to implement the auction rules in electronic systems. Some were complete failures like Vidifleur (Kambil & van Heck, 1998), others were very successful for example Tele Flower auction and later KOA. Critical is to automate the business rules with regard to auctioning without creating disadvantages with regard to the logistical business rules. Attempts to create a mixture of auctioning with demand orientation and new logistical forms – see for example Sample Based Auctioning (Kambil & van Heck, 1998) – were not successful. Some new business rules could be implemented in the electronic auction systems like “proxy bidding’ and a warning system when specific products will be auctioned.

Contribution to Network Performance

The network performance in terms of logistical performance and delivery of a variety products is caused by the combination of the strengths of the auction with the strengths of the logistics. The business network therefore is able to deliver within 24 hours flower products around the world. Smartness is related to the auction and logistical capabilities.

Based on the analysis the following hypothesis is formulated.

Hypothesis 1: *Better aggregation of demand information by the open electronic auction systems will increase the adaptability and therefore improve the network performance.*

Demand-driven Network

In the demand-driven network the (electronic) brokerage model is a logical choice due to its forward-driven nature. Business network coordination is steered by the wholesalers/retailers (given the feedback from the end-consumers). It is in terms of allocation mechanism less transparent and will usually lead to less optimal allocations. Usually price information from the open auction market plays a role as a (possibly inaccurate) benchmark. It can be argued that there is less stimulus for innovation (also due to the fact that products are more commodity type of products). Within the demand-driven networks reverse auction markets could be implemented (as we analysed in the fruit industry (Leijdekkers, 2001; van Heck, 2004)). In this reverse auction scenario buyers specify their demand and growers bid to fulfil that demand in terms of quality, lead-time, and price.

Important Business Rules

In the demand driven network business rules with regard to specifying the contract between buyer and grower(s) are important. The broker is connecting buyers with sellers and by specifying the details of the contract the future demand in terms of product, services and delivery time are specified.

Embeddedness in IT

The business rules with regard to direct contract between buyers and sellers could easily be embedded in electronic systems. Several attempts were made to create network wide systems which is much more difficult and most systems failed due to the power balance between flower cooperatives on one hand and wholesalers/retailers on the other hand. Electronic brokerage systems enabled better information exchange between the parties involved in the contract.

Contribution to Network Performance

The network performance in terms of product and logistical performance is related to the demand orientation of the network. Flowers are produced on demand. Smartness of the business network is related to determining the future demand of consumers with regard to flowers.

Based on the analysis the following hypothesis is formulated.

Hypothesis 2: *Better specification of demand information (from end-consumers to growers about consumers preferences and feedback) will increase the adaptation and therefore improve the network performance.*

It is not clear what the impact is of the two different logistical systems. In the supply driven network the hub-and-spoke system allows efficient distribution and transportation from growers to buyers. However, its weakness is that specific logistical demands are hardly being met. In the point-to-point system of the demand oriented network the individual logistical transaction is effectively carried but the overall efficiency is questioned.

Conclusions and Implications

This article makes three key contributions to the literature of electronic markets and smart business networks.

First, it shows that two types of network configurations (supply-driven and demand-driven) with each their own type of business logic and business rules can be distinguished in business networks. Smartness is related to the fact that a business network can handle both configurations at the same time.

Second, it shows how electronic markets function as a network orchestrator in a smart business network and how they manage adaptation and adaptability by facilitating the different network configurations by enabling multiple market-based coordination mechanisms. Both electronic auction markets as well as electronic brokerage markets create adaptability and adaptation capabilities respectively that impacts the overall network performance.

Third, it formulates hypotheses that show how specific business logic contributes to the adaptation and adaptability of the business network.

Although derived from the context of the flower industry it seems to be likely that these results also hold in other industries for example direct sales versus reseller models in the electronics industry or the insurance industry, and production-on-demand versus cash-and-carry in the furniture and automobile industry. Further research needs to develop and test hypotheses in these and other industrial settings.

References

Adler, P.S., B. Goldoftas, and D.I. Levine, (1999). "Flexibility Versus Efficiency? A Case Study of Model Changeovers in the Toyota Production System", *Organization Science,* 10 (1), pp. 43-68.

Basu, A., A. Kumar, (2002). "Research Commentary: Workflow Management Issues in E-Business", *Information Systems Research,* 13 (1), pp. 1-14.

Blok, J., S. Hageraats, E. van Heck, and S. van de Velde, (2003). *Flourishing E-commerce? Key Success Factors for E-commerce in the Dutch Floricultural Sector*, KLICT report, (October).

Brown, S.L., K.M. Eisenhardt, (1997). "The Art of Continuous Change: Linking Complexity Theory and Time-paced Evolution in Relentlessly Shifting Organizations", *Administrative Science Quarterly,* 42 (1), pp. 1-34.

Christensen, C.M. (1997). *The Innovator's Dilemma: When New Technologies Cause Great Firms to Fail*, Harvard Business School Press, Cambridge, Mass.

Christensen, C.M., J.L. Bower, (1996). "Customer Power, Strategic Investment, and the Failure of Leading Firms", *Strategic Management Journal,* 17 (3), pp. 197-218.

Eisenhardt, K.M., D.N. Sull, (2001). "Strategy as Simple Rules", *Harvard Business Review,* 79 (1), pp.106.

Delporte-Vermeiren, D., P.H.M. Vervest, and E. van Heck, (2004). "In Search of Margin for Business Networks: The European Patent Office", *European Management Journal,* 22 (2), pp. 167-182.

Ellis, P.D. (2003). "Social Structure and Intermediation: Market-Making Strategies in International Exchange", *Journal of Management Studies,* 40 (7), pp. 1683-1708.

Gatignon, H., J.M. Xuereb, (1997). "Strategic Orientation of the Firm and New Product Performance", *Journal of Marketing Research,* 34 (1), pp. 77-90.

Grant, R.M. (2003). "Strategic Planning in a Turbulent Environment: Evidence from the Oil Majors", *Strategic Management Journal,* 24 (6), pp. 491-517.

Hinterhuber, A. (2002). "Value Chain Orchestration in Action and the Case of the Global Agrochemical Industry", *Long Range Planning,* 35 (6), pp. 615-635.

Hoogeweegen, M.R., W.J.M. Teunissen, P.H.M. Vervest, and R.W. Wagenaar, (1999). "Modular Network Design: Using Information and Communication

Technology to Allocate Production Tasks in a Virtual Organization", *Decision Sciences,* 30 (4), pp. 1073-1103.

Kambil, A., E. van Heck, (1998) "Reengineering the Dutch Flower Auctions: A Framework for Analyzing Exchange Organizations", *Information Systems Research*, 9 (1), (March), pp. 1-19.

Kambil, A., E. Heck, (2002). *Making Markets: How Firms Can Design and Profit from Online Auctions and Exchanges*, Harvard Business School Press, Mass..

Kambil, A., P.F. Nunes, and D.D. Wilson, (1999). "Transforming the Marketspace with All-in-one Markets", *International Journal of Electronic Commerce*, 3 (4), pp. 11-28.

Kogut, B. (2000). "The Network as Knowledge: Generative Rules and the Emergence of Structure", *Strategic Management Journal,* 21 (3), pp. 405-425.

Kumar, K., H.G. van Dissel, and P. Bielli, (1998). "The Merchant of Prato - Revisited: Toward a Third Rationality of Information Systems", *MIS Quarterly,* 22 (2), pp. 199-226.

Lee, H.L., V. Padmanabhan, and S. Whang, (1997). "The Bullwhip Effect in Supply Chains", *Sloan Management Review,* 38 (3), pp. 93-102.

Leijdekkers, B. (2001). *Omgekeerde Elektronische Veilingen in Vraaggestuurde Ketens*, MSc. Thesis, Erasmus University Rotterdam, (May), (in Dutch).

Lorenzoni, G., C. Badenfuller, (1995). "Creating a Strategic Center to Manage a Web of Partners", *California Management Review,* 37 (3), pp. 146-163.

Lukas, B.A. (1999). "Strategic Type, Market Orientation, and the Balance Between Adaptability and Adaptation", *Journal of Business Research,* 45 (2), pp. 147-156.

Lukas, B.A., O.C. Ferrell, (2000). "The Effect of Market Orientation on Product Innovation", *Journal of the Academy of Marketing Science,* 28 (2), pp. 239-247.

Malone T., J. Yates, and R. Benjamin, (1987). "Electronic Markets and Electronic Hierarchies", *Commun. ACM,* 30 (6), pp. 484-497 (June).

March, J.G. (1991). "Exploration and Exploitation in Organizational Learning", *Organization Science,* 2 (1), pp. 71-87.

McKee, D.O., P.R. Varadarajan, and W.M. Pride, (1989). "Strategic Adaptability and Firm Performance - a Market-Contingent Perspective", *Journal of Marketing,* 53 (3), pp. 21-35.

Narayandas, D., M. Caravella, and J. Deighton, (2002). "The Impact of Internet Exchanges on Business-To-Business Distribution", *Journal of the Academy of Marketing Science,* 30 (4), pp. 500-505.

Podolny, J.M. (1994). "Market Uncertainty and the Social Character of Economic Exchange", *Administrative Science Quarterly,* 39 (3), pp.458-483.

Pollock, T.G., J.F. Porac, and J.B. Wade, (2004). "Constructing Deal Networks: Brokers as Network 'Architects' in the USIPO Market and Other Examples", *Academy of Management Review,* 29 (1), pp. 50-72.

Ritter, T., H.G. Gemunden, (2003). "Network Competence: Its Impact on Innovation Success and Its Antecedents", *Journal of Business Research,* 56 (9), pp. 745-755.

Sanchez, R., J.T. Mahoney, (1996). "Modularity, Flexibility, and Knowledge Management in Product and Organization Design", *Strategic Management Journal,* 17, pp. 63-76.

Slater, S.F., J.C. Narver, (1994). "Does Competitive Environment Moderate the Market Orientation-Performance Relationship", *Journal of Marketing,* 58 (1), pp. 46-55.

Slater, S.F., & Narver, J.C. (1998). "Customer-led and Market-oriented: Let's Not Confuse the Two", *Strategic Management Journal,* 19 (10), pp. 1001-1006.

Van der Aalst, W.M.P., A. Kumar, (2003). "XML-based Schema Definition for Support of Interorganizational Workflow", *Information Systems Research,* 14 (1), pp. 23-46.

Van Fenema, P.C., O.R. Koppius, (2003). "Repertoires of the Strategy Process", *working paper*, Rotterdam School of Management, Rotterdam.

Van Heck, E. (2001). "Innovative Electronic Auctions in Supply and Demand Chains: Empirical Research in the Flower Industry", *Journal of Chain and Network Science*, Vol.1, No.1, pp. 65-76.

Van Heck, E. (2004). "Innovative Electronic Reverse Auctions in Demand Chains: Prototype and Experiments in the Fruit Industry", in: Hendrikse, G., *Restructuring Agricultural Cooperatives*, Rotterdam School of Management, pp. 29-50.

Wathne, K.H., J.B. Heide, (2004). "Relationship Governance in a Supply Chain Network", *Journal of Marketing,* 68 (1), pp. 73-89.

Weick, K. E. (1979). *The Social Psychology of Organizing*, Addison-Wesley, Reading, Mass..

20 The Viable Systems Model Applied to a Smart Network: The Case of the UK Electricity Market

Duncan R. Shaw[1], Bob Snowdon[2], Christopher P. Holland[1], Peter Kawalek[1], and Brian Warboys[2]

Introduction

Beer (1979) and Checkland (1981) have written extensively on how organisations and networks exist within complex environments, which generate emergent demands upon them (Anderson, 1999, p. 218). In order to remain viable these networks have to be able to fulfill these demands but as Haeckel and Nolan (1996) pointed out: emergence cannot be *forecasted* and so a *sense and respond* capability is required. The object of the study is to understand how unforecastable, unplanned for and potentially devastating exogenous shocks to businesses can be mitigated by the benefits of being part of a Smart Network. The contributions of our article apply both to academics and business practitioners and are in its investigation of the concept of Smart Business Networks. In one such network, an electricity market, we illustrate how the smart capability functions at a strategic, business process and technical levels using Beer's Viable System Model (VSM) to analyze it.

Research Method

Our case study of the UK electricity market is an illustration of a complex system that generates highly volatile emergent demands for electricity supply businesses. These businesses use a Smart Network to help meet these demands, which are a legal obligation set by the industry regulator. We suggest that an embedded intelligence allows the accommodation of extreme flux in user demand. These environmental demands are of the nature of communications and control, which are cybernetic problems. Therefore we analyze this case using Beer's VSM, which was designed to analyze highly complex and recursive systems made up of medium term viable sub-systems such as businesses (Beer, 1979).

---

[1] Manchester Business School, Manchester Business School, Booth Street West, University of Manchester, Manchester M15 6PB, UK, dshaw@man.mbs.ac.uk
[2] Department of Computer Science, University of Manchester

We then use the VSM as a framework for delineating this complex system along lines of near decomposability (Simon, 1969, p. 99). We use Simon's concept of near decomposability, operationalised as Beer's VSM, to "modularize" a complex business network and investigate the interaction between its "modules". Of course near decomposability is not the same as complete decomposability so the subsystems exhibit module-like properties (Parnas et al., 1985). Their external connections are loosely coupled (Weick, 1974) *relative* to their internal connections. Their "intensity of interaction" (Simon, 1969, p 90) is greater for internal than external connections. This justifies us thinking of them as *subsystems* and of the overall network as having a heterogeneous structure rather than being a single homogenous object.

Beer describes a system as "a group of elements dynamically related in time according to some coherent pattern". The interrelations are the business processes that are shared between elemental businesses, for example when a vendor business' service or product is composed into that of a customer's meta-process. A business network is a system because the businesses in the network are interrelated via business processes and share dependences such as resources, (e.g. goods and information), and meta-resources such as trust and power.

VSM Analysis of the UK Electricity Market

The UK Electricity Market

The electricity sector in England and Wales is a connected set of electricity producers, suppliers and consumers joined by two networks. The first network carries electricity, the raison d'être of the system, and the second network carries data between the various diverse organisations and private individuals that this sector's supply chain consists of. The second network is used to control the first network.

In March 2001 the UK government introduced New Electricity Trading Arrangements (NETA) in England and Wales (National Audit Office, 2003). These arrangements were designed to use market forces to reduce electricity prices by making the electricity market operate more like other commodity markets. Prior to this the arrangements for trading electricity, known as the Pool, were thought to be uncompetitive and open to manipulation. In October 1997 the Minister for Science, Energy and Industry asked the Office of Electricity Regulation (OFFER), the regulator at that time, to review the way that electricity was traded in England and Wales and to suggest a number of improvements in areas that included reducing the price charged to the user and improving choice, quality and security of supply for electricity users (NAO, 2003).

OFFER's review of the Pool pointed to problems of over regulation that limited the effect of normal market forces such as competition in price setting, together with supply-side and demand-side price influencing. In short the Pool, one of the first examples of a wholesale electricity market in the world, was limited by the complexity of its bidding and price setting mechanism, the inflexibility of its regulations and openness to manipulation of its payment rules (NAO, 2003). The main proposal from the review was that the trading of electricity should become much more market-based. OFFER recommended that the electricity market should operate more like other commodity markets subject to special requirements for physically balancing supply and demand in order to maintain the security and quality of electricity supply.

These special requirements come from the fact that electricity is a commodity that is very difficult and costly to store; and whilst its supply cannot be varied instantaneously its demand does vary instantaneously. Balancing rather than buffering stores is used to stop frequent small power cuts caused by high user demand volatility. The Government demands that users should be shielded from short-term price volatility.

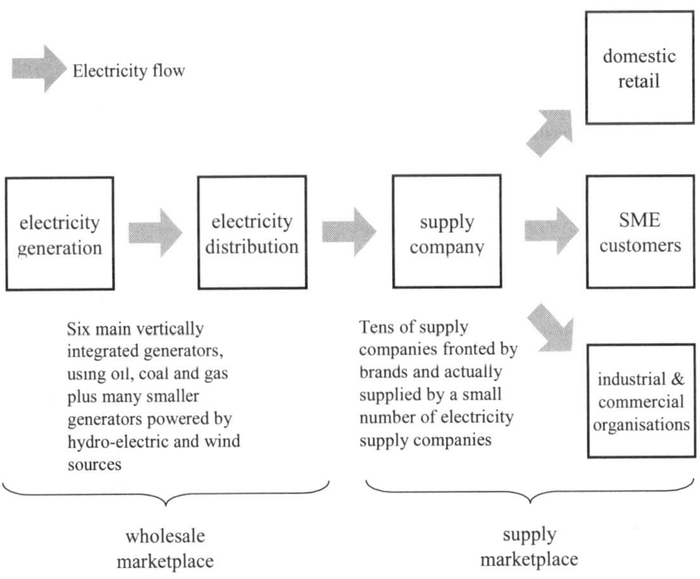

Fig 20.1 Elements of the English and Welsh electricity industry value chain in 2003

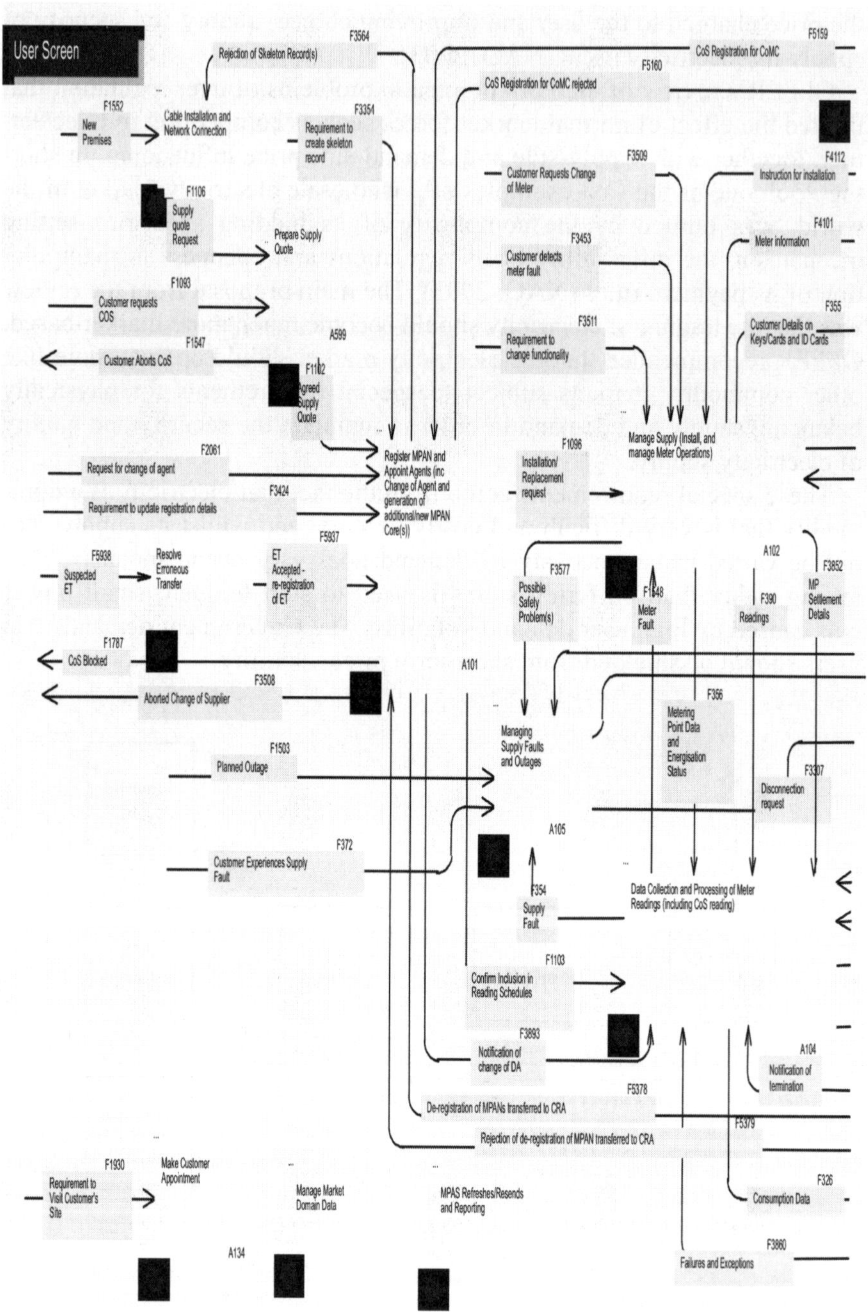

Fig 20.2 Overview diagram of the UK electricity industry key business processes (source: MRASCo)

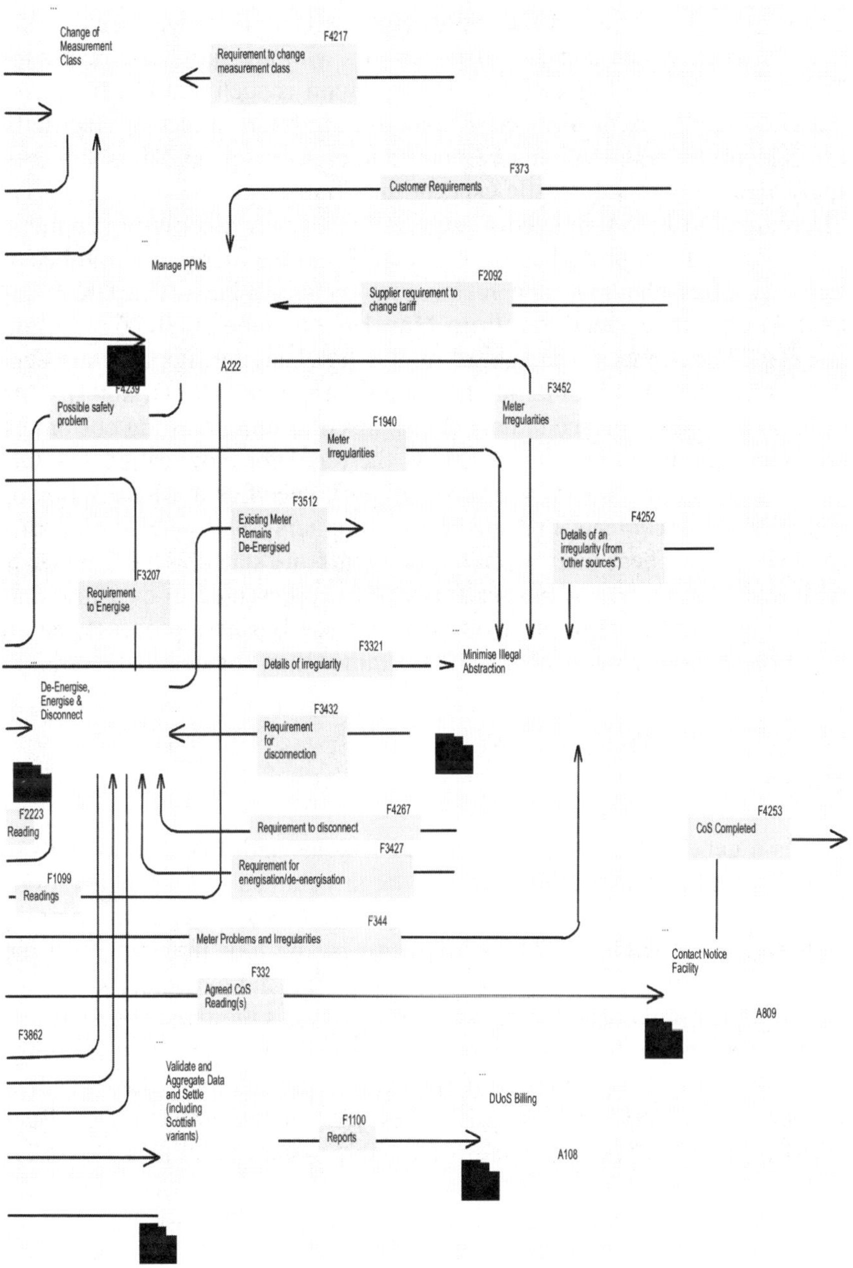

Fig 20.2 (continued)

These recommendations led to the current trading arrangements known as NETA. With NETA the value chain for the industry is divided up into the wholesale marketplace and the supply marketplace. Here we focus on the supply market, which consists of generators who are suppliers, pure suppliers and users (see Figure 20.1). Deregulation is such that Credit Suisse First Boston, a bank, is allowed to trade on the future prices of electricity in the electricity wholesale marketplace and a grocery firm, Sainsbury, can supply electricity to a domestic user for their home.

Deregulation has stimulated a large influx of new electricity suppliers. This increase in suppliers has been in parallel to the increasing number of electricity users changing and rechanging their suppliers. The UK's National Audit Office found that from May 1999 to June 2000, "6.5 million customers - one in four - had saved money by changing supplier, and customers were changing at the rate of 400,000 a month" (NAO, 2004). This has lead to a huge increase in user churn: disconnecting existing customers and connecting new ones. Furthermore, the regulator, now called The Office of Gas and Electricity Markets (Ofgem), specifies a whole series of service level agreements that electricity suppliers must meet during this change process. These mandatory requirements are stated in the form of a highly complicated set of business processes represented in dataflow diagrams. Figure 20.2 shows an overview of these business processes as an indication of how complicated they are rather than for detailed examination.

VSM Analysis

VSM is a general architecture for viable systems and it is used to analyze the ability of this network to deal with large volumes of user registrations and deregistrations by examining the registration and deregistration process from the viewpoints of the subsystems of the four major parties: the user of the electricity; the old electricity supplier; the new electricity supplier; and the regulator, Ofgem. Beer (1979) defines the five subsystems of a viable system and how they interact to control an organization (see Figure 20.3). The decomposition of a system into discrete but interdependent subsystems with different roles is a key part of the VSM model. Beer (1979) defined the five subsystems of a viable system as follows:

- Subsystem 1 consists of operational processes – the "plants",
- Subsystem 2 oversees System 1's processes,
- Subsystem 3 plans operational strategy inside the organisation,
- Subsystem 4 is concerned with outside the system and the future,

- Subsystem 5 sets policy for the system.

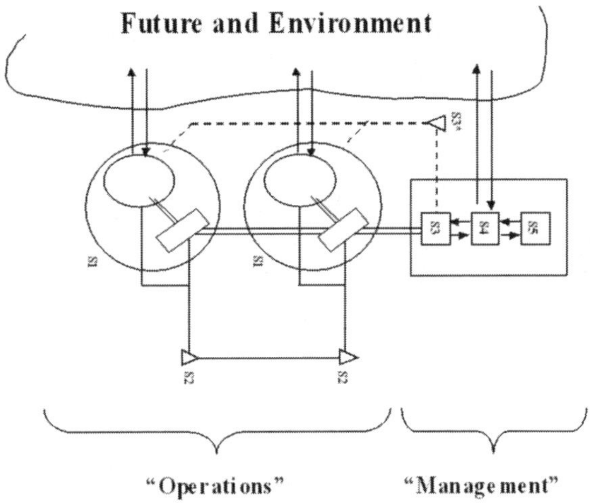

Fig 20.3 Standard VSM diagram showing subsystems

These five subsystems interact to produce all the VSM's behaviors and control the production of these behaviors. We can use the VSM to decompose the market into subsystem roles. We can also use the VSM to decompose the regulator, the electricity suppliers and the users. For example, Subsystem 1, the plant, is the subsystem that supplies electricity in the supplier's system and consumes electricity in the user. The separation of controlling subsystem and controlled subsystem is another property of the VSM.

- Subsystem 1 (operations) – supplying electricity (supplier), using electricity such as the operation of a hairdryer or electric furnace (user), regulating the supply and use of electricity (regulator),
- Subsystem 2 (oversight) – supervising day-to-day electricity supply (supplier), supervising day-to-day electricity use such setting the heat levels of a hair dryer or an electric furnace (user), regulating the supply and use of electricity such as availability and price levels (regulator).
- Subsystem 3 (operations strategy) – supplying electricity efficiently and effectively (supplier), using electricity efficiently and effectively (user), regulating the supply and use of electricity such as checking user satisfaction (regulator),

- Subsystem 4 (outside and future) – dealing with environmental and future requirements that affect the supply of electricity such as oil prices (supplier), dealing with environmental and future requirements that affect the use of electricity such as electricity prices (user), dealing with environmental and future requirements that affect, or are affected by, the supply and use of electricity such as global warming (regulator),
- Subsystem 5 (policy) – whether and how to supply electricity, diversify or change sector (supplier), whether and how to use electricity (user), how to regulate the supply and use of electricity such as for supplier satisfaction, user satisfaction, the satisfaction of both or the satisfaction of another party (regulator).

Herring and Kaplan have used the VSM to generate a Viable System Architecture (VSA) for the interfaces that link a viable system, that is itself a production subsystem (i.e. Subsystem 1) within a greater system, to the rest of the system and its environment (2001, p. 4). For example, a sales office of an electricity supplier is a viable system whose product is new customers. The VSA is developed as a software architecture but because it is based upon a general model for viable systems is applicable to our case. Here the production system is represented by the contents of any of the circles labeled S1 in Figure 20.3. Another example could be a single electricity supply business operating as part of the UK electricity network. It could also be a single factory using electricity. The value of this description of inter-subsystem and environmental interfaces is that it allows an examination of the interface structure and the interfacing protocol.

Herring and Kaplan classify adaptation capabilities into three types: homeostatic (maintaining control variables within parameters), morphostatic (changing the control algorithms that govern homeostasis) and morphogenetic ("acquiring new component and discarding others") (2001, p. 3). A user maintains profitability by incorporating an electricity price increase into the price of its products using homeostatic adaptability. A supplier displays morphostatic adaptation capability when it changes the method it uses to calculate profitability. The TXU Energy demerger is an example of morphogenetic capability used to maintain a threat to viability from negative profitability. All users, suppliers and the regulator display examples of all three types of adaptation capability to remain viable.

The interface structure is itself composed of an operational and a control hierarchy. Each interface between subsystems consists of a communications channel, such as a production manager (Subsystem 3) using an email channel to inform all factory supervisors (Subsystem 3) of the next week's production schedule. This is the operational level. If we were to view the interface itself as a VSM then it is the operational subsystem of the interface (Subsystem 3).

The control level of the interface is separate to the communications channel and acts to maintain homeostasis for its own viability. If this is not possible morphostatic, and ultimately morphogenetic, adaptation then occur. In other words an interface is used whilst it serves its purpose and if it fails to do so then its use is changed; and failing that another interface is used, i.e. the component is swapped out. An example of this from our case is the regulation of a single electricity supplier. If a supplier does not follow the strict business process guidelines set out by the regulator then the regulator takes action.

For example, we will now use the VSM in our analysis to show how the parties interact using different subsystems during a change of supplier process. The simple steps occur in this order:

1. Subsystem 4 of user becomes aware of a supplier offering a better deal,
2. Subsystem 3s of user and new supplier agree the deal parameters and how to connect,
3. Subsystem 3s of user and old supplier agree how to disconnect,
4. Subsystem 1s of user and old supplier disconnect,
5. Subsystem 1s of user and new supplier connect.

Changing supplier involves transferring user information from the old supplier to the new supplier. The regulator row of Table 20.1 shows how the regulator's Subsystem 1 checks the effectiveness of this transfer. If the old supplier takes too long then the regulator's Subsystem 1 communicates with the old supplier's Subsystem 4 to demand an improvement under threat of action to hinder that supplier's policy attainment. In other words the regulator threatens punitive action and the old supplier's Subsystem 4 asks its Subsystem 1 to hurry and its Subsystem 3 to plan how to stop the delay reoccurring.

The Subsystem 4 boxes of the user and suppliers in Table 20.1 are shaded to emphasize that the regulator only interfaces with Subsystem 4. However, if the interface that the regulator uses to communicate its threat is not capable of transmitting, or the supplier is not capable of receiving, then the interface is thus not capable of realizing its goals as an interface.

In our example this may be because the person that transmits the threat is not trained to use email or the person that receives it has left the supplier company. The control system of the interface acts to correct this by, for example, directing the transmitting person to use the telephone or, respectively, acquiring a new reception person. Here the control system for the interface is embodied in the responsibility of the manager in charge of communication with badly performing electricity suppliers.

Table 20.1. The functions of the subsystems of each stakeholder in the electricity user registration and deregistration process

	Subsystem 1: operations	**Subsystem 2: oversight**	**Subsystem 3: operations strategy**	**Subsystem 4: outside and the future**	**Subsystem 5: policy**
Electricity user	Uses and pays for electricity supplied by the old supplier then by the new supplier.	Checks use of, and payment for, electricity is in line with operational strategy.	Plans how to use electricity in line with policy. Plans how to disconnect with one supplier and then connect with the other.	Looks for other electricity uses, *suppliers* and *payment methods* in line with policy (least cost and most dependable service). Finds a better deal.	Use the cheapest electricity from the most dependable source.
Old supplier	Supplies electricity to user, charges and accepts payment. Stops supplying electricity after deregistration.	Checks the user is being supplied and is paying. Checks that supply is stopped after deregistration.	Plans supplying, billing and payment acceptance in line with policy. Plans disconnection and connection.	Looks for other electricity supply sources, supply methods, payment methods and connection/disconnection methods in line with policy. Attempts to forecast demand, regulatory change and other change drivers, including policy change drivers.	Maximize profit from supply versus payment for a high churn market.
New supplier	Starts supplying electricity after registration. Supplies electricity to user, charges and accepts payment.	Checks supply is started after registration. Checks that the user is being supplied and is paying.	As above.	As above.	As above.
Regulator	Checks that service level agreements are met by both suppliers and takes corrective action if they are not.	Checks that corrective action is effective.	Plans how to measure service levels, take corrective action and measure corrective action.	Looks for other ways of measuring service levels, taking corrective action and measuring corrective action effectiveness including external policy change drivers.	Use market forces to maximize service levels and minimize prices to users.

The description of inter-subsystem and environmental interfaces in the VSA also allows an examination of interfacing protocols, which is the description of the process for connecting and disconnecting interfaces (Herring and Kaplan, 2001, p. 6). But here we confine our analysis to a simple change of electricity supplier at the business level rather than at the interface level because this is all that is required to illustrate some of the smart properties of this network.

The final property of a viable system is self-reference. Self-reference is the property of a system, which makes the existence, design and behavior of one part of a viable system naturally complete, fit with and be a consequence of the existence, design and behavior of the other parts of the system. In our electricity market case an electricity supplier is a component of the viable system that is the electricity market. The very nature of the component causes it to strive to increase custom as its design allows it to do; and its behaviors, based upon the design and driven by its nature, actually cause this to happen. On a lower level (i.e. below the network level and below the organizational level) this driving nature, or policy subsystem, is fuelled by the personal and group motivations of humans that staff the policy role of the supplier's business. The same can be seen for the other subsystems of the VSM when we view them as roles that act to maintain system viability with respect to other subsystems via homeostatic feedback mechanisms.

Discussion and Conclusions

Our analysis shows the very high *structural flexibility* requirements placed upon the electricity suppliers during changes in supplier and the regulation of this process. A customer is able to choose to change to any other electricity supplier in the market; therefore each supplier potentially has to communicate data to any other. Furthermore, this complicated process occurs *every time* a user changes supplier so there is a very high *volume* of such interactions between all three parties. Each interaction involves the preparation, transfer and processing of large amounts of user data thus generating very high *volume flexibility* requirements. The suppliers have to change from transmitting zero data to a given competitor, to transmitting a high volume of data whenever a customer changes supplier.

The benefits of deregulation were that electricity prices fell (for the *users* and the *regulator*, i.e. the government) and new suppliers could enter the market (for the *new suppliers*). The current suppliers did not directly benefit. This was due to two reasons. Firstly, deregulation led to more market-like conditions that allowed the entry of more electricity suppliers and an associated increase in competition, which drove down prices. Secondly, as well as service levels the industry regulator specifies in great detail the business processes that the suppliers must enact. In other words the regulator describes how the suppliers should behave to each other and to the users.

One example of processes that are enacted by all parties is the description of the business processes that are required to produce a user disconnection and a connection, i.e. a change in supplier. These business processes are completely modeled in dataflow diagrams that are easily available and whose evolution is strongly controlled by the regulator (MRASCo, 2003). The model contains the sub-processes: disconnect, connect, check disconnection and check connection. This business process model is a standard for the interactions of all parties. It *limits variety* at any given stage in the process to a small set of well-defined stimuli and *response options*, i.e. problem types and associated solution types. Also, the publication and availability of the MRASCo dataflow diagrams ensures that all parties are familiar with these standard business processes. Thus *type flexibility* requirements are fixed to partly compensate for variable *structural flexibility* and apparent *volume flexibility*.

Extreme *structural flexibility* requirements come from the ability of any user to choose any supplier. This is mitigated by the Data Transfer Service (DTS) operated by Electralink (Electralink, 2004), which was formed after deregulation by the fourteen Public Electricity Suppliers of England, Scotland and Wales. The DTS is in itself a network that enables business-to-business data communications between any electricity suppliers connected to it, i.e. *there are two networks here*: the electricity supply chain and the DTS. Thus the transaction costs of suppliers-to-supplier and regulator-to-supplier communication is lowered. More importantly the incremental costs of such communication are lowered and so *volume flexibility* is greatly increased. This simple Flexibility Model, incorporating the *structural*, *type* and *volume flexibility* constructs was developed as part of the EPSRC funded Flexible Business Integration project.

Another product our VSM analysis, combined with Simon's insights on hierarchy, is that whilst the same number subsystems of the user and suppliers interact, the regulator's operations subsystem (Subsystem 1) interacts only with the meta-systems of the suppliers. This mixing of roles has the effect of enabling the network to exist on *three hierarchical levels*. If we divide the roles of a VSM into two: *production* (Subsystem 1) and the meta-process acting on *production* called *evolution* (all other subsystems) we can say that a single supplier, or the regulator, exists on two hierarchical levels. These are the *production* level where business processes directly further the goals of the subsystem (e.g. electricity supply or use) and the *evolution* level where meta-processes act upon the processes on the production level (Warboys et al., 1999, p. 26). The implications of this are discussed in the next section.

The 'smart' in smart networks is *distributed* across the whole network. One example of this concerns a network of actors. An actor can react faster if it is located *functionally local* to an emergent demand upon the network. The BBC, Reuters and other news networks exhibit this property by distributing foreign correspondents all over the world. By being located near to an unforecastable demand upon their network, such as a newsworthy event, foreign correspondents can report on the event faster. This is because they may hear about it faster and because they can get to the scene of the event faster. We use the concept of *functionally local* to emphasis that it is the functioning of the actor that needs to be local to the emergent demand rather than the actor's actual self.

Secondly, network smartness includes some *capability*. An emergent demand that requires a response exhibits variety, i.e. it is not of constant type. A response capability must consist of at least two components: a *decision-making* capability and *response production* capability. The *decision-making* capability is a choice between possible response production options and the latter is a set of business processes to execute, e.g. the choice a foreign correspondent has on if or how to follow the story.

The smart architecture of the UK electricity network is operationalised partly as a regulatory standard. The regulatory standard, or business process model, is an example of *embedded intelligence* within a network because it *distributes capability* to enact a common set of business processes across many organisations. This capability is *functionally local* because it is directly available to local decision-makers; humans or model-driven Business Process Management Systems (BMPS). Intelligence is embedded into this electricity market via an intelligently designed standard for behavior. A standard is a model projected onto the B2B interaction partners (like an ERP vanilla process model is forced onto one organisation). One can either abstract a model from an object process or project a standard onto an object. Both can be used to drive BMPS, or human, process enactment and be examples of network intelligence.

The business process interactions standardized by the regulatory standard are not the only example of smartness in this network. Another smart property of the UK electricity market is provided by the DTS. Infrastructural communications protocols are also standardized in the form of the DTS thus limiting the costs of *structural flexibility* by reducing the number of possible *response production* requirements to one standard DTS protocol. Thus the *decision-making* capability of each user only has to deal with choosing a supplier, not how to connect to them. Both the standard for business process (the data flow diagrams) and the standard for interconnectivity (the DTS) take advantage of Simon's concept of near decomposability by modeling *only* the salient properties of the complex system of users, suppliers and regulator. Thus, by having only to deal with an abstraction, the full complexity of business operation is reduced for all parties.

Finally, modeling a Smart Network as a viable system may be highly appropriate because viability is a product of a system's innate homeostasis. The interactions between subsystems are modeled using a control paradigm that by its very nature is *anti-oscillatory* and so strives to maintain a set point (Herring and Kaplan, 2001, p. 4). This set point can exist at any hierarchical level and so maintaining it can encompass automatic homeostatic, morphostatic and morphogenetic adaptation on the part of the viable system. This has the effect of making the system naturally stable and less prone to dissolution because of exogenous stimuli.

Smart Business Networks are viable systems themselves and can be decomposed into subsystems that either together or singularly must display smartness. These subsystems, such as process networks or telecommunications infrastructures are themselves networks that *must fully* overlay the main Smart Network. They display smart properties that contribute to the smartness of the greater Smart Network. This is aligned with the properties of "distributedness" and functional locality. If smartness is not *distributed* or *functionally local* then it is the business that is smart and not the network. This applies across the network *span* of businesses, in order to affect all members, and up the hierarchy of all its levels, for dealing with emergence.

Future research in this market is focusing on how business process management systems can be incorporated into the modeling of the industry. The current approach of using dataflow diagrams is static and is not architecturally designed in such a way as to facilitate its own evolution, i.e. it could be redesigned hierarchically to allow more single action changes using the concept of loose coupling.

Acknowledgements

We would like to acknowledge the support of the Engineering and Physical Sciences Research Council (EPSRC) in funding our Flexible Business Integration project. We would also like to thank the reviewers, whose original suggestions are listed below, for helping us improve this article.

References

Ashby, W.R. (1958). "Requisite Variety and Its Implications for the Control of Complex Systems", *Cybernetica*, 1 (2), pp. 83-99.

Anderson, P. (1999). "Complexity Theory And Organization Science", *Organization Science*, (10) 3.

Beer, S. (1979). *The Heart of Enterprise*, John Wiley & Sons Ltd.

Checkland, P. (1981). *Systems Thinking, Systems Practice*, John Wiley & Sons, Chichester.

Curtis, B., M.I. Kellner, and J. Over, (1992). "Process Modelling", *Communications of the ACM*, 35 (9).

Electralink, (2004). www.electralink.co.uk (accessed 11 May 2004).

Haeckel, S.H., R.L. Nolan, (1996). "Managing by Wire: Using IT to Transform a Business from Make-and-Sell to Sense-and-Respond", in: Luftman, J.N. (1996). *Competing in the Information Age: Strategic Alignment in Practice*, Oxford University Press.

Herring, C., S. Kaplan, (2001). "The Viable System Architecture", *Proceedings of the 34th Hawaii International Conference on System Sciences (HICSS-34)*, Theme III: Software Engineering and Related Issues, Software Architecture, IEEE Computer Society.

MRASCo (2003). *Master Registration Agreement (MRA) Process Diagrams* (August).

Mumford, E. (2000). *A Socio-Technical Approach to Systems Design, Requirements Engineering*, Vol. 5. Springer-Verlag, London.

Malone, T.W., K. Crowston, (1994). "The Interdisciplinary Theory Of Coordination", *ACM Computing Surveys*, 26 (1), pp. 87-119.

Malone, T.W., J. Yates, and R. Benjamin, (1987). "Electronic Markets and Electronic Hierarchies", *Communications of the ACM*, 30, (7), pp. 97.

National Audit Office (2003). *The New Electricity Trading Arrangements In England And Wales*, Report for the House of Commons, The Stationery Office, London.

National Audit Office (2004). "Advice for Consumers: Choosing the Best Electricity Supplier for Your Needs", www.nao.gov.uk/ publications/ electricity1.htm (last accessed 5 May 2004).

Newell, A. (1989). "Putting It All Together", in: Klahr, D. K. Kotovsky, (1989). *Complex Information Processing: The Impact of Herbert A. Simon*, Erlbaum Associates, Hillsdale, NJ.

Nolan, R.L. (2000). "Information Technology Management from 1960-2000", in: Chandler, A.D., J.W. Cortad, (Eds.), A *Nation Transformed By Information*, Oxford Press, Cambridge, England.

Parnas, D.L., P.C. Clements, and D.M. Weiss, (1985). "The Modular Structure of Complex Systems", *IEEE Transactions on Software Engineering*, Vol. SE11, No. 3, pp. 259-266.

Simon H.A. (1986). "Decision Making and Problem Solving, Research Briefings", *Report of the Research Briefing Panel on Decision Making and Problem Solv-*

ing, National Academy Press, Washington, DC, www.dieoff.org/page163.htm (accessed 11 May 2004).

Simon, H.A. (1969). *The Sciences of the Artificial*, MIT Press, Cambridge, Mass.

Warboys, B., P. Kawalek, I. Robertson, and M. Greenwood, (1999). *Business Information Systems: A process approach*, McGraw Hill.

Weick, K.E. (1974). "Educational Organizations As Loosely Coupled Systems", *Administrative Science Quarterly*, Volume 21 (March).

Williamson, O.E. (1991). "Comparative Economic Organization: The Analysis of Discrete Structural Alternatives", *Administrative Science Quarterly*, Vol. 36, pp. 269-296.

Review Comments

Reviewer: Katerina Pramatari
Rapporteur: Marcel van Oosterhout

The article gives the impression that the viable systems model is applied to components of the network, not the network itself. The regulator does act on the level of the network. Two suggested properties for smart business networks, i.e. 'sense and respond capability' and 'bounded rationality' are not clearly demonstrated in the UK Electricity Market case.

We expect deregulation should lead to benefits / gains for (some of) the business network actors involved. The article is not quite clear what benefits deregulation has brought, and which business network actors are having the benefits? Furthermore, is the whole system becoming more efficient / healthy? In the analyses not only the user should be considered, but all the other stakeholders. Consider the results of an earlier study on deregulated utilities by the World Trade Organization.

In the utilities sector smart business networks are formed and enabled by electronic marketplaces (like www.utilics.com). Via such marketplaces electricity can be auctioned, furthermore (aggregated) demands of industrial customers can be represented and brought on the market.

The regulator has a strong role in the further development and deregulation of the electricity market. What will happen if the whole EU market for electricity is deregulated? According to EU policy this needs to be in place in 6 years from now. Some countries have already deregulated their electricity market; others are still in the process of implementing the new market structure. Some global standards have been developed, however the implementation differs per country. Deregulation has led to more rules and more complexity in the business, thereby increasing the transaction costs. However, in the end prices for the final consumer should go down, because deregulation will lead to more market like conditions and competition (with new players entering the market). However, in some markets net utility cost went down, however total costs went up because all kinds of taxes were added (connection fees, usage fees, and local fees).

Business process standards (data flow diagrams) enforced by market regulators limit the behaviour for data transfer varieties. Dataflow diagrams are static models, which are not easy to make adaptive.

Due to deregulation of the market, in the future customers might sell their excess capacity of electricity on the market, which they had produced via home-electricity devices. This possibility is not taken into account in the models.

The question is whether the electricity business network is a structural system, with a number of generators, receivers and brokers of information (as posed by Dan Braha). It would be interesting to use his approach to analyze the electricity business network, including the switching behaviour (400.000 switching customers per month in the UK).

In the US deregulation forced separation of electricity suppliers (who control the electricity network) and electricity providers.

With regards to the smartness of a business network, the fundamental question is which percentage of the network has to be successful, to call it smart? You don't have to be successful to be smart. Smartness is usually related to uniqueness and novelty. In the analyses and design of smart business networks the authorities should be included as well, since they often constitute an important actor in the network.

21 Governing Smart Business Networks by Means of Distributed Innovation Management

Jens Eschenbaecher[1], Falk Graser[2], and Axel Hahn[3]

Introduction

With the recent acceleration of market dynamics, more flexible ways of collaboration need to be put in the place of traditional static supply chains. "Smart Business Networks" (SBN) are regarded an appropriate instrument to meet the challenges of future competition and better innovation management performance. Their temporary, flexible and dynamic nature requires the necessity to quickly exploit synergies between different enterprises to realize innovative common business objectives. Creating new ideas, transforming them into a product or service, and successfully bringing them to the market is a challenge that is yet difficult to manage within single enterprises where several players within one singular organization need to be streamlined to the common objective (O'Sullivan 2002). Innovation management is a major issue to make industrial collaboration in enterprise networks of companies more successful (Hauschildt 1993; Kleinschmidt et al., 1996). Within a collaborative network, the success of innovation processes highly depends on an efficient network government (Lentz 2003, Eschenbaecher 2004): Different intra-enterprise innovation processes run by several players from different organizations, sharing different company cultures and information systems, need to be harmonized to successfully realize an innovative idea.

This paper takes a three step approach to discuss how the Distributed Innovation Management can be applied for governing Smart Business Network. First, a case study will highlight the need of structured and innovation-driven governance for enterprise networks. Secondly, basic con-

[1] University of Bremen and Bremen Institute of Industrial Technology and Applied Work Science (BIBA) at the University of Bremen, Hochschulring 20, D-28359 Bremen, Germany, esc@biba.uni-bremen.de

[2] University of Bremen and Bremen Institute of Industrial Technology and Applied Work Science (BIBA) at the University of Bremen, Hochschulring 20, D-28359 Bremen, Germany, grs@biba.uni-bremen.de

[3] University of Oldenburg, Ammerländer Heerstr. 118, 26111 Oldenburg, Germany, hahn@wi-ol.de

cepts of Smart Business Networks and Distributed Innovation Management are to be exposed and integrated into a synthesizing life-cycle schema for collaborative networks. Thirdly, Distributed Innovation Management is discussed in more detail and a prototypical web-based platform supporting innovation-driven network governance is to be introduced.

Case study: The role of Innovation Management in Enterprise Networks

The following descriptions are based on the "Tooling Manufacturing" case evaluated by Behnken (2004). Within the last years, more and more large enterprises have taken strategic decisions to concentrate their procurement and collaboration on a small group of key suppliers (*strategic suppliers*). Participating in this exclusive group requires outstanding economical, technological and qualitative competences. For small companies, this requirement is difficult to fulfill and they must take significant efforts for remaining in business either in direct cooperation with the hub or as 2nd or 3rd tier supplier. Typically, these suppliers are small and highly specialized companies that have in-depth knowledge on their own individual businesses on hand. Designing an innovative product or service in a collaborative network fundamentally requires integration of each partner's specific knowledge into the item. Managing these innovation related information/ knowledge flows in a network is one of the most important tasks of distributed innovation management. Figure 21.1 shows the complexity of information and goods flows inside a collaborative aerospace engineering network of one hub and six partnering SMEs.

This clearly indicates the necessity for an inter-organizational, Distributed Innovation Management (DIM) to support governance and coordination activities within the network. Hence, establishing an efficient DIM is a success critical factor for the network's overall success. Later, we will give an approach to a methodology and a web-based portal addressing this problem.

The scenario pictured within Figure 21.1 holds true for a traditional static supply-chain, and it does not necessarily represent a Smart Business Network. Anyway, the imagination of a highly dynamic and flexible Smart Business Network points out even clearer the need for a flexible and adaptive DIM as a governance instrument: Whenever a partner enters or leaves the network, it has to be integrated into or disintegrated from the existing ICT infrastructures. Since a computer supported DIM must run on that infrastructure, the DIM methodology must be able to support flexibility among the partners.

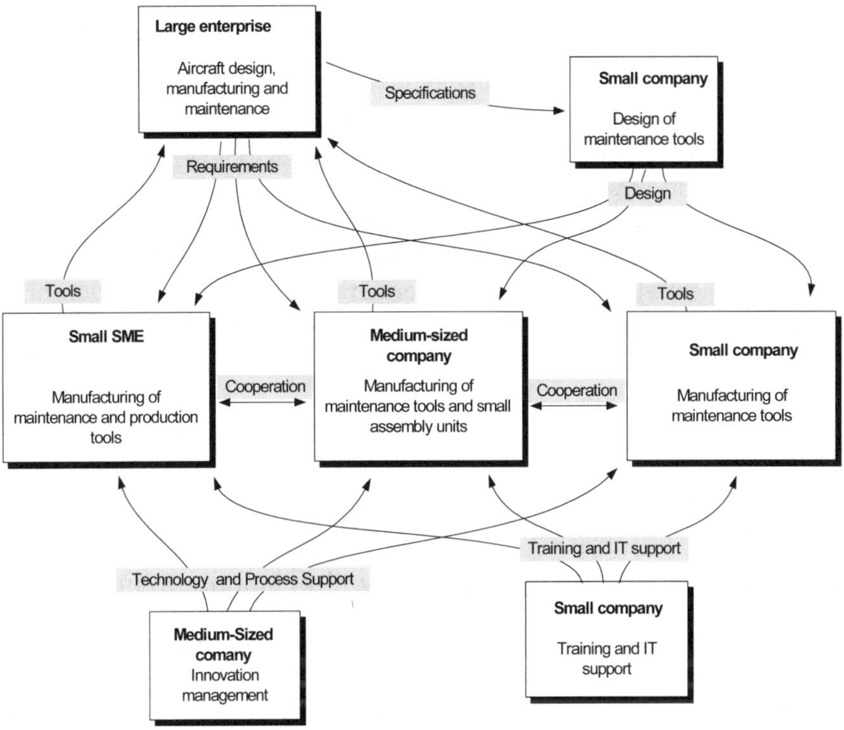

Fig 21.1 Interaction in Tool Manufacturing Scenario (Behnken 2003)

Distributed Innovation Management within Smart Business Networks

The term "Smart Business Network" is used for organizations that are knowledge-driven, internet-worked, dynamically adaptive to new organizational forms and practices, learning as well as agile in their ability to create and exploit the opportunities offered by the e-economy," (Filos, 2003). Therefore, adaptability is a crucial feature of the SBN. The concept of SBN is currently seen latest development in organizational development that started with traditional forms of organization (e.g. hierarchies) and had a first turning point with increased networking structures followed by the innovative concepts described before.

A smart organization is an organization that comprises best practice of various forms of organization. It is thus an excellence model. (Filos 2000) Three characteristics of the SBN make it unique (Ellmann, 2003).

- Its commitment to build collaborative partnerships which encourage and promote the clash of ideas. Customer focus and meeting (or even surpassing) customer expectations is recognized as a key success factor,
- The SBN survives and prospers in the new economy because it can respond positively and adequately to change and uncertainty,
- The SBN identifies and exploits new opportunities by leveraging the power of smart resources, i.e. information, knowledge, relationships, brands, and innovative and collaborative intelligence (Filos, Banahan, 2000).

It is therefore a “best-of everything organization” that can respond to the shift from supplier driven mass production to customer driven mass customization and all its consequences.

Evolution Towards Distributed Innovation Management

Throughout the last five decades, practices in Innovation Management changed significantly (Möhrle, 2003).

Pavitt (2003), Rothwell (2000), Dogson (1994) and others have put forward more than a decade ago non-linear innovation models, such as the systems integration and networking model or 5th generation model that conceives implementation as a non linear process of both explicit and tacit knowledge flows among a network of firms and their suppliers and customers. The authors structure innovation management in a four level model shown in Figure 21.2. The y-axis represents the different team structure (more information on teams at Cascio 1999; Zedtwitz und Gassmann 2002) and the X-axis represents the form of collaboration. The lower levels in the hierarchy (collaborative, project and individual innovation) are embraced by the distributed concept. In DIM, collaboration is extended beyond the limits of a single organization, cutting across the enterprise network. Next figure depicts an approach to this concept.

Individual innovation has been the main focus of much research in the past and involves the development of tools such as mind mapping and Triz to support innovation for the individual or small group of individuals.

Project innovation represents tools that support project teams, in particular virtual teams. This area is currently addressed with software tools such as MS Project and collaborative environments to support information sharing between small groups, over the intranet or internet.

Collaborative innovation is innovation among a large group of individuals sharing a portfolio of projects (rather than one single project). In this type of innovation department goals replace project goals. The tools available for collaborative innovation environments are typically referred to as "unstructured collaboration" tools. These types of tools provide an information framework where organizations can construct their collaboration environment to share and exchange any type of information including organizational goals, actions, teams and results. This type of innovation management is available as "state of the art".

Distributed innovation is innovation across a particular intranet within an organizations supply chain or even virtual organizations. This level of innovation is defined by all of the "collaborative", "project" and "individual" innovation, taking place lower in the hierarchy. This facilitates in enhancing innovation across supply chains by reducing the enterprise-centric perspective of individual organizations and seeking a more dynamic network-centered perspective that engages enterprises other than closest suppliers and customers. The tools required for effectively supporting distributed innovation are in their infancy.

In developing a DIM methodology and a software tool supporting this methodology's utilization, the authors have adopted the idea of non-linear innovation processes and introduce requirements and an approach for a flexible technological infrastructure. The Distributed Innovation Management approach provides the flexibility to support the application of different innovation methodologies to offer the ideal basis for innovation.

Distributed Innovation Management is defined as the process of managing innovation within and across groups of organizations joined to co-design and co-produce products and to over co-services to fulfill the customer's needs. For doing this, the companies must align their strategies for business models, organizational structures (processes), exchange of knowledge and last but not least ICT, to build a stable and efficient organization. In this context Behnken (2003) stated that enterprises that do not successfully master their own, intra-organizational innovation processes are expected to face immense problems in sharing their innovation processes with other networking companies.

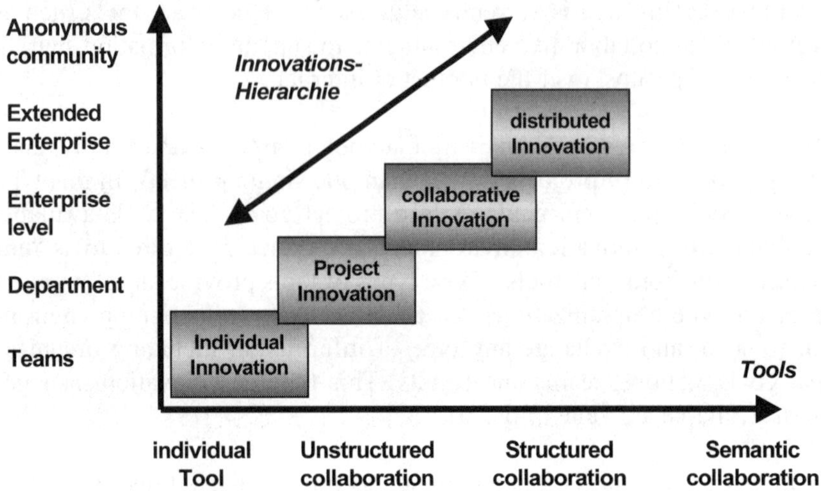

Fig 21.2 Structuring innovation management in teams (O' Sullivan, 2003)

An integrated Life-Cycle-Schema for DIM in SBN

Many life-cycle models for virtual organizations and SBN have recently been developed (Tølle et al., 2002). Analyzing the latest developments indicates that there is a clear focus on the "creation" which we summarize in more detail with the term breeding environment and "operation" phases of the VO life cycle. Every attempt to create a SBN must be accompanied by a careful analysis of the life-cycle in terms of partner configuration and mechanisms to organize the collaboration. Figure 21.3 shows the life-cycle of an enterprise network. A prerequisite for a frictionless operation is an efficient inter-organizational product data- and process management (Reinhart et al., 2000).

While in earlier projects the emphasis was mostly on supporting the operation phase, it can be noticed that in the latest projects the complete management of the innovation process phase is becoming important (Camarinha-Matos, 2004). Consequently, Figure 21.4 shows the concept of the Virtual Breeding Environment[4], which is embedded into the life-cycle of a SBN.

[4] A Virtual Breeding Environment creates a community of occasionally collaborating companies. The community ensures that the partners apply methods and procedures to ensure a certain quality standard .The term virtual breeding environment was recently developed by Camarinha-Matos and Afsarmanesh (2003)

This life-cycle has been detailed a bit more in order to better stress the various requirements. When the VBE created an operable SBN, the partners are ready to realize the innovative product and service that is objective of the partners involved. That objective represents the "Virtual Centre" of the life-cycle, to that all actions need to be adjusted.

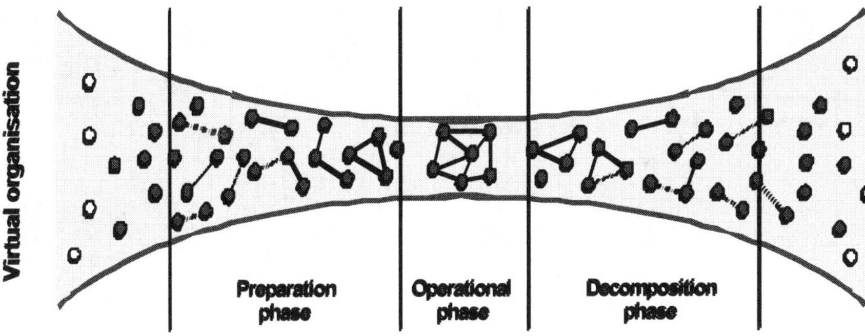

Fig 21.3 SBN Life-cycle from an organisational viewpoint

In the breeding environment the first phase deals with initiating a SBN. The main requirement for doing this is ultimate trust between the collaborating partners. The second phase is called draft planning. In this phase reduction of uncertainty is a major requirement for the network partners. An outline or initial plan will support the SBN enormously. Thirdly, the formation phase is responsible for partner selection. In this phase interaction and readiness to communicate to create any kind of common process in the SBN. This phase concludes activities in the breeding environment.

The second main area is called realization of innovation products and services in Figure 21.4. Here the clear focus is on successfully conducting the distributed innovation process. The detailed planning is a prerequisite for any realization activities in a SBN. Reciprocity and commitment from all SBN partner will ensure that all partner share objectives and visions. In the operation phase the requirements knowledge exchange and disclosure of competencies ensure that the network invests in the best possible solutions. Finally the SBN disassembles which again sets major requirements towards reliability and commitment. Figure 21.4 states the overall life-cycle a Smart Business Networks and integrates some prerequisites that must be met to run efficient DIM within that life-cycle.

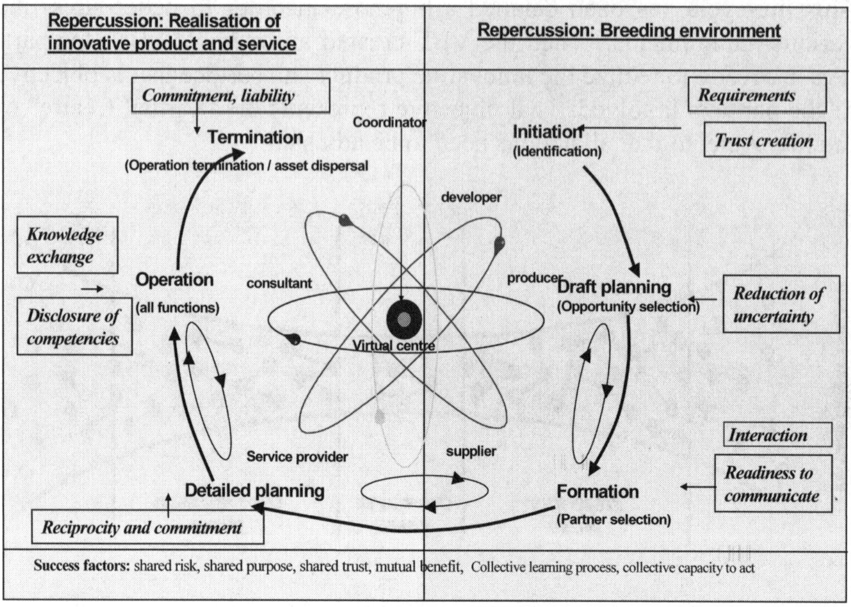

Fig 21.4 Requirements for DIM in SBN (Eschenbaecher, 2004)

In the authors' opinion DIM is a central instrument for governing SBN. Therefore a clear concept on the related DIM approach must be given. This is characterized by three main aspects:

- Coordination by using: Transparent structure of responsibilities, defined control mechanisms, power structures, structuring and governing phase model, definition of organizational forms of virtual teams, steering committee as project controlling and external support by consultants or non-team members,
- Communication by using: Portal structure to save, open and revise documents, e-mail, calendar, news editor, quick links, status window, category definition,
- Cooperation with: Subscription opportunity, Web-browser user interface (24 hours availability).

It is important to follow a holistic approach taking into account strategic, structural and technical aspects in order to implement an effective distributed innovation management in SBNs enabling the partners to share the success factors risk, purpose and trust. The organizational structure and infrastructure influences the costs and effectiveness of the collaboration.

Strategic Recommendations

Strategic alignment of singular companies must be the sum of their individual strategies (Marshall et al, 2001). Hence, the strategic aspects of innovation management must focus on the individual partner and its alignment. The innovation can be implemented on a green field or introduced into an existing VBE. In both cases these strategic aspects are (i) respecting individual strategies/ alignment, (ii) accepted mediation instance (iii) transparency and (iv) communicated individual mutual benefits.

In existing VBE it is strategically important to implement the aspects stated before to foster innovation processes. For the SBN a strategic innovation management methodology then can be selected and applied according to the individual interests of the involved partners.

DIM approach

The general idea is to support scenarios like the one shown in Figure 21.1 with a methodology to commonly conduct DIM. This would enable such networks to become smarter in the direction of a SBN. As a major component the concept of collaboration has a major impact on distributed innovation management in SBN. Our approach splits the innovation process into specific, discrete phases. Each phase is concluded by a review that clears the innovation process for the next phase by accepting the previous' phases results, or forces the process back into the previous phase for improvement.

These iterative recursions separate the model from traditional, linear innovation models. Hence, this model is a non-linear one. Within the phases "context", "assessment", "preparation", "achieving" and "auditing" many subordinate parallel activities take place, see Figure 21.5.

Every phase is finished by a review organized by an independent group of experts. This can be an internal management board, reviewers of a funding body or a steering committee of a distributed team. Furthermore the innovation process is separated in the two main stages innovation planning and innovation introduction. These areas are governed by project teams which coordinate the project. This methodology shows that conducting a DIM activity within a network makes a substantial effort in coordination, cooperation and communication necessary.

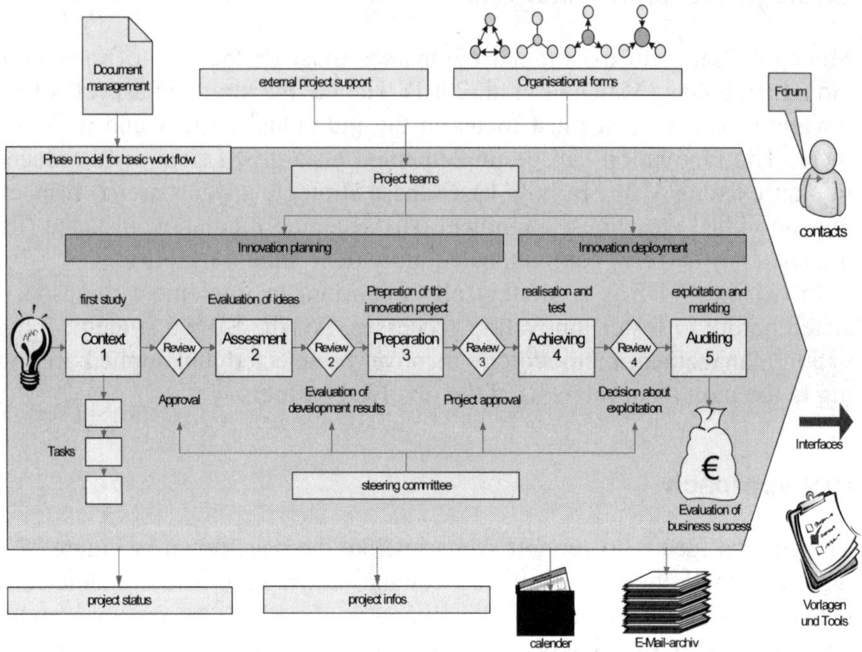

Fig 21.5 Approach for non-linear Distributed Innovation Management (Eschenbaecher, 2004)

Evaluation

The non-linear DIM approach stated above was incorporated into a prototypical web-based platform. This prototype has been prepared in 2003 (Bremermann 2003). Consequently the usage of the DIM methodology has been tested within a large user case (see Eschenbaecher 2004). 55 organizations participated in a study on their judgment on a web-based DIM methodology (www.expide.org/ecolead). The following screenshot shows the portal, see Figure 21.6.

As a main result, all the testing organizations agreed that a web-based DIM platform is the appropriate way to support innovation management in SBN.

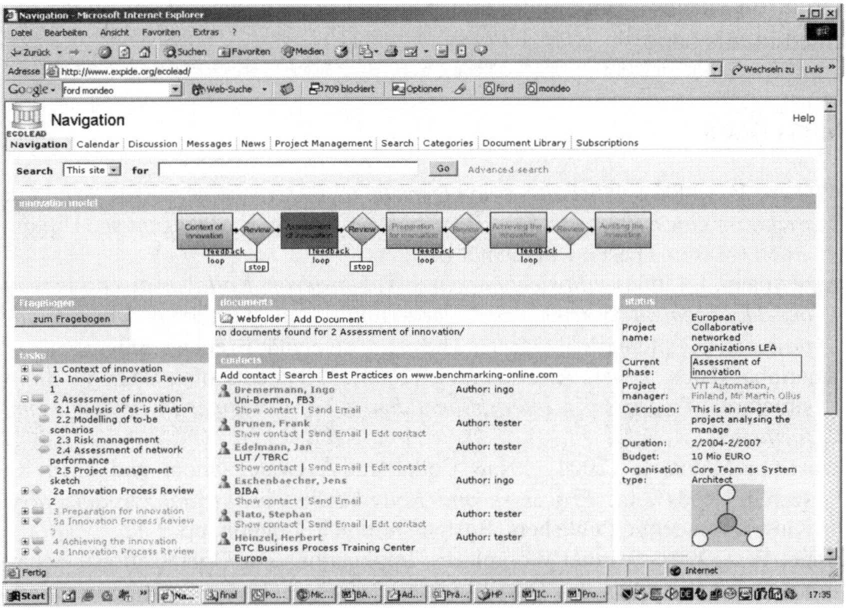

Fig 21.6 Web based distributed innovation management model

Summary and Findings

SBN impose enormous requirements on the ability of companies to collaborate and innovate. New methods and approaches are needed to provide those SBN with the appropriate instruments to face this challenge. Distributed innovation management has been highlighted as powerful approach to better govern and structure SBN. Yet, innovation management is not sufficiently implemented in that kind of organization. This is based on the large set of requirements shown and the missing common strategy development for the overall network as discussed in the paper. Recommendations for strategic and infrastructural aspects highlight the need to create a distributed innovation management system.

The main success factors for a SBN, shared risk, shared purpose, trust and mutual benefit have to be supported by clear and visible collaboration mechanisms. Consequently the practical implementation of an innovation strategy is a key success factor.

The evaluation of the DIM approach took place in a major case study in 2003 (Bremermann, 2004; Eschenbaecher, 2004). Further validation of these concepts is presently done by implementing them into a number of case studies. Assessment of these case studies will provide crucial information on success, potentials, and possible weaknesses of the ideas presented in this paper.

References

Behnken, E. (2004). *Innovationsmanagement in Unternehmensnetzwerken: Entwicklung eines Konzepts für „Distributed Innovation Management*, Diplomarbeit (Master Thesis) Universität Bremen.

Bremermann, I. (2004). *Entwicklung eines Webbasierten Kollaborativen Innovations-Management-Systems zur Steuerung von Verteilten Innovationsprozessen*, Diplomarbeit (Master Thesis), Universität Bremen, 2004.

Camarinha-Matos, L., H. Afsarmanesh, (2004). "Elements of a Base VE Infrastructure". To appear in *International Journal of Computer Integrated Manufacturing*.

Camarinha-Matos, L. (2004). "New Collaborative Organizations and Their Research Needs", in: *Processes and Foundations for Virtual Organizations*, Kluwer Academic Publishers, Boston/Dordrecht/London, pp. 3-12.

Cascio, W. (1999). "Virtual Workplaces: Implications For Organizational Behaviour", in: Cooper, C.L., D.M. Rousseau, (Eds.), *The Virtual Organization - Trends in Organizational Behaviour*, Vol 6, pp. 1-14, John Wiley & Sons.

Cormican, K. (2001). *Product Innovation Management for Networked Organisations*, Galway, Ph.D-Thesis.

Dodgson, M. (2000). *The Management of Technological Innovation*, Oxford University Press, England.

Drucker, P.F. (1986). *Innovations-Management für Wirtschaft und Politik,* Econ. Verlag, Düsseldorf - Wien, 3. Auflage.

Ellmann, S. (2003). *Collaboration in Enterprise Networks- Theory, Technological Background, Network Management and Roadmap.* Master Thesis at the University of Bremen in cooperation with the COMPANION Projekt (www. companion-roadmap.org).

Eschenbaecher, J. (2004). *Innovationsmanagement in Unternehmensnetzwerken.* To be published as Ph.D Thesis at the University of Bremen.

FILOS, E. (2003). "FP6 Roadmaps and Scenario - The Example of IST Key Action II", keynote presentation, *ISTC Meeting*, Brussels, (January 29). Available at: www.ekt.gr/news/events/ekt/20021219/FP6_021219_EFilos_part2%20.ppt, (accesses 20 January 2004).

Filos, E. (2002). *European collaborative R&D projects related to the Smart organisation,* ECPPM Papers, No. 356.

Gassmann, O., M. von Zedtwitz, (2002). "Organising Virtual R&D Teams", *R&D Management*, Vol. 33, No. 3, pp. 243-262.

Gerken, M. (2004). *Modell zur Gestaltung Intra-Organistorischer Innovations-Prozesse bei der Befundung von Schadmotoren*, Diplomarbeit (Master Thesis) Universität Bremen, 2004.

Hauschildt, J. (1993). *Innovationsmanagement*, Verlag Franz Vahlen, München.

Hess, Th. (2002). *Netzwerkcontrolling – Instrumente und Ihre Werkzeugunterstützung*, Deutscher Universitätsverlag GmbH, Wiesbaden.

Kleinschmidt, E.J., H. Geschka, and R.G. Cooper, R., (1996). *"Erfolgsfaktor Markt – Kundenorientierte Produktinnovationen"*, Springer-Verlag, Berlin.

Möhrle, M.G. (1999). *Der Richtige Projekt-Mix*, Springer-Verlag, Berlin.

Lentz, S. (2004). *Gestaltung, Analyse und Bewertung von Konzepten zur Steuerung von Interorganisatorischen Innovationsprozessen*, Studienarbeit, Universität Bremen.

Marshall, P., J. McKay, and J. Burn, (2001). "The Three S's of Virtual Organisations: Structure, Strategy and Success Factors", in: Hunt & Davnes (Eds.), *E-Commerce and V-Business*, pp. 171-192, Butterworth Heinemann.

O'Sullivan, D., K. Cormican, (2003). "A Collaborative Knowledge Management Tool for Product Innovation Management", *Int. Journal of Technology Management*, Vol. 26, No. 1, pp. 53-67.

Pavitt K. (2003). *The Process of Innovation*, SPRU working paper No.89, University of Sussex, Brighton.

Rothwell R. (1994). "Towards the Fifth Generation Innovation Process", *International Marketing Review*, pp. 7-31.

Schuh, G., B. Katzy, and K. Milarg, (1997). "Wie Virtuelle Unternehmen Funktionieren: Der Praxistest ist Bestanden", *Gablers magazin*, No.3, pp. 8-11.

Tølle, M., P. Bernus, and J. Vesterager, (2002). "Reference Models for Virtual Enterprises PRO-VE'02", *3rd IFIP Working Conference on Infrastructures for Virtual Enterprises*, (May), Sesimbra, Portugal.

Section 4

Design of Smart Business Networks

22 Sharing Process Knowledge in Business Networks

Amit Basu[1]

Introduction

Increasingly, firms worldwide are moving away from monolithic structures with vertically integrated businesses spanning large value chains and towards more tightly focused business capabilities that more effectively leverage each firm's core competencies. A major factor enabling this trend has been the dramatic improvement in inter-firm communication and coordination processes enabled through a broad array of information technologies, ranging from email and the Internet to EDI and Web services. This is consistent with economic theories such as Transaction Cost Economics that argue the merits of market mechanisms for business transactions (Williamson, 1981), but recognize the inherent risks and costs of using markets rather than intra-firm hierarchies (Malone et al., 1987). As a result, it is becoming necessary today for a firm to develop strategic plans that include consideration of the roles and activities of a variety of business partners as well as its own. In other words, such firms increasingly function as entities within a business network, or business web, rather than as standalone monoliths. Recently, there has been increasing interest in the design of *smart* business networks, which can be characterized by the following features:

- Value systems that have more complex topologies than linear chains or tree-structured hierarchies,
- Coordination mechanisms that can effectively manage the necessary interactions among component firms and their processes (recognizing that many firms participate in multiple business networks),
- The ability to adapt to changing markets and environmental conditions,
- The ability to learn from past performance.

[1] Cox School of Business, Southern Methodist University, Dallas, TX-75275, USA, abasu@smu.edu

The effective functioning of a smart business network depends upon three major factors:

1. effective management and implementation of key business processes within each component firm in the network,
2. effective communication and coordination between the various firms within the network, and
3. creation of an effective interface between the network and its environment.

Complicating these factors is the fact that each of the component firms within the business network may be an independent firm, with its own goals and priorities. In other words, it is unlikely that the firms would be willing to provide as much transparency about its internal operations and resources to its business partners as it would to other divisions/units within the same firm. Thus, an important yet nontrivial challenge in the design and implementation of a business network is the creation of suitable interfaces between the participating firms, geared towards addressing all three factors above. Furthermore, since the participants in the network and/or the structure of their business processes can change over time, it is also important to have tools to quickly and reliably analyze the effects of such changes on the functioning of the network.

In this paper, we examine the concerns and challenges to the effective implementation of mechanisms for sharing process knowledge among the participating firms in a smart business network, and propose an approach to formally model and analyze shared process knowledge. Our approach is based on a graph-theoretical approach to the specification of business processes and workflows, using a construct called a *metagraph* (Basu and Blanning, 1994), and presents the following advantages for designers and managers of smart business networks:

1. The approach is based on graph theory, which combines intuitive visualization capabilities with a mathematical foundation that supports robust algebraic analysis. An important benefit of this feature is that it enables sophisticated computer-based tools to support process analysis,
2. Metagraph-based representation of business processes enable all the important components of the processes to be considered, and also supports multiple views of the processes that highlight interactions between components such as documents, tasks and resources,
3. There are algebraic procedures that can be used to analyze the effect of changes such as failures or removal of components such as tasks and resources, and the synthesis and/or decomposition of multiple processes,

4. Metagraphs also support hierarchical abstraction operators, which enable simplified and focused views of complex processes, which reduce the complexity and visual clutter of "flat" representations.

The paper is organized in five sections. In the second section, we discuss the issue of knowledge sharing in business networks, and what capabilities would be needed to support this. In the third section, we briefly review the use of metagraphs for representing knowledge, processes and workflows. In the fourth section, we show how the formal properties and operators of metagraphs can be exploited to achieve the capabilities identified in the second section. And finally, the last section presents some directions for further research.

Knowledge in Business Networks

Relationships in business networks between two specific firms can of the following types:

1. Vertical relationships along the value chain: In this case, each partner performs business processes spanning a specific component of the value chain, such as raw materials sourcing, component manufacturing, assembly and manufacturing, marketing, distribution, sales and after-sales service (the chain in a service industry is similar, with manufacturing substituted with service assembly and composition),
2. Horizontal relationships across the value chain: In this case, the two firms may perform the processes in the same or overlapping portions of the value chain. Examples of this case include two suppliers of parts to an automobile manufacturer, or two content providers to a financial services provider,
3. A hybrid relationship, such as where a firm that is already performing a process engages a supplier (vertical) partner to augment its capacity and throughput for that process.

If all the relationships between connected firms are considered, the resulting business network can be huge, spanning multiple industries, mutually competing firms, and firms that have no non-trivial dealing with each other. Therefore, we use the term business network to refer to the network of firms that a particular firm interacts with. In other words, given three firms A, B and C such that A and B interact, and B and C also interact, the business network of A would include B, but not C (unless A and C also interact directly).

In order for each firm in a business network to function effectively, it has to not only manage its own internal processes, but also manage its relationships with its partners. This means that it needs to know how the business processes of each partner would impact its own processes, and similarly, it needs to provide its partners with sufficient information about its processes so that they can function effectively. In order to achieve *smart* business networks, we further assume that the specification of shared process knowledge is in a form that can allow the network to be reconfigured easily, with new partners and new relationships. Thus, not only the functional structures of processes, but also relevant business rules that govern the use of inter-firm process relationships, have to be specified.

In the next section, we show how the use of metagraphs for process representation can be leveraged to capture this type of information, and also to support formal analysis of the business processes spanning the network.

Metagraphs and Process Knowledge

A metagraph is a graph-theoretic construct in which edges are used to denote directed relationships between two sets of elements. These relationships can be represented visually, as shown in Figure 22.1. Each set of elements in a vertex is identified by surrounding them by a closed boundary such as an oval. Each arrow denotes a relationship, from its invertex to its outvertex. In addition to the visual representation, there is also a formal matrix representation of a metagraph, in terms of an adjacency matrix (Basu and Blanning, 1994). Furthermore, using appropriate algebraic operators defined on this matrix representation, a variety of transformation, connectivity-based properties and procedures have been defined on metagraphs, and these have also been applied to a variety of structural analyses of metagraphs. In particular, connectivity features of metagraphs are very useful. For instance, two kinds of paths can be defined on metagraphs. The first type is a simple path, which represents a sequence of edges linking two individual elements. This is similar to connectivity as defined for traditional graphs such as simple and directed graphs. The second type is special to metagraphs, and is called a metapath. A metapath defines connectivity between two *sets* of elements, and is a powerful construct that can be exploited for a variety of different analyses. An example of a metagraph, along with both simple and metapaths is provided below.

Figure 22.1 shows a metagraph consisting of five edges, e_1,..., e_5 defined over a generating set of eight elements, x_1, …, x_8 (the number below each edge will be explained in the next section). Associated with each metagraph is an adjacency matrix A, as well as the closure A* of the adjacency matrix. This closure matrix is particularly useful in connectivity-based analysis of any metagraph, since it reveals all the simple paths in the metagraph, and can also be used to identify all the metapaths in the metagraph. This ability to capture connectivity between sets is a powerful feature of the metagraph representation, since it also provides the basis for hierarchical abstractions of metagraphs, as discussed below.

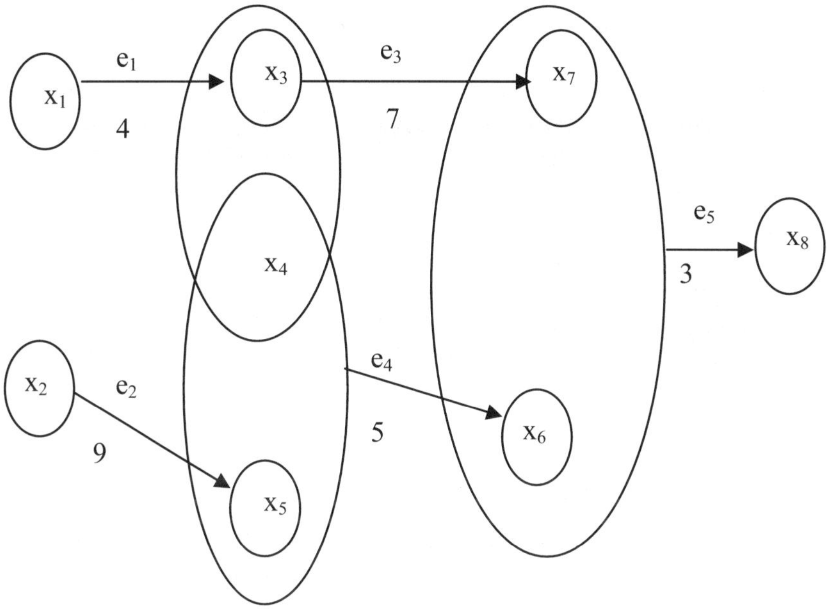

Fig 22.1 A metagraph

In the metagraph representation of business processes, each process is represented as a collection of tasks, and each task is represented as an edge linking sets of inputs and outputs (Basu and Blanning, 2000). The inputs and outputs may be organized as documents such as forms and reports. In effect, each edge provides a black-box representation of a task, since it does not reveal the task's internal structure or procedural specification; only what inputs are needed to drive it and what outputs are generated upon successful completion of the task. Each task can also have additional attributes associated with it, such as the resources (people, machines, etc.) needed to execute the task, the duration of the task, and the cost of the task. The representation has a formal algebra associated with it, which enables analysis of process structure. This analysis can also be extended to the synthesis of processes from several component sub-processes, and the decomposition of complex processes (Basu and Blanning, 2003).

An example of a metagraph-based representation of a process is shown in Figure 22.2, which depicts a simplified version of the process of loan evaluation in a bank. The vertices in the metagraph consist of information elements needed in the process, as well as conditions applicable as constraints on tasks (such conditions are prefaced by a "?'). To illustrate the representation, consider the edge e_2, which represents a loan risk assessment task. This task is performed by a loan officer l, and generates a value of LR, the risk rating of the loan, based on the credit rating of the applicant and the loan amount requested. Now consider the edge e_5, which reduces the feasible loan amount if the loan risk rating turns out to be unacceptably high. The condition "?Risk High' limits the use of this task to only these situations. On the other hand, if the loan risk is acceptable, the condition "?Risk Low' is satisfied, and a loan decision is made by following the decision rule embedded in the path $<e_8, e_9>$. In effect, this example shows many features of the metagraph representation of processes, such as the use of constraints on tasks, the responsibilities of each resource, the use of iterative sub-processes when necessary, and the sequential dependencies of tasks.

Processes in Business Networks

Assume that processes within each firm in the business network are represented as metagraphs. In fact, each firm may have several such process metagraphs corresponding to its various business processes. Each process has a specification that details its complete structure, and this specification is intended for internal use within the firm owning that process. However, the business partners of that firm may also need to have some understanding of the structure and scope of the process, so that they can align the process with their own related processes. An obvious challenge in this area is the representation of each business process at multiple levels of specificity, so that different entities involved with that process can not only be aware of the process, but also factor their understanding of the process into whatever process analysis they deem necessary.

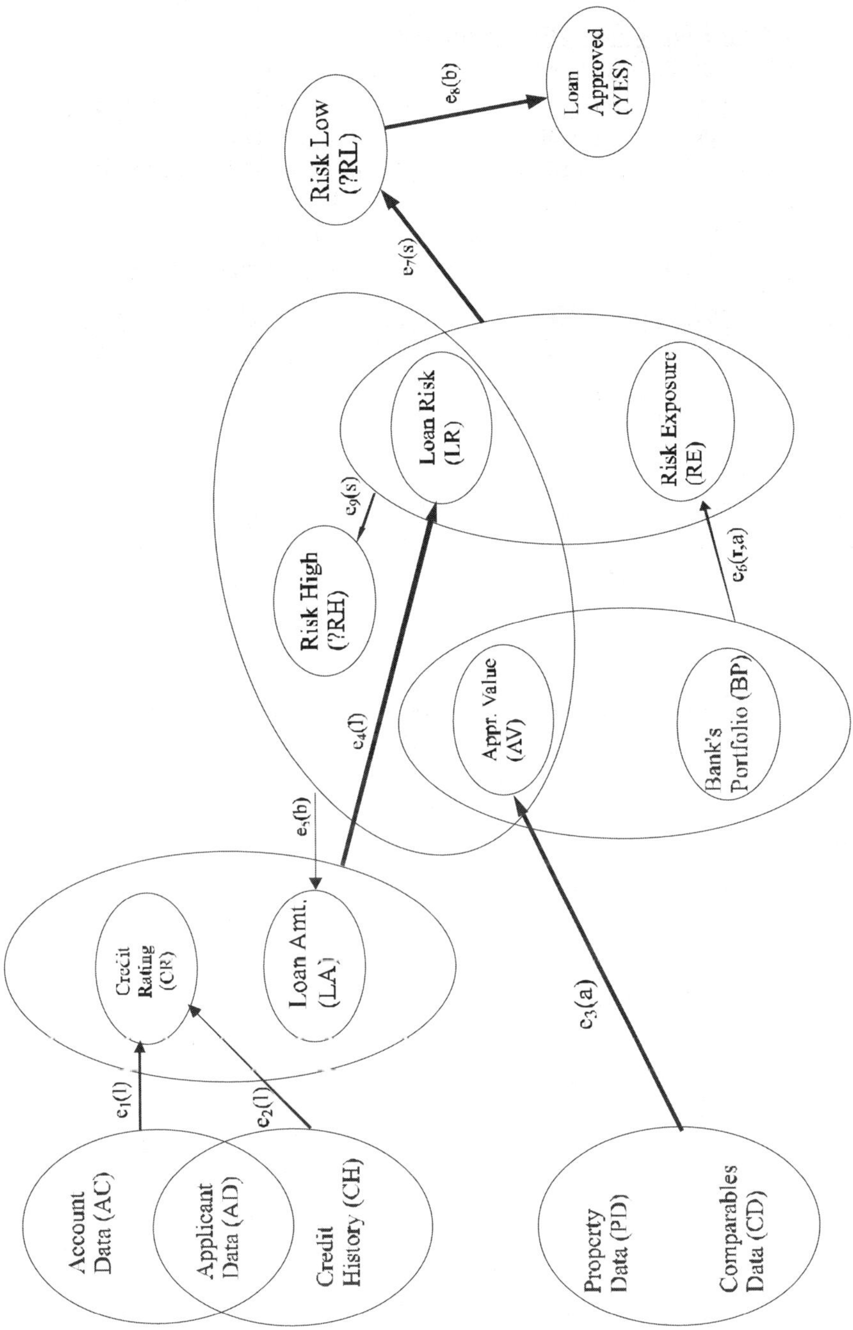

Fig 22.2 Metagraph of Loan Evaluation Process

Legend for Tasks and Resources:

e_1: Credit Rating Process
e_2: Alternative CR Process
e_3: Property Appraisal
e_4: Risk Assessment
e_5: Loan Amt. Reduction
e_6: Risk Exposure Assessment
e_7: Acceptable Risk Assessment
e_8: Loan Approval
e_9: Bad Risk Assessment
a: appraiser
b: branch manager
l: loan officer
r: risk analyst
s: risk categorization system

Fig 22.2 (continued)

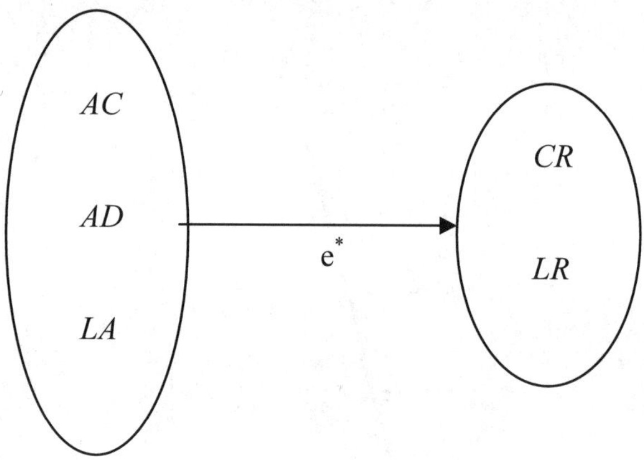

Fig 22.3 Projection of Loan Process Metagraph

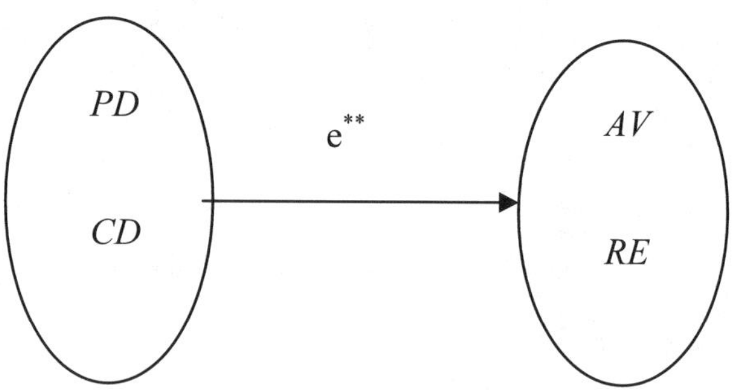

Fig 22.4 Projection of Risk Exposure Tasks

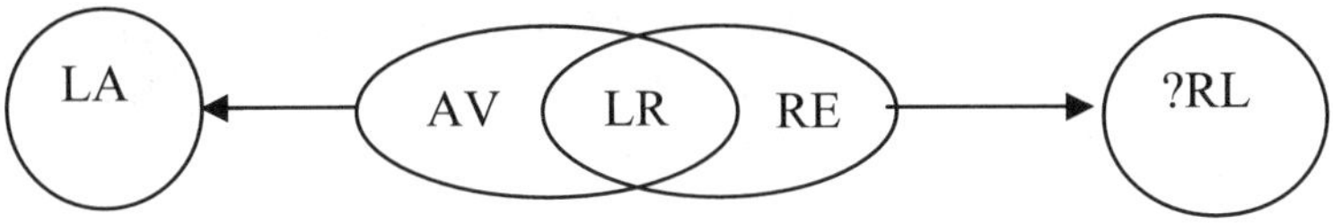

Fig 22.5 Projection of Branch Manager Tasks

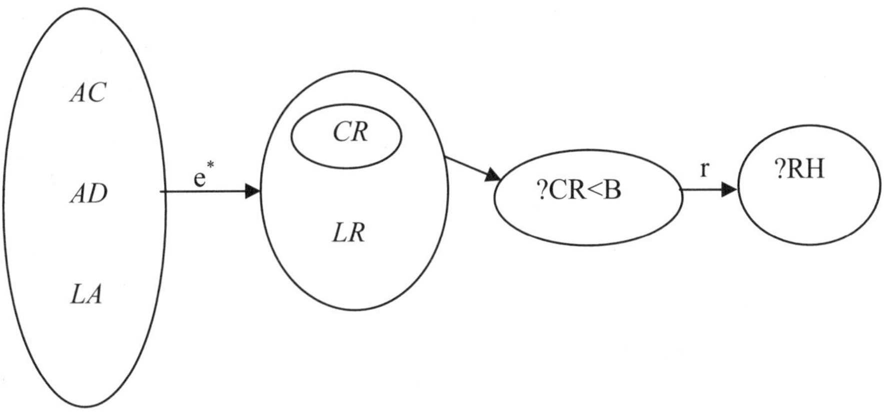

Fig 22.6 Figure 22.3 Augmented with a New Rule

Sharing Knowledge about Process Structure

A significant advantage of the metagraph approach to process representation is that it allows multiple representations, in various modalities. For instance, metagraphs support a *projection* operator (Basu, Blanning, and Shtub, 1997), which enables a large metagraph S defined on a set of variables X to be simplified into a corresponding view S_1 defined in terms of a specific subset X_1 X such that internal details of S that involve elements other than the specified subset X_1 are not disclosed, yet any changes in the original metagraph that impact the view are propagated to the view. In other words, if a process and its views are defined in terms of metagraphs, then any changes to process structure are propagated as relevant to the views, and can be factored into any analysis of the process at the level of the view. To illustrate the notion of the projection operator, consider Figure 22.3. This shows a metagraph consisting of a single edge, which represents the projection of the metagraph in Figure 22.2 over the subset of elements (*AC, AD, LA, CR, LR*).

The value of the projection operator is that it provides a simpler view of a process or system. In the context of business process modeling, this hierarchical abstraction serves another useful purpose. It enables selective disclosure of process knowledge, thus facilitating knowledge sharing across organizational boundaries. However, this requires a minor refinement of the projection operator. In the projection operator as defined in (Basu, Blanning, and Shtub, 1997), a projected edge represents a metapath from the invertex to the outvertex in the base metagraph. However, in the multi-organizational context, a firm may want to project an edge without necessarily showing all its invertex elements. To see this, consider the edges e_3 and e_6 in Figure 22.2. These represent tasks performed by a risk analyst and a property appraiser, and utilize information components PD, CD and BP as pure inputs. Of these, PD and CD may be externally procured items from applicant data or real estate reports. However, BP represents the bank's internal portfolio information, which may be private. In such situations, it is reasonable to consider an external view of the process as shown in Figure 22.4. Note here that BP does not appear in the projected edge, even though it is a pure input to the process. Nevertheless, the edge is a reasonable characterization of the risk exposure assessment process, for external purposes.
We formalize this external projection operator as follows:

Definition: Given a metagraph S = $\langle X, E \rangle$ with a subset X_1 of X being *private* elements, then an *external projection* of S over a subset *X'* of X such that $X' \cap X_1 \neq \phi$ is obtained by taking the corresponding projection of S over *X'* and then removing all elements of X_1 from it.

Note that the external projection can be easily derived from the regular projection operator, so no new procedures are needed. Also, by definition, each externally projected edge is a feasible task in an internal process once the private elements are also made available.

The external projection then allows for a very useful way to share process knowledge. We illustrate this using the example process in Figure 22.2, which reveals the loan evaluation process assuming that all the tasks are performed within a single organization. Now assume that the process is to be disaggregated into component sub-processes managed by three organizations. The first organization, which uses the loan officer resource, performs the tasks captured by the external view in Figure 22.3. The second organization, which consists of the risk analyst and property appraiser resources, performs the risk exposure sub-process represented by Figure

22.4. And finally, the third organization, consisting of the branch manager and risk categorization system resources, performs processes shown together in Figure 22.5 (for space reasons, the loan decision propositions are used to correspond to the approval and rejection decisions).

The strength of this approach is that each organization can represent, analyze and manage its own processes using the metagraph representation. At the same time, the external views of the processes collectively comprise a metagraph too, which can be analyzed using the same formal analytical tools and procedures.

Most business processes are also governed by business rules, which determine the specific conditions under which each task can apply. In the metagraph representation, rules can be incorporated seamlessly in the representation. This is because rules stated in the form "IF <A> and <B> and … THEN <C>" can be represented as edges in a metagraph, with the conditions (antecedent) forming the invertex of each edge and the consequent forming its outvertex. In other words, a collection of rules can be represented as a metagraph, and rule-based inference can be implemented using connectivity properties and procedures on the metagraph. This has been shown in (Basu and Blanning, 1997).

In the context of a business network, business rules show up in two ways. First, there are business rules that apply to a firm's own processes. Such rules can be incorporated into the metagraph representation of each relevant process. Furthermore, such rules would be abstracted out of the external view of the processes as seen through suitable projections applied to the process metagraphs. It is easy to see how each firm in the network can keep its internal rules secure, even while revealing the appropriate information about its processes to its partners. An internal rule would appear in a projected view of a process only if all the antecedents and the consequents of the rule were part of the projection set (which is controlled by the firm that owns the process). At the same time, a business partner may want to impose conditions upon its partner's processes. For instance, a manufacturer may insist that the component produced by a supplier meet a particular quality requirement.

The shared representation of inter-organizational processes can also be embellished with additional business rules that are visible to all partners, and can be used to refine the process. For instance, in our example, consider the addition of a negotiated rule among the partners that if the credit rating of the applicant is below B, then the risk is too high. Such a rule can be superimposed on the shared process, and also propagated to relevant organizations. Figure 22.6 shows how this rule, represented by the edge "r', can be added to the shared views. Note that the other new edge that is added merely evaluates the proposition "Is Credit Rating Less than B?" based on the value of the credit rating CR. In this case, this new rule provides an alternative workflow that could override the business rules embedded in the original processes. In fact, it is easy to see that it might reject loans that otherwise may be acceptable. The important point is that the shared rule can be applied in the context of this particular business network, without affecting how each individual firm may conduct its process internally, and with other partners. This is because each firm can construct different views for different networks in which it participates, and the collective processes in these networks could be very different, yet all managed in conjunction with each firm's internal processes, and without violating any privacy constraints for any of the internal processes.

Sharing Temporal Knowledge

So far, we have focused on merely functional dependencies between tasks in terms of the information elements they use and produce. However, there are other dimensions of processes that also can be shared. One significant area of concern among business partners interacting in terms of specific processes is the timing and scheduling of tasks within each firm that are dependent on related tasks performed at other firms within the business network. A significant advantage of the metagraph approach is that it allows attributes such as task duration and cost to be assigned to edges representing process tasks. These attributes can then be used in analyzing the schedule and cost aspects of each process. For instance, task duration attributes can be used in algorithms to identify the critical path through each process, namely the sequence of tasks that must be completed in time in order to complete the process in time. Identification of such critical paths can be beneficial, since each process workflow is a metapath involving multiple elements and tasks, and the critical path determines not just the tasks that are critical (which is what traditional PERT/CPM analysis does), but also which outcomes of each task must be achieved first (Basu and Blanning, 2001). In other words, within each workflow of a business process, the critical path analysis can identify the sequence of tasks as well as the affected elements that are critical to the timely completion of process execution.

To see how critical path analysis can be used with process metagraphs, consider again the metagraph in Figure 22.1 as a process metagraph, and let the numbers below each edge correspond to the expected durations of the tasks represented by that edge. Based on these, the earliest completion times and latest completion times for each outcome element can be computed as shown in Table 22.1. The table also shows the slack in the schedule for each outcome. From this, it is easy to see that not only is the set of critical tasks comprised of $\{e_2, e_4, e_5\}$, but furthermore, within these tasks, the elements x_5 and x_6 are on the critical path, while x_4 is not. This indicates than the tasks that generate x_4 have some slack, even though x_4 is an input to a critical task.

Table 22.1 Critical Path Analysis of Figure 22.1

Element	Earliest Completion	Latest Completion	Slack
X_1	0	3	3
X2	0	0	0
X3	4	7	3
X4	4	9	5
X5	9	9	0
X6	14	14	0
X7	11	14	3
X8	17	17	0

To see how critical path analysis can be used with process metagraphs, consider again the metagraph in Figure 22.1 as a process metagraph, and let the numbers below each edge correspond to the expected durations of the tasks represented by that edge. Based on these, the earliest completion times and latest completion times for each outcome element can be computed as shown in Table 22.1. The table also shows the slack in the schedule for each outcome. From this, it is easy to see that not only is the set of critical tasks comprised of $\{e_2, e_4, e_5\}$, but furthermore, within these tasks, the elements x_5 and x_6 are on the critical path, while x_4 is not. This indicates than the tasks that generate x_4 have some slack, even though x_4 is an input to a critical task.

In the analysis of interacting processes across a business network, such critical path analysis can be extremely valuable, since the view of each component process is at a high level that spans many specific tasks. In terms of the example, the tasks that produce x4 may be a sub-process within one firm, while the task that uses that information may be in another firm. Identification of the critical path can alert each organization to focus on the scheduling of the time critical tasks (and even the components of these tasks) that impact not only that firm's own processes but also those of its partners.

Sharing Other Process Knowledge

In this paper, we have focused our attention on two types of knowledge sharing about processes that can be valuable for managing inter-organizational processes. However, the metagraph representation supports a variety of other types of process knowledge that can be shared for effective process management. For instance, process metagraphs can be transformed into equivalent metagraphs that focus on the interactions between resources, rather than information elements. These resource interaction metagraphs (RIM) can be analyzed in the same way, since they are based on the same construct (Basu and Blanning, 2000). In other words, the RIMs of the interdependent processes of the different firms in a business network can be used to identify the resources that need to interact across organizational boundaries, and furthermore, the nature of these cross-boundary interactions. This can be a valuable tool in designing communication and coordination mechanisms across the business network.

Conclusion

In this paper, we have shown how representation of business processes and workflows as metagraphs can be used to share knowledge about process structure and scheduling across business networks in ways that support not only useful visualization and abstraction of processes but also useful structural analysis of these processes. In particular, we have focused on the projection operator and an extension of it called the external projection, and demonstrated how such abstraction of process structure can be exploited for inter-organizational knowledge sharing at appropriate levels of specificity and disclosure. We have also shown how temporal information about processes can be represented in process metagraphs, and demonstrated the use of critical path analysis to improve analysis and sharing of temporal knowledge about such processes, both within individual firms as well as across the participating firms in a business network.

The metagraph approach to business process analysis is unique in its ability to combine intuitive and powerful visualization capabilities with the representational power to include knowledge about many important aspects of processes such as information elements, tasks, constraints, rules, resources and durations (as well as possibly other attributes such as cost and reliability), along with a formal mathematical foundation that enables a variety of useful analytical procedures on the represented processes. Providing a single common basis for each firm to represent its processes and manage its internal processes as well as the sharing of appropriate knowledge about the processes with business partners is a key advantage, since it does not force each firm to have to use different methods and mechanisms for external knowledge sharing versus its internal knowledge management.

Finally, it is important to recognize that while the exposition in this paper has been largely in terms of the visual representation of metagraphs, all the features and analysis that we have discussed can be implemented in computer-based tools that manipulate the algebraic representation of process metagraphs in terms of the adjacency matrix and algebraic operations on it. Detailed description and discussion of such algebraic analysis is available in many of the archival papers cited in the references.

There are a number of additional aspects of process management that have not yet been explored in the metagraph representation. Examples of such features include specification of delegation rules for workflow control, compensatory transactions for aborted workflows in processes, and economic analysis of processes. These all represent promising areas for future research, along with the development of CASE-type computer tools based on metagraphs for knowledge sharing and process analysis.

References

Basu, A., R.W. Blanning, (1994). "Metagraphs: A Tool for Modeling Decision Support Systems", *Management Science*, Vol. 40, No. 12 .

Basu, A., R.W. Blanning, and A. Shtub, (1997). "Metagraphs in Hierarchical Modeling", *Management Science*, Vol. 43, No. 5.

Basu, A., R.W. Blanning, (1997). "A Graph-Theoretic Approach to Analyzing Knowledge Bases Containing Rules, Models and Data", *Annals of Operations Research,* Vol. 75 .

Basu, A., R.W. Blanning, (2000). "A Formal Approach to Workflow Analysis", *Information Systems Research*, Vol. 11, No. 1, pp. 17-36.

Basu, A., R.W. Blanning, (2001). "Workflow Analysis Using Attributed Metagraphs", *Proceedings of the 34th Hawaii International Conference on System Sciences*.

Basu, A., R.W. Blanning, (2003). "Synthesis and Decomposition of Processes in Organizations", *Information Systems Research*, Vol. 14, No. 4.

Malone, T.W., J.Yates, and R.I. Benjamin, (1987). "Electronic Markets and Electronic Hierarchies", *Communications of the ACM,* 30 (6), pp. 484-497.

Williamson, O.E. (1981). "The Economics of Organization: The Transaction Cost Approach", *American Journal of Sociology,* Vol. 87, No. 3, pp. 548-576.

23 How Much Business Modularity?

Martijn R. Hoogeweegen[1] and Peter H.M. Vervest[1]

Introduction

Interaction costs are further decreasing (Butler et al., 1997), influencing the trade off between in-house production and outside procurement in favor of the latter (Clemons et al., 1993). The opportunity for organizations is to improve profitability by outsourcing more capabilities to specialized business network partners. The threat is that organizations should clearly focus to their core capabilities and make sure to be among the best providers of these capabilities within their business network communities.

Decreasing interaction costs will lead to the break up of organizations in sub-units, which specialize in one or more core capabilities. Whole communities of business networks may disaggregate into fragmented organizational units operating independently in many different constellations to fulfill market opportunities. This process will transform relatively stable business networks into dynamic ones.

Business modularity is seen as an important enabler to dynamically operating business networks. Modularity "… is an approach for organizing complex products and processes efficiently" (Venkatraman & Henderson, 1998). The break up of organizations will be fostered by organizing around modular capabilities. The benefit of fragmented communities is that like other modular systems they can mix and match the right organizational units to create the appropriate value for every single customer. The drawback of fragmented communities is that they become more transparent and will not tolerate inefficiencies and imperfect markets. This will erode the possibility to generate an adequate margin. The question therefore is to what extend an organization should aim for modularizing processes and products (see Figure 23.1). In this paper we address the issue of business fragmentation opposed to the concept of granularity, which refers more to an information systems point of view.

Real smart organizations know to what level they should modularize products, processes and business networks. They know that too little modularization restricts the possibility to mix and match with other organizations in temporary alignments. Too much modularity on the other hand fosters the transparency of the offerings. Transparency will lead to

[1] RSM, Erasmus University Rotterdam, PO Box 1738, 3000 DR, Rotterdam, The Netherlands, mhoogeweegen@fbk.eur.nl, vervest@d-age.com

increasing competition resulting in lower margins and dangers of imitation.

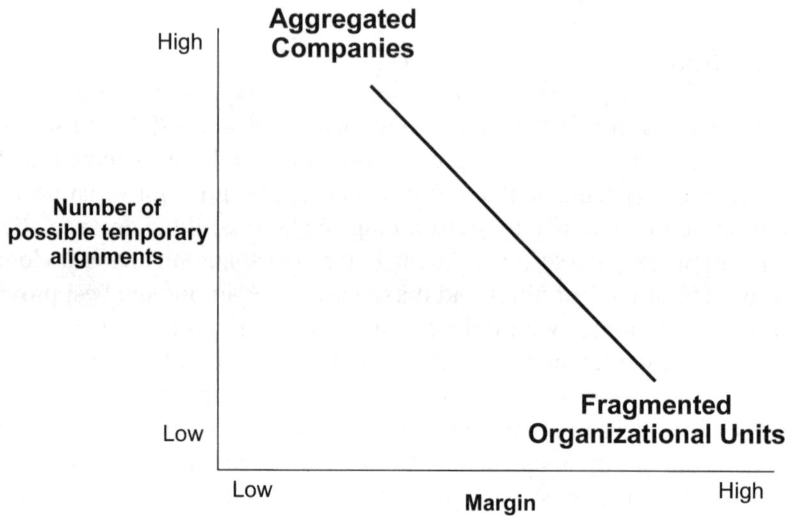

Fig 23.1 The trade-off between aggregation and fragmentation

This paper introduces a preliminary framework to assess the appropriate level of modularity. First the theoretical background is drawn before the framework is introduced. Then a case study in the automotive industry will serve as an example how to apply the framework. Finally conclusions are drawn.

Background

As interaction costs further decrease, businesses will fragment into smaller units organized around one or a couple of capabilities (see Aurik et al., 2002). Based on the Transaction Economics Theory of Williamson (Williamson, 1985), Clemons et al (Clemons, 1993) illustrate how IT affects the balance between in-house production and outside procurement. The cost of in-house production is the result of relatively *high* production cost and relatively *low* coordination cost. The cost of outside procurement is the result of relatively *low* production cost and the relatively *high* coordination cost. The lower interaction cost, the lower coordination cost, the more likely organizations will prefer outside procurement over in-house production. The move towards small organizational units, which are specialized in one or a couple of capabilities, will create dynamic business networks in which many units form all kinds of temporary alignments to combine their specialized capabilities to fulfill customer requirements (see also Miles&Snow, 1992).

The process of fragmentation is not only supported by decreasing interaction costs. Also the trend of customization is driving this process. Customers ask for more service and more personalized service: see also Ives & Mason, 1990, Pine, 1993 and Vervest & Dunn, 2002. Customized demand requires the instant mixing and matching of the right capabilities to exactly fulfill was has been asked. Organizations are forced to think in reverse (Jarvenpaa & Ives, 1993): first collect the (customized) customer order; then organize within your business network the right supply or delivery chain of organizations. The more customers ask for personalized goods and services the more business networks will evolve into dynamic ones. Dynamic networks of small organizational units are better capable of dealing with customized demand.

Organizations in dynamic networks are challenged to offer competitive capabilities and to form the right temporary alignments to serve customized demand. An interesting enabler is business modularity. Using modular production techniques to deliver modular products is the key to success in delivering customized goods and services efficiently. The idea of modularity is to standardize the components of a system (a product or process) in such a way that they can be separated and recombined fairly easily. This makes modularity a powerful approach to organize complex products and processes efficiently (Venkatraman & Henderson, 1998). The major expected benefits of applying modularity are the increase of customer satisfaction, the decrease of coordination costs and the decrease of production costs. Garud and Kumaraswamy, (1993) referred in this respect to the *economies of substitution*: in a modular process design only parts of a process have to be substituted by other processes to produce a different product. Modularity allows to mix and match service elements to the customers requirements and establish a these with a 1:1 relationship to the associated capabilities (Hoogeweegen et al., 1999).

Fragmentation Framework

The trend towards fragmentation is supported by decreasing interaction costs and the increased demand for customized goods and services. Organizations will streamline their activities to their core capabilities and will adopt modular business structures. The question is however to what extend modularity adds to an organization's profitability and whether there is a limit to the degree of modularity.

Too much modularity will have an economic drawback. The more modular a system the more visible this system is to the outside world how it works and functions. This will increase transparency and will give ammunition to customers and competitors to ask for lower margins or to imitate offered modules. Seen from an economic point of view an organization should always want to "cover up" its modules to justify certain sales prices. The more modules in-house and / or the larger the modules the better an organization is capable of hiding inefficiencies and calculate them in the sales price. However, the higher the level of modularity the less possibilities to mix and match them with other modules.

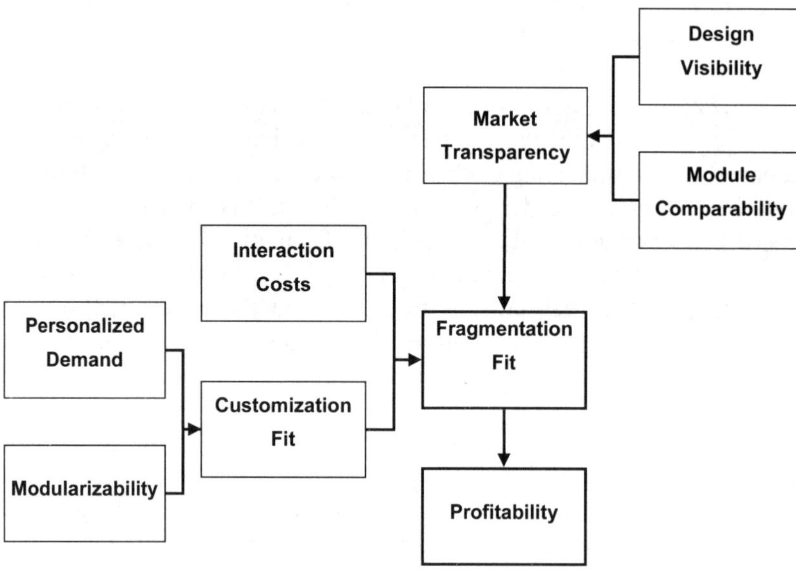

Fig 23.2 Fragmentation Framework

Defining the optimal level of fragmentation requires a constant deliberation about the forces driving fragmentation and those that resist fragmentation (see Figure 23.2). The forces that drive fragmentation are customization and decreasing interaction cost. The forces that resist fragmentation are the limited possibilities to form temporary alignments and the erosion of margins due to increasing transparency.

Fragmentation is positively influenced by lower interaction costs and a good customization fit. The (mis) match between the demand for personalized products and the "modularizability" of products, processes and networks explains the customization fit. Modularizability is described as to what extend products, processes and networks can be designed modularly. Modularizability is enhanced (1) when a system can be relatively easy divided into subsystems; (2) when the subsystems are compatible with each other and (3) when subsystems optimally can be used or ran in parallel.

The better the modular operators as defined by Baldwin & Clark (2000), are applicable to a system the higher the modularizability of this system. These modular operators are: *splitting* a system into two or more subsystems or modules, *substituting* one module for another, *augmenting* by adding a new module to the system, *excluding* a module from the system, and *porting* a module to another system.

Compatibility refers to the interfaces of modules (O'Grady, 1999). A standard interface is required to easily connect modules. The higher compatibility the higher the modularizability of a system.

Optimal parallel processing is supported by divisible load theory (Robertazzi, 2003). The more optimal tasks can be allocated to parallel operating subsystems to increase the modularizability of a system.

Fragmentation is negatively influenced by the anticipated level of transparency that will occur due to a modular design. Transparency is the result of two forces. First, the smaller the modules of a system the more visible the design of these modules, and thus the more easy to imitate. Second, the smaller the modules the better they can be compared (in terms of performance, quality and price) and thus the more competition.

The framework shows how forces enabling and resisting fragmentation should be considered to define the optimal fragmentation fit and therefore optimally support the profitability of a smart business network community.

Automotive Case

The case described here to illustrate our framework is a simplification of how automotive supply chains are currently organized. Recent trends in the automotive industry are customization, focus on core competences, move to modular production, and new internet-based players (Morcott , 2000).The current automotive supply chain consists of eleven main capabilities organized in four echelons: a supplier, manufacturer, distributor and a car dealer. All eleven capabilities are required to design, produce, distribute and sell cars. When three similar supply chains are considered we focus on a network consisting of 3 times 4 is 12 organizations (see Figure 23.3).

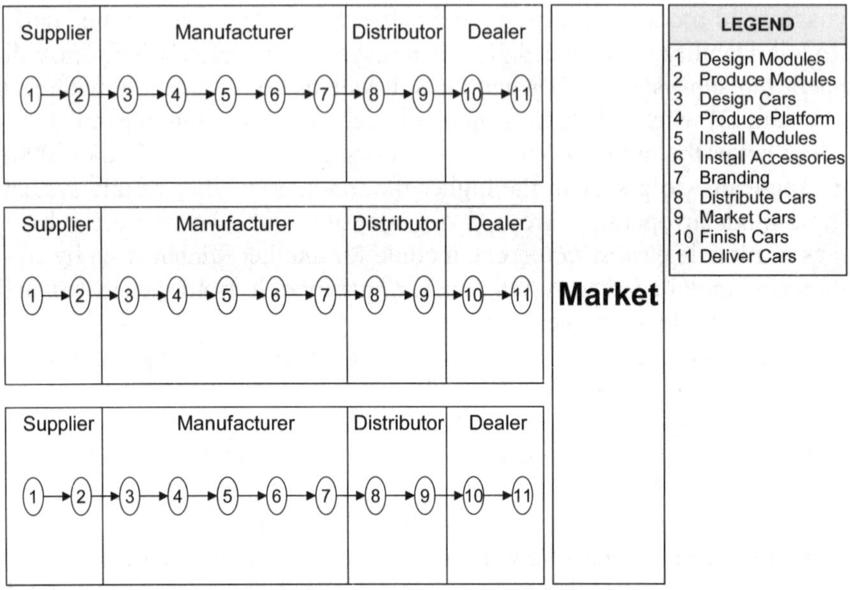

Fig 23.3 Current network design

In this case we define the level of fragmentation as the total number of organizations within a pre-defined network compared to the theoretical maximum number of organizations within that network. The theoretical maximum in this network is basically one capability per organization, meaning that this network would be broken up into 33 organizations (see Figure 23.4). Based on the current level of fragmentation within the network of 12 organizations we are going to assess the effects of the forces enabling fragmentation and the forces resisting fragmentation.

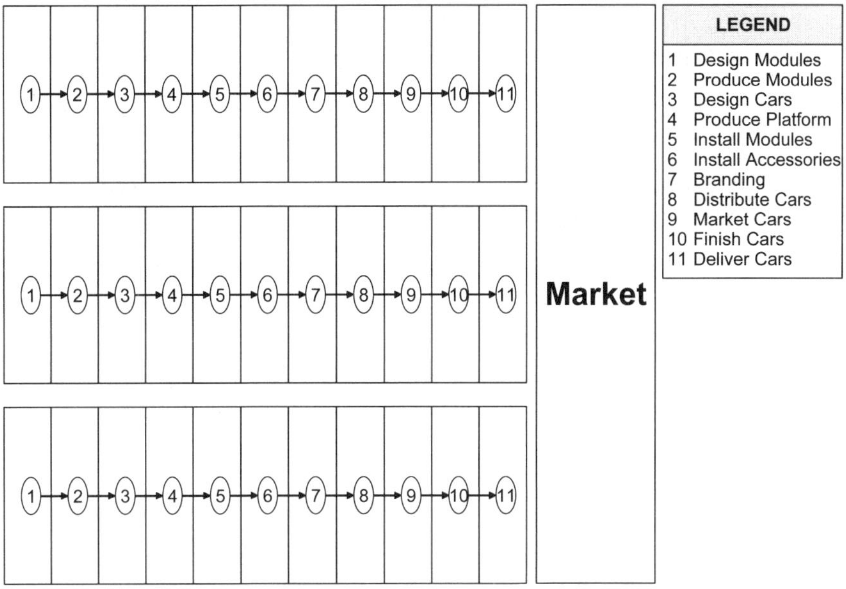

Fig 23.4 Theoretical Maximum Fragmented Network

Figure 23.5 illustrates how the current network design of 3 times 4 is 12 organizations could be further fragmented into a supply chain of eight organizations (and thus a network of 3 times 8 is 24 organizations). First of all, the design function will be separated from production (see capabilities 1, 2, 3, and 4). Decreased interaction costs will enable organizations to specialize in either production or design. The fourth capability, produce car platform, will be combined in one single organization with installing car modules, like doors, windows, etc. Second, due to the continuing trend of customization the market facing capabilities will be organized in separate organizations to fully prepare these capabilities for personalized demand. For example, finishing the car and installing accessories (capabilities 10 and 6) will be combined in a single organization as well as the branding and marketing of cars (capabilities 7 and 9).

Based on our framework a far reaching process of fragmentation in the automotive case could result in a new network consisting of 3 times 8 is 24 organizations. However, the framework also considers the factors resisting fragmentation. Figure 23.6 shows that the current supply chain of 4 organizations that face a break up into 8 organizations most probably want to fragment to a level of 5 organizations only.

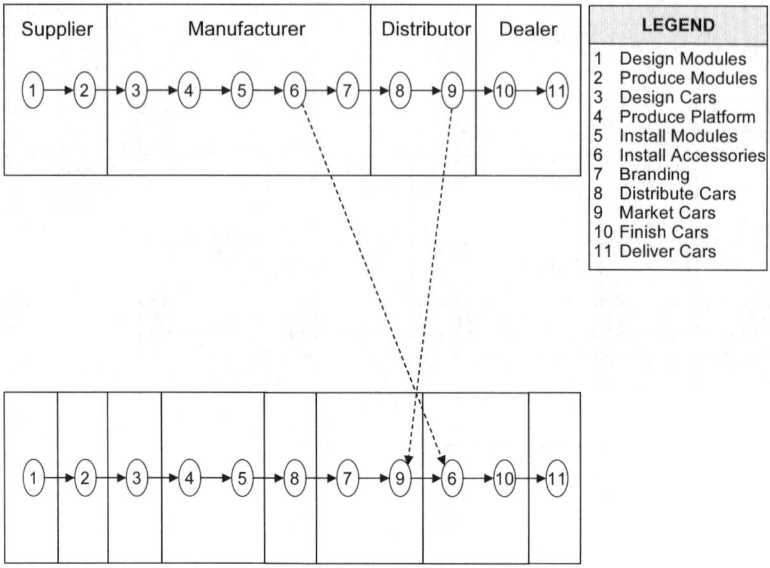

Fig 23.5 Maximum Expected Level of Fragmentation

The organizations owning production and design capabilities will try to prevent these capabilities to break up because they fear too much transparency. An organization only capable of producing car modules like doors can relatively easily be compared and replaced for another supplier. At the market facing side of the supply chain a similar process could be anticipated; indeed installing accessories and finishing cars will be combined into a single organization, as was shown in the fragmentation enabling section, however, organizations will try to combine these capabilities with the capability of delivering cars as well. In this way a more complete set of capabilities accrues that can be offered to the market.

This example shows that based on the framework the optimal level of transparency for this network is somewhere between 15 to 24 organizations.

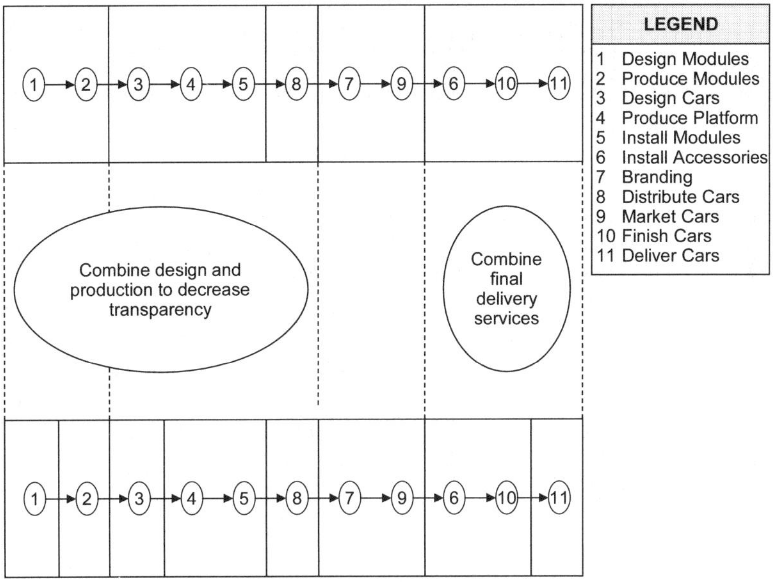

Fig 23.6 Minimum Expected Level of Fragmentation

Conclusion

Decreasing interaction costs and the increasing demand for personalized goods and services enable the further fragmentation of business networks into smaller organizational units. Too much fragmentation however, could lead to too much transparency enabling competition and imitation. Real smart business networks constantly assess the optimal level of fragmentation and adjust accordingly. To support the assessment of the optimal level of fragmentation we introduced the fragmentation framework. This framework considers both fragmentation enabling factors as well as fragmentation resisting factors.

References

Aurik, J.C., G.J. Jonk, and R.E. Willen, (2002). *Rebuilding the Corporate Genome*, John Wiley & Sons.

Baldwin, C.Y., Clark, K.B., (1997). "Managing in an Age of Modularity", *Harvard Business Review*, (September-October), pp. 84-93.

Baldwin, C.Y., K.B. Clark, (2000). *Design Rules: The Power of Modularity*, The MIT Press, Mass.

Butler, P., T.W. Hall, A.M. Hanna, L. Mendonca, B. Auguste, J. Manyika, and A. Sahay, (1997). "A Revolution in Interaction", *McKinsey Quarterly*, No. 1, pp. 4-23.

Clemons, E.K., S.P. Reddi, and M.C. Row, (1993). "The Impact of Information Technology on the Organization of Economic Activity: The 'Move to the Middle' Hypothesis", *Journal of Management Information Systems*, 10, 2, pp. 9-35.

Garud, R., A. Kumaraswamy, (1993). "Changing Competitive Dynamics in Network Industries: An Exploration of Sun Microsystems' Open Systems Strategy", *Strategic Management Journal*, 14, pp. 351-369.

Hoogeweegen, M.R., W.J.M. Teunissen, P.H.M. Vervest, and R.W. Wagenaar, (1999). "Modular Network Design: Using Information and Communication Technology to Allocate Production Tasks in a Virtual Organization", *Decision Sciences*, 30, 4, pp. 1073-1103.

Ives, B., R.O. Mason, (1990). "Can Information Technology Revitalize your Customer Service", *Academy of Management Executive*, 4, 4, pp. 52-69.

Jarvenpaa, S.L., B. Ives, (1994). "The Global Network Organization of the Future: Information Management Opportunities and Challenges", *Journal of Management Information Systems*, 10, 4, pp. 25-57.

Miles, R.E., C.C. Snow, (1992). "Causes of Failure in Network Organizations", *California Management Review*, (Summer), pp. 53-72.

Morcott, S.J., (2000). "Today's Automotive Supply Industry", *Vital Speeches of the Day*, 14, 4, pp. 431-434.

O'Grady, P., (1999). "The Age of Modularity", Adam and Steele Publishers.

Pine, B.J., (1993). *Mass Customization: The New Frontier in Business Competition,* Harvard Business School Press, Boston, Mass.

Robertazzi, T.G., (2003). "Ten Reasons to Use Divisible Load Theory", *Computer*, (May), pp. 63-68.

Venkatraman, N., Henderson, J. C., (1998). "Real Strategies for Virtual Organizing", *Sloan Management Review*, Fall, pp. 33-48.

Vervest, P.H.M., A. Dunn, (2002). *How to Win Customers in the Digital World: Total Action or Fatal Inaction*, Springer.

Williamson, O.E., (1985). *The Economic Institutions of Capitalism*, The Free Press, New York.

24 The Potential of Webservices to Enable Smart Business Networks

Jos van Hillegersberg[1], Ruurd Boeke[2], and Willem-Jan van den Heuvel[3]

Introduction

After the hype, the web still holds huge potential for B2B integration. Now that a majority of companies have realized some sort of, mostly static, web presence, the web's new promise is to enable smooth and cross-organizational business integration. Webservices (WS) seem to be among the key web-technologies that will allow this to happen. Eventually, these technologies should enable the transformation of current static supply chains into dynamic virtual networks of enterprises.

Proponents of WS-technology frequently claim that WS will lower barriers for "plug and play" B2B integration. Through WS-oriented architectures, current supply chains could become better integrated, more agile and eventually intelligent. Others have said that these technologies are not yet ready for large scale applications to supply chains and propose "traditional" cross-enterprise integration methods such as custom built point-to-point interfaces or centralized E-Hubs which are able to connect systems through custom made adapters.

Unfortunately, extensive reports from practice that address this debate are lacking. Dynamic business networks enabled through WS technologies are not yet a reality. The vast majority of current practical work is applying WS to improve intra-organizational integration rather than connecting different organizations together. Most research and industry reports in this area focus on new WS-technologies and standards. Few research addresses the potential benefits to current supply chains or addresses implementation issues. There is a lack of experience reports, case studies, demos, simulations and sample applications concerning the application of recent WS-technologies to illustrate and evaluate how WS could transform static and inefficient supply chains into more efficient and dynamic "smart" business networks.

---

[1] Erasmus University's Rotterdam School of Management, PO Box 1738, 3000 DR Rotterdam, The Netherlands: jhillegersberg@fbk.eur.nl

[2] Sitechno, The Netherlands: r.boeke@sitechno.com

[3] InfoLab, Tilburg University, PO Box 90153, 5000 LE Tilburg, The Netherlands, W.J.A.M.vdnHeuvel@uvt.nl

This paper attempts to start bridging this gap by focusing on the application of WS technologies to enable dynamic and smart business networks. The paper will address the following research questions sequentially:

Question 1: What are the current and near-future standardized components of WS-technology relevant to enabling smart business networks?(section 2)

This question is addressed through a literature review and by evaluating tools, technologies and methods for WS development.

Question 2: What is the current state-of-the-art in WS to enable smart business networks?(section 3)

This question is addressed through developing a typical scenario in which we transform a static supply chain into a "loosely coupled" business network. We implement the scenario using state-of-the art "enterprise application integration (EAI)" and WS orchestration technology.

Question 3: What are research issues regarding the use of WS technology to enable smart business networks? (section 4)

This question we deal with by reflecting on our experiences with the development of the scenario. From our development experiences we deduct research issues and an agenda for WS technology in the light of its application to enable smart and dynamic business networks.

Webservices

The Service Oriented Computing (SOC) paradigm (Papazoglou, 2003), with as its main materialization WS-technology, promises to deliver a profound new way of developing business applications and a significant step forward in the quest to maximize software reuse and integrate systems across different technology platforms. Although a variety of definitions of SOC exist, key to SOC is the process of constructing a software application by way of orchestration of pre-fabricated and pre-tested WS.

WS can be defined as self-describing, interoperable and reusable business components that can be published and invoked through the Internet, even when they reside behind a company's firewall. WS constitute in fact both design- and runtime, platform-agnostic distributed enterprise building blocks that can be composed into higher-order assemblies that support (inter- or intra-) organizational business transactions. Hence, WS enable enterprises to leverage massively distributed applications, cutting across "traditional" supply chains and vertical industries.

WS are considered an important candidate to overcome some severe obstacles of CBD. In particular, WS are described in a standard manner by their interface separating value-adding commodities from the actual implementation. WS employ open, text-based standards to achieve interoperation between applications that possibly reside at various collaborating organizations. While doing so, SOC overcomes one of the major disadvantages of object middleware technologies such as CORBA, which in fact were too complex, firewall unfriendly and hard to maintain. In addition, SOC puts greater emphasis on three complementary views on services: a client view, a provider view and a broker perspective (Burbeck, 2000). Software components usually needed to be licensed and integrated on the customer's site. WS reside at the supplier's site, thus supporting a federated architecture. The customer buys access to the WS instead of a license to download and integrate software code or a component. This model delivers potential benefits similar to application service provision (ASP). These include automatic upgrades to new versions, clear contracts through service level agreements and often specialized support from the vendor, etc. Lastly, services extend traditional class interfaces by including information that is vital to setup Service-Level Agreements by attaching information about extra-functional properties (OASIS, 2003), like performance, security, and pricing information.

The first wave of WS-technology standards has been devoted to developing infrastructural solutions for achieving interoperation at the level of messaging middleware. By now, industry has reached common agreement on interfacing standards for WS using W3C's WS Description Language (WSDL, (W3C, 2001)) that builds top of W3C's Simply Object Access Protocol (SOAP), (W3C, 2000). These technologies and standards allow organizations to expose their services and invoke services of other organizations using the Internet. For locating services, directory services have been developed such as UDDI (OASIS, 2003). Although these initial WS standards enable simple transactions using basic describe, publish, and interact mechanisms, they are not sufficient to support the more complex and long transactions that take place in a business network.

Therefore, several industry consortia are now developing higher-order WS stacks on top of SOAP that provide process composition languages. Current initiatives include ebXML Business Process Specification Schema

BPSS (ebXML, 2001) and the Business Process Execution language for WS, (BPEL4WS), (BPEL, 2003), an initiative of BEA, IBM, Microsoft SAP and Siebel. The W3C has initiated the Web Services Choreography Working Group to establish a vendor-neutral choreography specification which commands consensus and wide support. Today such as standard is not available and therefore for this study we focus on evaluating the current possibilities of the prominent current WS standards for transport (SOAP, XML), description (WSDL) and business processes (BPEL4WS), and explore their potential to support dynamic business networks. Thus, even though BPEL may be challenged or replaced, its current industry and development tool support made it a logical choice for this study. Figure 24.1 illustrates how the standards used fit into the WS standards stack.

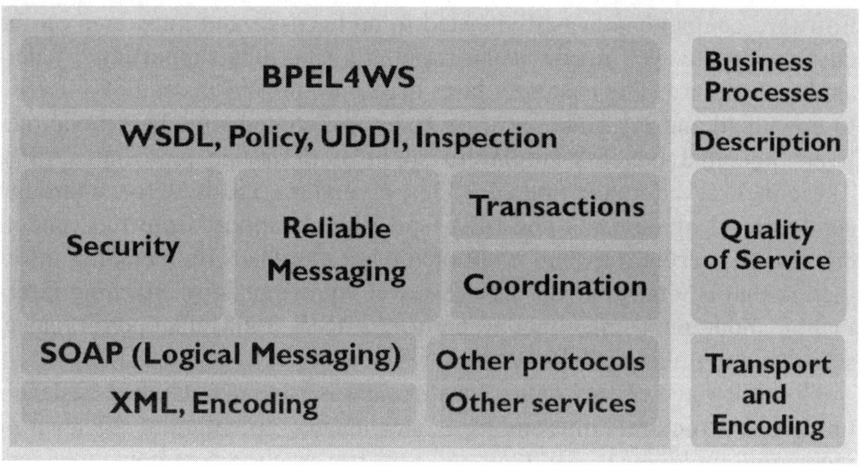

Fig 24.1 WS standards stack (Source Curbera et al., 2003)

The key properties of BPEL are summarized in (BPEL, 2003): "BPEL4WS defines a model and a grammar for describing the behavior of a business process based on interactions between the process and its partners. The interaction with each partner occurs through WS interfaces, and the structure of the relationship at the interface level is encapsulated in what we call a partner link. The BPEL4WS process defines how multiple service interactions with these partners are coordinated to achieve a business goal, as well as the state and the logic necessary for this coordination. BPEL4WS also introduces systematic mechanisms for dealing with business exceptions and processing faults. Finally, BPEL4WS introduces a mechanism to define how individual or composite activities within a process are to be compensated in cases where exceptions occur or a partner requests reversal". BPEL is built upon, and heavily uses WSDL. Every BPEL process is exposed itself as a WS described in WSDL. The BPEL process uses WSDL datatypes and WSDL to call external WS required (see Figure 24.2).

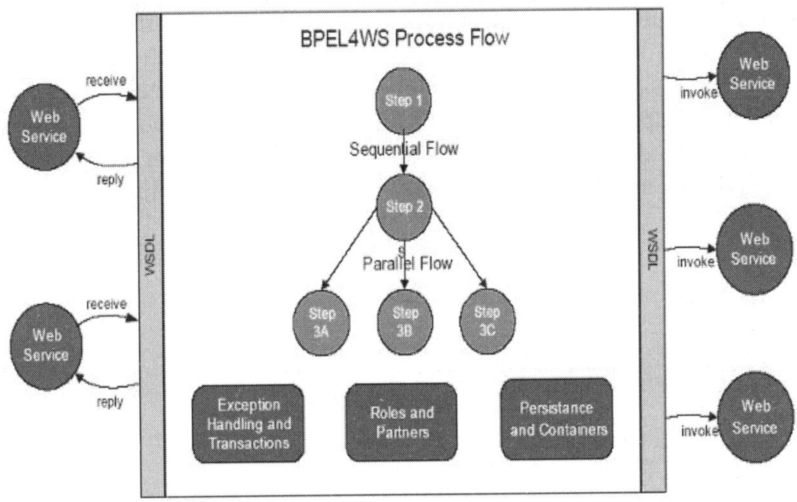

Fig 24.2 BPEL4WS process components (Source Peltz, 2003)

BPEL supports both WS-orchestration and WS-choreography. Peltz (2003) describes the difference between the two as; "*Orchestration* refers to an executable business process that may interact with both internal and external WS. For orchestration, the process is always controlled from the perspective of one of the business parties. *Choreography* is more collaborative in nature, in which each party involved in the process describes the part they play in the interaction". For our exploratory study, we focus on WS-orchestration. A WS-orchestration allows a party in a business network to quickly define and execute a business process incorporating the services of business partners in the network. Therefore, WS-orchestration technology seems especially useful for enabling dynamic business networks. The actual possibilities of BPEL combined with the early WS standards SOAP and WSDL will receive more attention in the next section when we implement a business network scenario.

Implementing a Business Network Enabled by WS

To explore the potential of the current WS technology to enable smart business networks we now develop a typical scenario in which we transform a static supply chain scenario into a "loosely coupled" business network that can be easily adapted and configured. We first implement the scenario using state-of-the art "enterprise application integration (EAI)" and then deploy WS orchestration technology. The scenario used here is partly based on a supply chain scenario developed by the WS Interoperability organisation (WS-I.org, 2004). WS-I has developed UML specifications of a Supply Chain Management scenario for the purpose of evaluating WS standards and tools. The specification documents include Use Cases, Use Case Scenarios, Activity Diagrams and a sample architecture.

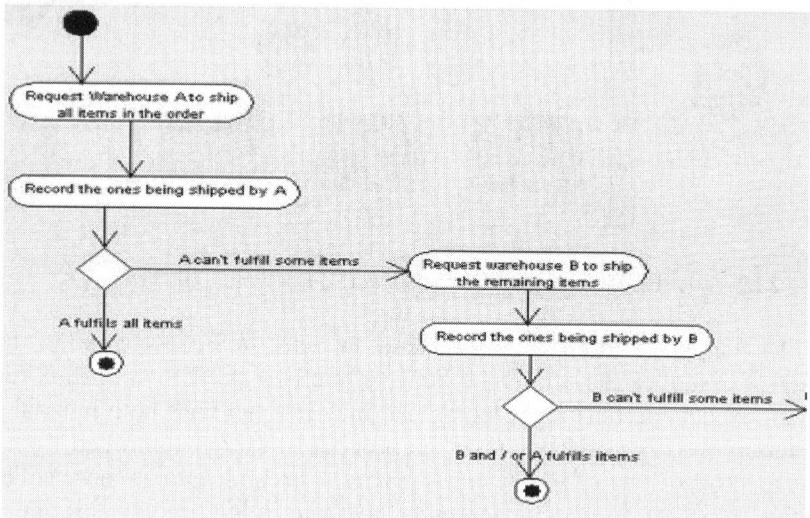

Fig 24.3 Sourcing process of a Retailer in the WS-I sample supply chain scenario (WS-I, 2004)

The WS-I supply chain scenario is based on a typical B2C model in which Retailer receives customer orders and has to fulfill these by ordering from a collection of warehouses. The retailer has to manage stock levels in warehouses and replenish by ordering from a Manufacturer's inventory (a typical B2B model). In order to fulfill a Retailer's request a Manufacturer may have to execute a production run to build the finished goods (WS-I,

2004). Figure 24.3 shows part of the WS-I scenario (Sourcing of goods from a Warehouse) in an UML Activity Diagram. The process flow shows that ordered goods are located and shipped from warehouse(s). The objective of this sourcing process is to deliver all goods ordered and prevent "out of stock".

The WS-I scenario is a useful basis for our study. However, it is quite broad and models a static supply chain. For example, the number of warehouses is fixed (3). Moreover, the business rules are very basic. For example, as Figure 24.3 illustrates, orders are shipped from the warehouses only based on a fixed sequence checking the available stock at warehouse A, B and finally C, thus not comparing cost information. Therefore we have developed our own scenario, which is based on the WS-I supply chain scenario, but adds dynamics to the business network and more complexity to the business rules.

Similarly to the WS-I scenario, the sourcing process will sequentially check multiple warehouses if the stock of a single warehouse is not sufficient. Differing from the WS-I scenario is the option to change the number of warehouses and the product assortment of each warehouse. The scenario can thus be used to experiment with "smart" WS orchestrations that use more complicated business rules to simulate the efficiency of order delivery for various business networks and warehouse product assortments. The Warehouse system stores product ID's, prices and stock levels and replenishes stock by ordering from a producer whenever the stock level drops below a minimum level. The Warehouse system keeps track of the number of items in stock, the number of items ordered by customers and the number of items in backorder with a producer (status awaited). Other than in the standard WS-I scenario, prices can be different for the same product in different warehouses. Using this information, smart WS orchestrations can be devised that optimize in time delivery and aim for the lowest price. Finally, producers are included in the scenario. Producers can be configured to produce certain products in certain batches. The warehouse can order from any producer in the business network. At this stage, the emphasis is on enhancing the Retailer-warehouse relationship.

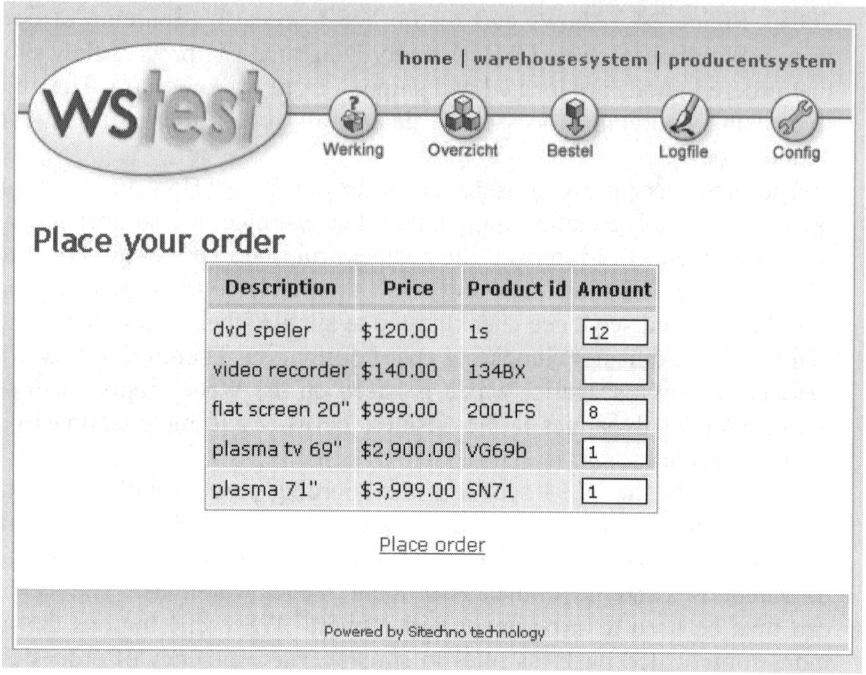

Fig 24.4 Sample webshop application

The scenario was implemented by building small software applications for each group of actors (producers, warehouses), a webshop application to serve the test-customer, and an application to configure the scenario. The user interface of the webshop is shown in Figure 24.4. Test consumers can order products order multiple products in a single session. The shop application checks the warehouses through calling their interfaces (services) to inquire about stock levels. Figure 24.5 shows the scenario configuration application. It can be used to configure the business network, e.g. setting the number of warehouses, their product assortment and prices.

Initially, the scenario was implemented in the Microsoft .Net framework. Using standard Enterprise Application Integration techniques (like Remote Method invocation), the communications between webshop, warehouse and producer were established. Then, the scenario was ported to WS-technology. By using a WS orchestration tool (BizTalk , 2004) and BPEL WS orchestration, the B2B processes were replaced by WS-orchestration. These were previously "hard coded" into the .net (C#) code. This exercise allowed us to clearly compare the potential of WS-orchestration languages and tools as compared to traditional Enterprise

Application Integration (EAI) techniques. In the following discussion, we focus on the sourcing process between the Webshop and the retailer.

In porting the standard EAI scenario to a WS-orchestration, we focused on the following questions: First, what is the power of BPEL to support more complex B2B interactions? Would it be limited to modelling simple straightforward interactions or could it also be used to quickly setup more complex and long business transactions? Second, how mature and compatible are the standards and tools? As mentioned in the previous section, orchestration standards such as BPEL are still under development. Does this cause unexpected side-effects and unpredictable behaviour of the supporting tools? Even more importantly, will WS-orchestration technology enable the end-user to quickly setup and adapt B2B processes? Will WS-orchestration technologies finally allow business users to escape from costly, and error prone traditional EAI technologies that they did not understand? In other words, will these technologies soon empower the end-user to become a "business network supervisor and configurator"?

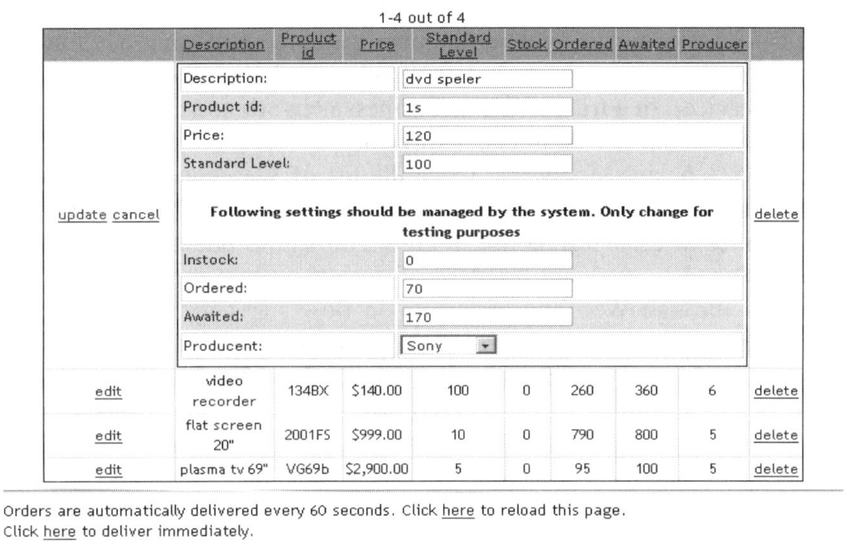

Fig 24.5 Managing the Warehouses & Product Assortment in the business network

The implementation project started in 2003. Initially, we used Microsoft BizTalk 2002 as the WS-orchestration product. However, the product had several shortcomings, and when BizTalk 2004 was launched in February 2004, we decided to migrate to this product. We have considered several other tools that supported WS-orchestration for this study, such as tools from Collaxa, BEA, IBM and Cordys. However, comparisons of several of these products illustrate that differences are minor (Peltz, 2003) and for our purposes any of these tools could have been used.

BizTalk 2004 includes several components such as a visual orchestration designer, a "message-mapper" to graphically translate and map different XML messages and a Business Rule composer that is meant to isolate business rules from the application. The BizTalk monitoring environment contains a performance measurement tool and a debugging tool. To get a feel for the usability and adaptability of BPEL WS- orchestrations in BizTalk, we will briefly discuss the WS-orchestration between the webshop and the Warehouses.

As mentioned earlier, a BPEL WS orchestration is itself setup as a WS. Therefore, the orchestration starts with an incoming request, which is a customer order requesting some quantity of a product. The orchestration monitors a "port" for incoming requests and starts an orchestration whenever an order message is received.

As our scenario uses a dynamic number of warehouses that have unique ID's, we built separate WS to locate Warehouses ID's (a kind of simple directory service). In a truly dynamic business network, indeed, an orchestration process could decide to check directory services to short-list potential partners in a business network. Once the list of Warehouses to check for stock has been identified, the orchestration can start checking product availabilities at each warehouse. Figure 24.6 shows one of the orchestrations designed to evaluate the ease of designing and implementing B2B processes through WS. The orchestration flow starts by retrieving warehouse ID's of three preferred business partners. It then proceeds by concurrently getting price and availability quotes from these three warehouses based on the customer order. The connection to the external Warehouse WS is quickly established in BPEL. An external "port" can be created by simply specifying the Web-address of the WS and the request and response messages are connected graphically by using "drag and drop" to the node "avail request". As all quotes have been received, a decision is built-in to evaluate if the quotes received can individually or jointly fulfill the order (The IF-THEN construct is visually shown by the diamond shape in Figure 24.6). If this is the case, another orchestration (Place Order) is invoked. If the quotes received cannot meet the order, an orchestration is invoked that requests quotes from additional warehouses.

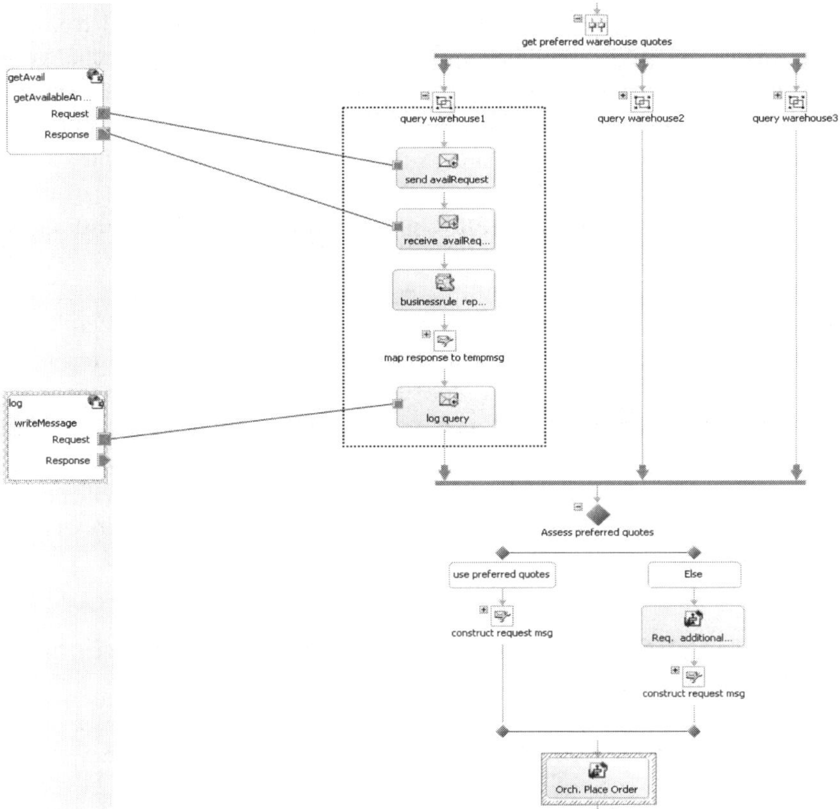

Fig 24.6 A BPEL flow to concurrently select a Warehouse for ordering

We have implemented several variants to test the adaptability of the orchestration language and tools. From the scenarios we developed and implemented using WS-orchestration, and the comparison to the initial traditional EAI approach, several conclusions can be drawn:

First, the well established and relatively simple SOAP and WSDL standards enable a true cross-platform distributed architecture. As long as these standards are well supported across platforms, WS will truly allow straightforward B2B integration using standard and low-cost Internet technology. This is a major advantage in enabling business networks, as small companies within these networks usually do not have the knowledge, time and money to implement traditional and complex EAI technologies.

Second, our scenario implementation clearly demonstrated that the network orchestration could be designed mostly separately from the various systems available in the business network. Thus, the network business rules (such as selecting a warehouse to order from) are isolated from the "back-office systems" and therefore more "visible" and easier to change. It could be stated that the B2B logic is extracted from the individual systems, and now resides in a separated WS-orchestration layer. This is a key advantage to creating dynamic business networks. Although it is hard to define what exactly is meant by a "smart" business network, the example also illustrated that basic decision logic could be easily built into an orchestration and adapted with relatively little effort.

Third, we found that orchestration technology has greatly advanced over the last 2 years that we have been carrying out this project. Still, although it has become much easier to put together orchestrations, it is in our opinion still the work of specialized consultants/developers. It is more likely that after some training, non-IT staff could adapt the business rules within an orchestration. However, businesses should handle these changes with care, as the impact of malicious code in a WS-orchestration will not be limited to the internal business, but will also impact suppliers, partners and even worst, customers.

Conclusion and Discussion: An R&D agenda for WS to Enable Smart Business Networks

WS are a promising technology to enable dynamic and smart business networks. However, the current WS stack of standards can no longer be considered a set of simple and coherent technologies as in the early days of WS. The technology is maturing, and as issues such as WS orchestration, choreography, security, quality of service and transactions are resolved, the set of standards gets richer and naturally also more complex. An area in which standards are still evolving and competing is the area of WS orchestration. In the last couple of years, we have seen many different standards rising and disappearing, and given this high technological pace, it is not surprising that businesses are reluctant to considerably invest in this part of WS-technologies. Thus, examples of business networks that already use orchestration technologies are scarce.

Therefore, to evaluate the state of the art and its potential to enable smart and dynamic business networks in the future, implementing scenarios is a useful research method. Work as done by the WS-I to develop standard sample specifications to serve as a test-bed, interoperability test and reality check for the new WS-technologies is very imperative. However, a downside of such initiatives is that mostly only vendors are providing sample solutions, and objective reviews of the possibilities of the tools and standards are scarce.

In this study we aimed to evaluate the current state-of-the-art in WS to enable smart business networks. The evaluation demonstrated that (1) SOAP and WSDL standards enable an easy to setup true cross-platform distributed architecture, (2) WS orchestration facilitates the creation of dynamic business networks by clearly separating B2B logic from the separate systems and making it easier to built-in "smart" and adaptable decisions, (3) although WS standards make B2B integration easier to put together orchestrations, it is certainly not yet an end-user task. Putting together successful orchestration will require close collaboration of business and IT specialists.

Our scenario has not tested performance, security and scalability of the orchestration tools, nor were the B2B processes complex enough to reach the limits of the expressive power of BPEL. Also, we have assumed that the various warehouses in the business network had adopted the same industry specific standards for quotes, orders etc. In reality, such standards are currently under development and often rivaling initiatives exists. Although orchestration tools included basic translation support, semantic differences in business processes can be non-trivial to resolve. Moreover, as business networks often lack a "chain director" designing the orchestration will in many cases be a collaborative process. We therefore claim that languages and tools to design B2B interaction should have features to support team collaboration.

Intelligence is required as the coordination cost (searching for appropriate services, negotiating for price and quality of services, monitoring B2B transactions) may become too high in dynamic business networks. Therefore, intelligence should be added to WS enabled business networks. This is where research on agent technologies in supply chains and WS technology are likely to meet in the future. It is our first assumption that both technologies are complementary and developing agents is more feasible in a B2B network that utilizes WS standards.

Nevertheless, the progress in WS-orchestration technologies has been substantial recently, and the scenario implemented in this paper has demonstrated that enabling a business network through WS-orchestration seems feasible. Real benefits are only expected in cases where supply chains can profit from transforming into a dynamic network of businesses. Especially when quick adaptability of the B2B processes or the configuration of the business network is an important issue, the use of WS-and WS-orchestration should definitely be considered.

References

BPEL, (2003). BEA Systems, IBM. Microsoft, SAP AG, Siebel Systems. *Specification: Business Process Execution Language for Web Services Version* 1.1, http://www-106.ibm.com/developerworks/library/ws-bpel/.

Burbeck, S., (2000). *The Evolution of Web Applications into Service-Oriented Components with Webservices*, http://www-106.ibm.com/developerworks/WSs/library/ws-tao.

Curbera, F., R. Khalaf, N. Mukhi, S. Tai, and S. Weerawarana, (2003). "The Next Step in Webservices", *CACM*, (October), Vol. 46, No. 10, pp. 29-34.

EbXML, (2001). *ebXML Business Process Specification Schema*, Version 1.01, http://www.ebxml.org/specs/ebBPSS.pdf.

OASIS, (2003). *UDDI* V 3.0.1, http://uddi.org/pubs/uddi-v3.0.1-20031014.htm

Papazoglou, M.P., D. Georgakopoulos, (2003). "Service Oriented Computing: Introduction", *CACM*, (October), Vol. 46, No.10.

Peltz, C. (2003). "Webservices Orchestration and Choreography", *IEEE Computer*, (October), pp. 46-52.

W3C (2000). *Simple Object Access Protocol (SOAP)* 1.1, W3C Note 08 (May), http://www.w3.org/TR/2000/NOTE-SOAP-20000508/.

W3C (2001). *WSs Description Language (WSDL)* 1.1, W3C Technical Report, (March), http://www.w3.org/TR/wsdl.

WS-I.org (2004). *Supply Chain Management Use Cases*, http://www.ws-i.org/.

25 Embedding Business Logic Inside Communication Networks: Network-based Business Process Management

Louis F. Pau[1] and Peter H.M. Vervest[1]

Evolution of Business Process Management (BPM) Architectures

The new BPM systems make it possible to define process logic as an applications program and run this on different 'organisational environments' (that is, different computer systems and application programs, and different human interactions in the process flows). This approach has particular attractions to business and technologists (Strong & Volkoff, 2004).

Processes can be properly defined in a runtime environment. Previous process modeling languages and tools often resulted in prescriptive recipes, were difficult, time-consuming and costly to implement. Now we can define and build small process modules, which can be templates in an organisational library, can be integrated within a complete process, plug-and-play in different environments, can be re-used, easily changed, and continually improved. Processes can be improved gradually: existing processes are viewed as black-boxes, so the BPM logic defines a certain expected behavior, or norm, of present computer systems and human beings. Deviations from the expected norm are reported to the process management console while the BPM kernel event manager keeps track of all process events and flows. The behavior of processes can be governed by rule-engines so that process results can be changed very quickly and in a controlled way (Krishnamurthy, 2003; Ben-Ameur, 2003). Outsourcing of elements of business processes is made easy and manage-able as well as insourcing or service provisioning to business partners and others.

In this paper we argue that changes in BPM's, but above all that a technical integration of the BPM execution networks and environments, enable to reduce duplication in modularized business processes and their support systems (Isenberg, 2003), and therefore to run business processes more efficiently and with more flexibility.

[1] Erasmus University's Rotterdam School of Management, PO Box 1738, 3000 DR, Rotterdam, The Netherlands, lpau@fbk.eur.nl, vervest@d-age.com

Example 1: Client authentication and credit checking do not need to be carried twice in the mobile networks and in the banking/credit card transactions processing systems, especially when the information security around mobile transactions resides mostly in the mobile network and its backbones. The benefit would be to move these two functions from financial institutions to communication operators or vice-versa.

Example 2: Digital rights management (DRM) is at source created and managed by content owners (or their proxies), although access network operators want to manage DRM as well while collecting end user profiling data the content owner does not get. The content payment also tends to be done by the access network operators and only reversed in part to the content owner. The main benefit from moving DRM and content payment initiation solely to the content owner reside in better access to end users.

Example 3: Many logistics supply chains rely on EDIFACT messages which at the same time serve as trigger events for subsequent physical transport or control steps, while the physical transport assets themselves need communication for the deployment of these resources at the proper location and time. By embedding the messages, inter nodal communications and the supply chain specifications in the same network with push facilities, much can be gained in handling delays and exceptions.

This paper suggests therefore as a first theme, to go with the technical current and to move major elements of business process logic (such as authentication, credit checking, DRM and others) into communication nodes for more flexible and efficient execution. Client behavior and regulatory rules as well as other changes are anticipated.

Unused Control Capabilities Resident in Communication Networks

All communication networks, whether connection based (e.g. SS7 signaling protocol and its derivations such as MTP-3, Camel, etc.), or connectionless (e.g. MPLS, flow control, or SIP on top of IP or ATM networks), need a control network for session establishment and many other derived functions. Such control networks are either physically separate, or common with separation, from the transport networks.

Traditionally network operators, and the bodies regulating them, have failed to see in the control networks the potential as "business control " networks performing, besides their session control and configuration functions, the command and configuration of elementary business processes depending on this communications infrastructure. The business control networks would not carry to data items or messages but the protocols enabling process module synchronization and execution.

This paper therefore, as a second main theme, proposes to use the control/signaling networks for business logic control. The next section will give more details.

From Business Process to Business Network

Once process logic can be abstracted from its runtime environment it is possible to divide process modules over a number of different actors (Hoogeweegen, 1999; Pedrycz, 2001) - defined as organizational entities - that are connected together via a communications infrastructure (see Figure 25.1). Generally, one of the major stumbling blocks to swift process coordination is the distribution of business and process logic over actors at the outside of the network. The business problem of path finding and resource allocation is also very similar to the issues surrounding naming/ addressing/ routing and capacity utilization in traditional communications network design and management.

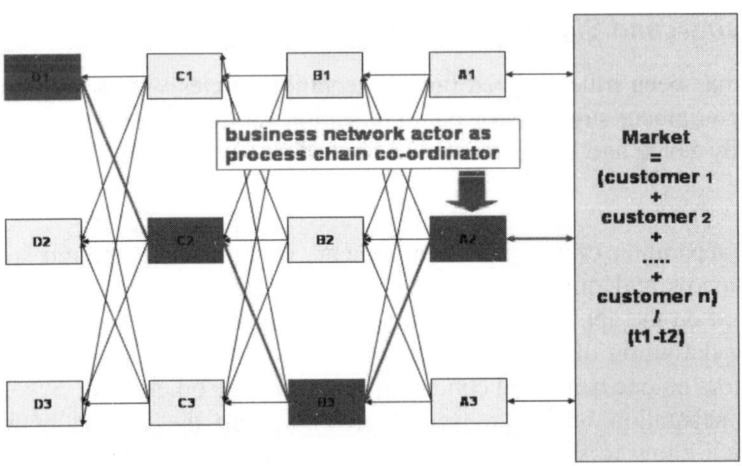

Fig 25.1 According to the Modular Network Design of business interactions, each actor pledges process modules (defined as service elements and production elements) that can be linked together to satisfy a defined customer order (Hoogeweegen, 1999; Wolters, 2002)

In total, this paper endeavours a novel approach for smart business networking relying on the embedding of business logic into the control layers of communications networks., with the resulting process simplification and specialization.

Needless to say, this is a bold proposition which some may feel to far from present realities and legacies. The next section will show facets of this proposal in terms of what is at stake.

Note to the Readers

Readers should note that in this paper, the notion of "bank" is reduced to the secure payment functions carried out by institutions like credit card companies, bank payment cooperatives, etc. Also, we implicitly assume that a communications network operator offering services, does not need to be also a backbone transmission owner.

The Business Process Impact of On-the-fly User-driven Management of Communication Architectures

Each the following subsections will map an a technical aspect in to business process, smart process, or regulatory consequences.

Transport and Signaling Networks

What has been little realized outside technical circles within communications equipment suppliers or communication service suppliers, is that historically voice and data flows have obeyed two underlying design principles:

1. the separation of transport and content (voice, data), although specific protocols and quality of service can regulate properties of the flows based on the application requirements; today this extends to the regulatory definition of backbone network operators and access network operators on one hand, and content providers on the other hand;
2. the separation of the transport networks from the control networks, which allow to set-up, manage, close and record the characteristics of connections or communication sessions; such control networks are often, for availability and security reasons physically separate from the transport networks, and execute control functions in a connection based or connection less way (SS7 and its equivalent for ATM networks in the

first case, TCP in the second case, and SCTP as an intermediate solution).[4]

However, because obviously a control network is required to run and get revenue from a transport network, the ownership of the two was traditionally the same, and thus the suppliers were traditionally supplying integrated transport and control networks with management thereof. Operators could embed via application-specific programming of the upper SS7 stack layers (MTP-3), so called "intelligent network" or "computational intelligence "functionality, such as call admission control, mobile agents, etc."(Pedrycz, 2001).

From the business process management point of view, the interest is not on the transport networks, but on the capabilities offered by the signalling/control networks. Admittedly, SS7, SCTP management exclusively by the operators gave them too much power in process management.

Open Signaling and Adaptive Networks

From a technical and research perspective, things have changed with standards such as the IEEE P1520 standards (IEEE, 2000) (Lazar, 1997) for interfaces to communication networks, as well as so called adaptive networks. Both define interfaces such that a user, e.g. the economic agent initiating a transaction, can determine the controls applicable to his own communication needs (connection, session, flow), and choose between transport networks or their dynamic configurations

From the business process management point of view, it should be possible to extend the IEEE P1520 programmable interfaces to networks, with corresponding programming model and binding mechanisms, to business logics and not just tariffs or quality of service.

Other Technical Capabilities

1. *Active networks*: The approach described above is especially appropriate for services implemented statically, usually of transactional nature, based on servers. Active networks cater to cases when the packet processing is distributed and performed by the routers along the path (or tree) to a destination (GCAP, 2000). From the point of view of business

---

[4] The Stream Control Transmission protocol SCTP allows companies to exchange signalling information between switching systems using IP.

process management, active networks enable the capability to identify, select and manage a set of economic agents involved in some of these processes, and to manage their links.

2. *Hot billing and prepaid services*: Whereas traditionally subscription based fixed or mobile voice and data services rely on the delayed payment to the operator, via payment intermediaries, of the subscription, plus traffic (or bundles thereof), the need to check the outstanding balance prior and during a call against the credit balance of a pre-paid non-subscription customer, have shifted the ultimate solvency testing of the end user away from the payment intermediary over to the mobile operator and it's associated rating systems. Communications equipment providers have thus engineered interface and control systems which link directly the control network (which establishes the connection or session) with the customer care system (which checks on prepaid balances), all this in real time. What this means, is that from being traditionally trusted with the collection, aggregation, and solvency checks of the end user, the payment intermediary has only the collection task left. This turns the mobile operators into de facto deposit banks. As to the end user authentification, it is still split and essentially done twice in different ways, because of different processes for authentification on the communications service provisioning side of the operator (typically AAA servers), and for the payee authentification of the payment intermediary (typically a financial collection system with account identification and authentification). From the point of view of business process management, hot billing illustrates altogether the ability of non-payment agents to take on financial deposits management, and even to extend this to other services, while managing the communication networks at the same time. Pre-paid services also illustrate the ability in mobile networks to activate and monitor service level agreements between parties in real time.

Embedding the Business Logics into the Communication Networks

A Communications-enabled Business Architecture

Figure 25.2 shows how communication networks can provide a basic business architecture, with:

- a transport and capacity level, which is a technical agent chosen by the next level up,

- a business and control level at which an economic agent determines his business logic around the information, transport and services he needs, to select and control the transport level; this level interfaces with enterprise internal systems and information,
- a verification and risk control level, where business logic vets and activates the control level.

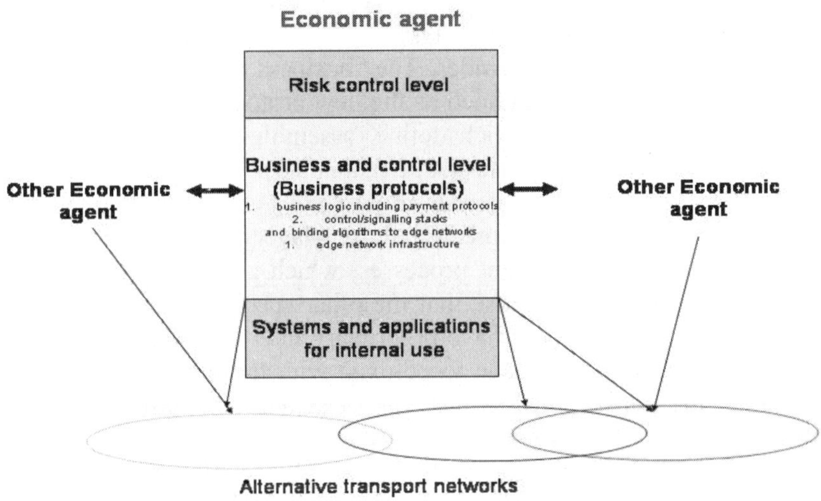

Fig 25. 2 Economic agent which interacts with other economic agents without general trade and payment intermediaries; this agent has imported into its communications and computer systems the network control functions, and merged these with his own business logic and processes (trade, payment, ERP, etc.)

The technical nodes and business logics or protocols, as well as the interfaces supporting this are defined and discussed below. It should be noted that some standards, such as UML, MDA, BPML (Arkin, 2002), allow to specify jointly the communications and business logic. It should also be noted that the proposed architecture indeed allows to embed only templates of business processes (or generic business protocols), as opposed to full processes with characteristics, so the end users can configure them at execution time.

Combination of Network Control Logic with Business Logics / processes and "Business Protocols"

Based on the above, we propose here in business terms to embed the business logics and processes of each economic agent into the Business and control level of that Economic agent's control Node in the communications networks at the edges (see Figure 25.2). Said in other words, but now formulated from a communications point of view, each economic agent would install the interfaces and control software of communication networks, and combine these with his own business logics and processes on both the trade and payment sides. The "business protocols" resulting from this embedding are here defined as the new protocols executed in the control/signaling networks, which define, assemble, synchronize or execute elements of business processes (see Figure 25.3).

This is of course only possible, in terms of genericness and availability of the corresponding software, for those players in the network control, trade processes and payment processes, which are best practices in each case – This implies of course that the other specialized trade or payment intermediaries, which only have proprietary interfaces and processes, may be doomed as they will have to co-exist with the main economic agents initiating the transactions, as the bulk of standardized processes will bypass them.

Figure 25.2 also highlights that, whereas all economic agents have engineered a possible choice of transports to support their needs at transport level, some of these may be shared between economic agents who interact. This is obviously the case both for communication carriers, ISP's as well as transport/logistics networks. However, the economic agent who initiates the transaction or business may, from his own business and control level, retain some control over such transport level resources.

Transport networks and the network controls for these are unaffected, except that binding interfaces or active network features resident at the economic agent's premises would interface with them. However, it is also possible, at the lower protocol level, to embed as well detailed transaction rules inside or alongside transport, network or application protocols; this is explained in detail in (Pau, 2003) and illustrated here in Figure 25.3.

Assuming process fit to be a measure of the alignment or correspondence between a set of common attributes of two different business processes, fit can immediately be set at a maximum value if several actors or business processes use the same business protocol. In another way, realizing that fit metrics are in general difficult to design and measure, they become much more explicit if and when standardized business protocols are used.

BPM Management Implications

Embedding the business logic inside the networks, with on-the-fly identification, selection, and management imply several consequences:

Proposition 1: End users can manage some communications and business processes to their liking and for competitiveness, whereas in the past they had to accept as given and use at best commodity specifications.

Proposition 2: Potentially a major competition will take place between those operators/network owners offering end users a freedom to create and manage business logic embedding mechanisms, and those operators/network owners who want to set and manage as a managed service deployment and operations of their users.

Proposition 3: New type of real-time business processes and services will become possible (e.g. document and order process synchronization and linking with company archives), paving the way to real-time service level agreements and order fulfillment across several business partners without necessarily involving restrictive network operator procedures and costs (Meij et al., 2003).

Proposition 4: Relying on Proposition 3, new types of on-the-fly reverse auctions will become possible (with multivariate attributes and constraints) (Pau, 2003) and will be executed inside the network without relying on a third party. The buyer can specify his process and service request inside the network, collect bids and validate the communications enabled process attributes with the bidders.

Proposition 5: Whereas now the execution of a business process across several parties is done relying on a neutral set of actors (network providers, data storage providers, ASP's, authentification centers, etc), the neutrality of which can sometimes been put in doubt, the proposed architecture would imply that groups of parties take control of their support nodes; this of course assumes changes to regulatory frameworks in some cases (e.g. granting communication licences to logistics or payment agents).

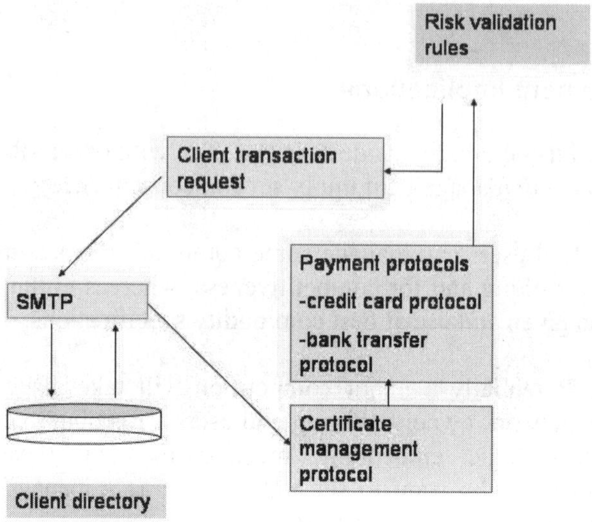

Fig 25.3 Example of a business control protocol (parts in green, interacting with internal system in grey and risk control level in brown) enabling a payment process in combination with the SNMP network control. This Figure 25.3 does not give the detailed flow of interactions between parties, but only aggregates thereof

Proposition 6: New insurance, risk management and legal frameworks are needed to support embedding business logics inside the networks. This is especially important to allow for fair and open trading not reduced by proprietary or incomplete process interfaces and communications control interfaces.

Future Developments of Integrated Business and Communications Control Logic and Conclusions

This paper investigates a novel way to embed business logic into the control layers of communications networks at the edges of the backbones. This is motivated e.g. by initial encouraging work at the Rotterdam School of Management in the fields of mobile networks and logistics (Pau, 2003). It has shown that process modularization requires formalized specifications but enables much faster exchange of process messages and result in improved logistical flows. In the area of mobile payments, it has been shown (Pau, 2003) that mobile operators owning a limited banking license actually perform payments more efficiently in terms of profitability and speed. Beyond these instances, but not covered here, UMTS/3G mobile networks used as business networks, and content distribution networks, represent important short term deployment areas, subject to regulatory changes.

Also, as process events can be linked very quickly, and economic agents may recompose themselves and/or their functions, the dynamic resource optimization across many economic agents will be increasingly complicated. We suggest that some genetic and bio-informatics algorithms are useful to realize the corresponding adaptation selection and recalculations of the business logic embedded at the communications level (Holland, 1992; Alemdar, 2003). Finally, such an approach opens the way technically to individualized communications tariffs and process costs or each agent, with settlement not only by operators or financial institutions (Pau, 2002).

As a conclusion, "smart business networks" cannot be defined and assume coordination at process level only, with resulting lack of control to end users and duplications. This paper offers a way to design and execute in practice smart business networks. However, it is also necessary to mention that it is not always possible to embed the business logic inside the communication networks (e.g. for internal and proprietary client-server systems, or 30 year old persistent processes), or that in some cases only some parts can be embedded.

References

Alemdar, N.M, S. Sirakaya, (2003). "On Line Computation of Stackelberg Equilibria With Synchronous Parallel Genetic Algorithms", *Journal of economic Dynamics and Control*, Vol 27, pp. 1503-1515.

Arkin, A. (2002). "Business Process Modelling Language - BPML 1.0", *BPMI*, www.bpmi.org.

Ben-Ameur, W., H. Keivin, (2003). "New Economical Virtual Private Networks", *Communication of the .ACM*, Vol 46, No 6, pp. 69-73.

GCAP Project, (2000). "EU Framework 4 program", *EU*, Brussels www.cordis.lu.

Holland, J.H., (1992). "Genetic Algorithms", *Scientific American*, Vol 278, No 1, pp. 66-72 .

Hoogeweegen, M.R., W.J.M. Teunissen, P.H.M. Vervest, and R.W. Wagenaar, (1999). "Modular Network Design: Using Information and Communication

Technology to Allocate Production Tasks in a Virtual Organization", *Decision Sciences*, 30, 4, pp. 1073-1103.

IEEE (2000). "Standard P1520 Programming Interfaces for Networks", *IEEE Standards Association*, NY.

Isenberg, D.S. (2003). "The End of the Middle", *IEEE Spectrum*, Vol 40, No 1, pp. 37-38.

Krishnamurthy, S., G.M. Pallavi, and G. Moakley, (2003). "Automatic Multi Business Transactions", *IEEE Internet computing*, Vol 7, No 3, pp. 66-73.

Lazar, A. (1997). "Programming Telecommunications Networks", *IEEE Network*, pp. 8-18.

Meij, S., L-F. Pau, E. van Heck, (2003). "Auctioning Bulk Mobile SMS/MMS Messages", 2nd *International Conference M-Business*, Vienna, www. mbusiness2003.org .

Pau, L-F. (2002). "The Communications and Information Economy: Issues, Tariffs and Economic Research Areas", *Journal of Economic Dynamics and Control*, Vol. 26, No's 9-10, pp. 1651-1676.

Pau, L-F. (2003). "Real Time SLA Provisioning for Mobile Operators Needing Spontaneously User-Defined Content", Research Report, Rotterdam School of Management, *Open Group QoS Task Force*, www.opengroup.org/qos_ taskforce .

Pau, L-F. (2004). "Mobile Operators as Banks or Vice-Versa?", *Proceedings Austin Mobility Roundtable*, University of Texas, Austin, TX, (March), ERIM Research Report, Erasmus University Rotterdam.

Pedrycz, W., A. Vasilakos, (2001). *Computational intelligence in telecommunications networks*, CRC Press, Boca Raton, ISBN 0-8493-1075-X

Strong, D., O. Volkoff, (2004). "A Roadmap for Enterprise System Implementation", *IEEE Computer*, Vol 37, No 6, pp. 22-32.

Wolters, M., (2002). "The Business of Modularity of the Modularity of Business", PhD Research Thesis, ERIM, Erasmus University Rotterdam.

Review Comments

Reviewer: Jups Heikkila
Rapporteur: Jimmy C. Tseng

The authors of this paper propose a simple but bold conception of embedding business logic within communications networks, or more specifically, using the signaling or control networks for business transactions control; it also proposes to push the industry-standard business logic traditionally residing on application layer (in the ISO model) down the protocol stack (L3 in CS and SNMP in IP networks). The examples lending support to this argument include, amongst other cases, to avoid the duplication of the GGSN / billing gateway overlapping with an IT transactions system for the payment services in GPRS and UMTS mobile communications networks. The authors observe that the services needed to support commercial transactions on both payment and mobile networks share certain common functions, like authentication and credit checking. The authors then present six propositions for the release of the network control function, to enable the development of new commercial infrastructure embedded inside the communications networks that will ultimately serve as the technological foundations of "smart business networks". Some of the propositions highlight the required regulatory changes.

The reviewer assessed the technological logic behind such a transition, examining the benefits of vertical network integration (e.g. to reduce latency) and horizontal application integration (e.g. to simplify complexity in the protocol stack). He did not address the business aspects. The reviewer then sought four points of clarification (responses by main author are summarized in *italics*):

1. Do you have a specific use scenario in mind, or is this a generic approach? *Operating payment services over the mobile networks and over ATM should be similar and they will share common functionality and infrastructure elements, recognized by third parties. With the convergence of telecommunications, you will start seeing new arrangements, for example, in Sweden, telecom identifiers maintained inside the MGW or GGSN, are recognized by the tax authorities.*
2. Does the approach imply a specific topology? Static networks handling transactions (e.g. SS7 hierarchy) or a network of mobile networks? *Old networks are a mess, the future is in the 3GPP supported common control for wireless and fixed networks (hopefully soon to be extended to control of 802.11x hot-spots).*
3. Can this provide a global "platform' for business? *Yes, consider for example current roaming arrangements and platforms. They share the same requirements for authentication, privacy, and trust and above all they manage in real-time SLA's between operators.*
4. Who would reap the benefits? There are already so many banks and so many telecom operators? *The convergence is evident in transaction handling cooperatives like SWIFT and in IBAN communication between credit card companies and banks.*

Participants in the workshop reacted with questions concerning (responses by main author summarized in *italics*):

1. Is moving the business logic down the protocol stack essential? *We are no longer in a circuit switched paradigm, but formal verification and traceability of the business processes are needed more then ever with the formal linking akin circuits based sessions.*
2. Would the traffic be able to handle digital assets and rights? *Yes, content providers want to enable one-stop service for digital rights management and payment and not let third parties (such as operators) reap all the benefits derived from user profiling and DRM management.*
3. Is provision of business logic compatible with the provision of bulk capacity and access points? *The evolution of what ITU calls "converged networks" combining transport infrastructure, access point, and service points means that the business models of telecom operators will change over time, and that they suddenly have a chance to become provision platforms for user-configurable business processes (instead of just being "pipes" for communication.*
4. Can you draw a parallel to application logic and give an example of a business protocol? *Modifying SNMP for a payment transaction is described in the ERIM report by L-F Pau, "Network-based Business Process Management: Embedding Business Logic in Communications Networks", ERIM Report Series Research in Management, ERS-2003-086-LIS, Rotterdam 2003.*
5. Is the convergence of the banking and telecom business probable given the different core competencies and strategic intents? Telecoms emphasize transaction, volume, and cash flow while banks emphasize management of wealth and assets. *The payment services addressed in this paper do not encompass all banking services. The focus is on payment services, mainly credit card operations, not knowledge intensive treasury functions.*
6. Would current telecom and banking regulations allow joint operations since telecom and banking licenses are very different? *There is a trend towards convergence of the two sets of regulations.*

The audience ended the discussions with a different perspective on possibilities offered by mobile networks, and the opportunity to re-evaluate business functionality on the network protocol stack.

26 What Is SMART about Credit Card Payments?

Jimmy C. Tseng[1]

Introduction

Businesses deploying electronic commerce applications are often required to coordinate their activities with external parties. For example, some online businesses provide their customers the ability to track and trace shipments through a service actually provided by external logistics service providers (e.g. UPS). Likewise, many Internet retailers integrate their online storefronts with payment services actually provided by third party payment service providers (e.g. WorldPay). Even individual traders on online auctions now have access to payment services provided by person-to-person payment processors (e.g. PayPal and Nochex). The deployment of these modular business components from different service providers is making it easier for businesses to share information in a seamless manner, and even coordinate activities between different organizations.

Building on existing literature on inter-organizational systems (IOS), business process re-engineering (BPR), and supply chain management (SCM), some researchers envisage a future for even more dynamically configured business networks (Smith and Fingar, 2003). Revitalized by recent developments in software, businesses are shifting from the deployment of monolithic applications dictated by functional requirements as in Enterprise Application Integration (EAI) towards modular business components. The new generation of Business Process Management (BPM), Web Services (WS) and Extensible Markup Language (XML) standards now provide a software architecture for integrating applications residing on different systems and business processes spanning multiple organizations. The Web Services architecture provides service description, publication, and discovery, which collaborators in the business network can utilize to bind and invoke services in a dynamic manner. When deploying applications in the services oriented architecture, application integration becomes a matter of making the relevant web services call instead of a complicated redesign effort (Miller, 2003). Despite these efforts, challenges remain in the standardization of web services (Kreber, 2003), and out-

[1] Erasmus University's Rotterdam School of Management, PO Box 1738, Rotterdam 3000 DR, The Netherlands, jtseng@fbk.eur.nl

standing issues remain in the area of security and interoperability. With the increasing maturity of these new business data processing technologies, attention is now turning towards the coordination and management of business processes spanning multiple organizations. The metaphor often used for software that coordinates and orchestrates such interaction within the web services architecture is the business operating system. While the business operating system metaphor is a powerful one, business process orchestration and management remains one of the least developed areas within the current protocol stack. Understanding the complex array of technology standards proposed in the Web Services architecture can sometimes be daunting as information technology vendors come up with an increasing array of technical standards and middleware technologies to address the challenges.

To realize the new opportunities for dynamic business networks, business cases are needed in conjunction with the rapid advances in the underlying technologies. We argue that online payments services provide a good context for a closer examination of these business network formations in operation.

Firstly, commercial payment service providers are already providing payment services in a modular manner, enabling easier integration with existing software platforms.

Secondly, payment services can adapt easily to different payment methods and payment networks (e.g. Visa, MasterCard, American Express).

Thirdly, payment processes are synchronized through online access to almost real-time data.

And finally, payment transactions place stringent security requirements on each partner on the network, and hence there are already well developed framework of contractual arrangements and business rules to allocate risk and liability. The inherent characteristics of online payment services make it a good business case for coordination of business activities through either manual procedures or automated means. Empirical business cases show where effective solutions exist without requiring extensive technology. Business cases also explain how technology actually changes business processes and relationships.

We describe in the next section the contractual arrangements in credit card payments. These arrangements provide the framework for partners in the network to coordinate their activities, thereby replacing the guiding hand of an orchestrator with a set of business rules. In section 3, we describe the changes in business rules for online credit card payments, in particular, the business rules that deal with procedures for authentication and authorization, the mechanisms for retaining evidence dispute resolution, and the enforcement of transactions. In section 4, we apply the lessons from the credit card sector to discuss the characteristics of smart business networks. We propose these characteristics as design principles for SMART business processes. And in the final section we discuss the future implications of SMART payment services for electronic commerce.

Contractual Arrangements in Credit Card Payments

Since payment transactions place stringent security requirements on each partner on the network, there is a need to map from functions, the roles and responsibilities, obligations and liabilities of each partner. The business and legal model for credit card transactions has been referred to as the four cornered model, because an explicit business relationship exist between two parties in the network, for example, the cardholder with the issuing bank.

By maintaining cardholder accounts, cardholders agree to the terms and conditions in the cardholder's agreement with the issuing bank. Likewise, there is an explicit business relationship between the merchant with the acquiring bank.

To keep their merchants accounts, merchants also need to agree to the terms and conditions of the merchant agreement. The issuing and acquiring banks are bound together by their membership in the banking associations. All four parties are bound together through a series of contractual arrangements illustrated in Figure 26.1. The payment flow and business processes for credit card transactions has been elaborated elsewhere (O'Mahony, Peirce, Tewari, 1997). The purpose here is to show how contractual arrangements between the different parties in a credit card transaction make it possible to coordinate activities between different parties.

In brief, for every new credit card account, an issuing bank offers credit to a consumer to make purchases in what is also known as consumer credit (Mandell, 1990). When a consumer initiates a purchase with a merchant using the credit card account, the merchant applies standard authentication and authorization procedures. Provided the bank procedures are followed (i.e. the account holder is authenticated and transaction has been authorized), the merchant passes the sales voucher to the acquiring bank (i.e. there is evidence to support the transaction).

Acquiring banks then clear the payment with the consumer's credit card issuing bank. For every transaction the acquiring bank charges a percentage of the transaction for the use of the payment service. Merchant Service Charge is negotiated based on the industry rate, the volume that a merchant generates. Settlement occurs through the card brand's payment infrastructure. International banking associations like Visa and MasterCard provide the payment infrastructure and rules and regulations regarding their payment networks. These rules and regulations provide the framework for further contractual arrangements in credit card payments.

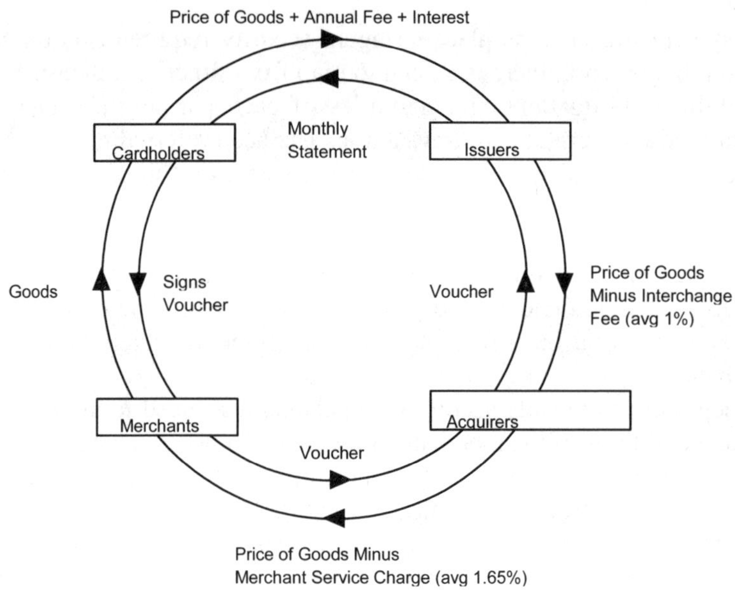

Fig 26.1 Credit Card Arrangements (*Source: Office of Fair Trade, March 1994)*

The business rules in credit card networks dictate how activities are to be coordinated (e.g. how disputes are resolved and enforced within the payment network). The fees and charges can be adjusted based on type of merchant (e.g. Mail Order/Telephone Order), and transaction (e.g. Cardholder Present transaction/Internet transaction) in order to allocate risk in an economically efficient manner. Interchange rates are also adjusted to serve as incentives for banks to adopt new technologies.

Business Rules for Online Credit Card Payments

From the merchants' point of view, credit card payment processing used to be provided by an acquiring bank that leases special terminal equipment and communication lines for initiating transactions. With the prevalence of the Internet, terminal equipment and dedicated communications lines are no longer necessary. Instead, most online payments are acquired through payment gateways, or hosted and managed payment services. The modular payment services typically provided by large acquiring banks and dedicated payment processors today allows businesses to better integrate their business applications with their payment system. For example, internet retailers can seamlessly integrate their shopping cart software with the payment modules provided by the payment service provider. This however, requires changes in the way business processes are coordinated between various parties. We examine in the remainder of this section the changes to payment processes, in particular those that deal with procedures for authentication and authorization, the mechanisms for retaining evidence dispute resolution, and the enforcement of transactions.

The changes in these processes can be a combination of manual and automated procedures. To illustrate, the security mechanisms traditionally built into a plastic card for a credit card transaction has been reduced to a series of private information like account number, expiry date, and billing address during an online transaction. An example of manual procedure is a series of security best practices designed to enhance the protection of cardholder sensitive information and transactional data called the Visa Account Information Security (AIS) program. An example of an automated procedure to enhance security is the Secure Electronic Transactions (SET[2]) specification (Visa International and MasterCard, 1997). SET was designed to operate from insecure public networks, making each web site a potential sales point, and each PC a potential entry point into the credit card network. SET is a complex monolithic system using proprietary technologies that was not adopted by the market. Visa's next solution called Visa Authenticated Payment Program "3D Secure" is much more modular, specifying security solutions for three different domains, the issuer domain, the acquirer domain, and the interoperability domain, using readily available technologies.

[2] SET is a trademark of SET Secure Electronic Transaction LLC (SETCo)

Authentication and Authorization

Authentication of a cardholder in a credit card transaction where the cardholder is not physically present presents several new challenges. Because the security mechanisms built into the plastic card can no longer be used, additional security mechanisms were introduced like the Card Verification Value (CVV) and Address Verification System (AVS). These private information are now used as part of the authentication process, and needs to be incorporated into the transaction process. Because such information is highly sensitive, they are not supposed to be retained by the business, but many still do so in the name of customer convenience.

Authentication under SET is very different from traditional credit card transactions that are initiated by the retail merchant, within the secure premises of the merchant's store. SET transactions are cardholder initiated transactions, rather than merchant initiated transactions. Part of the reason SET was not widely adopted can be explained by the need for extensive changes for all parties.

In contrast to the high-tech approach in SET to authenticate account holders, PayPal uses a simple low-tech mechanism to authenticate account holders. For each new account registered on PayPal, a small one-off billing is debited from the account. If the customer is able to provide the exact amount and the corresponding reference number, the customer and hence the account is considered to be authenticated.

Visa introduced in 2003 the "Verified by Visa" programme to add an additional level of cardholder authentication for online credit card payment transactions. This programme allows registered cardholders an additional level of protection against misuse of their accounts in an online environment.

In addition to authenticating a cardholder, each transaction above a merchant floor limit needs to be authorised. Prior to the development of automated authorization systems, a merchant employee had to make a telephone call to the acquiring bank with which they had contracted. With the advent of authorization systems for credit card transactions (e.g. Visa's BASE I), magnetic stripe terminals and payment gateways can now be used to reduce the authorization process from minutes to seconds. The authorization systems responds with an "authorization code" that needs to be linked to the transaction, and referred to when settling disputed transactions. Merchants are required to retain the authorisation code as evidence of an authorized transaction. With the advent of the clearing and settlement systems for credit card transactions (e.g. Visa's BASE II), the sales receipts with the cardholder's signature are no longer used in the clearing and settlement process, but again retained as evidence for resolving disputes.

BASE I (1973) Authorization System - Originally only 5000 authorizations per hour - Now 2800 transactions per second (3800 peak, theoretical 10,000 transactions) BASE II (1974) Clearing and Settlement System - Computerize processing and interchange of paper draft - Fourth update in July 2001, BASE II now processes 50 to 100 million transactions per day (valued between US$2 billion to $4 billion)

Fig 26.2 Visa Authorization and Clearing Systems (Source: Visa USA, 2004)

Evidence and Dispute Resolution

Should a dispute regarding a transaction occur, the operating rules and regulations of the international card brands provides provisions for passing the cost of claims back to the acquiring banks, which may in turn pass the cost of claims back to the claims to the suppliers under the conditions of the merchant service agreements. When such a dispute occurs, the issuing bank would suspend the charges to the consumer, and instigate an investigation, also called a chargeback. The resolution of the dispute depends on the merchants and hence acquiring bank's ability to provide proof of the transaction. The allocation of liability then falls on the acquirer responsible for recruiting the supplier to the card network (if no proof of transaction), and the issuing bank which is the extender of credit to the consumer (if there is proof of transaction).

For online transactions, a different set of business rules apply because there is no longer a cardholder's signature. In these situations, the chargeback is automatic and the burden is on the merchant to reclaim the disputed amount from the customer. When a chargeback occurs (historically less than 0.2% of all transactions), the issuing bank asks the acquiring bank to provide the physical voucher with the customer's signature (also known as transaction receipt retrieval). Because such an investigation incurs a cost (retrieval fees, chargeback, and filing fees), the customer is charged an additional fee if there is a valid physical signature (or evidence that the transaction was authorized). But if the mistake is with the merchant, a chargeback is placed on the merchant, and the threat of losing the merchant account if chargeback rates are too high. A variety of errors could also account for a chargeback, for example a stolen or forged credit card, a banking error, in which case there is all the more reason to examine fraud control and working practices (Visa International and MasterCard, 1997).

SET places heavy demands on storage requirements for evidence, which is not unusual for payment systems. For example, the merchant software needs to store the "auth code" before the payment is cleared, and retain it for a period of time to counter chargebacks. The associations believe that cardholder signatures are no longer required in SET since their digital signature is assumed to be sufficient evidence that the cardholder was involved, and an "auth code" is sufficient to prove that the transaction was authorised by the issuing bank. This design was supposed to remove "cardholder denies transaction" type of chargebacks, shifting the risk from online merchants, that in turn translates to reduced merchant service charges.

Enforcement and Chargeback

Parties in a credit card network are contractually bound to each other through a series of contracts, using the framework provided by the banking associations operating rules and regulations. All transactions have to be accounted for, and in the case of disputes resolved through the dispute resolution rules. Decisions are enforced by issuing chargebacks, or credit reversals. The mechanisms for debiting and crediting these accounts automatically are an integral part of the banking associations clearing and settlement systems. In order to enforce the decisions, the chargeback system is used to shift the burden of proof from one party to another based on the available evidence and applying the relevant dispute resolution rules.

In the absence of fraud, the individual amounts disputed are usually very small compared to the cost of instigating an investigation. Some of these disputes are written off by either issuers or merchants as bad debt. Historically, such debt has been relatively low compared to transaction volume, but can chargeback strains the resources of both the acquiring and issuing bank in other ways. Allowing disputes is costly for both issuing and acquiring banks, due to the need to staff call centers. As a result, the banking associations are still trying to work to change the business rules through introducing emerging technologies like SET and 3D Secure.

It can be argued that the perception of insecurity in electronic networks is often due to the lack of enforcement mechanisms. Despite the challenges created by new technologies and new ways of working, credit card networks can be said to be relatively safe because it has a built-in mechanism for resolving disputes and enforcing them.

Characteristics of SMART Payment Processes

Applying the lessons from the credit card sector in the previous section, we would like to highlight the characteristics of payment processes today. We use the acronym SMART to represent these characteristics of dynamic business processes, and suggest that characteristics serve as design principles for other SMART business processes.

Service Oriented Model

Payment systems are now increasing service-oriented. Payment processors are increasing providing a payment service, rather than a separate payment platform or software system. Address Verification Systems, and the "Verified by Visa" program are in reality authentication services provided by the payment network. Online authorization is another service provided by the payment networks. As increasing number of applications migrate to Web Services standards, certain functions can be replaced by the service model.

Modular Business Processes

Payment services are already modular in design. Business applications link to payment services through software modules that can be changed easily when business processes change. Visa gave up the monolithic architecture in SET for the modular architecture in 3D Secure. Merchants developing authentication processes using the "Verified by Visa" services are in essence coordinating business processes between multiple organizations, integrating business applications with the payment service.

Adaptive Networks

Payment services are flexible and can accommodate change easily because there are standards for interchange. Payment services can easily accommodate different payment instruments and payment brands, re-routing transactions to different payment networks as necessary. A customer can easily switch from a Visa account to a MasterCard account, and still use the same payment service. Payment gateways are capable of routing these messages to the relevant payment networks.

Real-time Data

Real-time data is essential for coordinating business processes across multiple organizations. With the current versions of the authorization systems, payment services can be coordinated using real-time data. When a merchant makes an authorization request, authorization codes are increasingly based on up-to-date credit availability on a particular account supplied by an issuing bank. Likewise, an authentication service like "Verified by Visa" needs to retrieve passwords from millions of accounts within a matter of seconds.

Trustworthy Business Rules

Credit cards currently are, and will likely remain the predominant form of payment for Internet commerce due to its widespread acceptance (Evans and Schmalensee, 1999). Despite the inherent security weaknesses in online credit card payments, credit card networks have a framework of business rules for allocating risk and resolving disputes. Although the chargeback mechanism was not designed to deal with the consumer issues regarding product and service (e.g. mis-representation, satisfactory quality, fit for purpose), it can cover circumstances where goods and services have been paid for, but not received, a feature not available for transactions without a financial intermediary. It therefore encourages spending, and builds business confidence.

The future for SMART Payment Services

The use of information and communication technologies to share information and coordinate activities in the supply chain has already been elaborated elsewhere. Integrating electronic commerce applications frequently involves the combination of information from external parties like logistics service providers and payment service providers. E-business technologies are used increasingly for tighter integration of transactional and logistical processes between parties in the supply chain, for example automatic track and trace of deliveries and the calculation of shipping charges and taxes.

However, in many organizations, improvements in transaction and logistics flows can be overshadowed by performance in payment flows (Killen and associates, 2001). While order, delivery and invoicing times have reduced dramatically, payments can still take between 30-60 days. Better coordination and automation of payment flows are now essential to the performance in the supply chain. The goals of improving throughput time, transparency, error handling through information sharing in the physical supply chain can also apply to the financial supply chain. For example, automated payment processing can reduce invoicing costs, and provide CFOs with better reporting, monitoring, and control through visibility of cash flows. Faster payment processing can significantly reduce float, and working capital required by a firm. Better exception handling can resolve errors and disputes more quickly and improve relations with customers.

Yet all of these potential benefits can only be reaped through collaboration since it requires a common transaction and payment platform that is accepted by all parties in the supply chain. Payment flows in the supply chain suffer from some of the same bottlenecks facing logistics flows in the supply chain. Orders need to be matched with delivery and invoices. Bills of Lading need to be matched with insurance and other trade documents. Freight payment involves matching invoices and bills. Reconciliation of these documents is usually necessary to take further action in the supply chain. In spite of the opportunities, research in business processes management still need to overcome the some of the challenges in orchestrating business processes across multiple organizations. Dynamic configuration of business processes requires effective coordination of activities between business partners.

We examine in this paper the credit card network as an example of a business network in operation. Unlike other business networks that focus predominantly on the information exchange processes, credit card networks provide a contractual framework of business rules for authentication and authorization, evidence and dispute resolution, and enforcement. The changes taking place in credit card networks shows that payment services are now offered in a modular manner, can adapt easily to different payment methods and payment networks, coordinated through online access to almost real-time data, which ultimately provides a framework for trustworthy business.

References

Evans, D.S., R. Schmalensee, (1999). *Paying with Plastic: The Digital Revolution in Buying and Borrowing*. MIT Press, Cambridge, Mass.

Howard, S, Fingar R., (2003). *Business Process Management (BPM): The Third Wave*, Meghan-Kiffer Press.

Killen and Associates, (2002). "Optimizing the Financial Supply Chain (FSC): How CFOS of Global Enterprises are Succeeding by Substituting Information for Working Capital", (April), accessed from www.killen.com/whitepapers/index.html.

Kreber, H., (2003). "Fulfilling the Web Services Promise", *Communications of the ACM*, (June), Vol. 46, No. 6.

Mandell, L. (1990). *The Credit Card Industry: A History.* Twayne Publishers, Boston.

Miller, G. (2003). ".NET vs. J2EE", *Communications of the ACM*, (June), Vol. 46, No. 6.

Office of Fair Trade (1994). *Connected Lender Liability - A Review by the Director General of Fair Trading of Section 75 of the Consumer Credit Act 1974*, OFT 097 (March).

O'Mahony D, M. Peirce, and H. Tewari H, (2001). *Electronic Payment Systems for E-commerce*, 2nd ed., Artech House, Norwood, Mass.

Visa International and MasterCard (1997). *Secure Electronic Transactions 1.0 Specifications Vol. 1 Business Guide.* (Visa International), Purchase, NJ.

Visa USA (2004). "A Legacy of Payment - Anytime, Anywhere, Anyway", (March), accessed from http://usa.visa.com/personal/about_visa/who/who_we_are_history.html.

27 Smart ICT Support for Business Networks

Jukka Heikkilä[1], Marikka Heikkilä[2], Jari Lehmonen[2], and Samuli Pekkola[1]

Introduction

Modern companies lean increasingly towards innovating and renewing their business operations in a more value-adding and customer-centric direction. As a prerequisite to this, a number of companies are willing to combine their knowledge and resources, for instance by forming strategic alliances supported by a mixture of open ICT infrastructure and proprietary and interoperable ICT applications.

This study examines a network of three focal companies that are seeking cost-efficient expansion of their services. As the potential market for these complex customer services is worldwide, the objective is expected to be met only with the help of ICT. Furthermore, the view among the companies is relatively unanimous regarding the necessity for co-operation. The joint business model is aimed at providing customized b-to-b services to a limited customer base. The model is based on long-lasting relationship with the customers and builds on in-depth knowledge of the customers' facilities, i.e. production equipment, software, labor skills and local circumstances, etc. The required information on customers' facilities to be analyzed, synthesized, and exploited originates from a variety of sources and differs in terms of confidentiality and reliability. The relevant information must ultimately be shared and jointly interpreted by the consortium companies, as this is essential to their complementary roles.

Often e-commerce, inter-organizational systems and business networks are formed by integrating existing ICT-infrastructures in order to make trading and production networks or supply chains more efficient (van de Ven , 1976; Wolters et al., 1999; Hoogeweegen et al., 1999). It is most often assumed that due to ICT, the transaction costs are reduced to the extent that it is worthwhile to outsource ancillary operations and concentrate on core competencies (Malone et al., 1987; Picot et al., 1997). Alternatively, the networks between partners and even competitors can also be seen as – not only a means of cutting costs – but a source of new, innova-

[1] Department of Computer Science and Information Systems, University of Jyväskylä, Finland
[2] Information Technology Research Institute, University of Jyväskylä, Finland

tive business ideas, where the network provides the customer with more added value than if the companies were operating independently (Nalebuff and Brandenburger, 1996; Dyer and Singh, 1998).

As shown in earlier studies (e.g. Andersen and Christensen, 2000; Törmänen and Möller, 2003), a vital prerequisite for the success of a network is a mutual adjustment process (Ciborra and Andreu, 2001). Although it is essential to learn from previous experiences, enhance the resource base and assimilate knowledge, it is also required that the companies engage in mutual adjustment processes despite their individually crafted strategies and legacy systems (Powell, 2000; Nielsen, 2002; Nooteboom, 2000). In this way, it is claimed that the participating organizations are thus able to reap the benefits of both the expanded resource base and innovative capacity (Powell, 2000).

ICT can be expected to have a strong role in business networks. Yet, the reality is that ICT projects for business networks have been hampered by difficulties in integrating (legacy) information systems to a sufficient level, differences in organization cultures and processes (e.g. inability to seamlessly unify processes due to differences in production modes), doubts concerning the pay-off of investments, fear of lock-in to focal companies and uncertain future profits and profit sharing (Kumar and van Dissel, 1996; Heikkila et al., 2003a, 2003b).

To summarize, ICT is not a panacea, rather it is both an obstacle and enabler. Moreover, establishing and operating a business network seems to require substantial effort in learning and coordinating the activities of the separate parties of a given network. This process serves also as a mechanism of indicating, creating and maintaining the trust and confidentiality between the network parties.

Against this backdrop, we reflect upon the role of ICT in the stages of creating and operating a joint business model, also taking into account the situation when a party exits or enters the network. As we have participated in the creation of such a network ourselves, we are well positioned to analyze the actual process of joint creation of a new business model and draw some initial conclusions on the functional requirements of ICT in operations and entry/exit situations. We propose that because of the high costs involved, ICT should support not only the operation of the networked business model in the steady state, but in particular also in the earlier phases and in the creation of business models for these services. In addition, ICT should support dynamic networks where new participants may enter and/or old participants may leave the network at some time point. These characteristics pose major challenges for ICT-support in all stages.

Indeed, our analysis shows that these features may not be available from the existing IT-infrastructure, or on the software market.

From Internal Applications to a Networked ICT-Infrastructure

Figure 27.1 illustrates the generations of organizational IS application archetypes on a Porter's (1980) value chain of a single firm. In most competitive organizations all of these archetypes can often be found. This study briefly summarizes the worldviews related to IS applications and illustrates that they were born in response to specific organizational problems. Figure 27.1 also depicts a typical ICT-infrastructure of an organization, which may also be of help when applied in a networked organization mode.

When considering ICT within a given firm, multiple archetypal applications exist. We can start by identifying some organizational functions which have traditionally been automated, i.e. those functions that have a clear and explicitly defined domain, such as general ledger, payables and receivables, MRP etc. These automated functions provide a vertical view of the organization's business activities (area 1 of Fig. 27.1) and aim at cutting costs, expanding capacity, reducing errors etc. The role of ICT is to formalize activities by creating a centralized view of the activity.

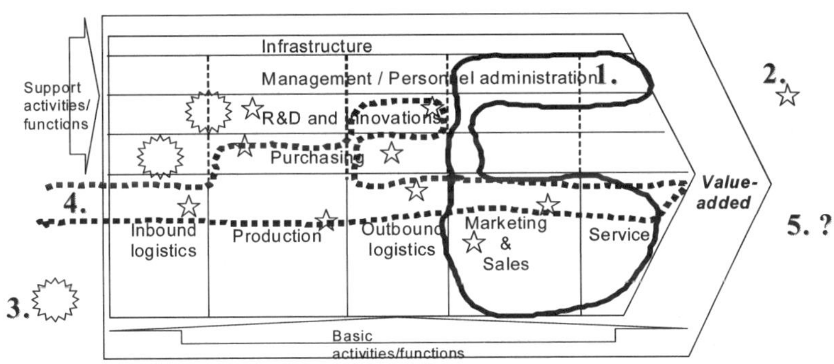

Fig 27.1 Archetypes of IS applications on Porter's single firm value chain

It is typically expected that all communication occurs via the database – with all operations data being aggregated for those in charge of management and decision making. This is also reflected in the development of such applications; they are clearly confined to specific functions and the concepts and tasks are well defined. At the same time, they easily neglect the differences in personal information processing and working styles.

Since it is difficult to cover business activities completely with functional ICT, the above approach left certain "holes' in the application map. Hence, personal IT tools have been emerging to increase the productivity of individual, sophisticated and skilled users with the objective of rationalizing and augmenting the individual's work (star 2 in Figure 27.1). These benefits also stem from compatible and interoperable standard toolsets, which enable tasks to be shared and swapped between employees without losing efficiency and productivity from the organization's viewpoint. Furthermore, individuals can patch any defects in the functional systems and compensate its weaknesses. Nevertheless, as the ongoing discussion on TCO (Total Cost of Ownership) illustrates, there are significant side effects in terms of breakdown situations, inadequate skills and consequent support needs.

Groupware and knowledge management tools (e.g., Notes, BSCW) aim at interconnecting shared toolsets and data for time and place independent remote work (Grudin, 1994; Robinson, 1992). It is assumed that a group using a groupware application maintains a common goal (multi-pointed star 3 in Figure 27.1) so that the application can support the accumulation of expertise. This may further shorten the time-to-market-cycle and improve coordination and co-operation within the group. Here the focus is clearly on group level as opposed to individual or organization level. In many cases the underlying social structure is challenged by the vision of shared information, for example the ownership of information is often unclear, which consequently obscures its trustfulness; it is in conflict with different reward structures (Schmidt and Bannon, 1992). It is most likely that these problems escalate when shared activities span across organizational boundaries.

Business process software (e.g. SAP, BAAN) offers a customer-oriented perspective on the organization's core processes by representing processes of service or production (area 4 in Figure 27.1). They aim at simplifying and streamlining the processes, minimizing the number of hand-offs, cutting lead-time and ensuring quality and delivery control. This focus is also their drawback – the systems usually tend not to tackle wide-ranging processes across the whole organization nor the multitude or interconnectivity of different processes. So, although the support for standardized processes is good, exceptions and exceptional behavior hamper full utilization of the systems.

The fifth type of system (5 in Figure 27.1) is designed for conducting business transactions on the market. Typically, it describes how the above mentioned systems form a steady state system infrastructure upon which the offerings to the customers are built. There has been recent growing interest in dynamic configuration of *multiple value chains* to meet customer requirements efficiently. Examples of such archetypal prototypes are reported by Hoogeweegen et al. (1999).

Analysis of the above mentioned archetypes shows that the systems are designed for particular purposes and situations and for recurring transactions. Put in another way, their ISs consist of automated operations, information gathering for management and assist in acting towards a common goal (de Michelis et al., 1998). However, using the systems always involves additional know-how that requires coordination and communication between people (ibid.). Although systems exist for coordination and communication purposes (e.g. abovementioned business process control systems, to some extent also groupware), users are expected to use them in accordance with formal instructions and informal social conventions – both of which share equal importance (Robinson, 1991). Furthermore, coordination and communication is also needed in resolving instructions and social conventions.

In summary, the current ICT-infrastructure does not, in fact, work without a considerable amount of human intellectual effort. Although it is possible (in principle) to codify the activities and the process in the form of ICT applications, it is evident that a substantial amount of know-how concerning the organizations' codes-of-conduct must always be articulated, exchanged, learned and made explicit in the networked environment. In short, the systems are not transparent enough to be easily integrated with each other.

Research Approach

This empirical in-depth study focuses on three companies starting a process of joint service development for global markets. We, the authors of the study, have the privilege of being a member of this consortium, in which the three companies for the first time undertake in-depth co-operation with the aim of creating a common business model. We actively take part as researchers and to a certain extent also as conciliators and facilitators in this process. Our research method resembles action research: we are involved in the practical actions of the consortium and our actions naturally also have an effect on the decisions made by the companies. Despite the obviously limited generalizability of the results, our study offers a view on the process of business network creation and the role of ICT in supporting it.

Our involvement in these topics spans the past 1.5 years. The synthesis here is based on a pre-study undertaken in 2002 and on the on-going research project of 2003-2004. Within the period of October 2002 and May

2004, we had eight workshops, five open discussion steering group meetings, around 40 one-partner meetings and 16 transcribed theme interviews with specialists on the topic. The data has been further supplemented with personnel meetings held at the Company A hcadquarters. Observations (with field notes and diary) have been recorded throughout the research project. The research diary (Newbury, 2001) facilitates analysis of the evolution of the process throughout the duration of the study.

All interviews have been taped, transcribed and checked by the interviewees and all memos of meetings and workshops have also been written and distributed to the participants. Peer researchers and independent "observers' have been used to ensure validity. Finally, the findings have been evaluated and their correctness checked with partner companies.

Case Description

Our research object, the business network (consortium), consists of three corporations (hereafter referred to as A, B, and C) and two research organizations. The primary focus is on the clientele of the two consortium members (A and B). Figure 27.2 below illustrates our interpretation of the changes that Company A underwent throughout its transition to its present situation. It depicts the changes in core competence, mode of co-operation and business network topology alongside the evolution in IS-architecture that emerged to support these changes.

Company A has become the leading supplier of capital goods within its own global segment and is generally considered the technology leader in its field. It was Company A that initiated negotiations for the establishment of this consortium. During the 90's, the company's core competence has evolved from manufacturing to the management of complex manufacturing machinery delivery projects. Next, as its business strategy states, Company A is expected to move towards customer oriented service. A subsequent result of this development might, in the extreme case, constitute the outsourcing of operation and maintenance of customer equipment to an affiliate of Company A and its partners. These possibilities emerge along with advances in ICT, remote diagnostics, control and coordination systems and constant pressure to cut costs.

This development has had implications for the IS-infrastructure of Company A. In the early stages it was rather simple (in relative terms); its own IS solution with appended functional application software. Its purpose was primarily to coordinate the intra-company product design and the planning of production. In the second stage, the architecture was enhanced with distributed work support and document management, with an emphasis on creating a knowledge base for the machinery supplied to the customers and the configuration thereof. The last phase, now at hand, requires a significant degree of synchronization with clients, partners, and even with competitors' information systems to build up a profitable, high-quality service offering.

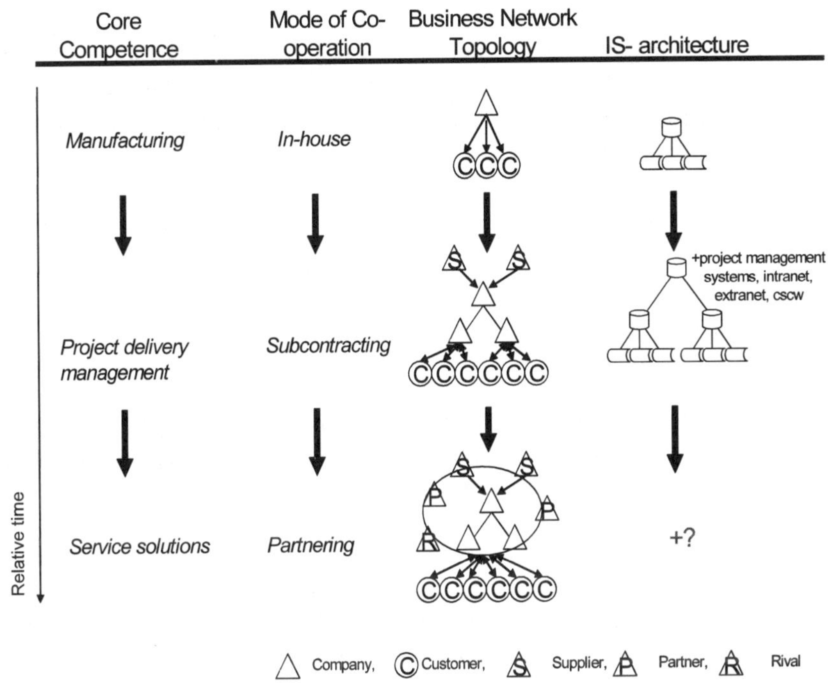

Fig 27.2 Evolution of core competences, mode of co-operation, business network topology and IS-architecture of Company A

Company B, a software house, has been moving towards a more customer-centric strategy. The company previously acquired its necessary additional industry-specific knowledge primarily through company acquisitions. Its clientele includes, among others, Company A and C (dyadic relationships over 30 years with the former and around 10-15 years with the latter) and also numerous customers of Company A. They therefore share the same clientele and are partial competitors within certain product groups.

Company C has been serving both Company A and B, as well as some of their clients. By participating in the consortium, Company C primarily seeks markets for its value-added infrastructure services, both by expand-

ing existing clientele and by providing new services for and with the companies of the consortium.
In order to carry on with their espoused strategies, the companies can no longer operate alone. They need each other to complement their services cost-efficiently. Most likely they also need capabilities, knowledge and innovations from outside their own competence. This development is paced by the growing tendency of the "end' clients to outsource parts of their business and on the increasing use of networks for creating, storing and accessing knowledge to share and appropriate information that cannot be produced internally. Because the companies operate on global markets, the network might need to be expanded so that similar benefits can be gained from local companies. As a result, our consortium is facing the question of how these kinds of new partnering services can be established and what changes should be made to the IS architectures in order to support these activities.

Observations

In our introduction we cited the main reasons for failure of ICT-based service development projects. Four out of every five failures were down to human error. However, as our case and numerous others demonstrate, it is possible to establish successful long-term business relationships with partners and competitors without the use of any ICT. Why, then, do ICT-solutions fail if the organizations have mutual interests in cooperation? Why is the integration of IS insufficient for their needs?

We believe that both the lack of trust and shared vision can be resolved if both organizations are made aware of the technical limitations and can be convinced of the inherent profits or cost savings; the latter of which we will now illustrate. Costs are principally incurred through the attempts of the organizations' employees to negotiate and understand the joint business model and the activities of other partners. To facilitate the cost-saving schema, organizations need inter-organizational, confidential workshops and meetings to sharpen shared vision and foster trust and explicit methods for cost and revenue estimation in order to relinquish uncertainty and misunderstandings, as well as clearly stated responsibilities and rights to the material. Unfortunately, again, only a few ICTs support these kinds of functional requirements.

The initial phases of our case network's lifecycle started 1,5 years ago. Even though the companies already had a long history of dyadic business relationships at the time, the goal of this consortium as a coequal partnership dictated that the first phase consisted of initial negotiations. The negotiations required each of the participant companies to make a strategic decision to engage in the project, to agree on which companies or business units were to be accepted into the consortium and to agree on funding and division of work. Initially, we negotiated with several business units of each of the companies A, B and C, two other ICT solution providers, a consultancy company and also with one customer corporation. Due to either a lack of resources or competitive reasons, the consortium membership settled to remain as it stood in the spring of 2003. The initial negotiation phase was largely concerned with communication and understanding the ambitions of the potential parties and selection of a "right' or suitable combination of capabilities and resources.

The following six months were spent in negotiations within the consortium regarding its specific goals. A great deal of discussions revolved around aligning the needs of the member companies. For example, one of the companies aimed towards a more abstract level when the consortium was first working out the necessary and sufficient conditions for a coequal network, whereas the others demanded practical results - and to get down to business as soon as possible.

This process involved numerous face-to-face meetings of the three companies, or pairs of companies, and presentations of slideware by all parties. Once an initial agreement on the abstraction level was finally reached, commencement of development work for joint business got underway in December 2003. At the time of writing, this iterative process remains ongoing and has until now mainly been carried on in joint workshops and pairwise meetings between the companies and the researchers. Whenever a new member, whether an individual or a company, enters the consortium the negotiation and sense-making rounds are restarted.

Figure 27.3 presents the total man hours spent by the participants of the consortium in workshops, meetings, phone meetings, interviews, and e-mail conversations. To date, around 1400 man hours have been spent in the above mentioned joint activities. The figures do <u>not</u> include any internal meetings of the companies, <u>nor</u> preparations or traveling to the consortium meetings. One can thus assume the actual amount of hours spent to be easily in excess of these figures, for instance using the 80:20 rule, as much as over 6900 hours (approx. 3,8 man years). Nevertheless, the consortium currently remains in its early phases, i.e. those of creating the joint service concept and laying the groundwork for the actual operation phase.

Qualitatively, time is spent on a myriad of complementary activities contributing to the articulation of specific aspects of the business models. Workshops, brainstorming sessions (inter-organizational/dyadic relations), person-to-person confidential discussions, scenario work, role plays, homework, and benchmarking analogies in addition to normal meetings. All in all, in our case, all of these methods were brought into play.

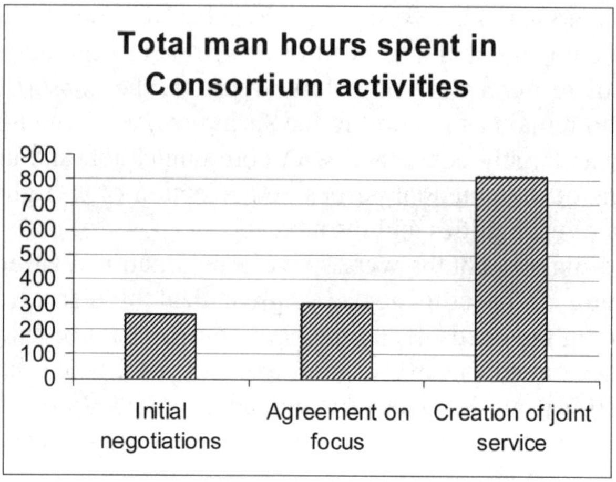

Fig 27.3 Total man hours of joint activities (excluding internal meetings, preparations for and traveling to meetings)

Suggestions for Smart ICT

The topic of our article was to examine the functional requirements for ICT in the context of business networks. We summarized the generations of organizational IS application archetypes and illustrated that they were born in response to specific organizational problems. Comparison of our case study with earlier theoretical discussions reveals that previous IS generations do not seem to fit the needs of co-operation in business networks. We therefore propose the following recommendations for future ISD development.

Based on the case study findings, our conclusions are threefold. Firstly, in the context of a business network we should pay *special attention to the joint development process* of the business model. According to our observations, the creation of a joint business is a learning-intensive intellectual activity involving the creation, interpretation and exchange of vast quantities of information. There is no doubt therefore that smart ICT solutions are needed to assist in such time consuming processes as these. Secondly, because of the special characteristics of our business area, i.e. designing new services for shared customers with a common long-term artifact, there is a need to revise and update the contract on a continuous basis throughout the duration of the customer relationship. In the global setting this means that ICT should support distributed intellectual work both in the model creation and operation stages. Thirdly, as partners may enter or exit the consortium, a set of new demands are placed on the ICT-infrastructure of the consortium as follows:

Shared knowledge management concerning the customer and facilities: As the relationship with shared customers is multifaceted and long-term, situations will likely emerge when one of the parties comes into direct contact with the customer (facilities). Ideally, the parties should gather common information about the configuration and customer situation and record any modifications made, along with any anticipated changes in the performance of the facility.

Contract management: The consortium members must have the contracts at hand whenever needed. In our case it is evident that almost all customer facilities are different and develop at different paces in their individual directions. This means that the consortium must analyze the status of the facilities and be prepared for surprises if the configuration of the facility has become changed. In a similar manner, the contract between parties is subject to the strategic changes of the individual companies; thus the contract is amended to allow for such resulting changes in situation (the burden of managing contracts has been investigated in earlier studies on outsourced operations) (Heikkila et al., 2003a, 2003b).

Access rights: As an example, the researchers of the consortium installed a groupware application as a common shared workspace and document database for intra-consortium coordination in order to support work activities and to make information sharing easier over distance. In this case, however, the classification of information sharing rights appeared to be a problem. A much more fine-grained classification of information was needed than any groupware was able to provide. At present, we have identified needs for the following categories: open to everyone, to group members only, various subgroups or private. In addition, exchange of confidential business information is found to only occur within dyadic relationships. These factors call for a sophisticated *role- and metadata-based* single-sign-on solution (Priebe et al., 2004), which would provide a role with access to all of the above mentioned categories of information securely via a uniform interface. As parties are at liberty to enter/leave the relationship, there is an evident need for metadata-based access control to establish, terminate and clear information instances of a specific party.

Authenticity and Digital Rights Management: Again, as the parties are numerous and the relationships long-term, metadata should exist on the creator, responsible organizations, version history, variants and general rights-of-use of any digital documentation – including a description of the means of gathering the necessary metadata. This is needed in order to facilitate tracking of fair and responsible use of the consortium material. It is also a necessary prerequisite for charging on, e.g., pay-per-use basis (Iannella, 2001).

Explicit process descriptions and change procedures: In essence, we are suggesting that continuous updates and revisions to the business model should become regular practice. Consequently, there is a need to be explicit about the processes involved in creating a new model (e.g. in the form of a computerized checklist connected to document repositories) and changing an existing model. Our belief is that the processes involved in engineering change management (ECM) represent good current candidates for such purposes.

However, most information and discussions are shared with consortium members and with trusted parties (sub-contractors, new partners in the future). Additional problems arise if one party leaves the consortium, if a joint business model becomes obsolete, if a new party enters the consortium, or when deciding what information should be granted to the newcomer. Who actually owns the customer data and how can it be shared? Can it be copied or replicated at all? Aside from the normal technical problems experienced in the handling of documents and permissions of a joint workplace, the conceptual shortcomings of the groupware regarding network learning support are severe.

As explained earlier, although the availability of information is extensive, its utilization requires new ways of interpreting and combining the data. Ultimately, this will require some form of metadata development to meet the functional requirements of the creation and operating process of the joint business model (Yates and Orlikowski, 1992; Päivärinta et al., 2001), such as domain descriptions, common terms, definitions and functions in order to facilitate data exchange and process integration.

Our conclusions are therefore in opposition to the mainstream integration approach. We suggest that seamless integration of the systems of the participating companies into a single IOS should be avoided due to the sheer number of relationships, consequent adaptation processes and non-compatible systems that come about as a result of various operational, structural, strategic, or even institutional factors. As an alternative, we recommend aiming at developing more generic ISs to meet the challenges of network management and innovation. In short, we see the need for inter-organizational, confidential workshops and meetings to sharpen shared vision and foster trust, for cost and revenue estimation in order to relinquish uncertainty and misunderstandings and the need to state all responsibilities and rights on the material. The challenge for ICT is to provide smart support for these intellectual dynamic processes within business networks. Might these solutions form the next generation of ICT archetypes?

Acknowledgements

This research is financially supported by the Academy of Finland, National Technology Agency of Finland, and the participating companies.

References

Andersen, P.H., P.R. Christensen, (2000). "Inter-Partner Learning in Global Supply Chains: Lessons From NOVO Nordisk", *European Journal of Purchasing & Supply Management*, 6, pp. 105-116.

Ciborra, C.U., R. Andreu, (2001), "Sharing Knowledge Across Boundaries", *Journal of Information technology*, 16, pp. 73-81.

De Michelis, G., E. Dubois, M. Jarke, F. Matthes, J. Mylopoulos, J.W. Schmidt, C. Woo, and E. Yu, (1998). "A Three-faceted View of Information Systems", *Communications of the ACM*, 41 (12), pp. 64-70.

Dyer, J., H. Singh, (1998). "The Relational View: Cooperative Strategy and Sources of Interorganizational Competitive Advantage", *Academy of Management Review*, 23 (4), pp. 660-679.

Grudin, J. (1994). "CSCW: History and Focus", *IEEE Computer*, 27 (5), pp.19-26.

Heikkila, J., H. Vahtera, and P. Reijonen, (2003a). "Beliefs and Perceptions on IOS Adoption on a Supply Network", in: *Proceedings Information Systems Research Seminar in Scandinavia, 26th IRIS*, Haikko Porvoo, 9-12.8.2003.

Heikkila, J., H. Vahtera, and P. Reijonen, (2003b). "Taking Organizational Implementation Seriously: The Case of IOS Implementation", in: *Proceedings of IFIP 8.6. Working Conference: The Diffusion and Adoption of Networked Information Technologies* (October), 6 – 8, Elsinore, Denmark.

Hoogeweegen, M.R., W.J.M. Teunissen, P.H.M. Vervest, and R.W. Wagenaar, (1999). "Modular Network Design: Using Information and Communication Technology to Allocate Production Tasks in a Virtual Organization", *Decision Sciences*, 30, 4, pp. 1073-1103.

Iannella, R. (2001). "Digital Rights Management (DRM) Architectures", *D-Lib Magazine*, 7 (6).

Kumar, K., H.G. van Dissel, (1996). "Sustainable Collaboration: Managing Conflict and Cooperation in Inter-Organizational Systems", *MIS Quarterly*, 20 (3), pp. 279-300.

Malone, T., J. Yates, and R. Benjamin, (1987). "Electronic Markets and Electronic Hierarchies", *Communications of the ACM*, 30 (6), pp. 484-497.

Nalebuff, B., A. Brandenburger , (1996*). Co-opetition*. Profile Books.

Newbury, D. (2001). "Diaries and Fieldnotes in the Research Process - Research Issues", in: *Art Design and Media*, Issue 1, The Research Training Initiative, University of Central England.

Nielsen, B. (2002). "Synergies in Strategic Alliances: Motivation and Outcomes of Complementary and Synergistic Knowledge Networks", *Journal of Knowledge Management*, Practices 3.

Nooteboom, B. (2000). "Learning by Interaction: Absorptive Capacity, Cognitive Distance and Governance", *Journal of Management and Governance*, 4, pp. 69–92.

Picot, A., C. Bortenlänger, and H. Röhrl, (1997). "Organization of Electronic Markets: Contributions From the New Institutional Economics", *The Information Society*, 13, pp. 107-123.

Porter, M.E. (1980). *Competetive Strategy: Techniques for Analyzing Industries and Competitors*, The Free Press, New York.

Powell, W.W. (2000). "The Capitalist Firm in the 21st Century: Emerging Patterns", in: DiMaggio, P., (ed.), (2003). *The Twenty-First-Century Firm: Changing Economic Organization in International Perspective*, Princeton University Press.

Priebe, T., E.B. Fernandez, J.I. Mehlau, and G. Pernul, (2004). "A Pattern System for Access Control", in: *Proc. 18th Annual IFIP WG 11.3 Working Conference on Data and Application Security*, (July), Sitges, Spain. www-ifs.uni-regensburg.de/top/indizes/index_forschung.htm (accessed 15 May 2004).

Päivärinta, T., V. Halttunen, and P. Tyrväinen, (2001). "A Genre-Based Method for Information Systems Planning", in: Rossi, M., K. Siau, (Eds.), *Information Modeling in the New Millennium*, Idea Group, Hershey, PA, pp.70-93.

Robinson, M. (1991). "Double-Level Languages and Co-operative Work", *AI & Society*, 5, pp. 34-60.

Robinson, M. (1992). "Computer Supported Cooperative Work: Cases and Concepts", in: Baecker, R. (Ed.), *Readings in Groupware and Computer Supported Cooperative Work: Assisting Human-Human Collaboration*, Morgan Kaufmann, San Mateo, CA.

Schmidt, K., L. Bannon, (1992). "Taking CSCW Seriously: Supporting Articulation Work - Computer Supported Cooperative Work", *The Journal of Collaborative Computing*, 1 (1), pp. 7-40.

Törmänen, A., K. Möller, (2003). "The Evolution of Business Nets and Capabilities - A Longitudinal Study in the ICT Sector", in: Fiocca, R., C.J. Hatteland, and I. Juon, (eds.), *Abstracts Proceedings from the 19th Annual IMP Conference*, (4-6 September), Lugano, Switzerland., pp. 99-100. Full article available at: http://www.impgroup.org/papers.php?viewPaper=4436.

Van de Ven, A.H. (1976). "On the Nature, Formation, and Maintenance of Relations Among Organizations", *Academy of Management Review*, pp. 24-34.

Wolters, M.J.J., E. van Heck, M.R. Hoogeweegen, and P.H.M. Vervest, (1999). "A Business Network Redesign Approach: Conceptual and Practical Issues", *working paper*, Erasmus University Rotterdam, Rotterdam.

Yates, J., W.J. Orlikowski, (1992). "Genres of Organizational Communication: A Structurational Approach to Studying Communication and Media", *Academy of Management Review*, 17 (2), pp. 299 – 326.

28 Web Information Extraction and Mediation as a Basis for Smart Business Networking

Hannes Werthner[1], Oliver Fodor[2], and Marcus Herzog[3]

Introduction

The paper describes an ontology-based mediation platform, enabling seamless information exchange between participating entities, thus, forming the "semantic" base for business networking. The Tourism industry serves as an example application domain. The Semantic Web platform described was developed within this context. This choice can be explained by the fact that this industry is highly networked, based on a worldwide cooperation of very different types of stakeholders.

The specific characteristics of the industry together with the fast evolution of the Web influences consumer behaviour, involving them directly in the "online" travel planning process and making them their own travel agents. As a consequence, most of the market players developed their own distribution strategy utilising online information systems to present and to sell their products. The fast evolution of e-commerce together with the fragmentation of the industry has led to a large number of different systems following diverse, often proprietary standards, thereby introducing heterogeneity at all levels of information processing. The resulting fragmentation of the entire e-tourism market represents a major obstacle in its further evolution towards a more cooperative environment.

The paper introduces the rationale of a distributed ontology-based mediation tool and describes the technological as well as methodological approach based on Semantic Web and Web Services technologies. The paper is organised as follows: Section 2 gives an overview of the travel and tourism industry. Section 3 describes the project Harmonise and its results; based on this experience the next section introduces the semi-automatic

[1] Department of Computer Science and Telecommunications, University of Trento, Trento, Italy, werthner@dit.unitn.it

[2] E-Commerce Competence Center - EC3, Vienna, Austria, oliver.fodor@ec3.at

[3] Institute of Information Systems, Vienna University of Technology, Vienna, Austria, herzog@dbai.tuwien.ac.at

Web information extraction tool Lixto Visual Wrapper. We conclude by providing a short outlook into our foreseen work.

The Travel and Tourism Industry

The travel and tourism industry is a global industry exhibiting very specific features: Travel and tourism represents approximately 11% of the world wide GDP (following the tourism satellite account method of the World Travel and Tourism Council). There will be one billion international arrivals in the year 2010 (following the World Tourism Organization) and tourism grows faster than the other economic sectors. It represents a cross-sectoral industry, including many related economic sectors such as culture, sport or agriculture, where over 30 different industrial components have been identified that serve travellers. This explains the industry's heterogeneity, and due to its SME structure it has a huge importance for regional development.

The supply and the demand side form a worldwide network, where both production and distribution are based on cooperation. The product is perishable, complex and emotional:

- a hotel bed not sold for one night represents a lost income. Suppliers are in a risky situation, which can be reduced if access to information is available,
- the tourism product is a bundle of basic products, aggregated by some intermediary. To support the rather complex bundling, products must have well defined interfaces with respect to consumer needs, prices, or also distribution channels,
- vacations are emotional experience structures that involve cognitive and sensory stimulations as well as affective responses to certain events.

Tourism is an information-based business; the product is a "confidence good". Tourists have to leave their daily environment for consuming the product. At the moment of decision-making only a model of the product, its description, is available. This characteristic entails high information search costs and causes informational market imperfections. Consequently, the industry has comparably long information- and value-chains. Figure 28.1 differentiates between the supply- and demand-side and the respective intermediaries. Links mark the relationships as well as the flow of information, showing only the most relevant links. Nodes indicate the relevant types of players. On the supply-side we denote with "primary" suppliers enterprises like hotels, restaurants, etc., which are mostly SMEs.

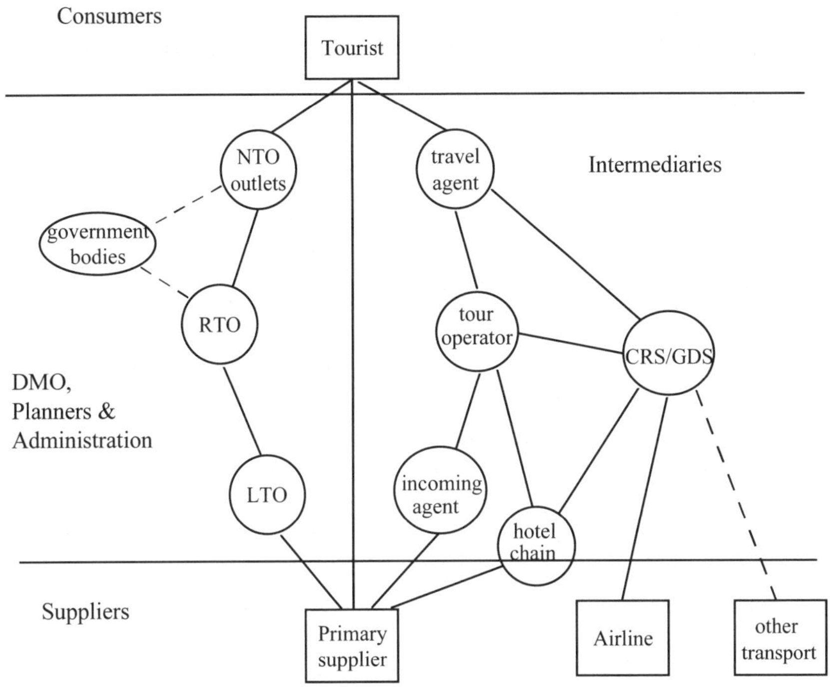

Fig 28.1 Structural view of the market (Werthner and Klein, 1999)

Tour operators can be seen as product aggregators, travel agents act as information brokers, providing final consumers with the relevant information and booking facilities. CRS/GDS (Central Reservation Systems/Global Distribution Systems), stemming from the airline reservation systems already developed in the 1960s, include also other products such as packaged holidays, or other means of transport. Whereas the intermediaries on the right side can be seen as the "professional connection between supply and demand (mainly based on the electronic infrastructure of the CRS/GDS). The left side is relevant for the management, planning and branding of a destination. Normally, these entities have to act on behalf of all suppliers within a destination and are not engaged in the booking process. The links to governmental organizations – as dotted lines – indicate that Destination Marketing Organizations are often governmental organizations.

The upstream flow of Figure 28.1 consists of product information, whereas the downstream flow reports on market behaviour, mostly represented in terms of statistical aggregates. Both information flows create a tourist information network tying together all market participators and, apparently, reflecting the economic relationships between them.

The Web facilitates new ways to meet changing consumer behaviour and to reach new market segments, leading to an "informatization" of the overall tourism value chain. This allows different strategies to generate value (Sweet, 2001). Such strategies allow for the design of new products and services, enlarging the range of options to customize and to configure products. IT and improved organizational procedures lower the price of customisation, enabling individual offerings based on mass-customisation.

Harmonise – an Approach to Semantic Mediation

The European project Harmonise is a concrete and implemented example of a semantic mediation platform (Dell'Erba et al., 2002). Its scope is to allow participating tourism organisations to keep their proprietary data format while cooperating with each other by establishing the so-called Harmonise Space – a networked harmonised environment.

From a technical perspective Harmonise focuses on the problems associated with the different representations of similar conceptual and semantic items in the domain. As previous standardisation initiatives in the tourism domain attempting to solve the harmonisation issues directly on the physical level have failed, Harmonise proposes a solution independent from the physical aspects, but promoting a harmonisation on a conceptual (or semantic) level instead.

The Mediation Platform

The Harmonise mediator service is dedicated to the "translation" needs between different participating systems facilitating the mutual information exchange. This is done via a mediating ontology, a shared conceptualisation of the domain which serves as a common reference for all participating actors. A mediator looks at information from a higher conceptual (semantic) level using this level of abstraction for the alignment purposes between local data models and the mediating ontology (Wiederhold ,1992). Harmonise tackles the information heterogeneity problem only. It does not intend to deal with process interoperability, as shown in Figure 28.2. The approach of "weak" coupling takes into consideration the specific industry context with its majority of SMEs and with many different, also legacy, solutions.

Semantic aspects, e.g., the meaning of entities of a problem domain, their characteristics and relationships to other entities, are specified independently of their physical representation, e.g., their storage structure. The same concepts can then be used for different technical solutions and changes on the physical level can be done independently from the conceptual level (Omelayenko and Fensel, 2002). The agreement of all market participants can be restricted to the semantic level, i.e., to the concepts behind exchanged messages, and thus be reached easier. The common semantic level enables mapping between conceptual models of different specific message formats focusing on the differences in the understanding of the domain whereas the definition of the exact structure and format of the messages can be neglected.

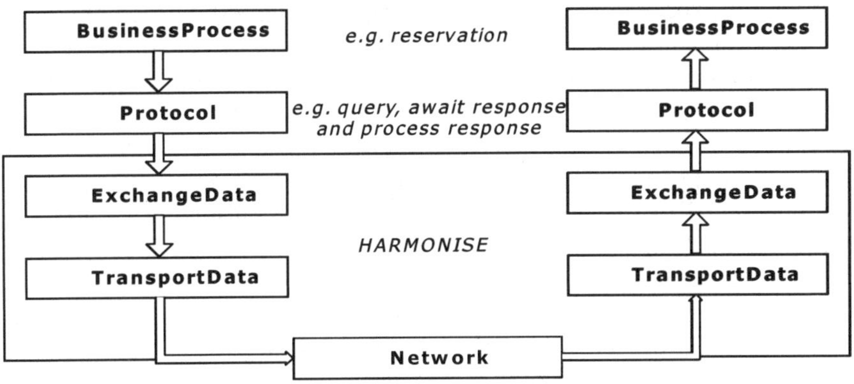

Fig 28.2 The scope of Harmonise in the overall business process: Harmonise supports information exchange only; business process integration is not supported

To adopt the Harmonise solution an actor must define a mapping from its native conceptual model to the Harmonise ontology (to perform the semantic mapping process) and vice-versa. Afterwards, the actor's information can be automatically translated (reconciled) into an intermediary representation "understandable" for all partners who have performed the same process. A leading principle in the mediator's design was the decentralisation of services in order to avoid performance bottlenecks. Thus, the resulting architecture introduces a distributed service relying on the central domain ontology but performing the translation operations directly at the actors' nodes. Given this, each actor participating in the Harmonise Space has to maintain only one mapping (to the central ontology) to be able to communicate with all other participants. The actual communication is conducted via peer-to-peer links.

Consensus Process

The real value of Harmonise is based on a possibly large number of participating organisations. It needs a sound organisational framework and business model to set up and to manage this network for the full deployment of the mediation service. The so-called Tourism Harmonisation Network (THN) constituted within the Harmonise project is the body to assume this responsibility. Its task is also to define and to version the ontology based on a social consensus building between the stakeholders involved.

Within the social consensus process, the THN was established as a leading open organisation concentrating domain experts, IT professionals, standardisation initiatives and tourism organisations worldwide with the role to coordinate the harmonisation effort and to foster new technologies for interoperability in the travel and tourism arena. The key role of the THN is to build and maintain the mediating domain ontology, the so-called Interoperable Tourism Harmonisation Ontology, representing the consensual agreement on the domain concepts and their characteristics. During the Harmonise project, the first version of the so-called Interoperable Minimum Harmonisation Ontology (IMHO) was created, initially covering the sub-domains of Accommodation and Event & Activities.

Harmonisation Process

Considering the two-level architecture of the mediator we distinguish two phases of the harmonisation process:

- *customisation phase* where the actors customise their gateways by establishing mappings between their local data models and the mediating ontology,
- *cooperation phase* when the actors' information is automatically reconciled (translated) to the target format reusing the defined mappings.

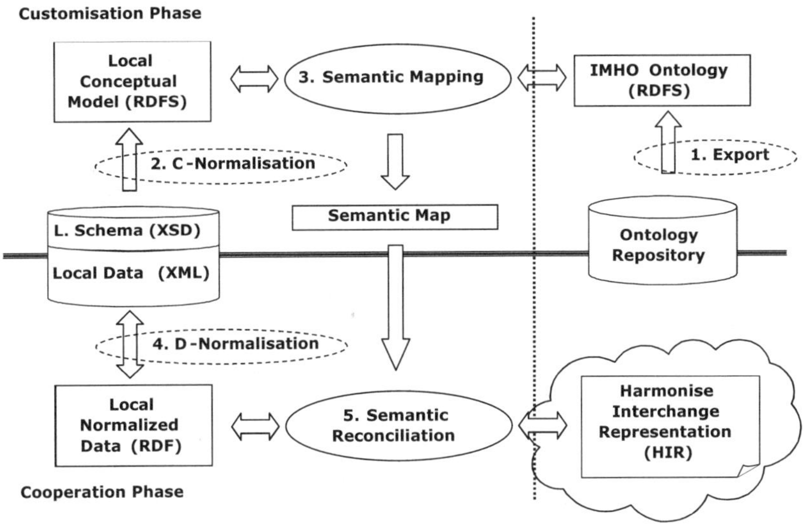

Fig 28.3 During the harmonisation process between two actors the processes shown are deployed twice in a symmetric fashion. Both actors have to map to the central ontology and data are reconciled at both sides

Figure 28.3 shows the harmonisation process of the mediator with the customisation and cooperation phase on both the conceptual and physical level. The figure shows only the harmonisation of a single actor participating in the overall harmonisation process. In case a complete communication path between two actors is established, the illustrated processes are deployed twice in a symmetric fashion. At the side of information provider the process is called forward *harmonisation*, on the information consumer side the term *backward harmonisation* is used. The harmonisation procedure takes the following steps:

Customisation Phase

Step 1: Ontology Export

The mediating ontology was built and is currently maintained in the ontology management tool SymOntoX enabling modelling and storing information with a high expressive power based on the OPAL methodology. In the customisation phase, a simplified RDFS representation of the mediating ontology is exported from the ontology repository. This step allows for hiding the complexity of different ontology constructs and provides the ontology as an "input" to the manual semantic mapping process.

Step 2: Conceptual Normalisation

The governing schema of a source document (in our case XML Schema or DTD) is "lifted" to a local conceptual model also represented in RDFS format. This process is called *C-Normalisation (Conceptual Normalisation).* The purpose of this step is to reverse engineer the conceptual information hidden in the schemas of local data sources and to align the re-engineered models to the representation of the mediating ontology. This step eliminates the differences in the representations of conceptual information models, which have to be semantically mapped.

The rationale behind this process is twofold: Firstly, as already explained, the normalisation step eliminates the representational differences between local models and the ontology. In Harmonise, we currently provide a semi-automated support for normalisation of XML Schemas, however, as described in Section 5 we extend the approach by applying a general and semi-automatic extraction engine in order to integrate with different local data formats such as HTML files. Secondly, the conceptual models produced by the reverse engineering process can be seen as simple ontologies providing a good base for the ontology building process at local sites. This is particularly important in the cases of, e.g., established national standards for representation of tourism information with an existing closed group of users. Thus, we understand the "simple" C-Normalisation process as a convenient "tool" for applying Semantic Web technologies to these legacy systems.

Step 3: Semantic Mapping

The semantic mapping step is the central task of the entire harmonisation process. In Harmonise we currently utilize the mapping methodology MAFRA supported by a GUI mapping editor tool and a transformation engine (Maedche et al. 2002). In the first instance of the mediator we use a fully manual mapping process only, partially with the aim to obtain a deeper practical experience to grasp the specialties of the process as well as due to the reason that there are no mature (semi-)automated solutions available in the open source market.

The local normalised conceptual model is semantically mapped against the shared IMHO ontology with the aim to eliminate semantic clashes. The concepts of the source model are projected onto the concepts of the target ontology (or vice-versa in the case of backward harmonisation) specifying dedicated bridges and customizing services driving the corresponding instance data manipulation. The product of the mapping process is a *Seman-*

tic Map carrying the necessary information for the semantic reconciliation step in the cooperation phase.

Cooperation Phase

Step 4: Data Normalisation

In the cooperation phase, the local instance data (e.g., in XML format) are transformed into an image of the local conceptual model. This step is named *D-Normalisation (Data Normalisation)* and is carried out by the *Normalisation Engine*. This process is driven by the information produced within the corresponding C-Normalisation reverse engineering step. The output of the D-Normalisation process is a set of local normalised (with meta-information annotated) data in RDF format.

Step 5: Semantic Reconciliation

After obtaining the normalised local instance data in RDF format, these are transformed into the Harmonise Interchange Representation (instances of IMHO) using the Semantic Map, the output of the corresponding mapping process. This transformation is conducted by the *reconciliation engine*, which uses the semantic map repeatedly, i.e., each time new instance data arrive at the input. The representation of the data is considered as universally "understandable" within the entire Harmonise Space and can be processed by each actor conducting the backward harmonisation procedure or another IMHO compliant system.

Harmonise and Related Approaches

Ontology mapping issues are discussed in several sources with respect to the following application categories (Noy and Musen, 1999; Kalfoglou and Schorlemmer, 2003):

- Ontology alignment
  - Information retrieval – in this case ontology mapping is used to facilitate search for and retrieve necessary information from the large number of information sources available (Zhu et al. ,1999),
  - Information integration – ontology mapping enables to ask queries in an uniform fashion over several information sources without having to access each source independently. In the ontology supported information integration scenarios the coordination between these data sources is achieved using a central ontology and the mappings be-

tween local ontologies and the central one allows for distributing and translating the queries (Visser and Schuster ,2002),
  - Data (information) migration/exchange – here the goal is to transform the information stored in an external source into the local representation using different schemas/ontologies. In this case the mapping between these ontologies usually defines the way the information is being translated during the migration process (Fagin et al., 2003).

- Ontology merging
  - the mapping is used to combine multiple partially overlapping ontologies into a single coherent ontology. The mapping information then allows for identifying relationships between concepts during the merging process (Noy and Musen, 1999; Stumme and Maedche, 2001).

The driving aspect of all the above listed problem areas are semantic relationships between ontologies. The purpose of the mappings is to explicate these relationships in a machine understandable formalism with a clearly defined semantics. Thus the mappings can be utilized to drive "intelligent" processes. By analysing different ontology mapping approaches one can identify differences in the depth of the information necessary to be captured by the mapping process, where these differences depend on their particular purpose. Thus, e.g., in information retrieval it appears to be sufficient to define semantic relationships between terms (concepts) of the ontologies (thesauri) to be mapped in order to enable re-classification of items to facilitate the search and retrieval process from multiple information sources. Usually, semantic relationships such as *broader term*, *narrower term* and *related term* are sufficient to satisfy the need of information retrieval. Similarly, in ontology merging, mostly explored by dedicated semi-automated algorithms, the encompassed information does not necessarily need to carry in-depth details on semantic relationships between the different ontologies. Ontology merging occurs mostly at the intentional level where the participating ontologies are not yet populated. On the other hand, in the information integration and exchange scenarios it is often required to establish detailed mapping definitions capable to drive information translation with limited information loss. The mapping definitions need to provide sufficient information for translating not only single concept instances but also to reconstruct the entire context of these instances preserving their semantics.

Commercial EAI (Enterprise Application Integration) and B2B (business-to-business) integration tools comparable to Harmonise, e.g., Microsoft BizTalk, IBM WebSphere, BEA WebLogic or Tibco ActiveEnterprise, aim rather at an integration of data sources to provide a common interface for applications. These solutions rely mainly on well-established technologies like XML and/or Web Services following primarily a service-oriented approach. Harmonise, in contrast, exploits the emerging Semantic Web paradigm (Bussler, 2003; Ding et al., 2004; Fensel et al. ,2003) where the application of domain ontologies facilitates the alignment of the diverse representations. An ontology, enabling the explication of a shared understanding of the domain concepts in a human as well as a machine understandable way, supports the mapping and alignment process on each level of automation: in a human expert driven scenario where the user is provided with an ontology explicated knowledge about the concepts to be mapped as well as in semi-automated scenarios where intelligent inference algorithms (Ehrig and Sure, 2004; Hernández et al., 2001) can be applied to deduce relationships between the concepts based upon the ontology explicated knowledge. In particular, the application of ontology supported (automated) inference methods to the interoperability problem enable to build more efficient and more accurate solutions in the matchmaking processes between the parties involved. The so obtained more flexible interfaces enable the creation of dynamic configurations and intelligent cooperation frameworks.

The Use of Harmonise in an Empirical Setting

Harmonise was evaluated with the first version of the IMHO (Events & Activities, Accommodation) defining mappings between schemas of participating systems and standards (TourInFrance, SIGRT Portugal, MEK Finland, WhatsOnWhen, TIScover and OTA). The main goal of this "business test" was to demonstrate the feasibility of the proposed solution and to obtain first experiences from the "real world" deployment of the Harmonise mediator. The tests were focused at the functionality and services provided by the Harmonise components to the users. The core indicator of the tests were the accuracy and completeness of the information translated among a set of participating actors. Further indicators were usefulness and user friendliness of all user interfaces. These "qualitative" indicators were evaluated directly by the actors' representatives (who were not part of the Harmonise team), giving them direct access to the system and performing interviews with them after the respective tests. All these tests showed satisfactory results and were positively evaluated by those persons. One limitation, however, should be noted: not all participating organisations were able to provide the needed XML schema or DTDs. Consequently, an extension to our approach by incorporating an information extraction engine seemed to be needed. This extension is described in Section 5.

Performance issues were not directly addressed by the evaluators mainly due to the reason that Harmonise is not primarily dedicated to perform time critical executions. However, a sample testing of the Normalisation Engine performance with a set of 1000 complex data sets (event descriptions in "WhatsOnWhen" schema with an XML to RDF lift) produced results within the range of 10 seconds on a Pentium IV, 1.4 GHz class machine.

Web Information Extraction

As of today most documents on the Web are formatted in HTML. Although XML is an important and well-accepted standard for data exchange, HTML is still the dominant document formatting language on the Web. While both HTML and XML are languages for representing semi-structured data, the first is mainly presentation-oriented and is not really suited for data representation in database applications. XML, on the other hand, separates data structure from layout and is much more suited for data representation. The lack of accessibility of HTML data for querying has dramatic consequences on the time and cost spent to retrieve relevant information from Web pages.

The solution to this problem is to use so-called wrapper technology to extract relevant information from HTML documents and translate HTML into XML documents which can be easily queried or further processed by applications. Lixto Visual Wrapper (Baumgartner et al., 2001) is a tool to interactively generate logic-based Web data extraction programs. Once a wrapper is built, it can be automatically applied to continually extract relevant information from a permanently changing Web page. The Lixto technology is particularly well-suited for building HTML-to-XML wrappers. It also introduces new ideas and programming language concepts for wrapper generation.

Figure 28.4 shows the main building blocks utilised in the wrapping process. We can differentiate the Visual Wrapper Designer, the Visual Wrapper Executor, and the Wrapper Program. The Visual Wrapper Designer allows for generating a Wrapper Program by means of an example HTML page and an interactive configuration process. The user highlights areas of interest on the Web page and the tool generates extraction rules that extract the data in the highlighted region. A Wrapper Program is a set of extraction rules that translates the HTML document into a so-called

XML companion document. The Visual Wrapper Executor takes as input a set of HTML documents and a Wrapper Program to automatically perform the conversion process on all HTML input documents.

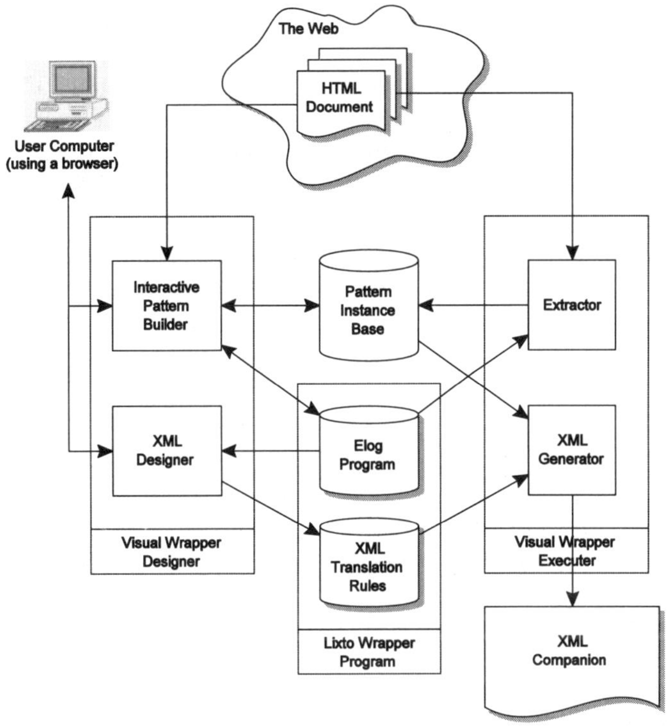

Fig 28.4 The main building blocks of the Lixto Visual Wrapper architecture

By applying this technology we can generate XML documents that represent data locked up in otherwise inaccessible HTML pages of Web applications. The Harmonise technology can utilize these XML documents in the harmonisation process. The wrapper technology can be furthermore used to provide Web Service interfaces for existing Web applications (Baumgartner et al., 2004) without the need to change or extend the implementation of these Web applications. This is a very powerful feature for application integration in a non-cooperative setting. E.g., in the tourism domain, most information is provided on Web pages without the possibility to access this information in a machine readable form which is needed for the harmonisation process.

Conclusions

We presented an approach to semantic mediation and information extraction as a first step towards intelligent business networking. As an example domain we chose the tourism industry. We can state that, at least in this domain, the application of „weak“ coupling can be seen as a successful first step, given that we extend it with information extraction. The application of ontologies in the tourism domain shows to be more acceptable than earlier physical level standards since they provide more flexibility to the stakeholders.

However, this is only a first pass: we see our approach as part of an overall suite to intelligent business networking, combining it with flexible means for dynamic cooperation including business rules, approaching the higher levels business process integration within a networked economy.

References

Baumgartner, R., S. Flesca, and G. Gottlob, (2001). "Visual Web Information Extraction with Lixto", in: *Proc. of 27th Intl. Conf. on Very Large Data Bases*, Rome, Italy, pp. 119-128.

Baumgartner, R., G. Gottlob, M. Herzog, and W. Slany, (2004). "Interactively Adding Web Service Interfaces to Existing Web Applications", in: *Proc. of 2004 Intl. Symposium on Applications and the Internet*, Tokyo, Japan, pp. 74–80.

Bussler, C. (2003). "The Role of Semantic Web Technology in Enterprise Application Integration", *IEEE Data Eng. Bull.*, 26, 4, pp. 62–68.

Dell'Erba, M., O. Fodor, F. Ricci, and H. Werthner, (2002). "Harmonise: A Solution for Data Interoperability", in: *Proc. of IFIP I3E 2002 Conference*, pp. 114–127.

Ding, Y., D. Fensel, M. Klein, B. Omelayenko, and E. Schulten (2004). "The Role of Ontologies in E-commerce", in: *Handbook on Ontologies*, pp. 593–616.

Ehrig, M., Y. Sure, (2004). "Ontology Mapping – An Integrated Approach", in: *Proc. of the 1st European Semantic Web Symposium*, Greece, Springer.

Fagin, R., P.G. Kolaitis, R.J. Miller, and L. Popa, (2003). "Data Exchange: Semantics and Query Answering", in: *Proc. of the 9th Intl. Conference on Database Theory*, Springer, pp. 207–224.

Fensel, D., J. Hendler, H. Lieberman, and W. Wahlster, (2003). *Spinning the Semantic Web: Bringing the World Wide Web to Its Full Potential*, MIT Press, Mass.

Hernández, M.A., R.J. Miller, and L.M. Haas, (2001). "Clio: A Semi-Automatic Tool For Schema Mapping", in: *Proc. of the ACM SIGMOD International Conference on Management of Data*, ACM Press.

Kalfoglou, Y., M. Schorlemmer, (2003). "Ontology Mapping: The State of the Art", *The Knowledge Engineering Review*, 18 (1), pp. 1–31.

Maedche, A., B. Motik, N. Silva, and R. Volz, (2002). "A Mapping Framework for Distributed Ontologies", in: *Proc. of the 13th European Conference on Knowledge Engineering and Knowledge Management*, Springer, pp. 235–250.

Noy, N.F., M.A. Musen, (1999). "SMART: Automated Support for Ontology Merging and Alignment", in: *Twelfth Banff Workshop on Knowledge Acquisition, Modeling, and Management*, Banff, Alberta, Canada.

Omelayenko, B., D. Fensel, (2002). "Analysis of B2B Catalogue Integration Problems - Content and Document Integration", in: *Enterprise Information Systems III*, Kluwer Academic Publishers, pp. 270–277.

Stumme, G., A. Maedche, (2001). "FCA-MERGE: Bottom-Up Merging of Ontologies", in: *Proc. of Intl. Joint Conference on Artificial Intelligence*, pp. 225–234.

Sweet, P. (2001). *Designing Interactive Value Development*, Ph.D Thesis, Lund University, Lund Business Press, Sweden.

Visser, U., G. Schuster, (2002). "Finding and Integration of Information - A Practical Solution for the Semantic Web", in: *Proc. of the ECAI 02 Workshop on Ontologies and Semantic Interoperability*, pp. 73–78.

Werthner, H., S. Klein, (1999). *Information Technology and Tourism - A Challenging Relationship*, Springer, Wien.

Wiederhold, G. (1992). "Mediators in the Architecture of Future Information Systems", *IEEE Computer*, 25 (3), pp. 38-49.

Zhu, X., S. Gauch, L. Gerhard, N. Kral, and A. Pretschner (1999). "Ontology-Based Web Site Mapping for Information Exploration", *ACM SIGIR 1999*, Berkeley, CA.

29 Public Administration Networked with Business: Towards Architectures for Interoperable and Retrievable Law

Rob M. Peters[1] and Marijn F.W.H.A. Janssen[2]

Introduction

The organization of law and the updating and incorporating of new laws as part of existing rules is an information intensive and complex endeavor. The adoption of new or updated rules requires a translation from the abstract laws in order to apply them to practical situations. This translation requires often the interpretation by jurists. The implications of new or updated laws need to be communicated to legal departments in order for them to comply with these new or updated rules. We will denote the creation, implementation, execution, enforcement and maintenance of laws as *production cycle* in this paper. Governments are looking for ways to increase their efficiency, decrease the administrative burden and reduce the lead times for adopting new legislations. The consequences of new laws at production phase are often not clear before introducing them or upholding them. The translation to practical implications takes place at many local government bodies and it is often not possible to inform the businesses, who are affected by the new law, pro-actively, as no information is available. This whole process is supported by heterogeneous information systems of various parties involved.

It does not require extensive explanation to stress the need for smart public-private networks from a production perspective. Most of the ERP software components companies run on need to be updated quite frequently to be in, and keep being in accordance with small changes in administrative legislation. The same holds for Human Resources software, Time reporting software, Tax reporting software and, more indirectly, Logistics software. All have to be updated due to changes in legislations. One dominant driver complicating this process, is the need to adapt legislation from the European Union. Nowadays businesses expect that government reduces the administrative burden of businesses. One aspect of creating a smart, service oriented, public administration is to make legislation inter-

[1] Leibniz Center for Law, University of Amsterdam, Peters@lri.jur.uva.nl

[2] School of Technology, Policy and Management, Delft University of Technology, marijnj@tbm.tudelft.nl

operable, contextual, and more understandable within the context of the business activity.

From the *demand* perspective, citizens and businesses find it very hard to find relevant legislation, local procedures and rules, policy documents etc. Governmental bodies are engaged in a flurry of policy and law making activities. Not only is this a complex myriad of legal issues, but the information is produced at different levels of public administration, including local, regional, national and European Union. A requirement is that online state legislative information should be equally accessible to all (Fage & Fagan, 2004). As such governments are searching for ways to make their information accessible and retrievable. This involves issues regarding terminology, explaining the type of legislative document, understandable and easy-to-use search interfaces and accessing the official status of online documents.

In this paper, *smart public-private collaborations* are investigated that are aimed at the seamless integration of law updates between various kinds of public agencies, software vendors and businesses and the creation of retrievable legislation. Analysis of projects supporting the production and demand cycle can produce a wealth of valuable data for local and central government, their partners and suppliers, as well as those researching smart public-private networks.

Research Methodology

The research methodology of combined action research and case studies was chosen to answer the goal of this research: the examination of the state-of-the-art of smart legislation networks and identification of feasible directions. Case study research can be characterized as qualitative and observatory, using predefined research questions (Yin, 1989). Action research or applied case study research is focused on "how to" questions (Checkland, 1981). Action research can be seen as a subset of case studies (Galliers, 1992). The amount of case studies should cover the demand-side of business, the perspective of legislation makers. Four case studies were selected satisfying the above criteria:

- Practical feasibility: the approach taken should be proven in practice, not just merely an idea,
- In depth data availability,
- Relevance for a large geographical area,
- Operating at both a national level and local level,

- Aiming at reducing administrative costs for businesses.

Hereafter a summary of the main characteristics of the case studies is given. The case studies are described in more detail below.

1. *IMRO*: This case deals with the retrieval of structured and unstructured spatial legislation and spatial policy documents and takes the perspective of businesses,
2. *ePower/Metalex*: This case study focuses on the creation of legislations and translating to maintainable format for participants in the network and using a structured approach based on object oriented technology,
3. *Overheid.nl*: This case study focuses on making unstructured legislation accessible by adding metatags and URL spider technology,
4. *OTP*: The OTP and other central registries is one of the many initiatives aimed at administrative process collaboration between governmental ministries and between agencies like the TAX office, the National bureau of statistics (CBS) and the chamber of commerce. This registry-effort has a history of more than a decade and is renewed for its impact on the collaboration between agencies and should therefore included in this research.

A Conceptual Framework

The OTP was investigated using interviews conducted with program manager, municipalities and departmental representatives. The other case studies were conducted using action research and structured interviews with end-users from businesses. The researchers were involved in the project as project managers or as participants in the project design. The case studies were analyzed using the conceptual framework that will be presented in the following section. Thereafter the case studies are described, discussed and evaluated

If smart legislation networks are the ideal, what specific conceptual framework can be used to evaluate current initiatives and guide developments? A large number of initiatives having different conceptual perspectives can be found, fuzzy searching mechanisms, object-oriented rules and more conventional methods like meta-data definitions. Which initiatives should be chosen and why?

Life-cycle, Architecture and Coordination Approach

The smart public private networks case studies we investigate aim to support the efficiency and time to adopt legislation or to find legislation. We do not consider the content of the laws and regulations, but the process for the businesses to comply with them in all their complexity and interacting influence. Since those businesses require access to the regulations and related public services and since those regulations change at all levels of government, it is justifiable to look at elements in the production, enforcement and maintenance of the laws throughout the whole life cycle at the four public administration layers: (1) Cross-national (European), (2) national, (3) regional and (4) local.

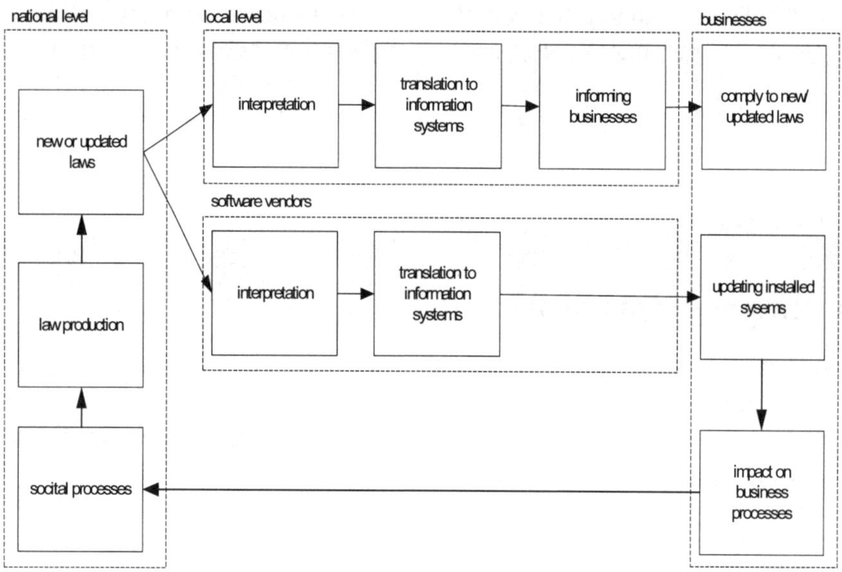

Fig 29.1 Law cycle

When taking the perspective of the *production* life cycle the production of laws is performed at a cross-national or national level, whereas often the implementation (service provisioning) and enforcement of these laws is executed at a regional or local level. As a result of new or updated legislation, information systems of businesses might need to be changed or other measures need to be taken to comply with them. After laws are implemented and imbedded in business processes (for example law might influence the annual reports), the society might influence the politics at a national level and new laws are made or existing laws are updated as shown schematically in Figure 29.1.

From a *demand* life cycle perspective, businesses have to cope with vast amounts of often interfering regulations. For businesses it is of vital importance to know which regulations are valid within particular geographical region. Businesses become only conscious of the implications of law after a permit request or renewal. Businesses also typically orient themselves at a larger geographically area than municipalities, whereas currently the information availability is often concentrated around local government bodies (municipality websites), so businesses are left to searching local level portals. The cases were assessed from a production and demand perspective, using evaluation criteria as proposed in the competing value approach of (Quinn and Rohrbaugh , 1983). The *production cycle* aims at the quick and efficient adaptation of laws. This also requires interoperability between information systems of various government organizations. As such the evaluation criteria from the production view are primarily based on the time and efficiency aspects as shown in Table 29.1. In contrast to the demand view, where non-expert should be able to search the legislation, government employs all kinds of judicial experts to translation of laws to implementation. The easiness of translation of the context will not be judged and considered outside the scope of this research.

Table 29.1. Evaluation criteria of legislation adaptation (production perspective)

Criteria	Description
Adaptation lead time business (software vendors)	Time to implement changes in legislations in information systems of businesses. In practice this means the time necessary for software vendors to update their system and install new versions of their systems.
Adaptation lead time government bodies	Time to implement changes in legislations in information systems of government organizations
Efficiency of adaptation	Resources needed by public bodies and businesses to implement changes/new legislations
Fairness of costs/benefits allocations	The perceived fairness of the interviewees about the division of the costs and benefits over the parties involved
Evolutionary balance	Any public private partnership faces stakeholders and conflicting interests. Initial investors need to have a long-term perspective on pay back and protection against "free riders". New participants have to perceive the added value of the network in order to contribute.
Interoperability	The level of automation between the layers of government (organizations) involved in this case study
Maintainability	The smoothness of updating existing laws between the layers of government (organizations) involved in this case study

The *demand cycle* deals with making legislation retrievable. Precision and recall are two traditional effectiveness measures: precision means the proportion of relevant documents out of those returned, whereas recall that of returned documents out of the relevant ones (Buckland and Gey, 1994). Corresponding to the competing value theory, a tradeoff between recall and precision is almost unavoidable. If you retrieve one relevant document, the precision is 100% but recall is very low. If you retrieve all documents, recall is 100% but precision has dropped.

Recent research shows that search engines should not only be regarded in terms of precision and recall. The easy production of textual content and related sources in content managements systems and fast feed back loops based on user behavior is as relevant as the smartest search algorithm when searching for legislation. The evaluation criteria are depicted in Table 29.2.

Table 29.2. Evaluation criteria of information retrieval (demand perspective)

Criteria	Description
Precision	The number of relevant documents retrieved divided by the number of documents retrieved
Recall	The number of returned documents out of the relevant ones
Usability	The easiness of using the retrieval mechanism
Intuitive	The way queries can be entered (human speech language, keywords, categories)
Fast	The time necessary for businesses to find an answer on a question
Administrative costs business	The total costs of business to find an answer on the questions (e.g. to which location might our LPG gas station be moved?)

Case Studies

In this section four case studies are presented. In the following section these criteria will be evaluated and discussed using the conceptual model.

IMRO

The Information Model for Spatial Planning (IMRO) (www.ravi.nl) in The Netherlands is a standardized unique codification of all spatial purposes or functions attached to a piece of territory. It maps the country in terms of operational function per geographical object. Operational function refers to as the legally defined purpose the geographic location is dedicated to. The legal implications are most interesting because of the fact that law defines those operational functions. The combination of operational function and legal constraints together form a natural ontology of societal activities or functions like housing, industry, parking, transportation, recreation, shopping, and so on. A map displaying the geographical objects now implicitly tells you what the spatial law dictates about that spot on earth in The Netherlands. By reversing the query it tells a business where some economic activities are allowed and where they are not.

Fig 29.2 Illustration of the navigation of legal constraints while relocating a tank station using IMRO

ePower/Metalex

It is only very recent that IT trained people have challenged the domain of law. A clash between law and IT trained people seems inevitable, as the constitutional law is the product of parliament and it is processed in a 2000 years old language only legal specialists are able to read. Given the fact that business back office processes are being linked more and more to government processes and given the fact that government is based on The Law, the old legal language is becoming legacy that needs to be accessed. It has been tried before to automate legal (contracting) procedures when EDI enabled some formal representation of rule-based systems (Bons, Lee & Tan, 1999). Most of those efforts were tedious and very time consuming. Today we see a number of efforts where the law is treated like a piece of machine-readable code, or at least attempts to cross the bridge between software and legal codification.

The first version of the "Metalex" legal XML standard developed by the University of Amsterdam during the last year (www.metalex.org). In combination with the Tax office an attempt was made to apply this standard to legal tax reporting procedures in the EC funded ePower project. Metalex covers the deontic legal constraints language which "jurisprudence" did for the last centuries. Only this time a machine can read it. The power project resulted in a method to create an ontology for a certain procedural domain. It has been applied successfully on tax deduction rule systems and pension calculation systems. It is now being tested in the area of the State Council (Raad v State). This important distinction is also visible in the usage of the term "taxonomy" and the term "ontology" (Boer, Engers and Winkels, 2003).A taxonomy as it is used in the context of XBRL (and other xml standards) is an agreement about the notification of a certain field in a message between two organizations or two machines. Ontology as it is used in the context of Metalex and lawis a standardized network of meaning and relations attached to the key concepts we want the government to regulate. A legal ontology expressed in machine-readable components is so important because of the impact the law has on other processes, its interoperability and maintainability.

Overheid.nl

The build of www.overheid.nl, version 3.0 (2002-2003), the National access portal for Dutch National law and government services provides the general entry point for citizens and businesses using a complicated URL management technology for 4000 websites of governmental agencies, a custom build search engine and a custom build retrievable XML structure for the whole of Dutch National Law. It has a considerable amount of users per day and it is well regarded by people within government to find laws and colleagues. It did not provide provincial law or local/municipality law and that was one of the main points of critique as was the crude characterization of the world into the profile "citizen" and "companies" as navigating user profiles. Currently the responsible Ministry is investigating the possibility to develop a new search engine on the one hand and a National metadata standard/infrastructure for ALL public (legal) information, standard services and unstructured content on the other. This approach may solve the mismatch between the demand side and the supply side of the chain because both perspectives are incorporated in the architecture of the whole process. eGIF eGMS in the UK is an eGovernment metadata standard based on Dublin Core and Warwick Framework and is now also used for the metadata standard initiative in The Netherlands (http://www.govtalk.gov.uk/schemasstandards/gcl.asp). Such an international exchange is perhaps unusual for a National agency and probably very helpful for interoperability within Europe in the Future. The applicability of Metadata at National level for all other government agencies proved to be a difficult case. It is very hard to agree on a generally acceptable taxonomy, which is specifically still useful within one service domain. As a result the Aplaws project in the UK found that local governments had to adapt the metastandard for their needs into thc Local standard (http://www.esd.org.uk/standards/lgcl). It remains the question if civil servants will actually use these in the long run.

ICTAL and OTP

A number of promising developments have been going on since EDIFACT was implemented in the early nineties. The Dutch Ministry of Internal affairs, The DutchTax office and the Dutch National bureau for statistics (CBS), adopted the XBRL (eXtensible Business report Language, www.xbrl.org) standard for financial record keeping and since 2003 the National Administration Transaction Portal (OTP) is taking shape (www.ictal.nl). The OTP is aimed at serving as the one-stop-shop for large amounts of structured data and transactions and it is relevant for our research because of the high level of standardization these automated processes require. The main point of criticism on Edifact used to be the costs and labor involved in the translation of processes in EDIFACT norms and messages. The OTP could well succeed in establishing a harmonized National business registry enabling electronic transaction for all governmental agencies. There is already resistance from a number of players to adopt the XBRL/XML technology to enable financial reporting to numerous government "shops" trough the OTP. Currently the main point of criticism sccms to bc thc changc from traditional Excel reporting habits to more complicated reporting using XBRL given the costs involved of alternated processes. The strongest opposition at the moment resided with the lower level government agencies, which see little benefits for them and a lot of costs in creating a cross-agencies one stop-shop-chain. This project as a case still has to deal with the question of fair allocation of costs at the relevant government level.

Discussion and Evaluation

In Table 29.3 some of the distinguished characteristics are presented, based on which life cycle and which activities the case study aims to improve, the interactions between which kinds of actors, the structured ness of the legislation and the technology used in the case study. Only the IMRO case study focuses on both the production and demand cycle. The case studies are systematically evaluated using the criteria of our conceptual framework. Some of the criteria are not applicable to all cases.

Table 29.3. Overview of the characteristics of the case studies

Name case study	Life cycle	Interoperability between actors	Structure of legislation	Technology used
IMRO	Production cycle: interpretation/translation demand cycle: and retrieve information	Public-to-public Public-to-business	Structured and unstructured	Object oriented GIS and standardization
EPower/Metalex	Production cycle: interpretation and translation	Public-to-business	Structured	object oriented technology , XML deontic legal constraints language
overheid.nl	Demand cycle: retrieve information at various level	Public-to-business	Unstructured and structured	Metatags, XML and search
ICTAL	Production cycle: translate	Public-to-public	Highly structured	XML and XBRL

It should be mentioned that the scoring of case studies was found to be difficult and sometimes subjective. From the investigation and evaluation of the case studies a number of conclusions can be drawn which will be discussed hereafter. The Dutch national governmental portal site provides access to the national laws using a sophisticated hierarchy of XML tags. Adding the metadata using document type definitions (DTD) and XML-schema's slightly reduces the precision problem, while increasing the number of relevant documents retrieved. The retrieval problem is not completely solved however, since one still has to know the right keyword or jargon to find the relevant law for our business life event. The production of a document type description of the law based on the legal linguistic notification as it has been applied for hundreds of years may prove to be a fruitless effort for the purpose of automation and interoperability. Another issue is that XML schema's for more unstructured data are totally dependent on appropriate meta tags and the debate about the appropriate tags will be endless without some link to the legal and economic fundaments of our society. The value of the content to the outside world remains invisible by means of normal navigation techniques like portals or search engines.

Other case studies show that decomposing the law in objects and relations between objects is a viable approach.

Table 29.4. Overview evaluation case studies

	IMRO	Epower/ Metalex	overheid.nl	ICTAL
Production cycle				
Adaptation lead time business (software vendors)	good	excellent	-	excellent
Adaptation lead time government bodies	excellent	excellent	good	good
Efficiency of adaptation	excellent	excellent	good	excellent
Fairness of costs/benefits allocation	excellent	-	not good	not good
Evolution	good	not good	not good	unknown
Interoperability over layers off gov agencies	excellent	excellent	good	good
Semi automated Maintainability	excellent	excellent	not good/good	-
Demand cycle				
Precision	excellent	good	good	excellent
Recall	good	good	good	good
Usability	excellent	not good	good	-
Intuitive	excellent	not good	good	not good
Fast	good	good	good	excellent
Administrative costs business	excellent	excellent	good	excellent

Objectification of the law in the Netherlands was found in the IMRO case study and seems to be preferred over representing laws as texts using an (XML) hierarchy. Objectification enabled business to search among laws at various levels using queries. Spatial law is constructed from a much better user-centered perspective than the national law or the penal law. The retrieval mechanism there is based on the numeric codification of the zoning area. There is a much more transparent link between the life event or business goal of the end user and the triangle of zoning area, zoning regulation and zoning policy in comparison with national law. Businesses have more access to the practical terminology of locations and functions of that location in relation to what they want to achieve. A spatial orientation provides us with a solution for two problems: retrieval and representation. The layered data structure of GIS enables the user to open thematic maps in relation to a certain area. When combined with traditional SQL queries on the textual databases the application provides a powerful navigation tool. The user navigates information like he used to navigate real life for centuries anyway: by using "maps". The relevancy of a document is always anchored to the geographical coordinate and so are all objects like infrastructure, business, laws, maintenance schedules, ownership statues, environmental interests and so on. The need to retrieve information from many places at different levels of government organization is a resource-intensive job as shown in Figure 29.3.

Legislation production efforts are distributed over the European, State, Region and local level, and within each level many agencies of various types exist. Where most of the investigated case studies were aimed at improving production or retrieval using technology, only the IMRO case was focused on the restructuring of the public administration building blocks itself. It enabled businesses to query form the demand perspective: Instead of "what can I do here?", the questions should be "where can I do this?" Although we did not investigate the structure of the public administration interoperability in the Netherlands, it seems that investigating the restructuring of public administration to enhance the support the demand perspective would be a viable research directions.

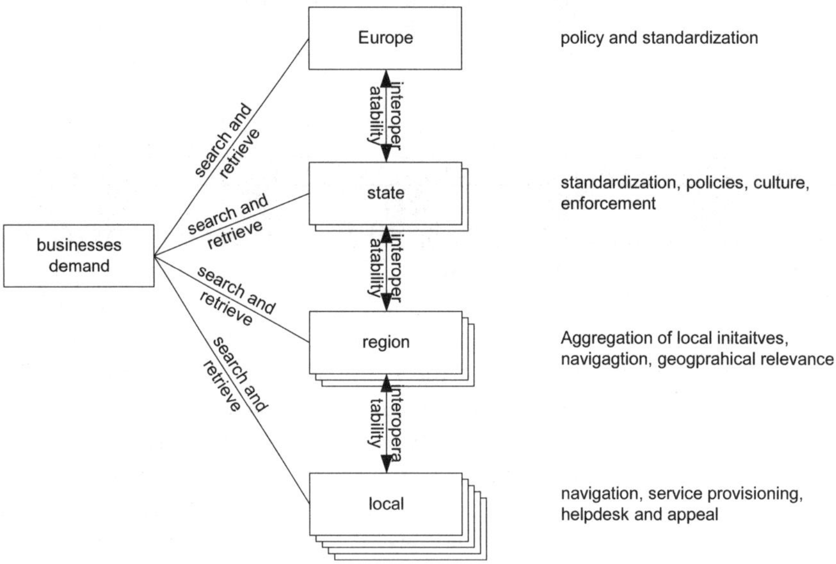

Fig 29.3 Fragmented nature of public administration

Conclusions

Politicians and civil servants at a central level develop new legislation and procedures. The continuous updating of laws and rules and the enforcement is performed by governmental organizations at a decentralized level.

Local governments have to translate the law to their local situation. Businesses and citizens have to comply with those regulations interacting at decentral level and at central level. These participants in the network use different applications, different ways to describe and incorporate laws in information systems, need different amount of resources and have various lead-times to comply with changes in law. A smart network is a network with more efficiency, lower risks and less costs, where the gap between policy makers, administrative organizations and businesses is bridged. It is vital that the architectural design fundaments of eGovernment services supporting economic activities are designed in consistency with (new) design principles for legal systems and the operational activities companies perform.

Object Oriented (legal) components which business software can process seem to be necessary to create a smart network. Those components need to be retrievable at the demand side of businesses. Retrieval requires usability and contextual relevance.

Geographical elements for retrieving localized legislator or jurisdiction is a feature necessary. This featured is gaining more importance, as legal systems need to be interoperable at a European scale. The combination of object oriented law and geographical systems combines finding relevant laws by easy navigation. The next generation of web services between government and businesses should be based on both (1) legal object oriented building blocks and (2) geographical relevance around the same ontology's. These can be taken as a starting point for creating interoperable and retrievable law.

References

Arendse (2003). *The OTP Architecture*. Report ICTAL, www.ictal.nl/.

Armour, F.J., S.H. Kaisler, and S.Y. Liu, (1999). "A Big-Picture Look at Enterprise Architectures", *IEEE IT Professional*, 1(1), pp. 35-42.

Boer, A., T. van Engers, and R. Winkels, (2003). "Using Ontologies for Comparing and Harmonizing Legislation", in *Proceedings of the International Conference on Artificial Intelligence and Law (ICAIL)*, Edinburgh (UK), ACM Press.

Bons, R., R.M. Lee, and Y-H. Tan, (1999). "A Formal Specification of Automated Auditing of Trustworthy Trade Procedures for Open Electronic Commerce", *Hawaii International Conference on System Sciences (HICCS).*

Buckland, F. Gey, (1994). "The Relationship Between Recall and Precision", *Journal of the American Society for Information Science*, 45 (1), pp. 12-19.

Checkland, P. (1981). *Systems Thinking, Systems Practice*. Wiley, Chichester.

Coase, R. (1937). "The Nature of the Firm", *Economia*, 4, pp. 386-405.

European Commission (2004). *Green paper on Public-Private Partnerships and Community Law on Public Contracts and Concessions*, European Commission, No. 327.

Fagan, J.C., B. Fagan, (2004). "An Accessibility Study of State Legislative Web Sites", *Government Information Quarterly,* 21, pp. 65-85.

Galliers, R.D. (1992). *Information Systems Research - Issues, Methods and Practical Guidelines*, Alfred Waller, Fawley, England.

Jensen, M., W. Meckling, (1976). "Theory of the Firm: Managerial Behavior, Agency Costs, and Capital Structure", *Journal of Financial Economics*, 5, pp. 305-360.

Malone, T.W., K. Crowston, (1994). "The Interdisciplinary Study of Coordination", *ACM Computing Surveys*, Vol. 26, No. 2, pp. 87-119.

Peters, R., F. Wilson, (2003). "Natural Language Access to Regional Information Sources: The Port-of-Rotterdam Case", *4th International Workshop on Image Analysis for Multimedia Interactive Services*, WIAMIS.

Rohleder, S.J., et al., (2004). *eGovernment Leadership: High Performance, Maximum Value. Fifth Annual Accenture eGovernment Study*. Accenture Government Executive Studies, www.accenture.com/xdoc/en/industries/ government/gove_egov_value.pdf

Quinn, R.E., J.W. Rohrbaugh, (1983). "A Spatial Model of Effectiveness Criteria: Towards a Competing Values Approach to Organizational Effectiveness", *Management Science*, 29, pp. 363-377.

Williamson, O.E. (1975). *Market and Hierarchies, Analysis and Antitrust Implications. A Study in the Economics of Internal Organization*. Macmillan, New York.

Yin, R.K. (1989). *Case Study Research: Design and methods*. Sage publications, Newbury Park, California.

List of Participants and Authors

Last Name	First Name	Affiliation
Baan	Jan	Cordys (NL) jbaan@cordys.com
Bar-Yam	Yaneer	New England Complex Systems Institute (MA, USA) yaneer@necsi.org
Basu	Amit	Southern Methodist University (TX, USA) abasu@smu.edu
Braha	Dan	Ben Gurion University of the Negev (Israel) brahad@bgumail.bgu.ac.il
Burke	Helen	Kenny's Bookshop & Art Galleries Ltd (Ireland)
Chen	Hong	RSM - Erasmus University Rotterdam (NL) hchen@fbk.eur.nl
Doukidis	Georgios	Athens University of Economics & Business (Greece) gjd@aueb.gr
Dunn	Al	D-Age Management Ltd. (UK) dunn@d-age.com
Eschenbaecher	Jens	University of Bremen (Germany) esc@biba.uni-bremen.de
Fodor	Oliver	E-Commerce Competence Center - EC3 (Austria) oliver.fodor@ec3.at
Golden	Willie	National University of Ireland (Ireland) willie.golden@nuigalway.ie
Graser	Falk	University of Bremen (Germany) grs@biba.uni-bremen.de
Gurevich	Greg	Lehigh University (CA, USA) ggurevich@lehigh.edu
Hagdorn	Lorike	RSM - Erasmus University Rotterdam (NL) lhagdorn@fbk.eur.nl
Hahn	Axel	University of Oldenburg (Germany) hahn@wi-ol.de
Harris	Ian	The Big Word (UK)
Heck, van	Eric	RSM - Erasmus University Rotterdam (NL)

		eheck@fbk.eur.nl
Heikkilä	Marikka	University of Jyväskylä (Finland) marikka.heikkila@jyu.fi
Herzog	Markus	Vienna University of Technology (Austria) herzog@dbai.tuwien.ac.at
Hilligers-berg, van	Jos	RSM - Erasmus University Rotterdam (NL) j.hillegersberg@fbk.eur.nl
Holland	Christopher	University of Manchester (UK) chris.holland@mbs.ac.uk
Holland, van	Winfried	Cordys (NL) wvholland@cordys.com
Hoogewee-gen	Martijn	RSM - Erasmus University Rotterdam (NL) mhoogeweegen@fbk.eur.nl
Hughes	Martin	National University of Ireland (Ireland)
Janssen	Marijn	Delft University of Technology (NL) marijnj@tbm.tudelft.nl
Kamsteeg	Eeuwe	Cordys (NL) ekamsteeg@cordys.com
Kawalek	Peter	University of Manchester (UK)
Kini	Deepak	Cordys (NL) dkini@cordys.com
Konsynski	Benn	Emory University (GA, USA) benn.konsynski@bus.emory.edu
Koppius	Otto	RSM - Erasmus University Rotterdam (NL) okoppius@fbk.eur.nl
Kourouthanassis	Panos	Athens University of Economics & Business (Greece) pkour@aueb.gr
Lehmonen	Jari	University of Jyväskylä (Finland) jari.lehmonen@sonera.com
Liere, van	Diederik	RSM - Erasmus University Rotterdam (NL) dliere@fbk.eur.nl
Ligtenberg	Diberna	Cordys (NL) dligtenberg@cordys.com
Moonen	Hans	RSM - Erasmus University Rotterdam (NL) h.moonen@fbk.eur.nl
Muller	Peter	ABZ (NL) pmuller@abz.nl
Nagel	Roger	Lehigh University (CA, USA) rnagel@lehigh.edu

Nunen, van	Jo	RSM - Erasmus University Rotterdam (NL) jnunen@fbk.eur.nl
Oosterhout, van	Marcel	RSM - Erasmus University Rotterdam (NL) moosterhout@fbk.eur.nl
Pau	Louis	RSM - Erasmus University Rotterdam (NL) lpau@fbk.eur.nl
Pekkola	Samuli	University of Jyväskylä (Finland) samuli@cc.jyu.fi
Peters	Rob	University of Amsterdam (NL) Peters@lri.jur.uva.nl
Pramatari	Katarina	Athens University of Economics & Business (Greece) k.pramatari@aueb.gr
Preiss	Kenneth	Ben Gurion University of the Negev (Israel) preiss@bgu.ac.il
Radkevitch	Ulad	RSM - Erasmus University Rotterdam (NL) uradkevitch@fbk.eur.nl
Rai	Arun	Georgia State University (GA, USA) arunrai@gsu.edu
Ruiter, de	Henk	Cordys (NL) hdruiter@cordys.com
Samba-murthy	Vallabh	Michigan State University smurthy@bus.msu.edu
Sangle	Vivekanand	Cordys (NL) VSangle@cordys.com
Schipper	Gerrit	ABZ (NL) gschipper@abz.nl
Schmid	Patrick	Lehigh University (CA, USA)
Shaw	Duncan	University of Manchester (UK) dshaw@man.mbs.ac.uk
Snowdon	Bob	University of Manchester (UK)
Tiwana	Amrit	Emory University (GA, USA) atiwana@bus.emory.edu
Tseng	Jimmy	RSM - Erasmus University Rotterdam (NL) jtseng@fbk.eur.nl
Vervest	Peter	RSM - Erasmus University Rotterdam (NL) vervest@d-age.com
Visser, de	Hans	Cordys (NL) hdvisser@cordys.com
Voorde, ten	Henk	Cordys (NL) htvoorde@cordys.com

Walters	Jason	Lehigh University (CA, USA) jwalters@lehigh.edu
Warboys	Brian	University of Manchester (UK)
Wareham	Jonathan	Georgia State University (GA, USA) wareham@acm.org
Werthner	Hannes	University of Trento (Italy) werthner@dit.unitn.it
Westwood	J.B.	University of Manchester (UK)
Wolters	Matthijs	Free University (NL) mwolters@feweb.vu.nl
Zuidwijk	Rob	RSM - Erasmus University Rotterdam (NL) r.zuidwijk@fbk.eur.nl

Index

Printing: Strauss GmbH, Mörlenbach
Binding: Schäffer, Grünstadt